Retrieving for All Occasions

Foundations for Excellence in Gun Dog Training

Elsa Blomster
Lena Gunnarsson

Translation by Charlotte West

KLICKER
FÖRLAGET

Retrieving for All Occasions

© Klickerförlaget Göteborg AB, 2015

Authors:	Elsa Blomster and Lena Gunnarsson
Translation:	Charlotte West
Editor:	Emelie Johnson Vegh
ISBN:	978-91-981613-4-2
Publisher:	Klickerförlaget Göteborg AB
Graphic design:	Johanna Simonsson, Formando Ludvig Aust, Aust Kommunikation AB
Illustrations:	Jenny Nyberg
Print:	Livonia Print, Latvia 2015
Photography:	Elsa Blomster and Lena Gunnarsson except for the following:

Bittan Börjesson	Back cover: Flat-coated Retriever
Carin Träffe	107, 109, 204, 205, 208, 210
Cecilia Svensson	251
Eva Carlsson	163
Håkan Hansson	159, 175, 178, 180, 210, Back cover: Yellow Labrador Retriever
Jonas Andersson	66, 111, 126, 184, Back cover: Golden Retriever
Joni Paananen	88
Låtta Bergstrand	243
Ludvig Aust	47, 165, 251
Malin Karlsson	221, 255
Mary Wright	108, 117, Back cover: Nova Scotia Duck Tolling Retriever
Per Christoffersson	181
Shadi Kajevand	72

Foreword

I am often asked if I have written a book that details my positive training methods, and sadly the answer is no. I am also often asked if there is a book I could recommend that follows the approach and again sadly I had to give the same answer, until now.

I deeply respect the amount of knowledge and time that has gone into making this book so informative and easy-to-follow. You just know as you are reading it that these are tried and tested methods by people who have an in depth understanding of how dogs learn and respond.

Each exercise is carefully explained but without going into to so much detail that you get bogged down. Exercises are mapped out in short, easy stages that demonstrate an intrinsic understanding of the training process, which is further shown through explanations of the "what ifs" when training might not go according to plan.

This book is long overdue in gundog training and I only wish I had written it. I take my hat off to Elsa and Lena for making gundog trainers' lives easier by writing this, because without this book people might not understand the way forward with their dogs, would not have the same pleasure and fun with their dogs, and might not succeed with their dogs.

December 2014

Philippa Williams

KCAI (CDA WGA FT)
Dogs for Life, UK

Contents

Rewarding and Fun Dog Training!

We have written this book because we love dogs and dog training. We also really enjoy field trial training and we couldn't find a book of this kind when we started our own field trial training. We wanted a book that could help us train our retrieving and flushing gun dogs, an accessible book in which we could find concrete suggestions for exercises that would also provide an understanding of where our training would lead. Much to our surprise, we discovered that there was no such up to date book available!

You see, we had an additional requirement: that all training would use positive reinforcement methods, without physical or verbal corrections. Traditionally, correction based training is considered a necessity, but we know there are alternatives. Our training is reward based and we've seen that the dogs learn very quickly and that it's easy to "re-teach" them if something goes wrong.

Above all, our dogs are highly valued members of our families. For us, spending time together is the best thing in the world. There's nothing better than the feeling of being in a partnership with our dogs, following their signals and learning their language. And it's hard to beat the wonderful feeling of when our dogs – happy, engaged, and confident – respond to our smallest signals when we go out together.

We own spaniels and retrievers, and we see it as our duty to allow the dogs to do what they are genetically programmed to do. In the simplest terms, you might say that we can only hone and direct their innate character.

We started using reward based training because it was effective and because it didn't cause any discomfort to our dogs. Training should be fun and enjoyable for both handler and dog. We like to think of our training as a form of exercise where the participant is allowed to reflect on things. We find it exciting and challenging to look at what we do from multiple viewpoints and question the status quo – is what we regard as "correct" really correct? Yes, this means that we even question our own training methods. We do not believe that there is a single way and are immediately suspicious if someone claims that there is a universal solution. So we are always on the lookout for ways to improve.

We hope you will find some new ideas in this book. For example, there are examples of basic training exercises for your gun dog from completing a first retrieve to how to begin organizing marked retrieves, to completing finding and retrieving exercises. But you can also read about the training method itself – what does it actually mean to incorporate a reward based philosophy into your training? What are the building blocks? Why do we do what we do? What are the results?

With that said, we want to emphasize that we are not the slightest bit interested in polarizing the issue. There is a lot of knowledge out there about field trial training. We are more than happy to listen to other points of view and we do pick up tidbits here and there and apply them to our own training. It's our hope that you will read this book in much the same way and pick out the bits that suit you best.

We want you and your dog to get started on training as soon as possible! This is why we have chosen to organize our book according to a combination of thematic chapters with practical exercises (in blue), and theoretical chapters (in pink). There is also a glossary at the end of the book.[1]

The book is written for you who want to enjoy daily training with your gun dog, and for you who want to take part in your first field trial. We talk about retriever training but we also outline where spaniel training and retriever training differ. Most of what you teach a retriever is also useful when training a flushing or pointing dog, especially with regard to retrieving. However, when it comes to finding and retrieving, spaniels and retrievers need to be trained differently. As indicated by its title, this book focuses on retrieving during field trials, but we will briefly touch upon

---

[1] On our webpage, www.retrievingforalloccasions.com, you can find even more resources

what a spaniel does prior to the shot. We will not, however, discuss what pointers and setters do prior to the shot.

You now have it in your hands – the book we wish we had when we first started field trial training. The title of the book means exactly what it says – it is intended for both daily use and for special occasions. This book has been written for you and your dog. It's for beginners in the world of field trials, and for those who might not be familiar with reward based training. Or perhaps you already know some of the basics and just want to further your training? This book is for you too. We have also included several advanced exercises for those who want to know what to expect in more advanced classes. Our hope is that you will read this book with an open mind and be willing to take on a fun and challenging training method.

Good luck!

Elsa Blomster &
Lena Gunnarsson

Diesel

Rewards

Effective rewards are a prerequisite for getting the most out of this book and being successful with your training. Rewards form the foundation of our entire training system. But what is a reward? It can be anything your dog is willing to work for. Now reread the previous sentence and let it sink in. What does it really mean?

You and your dog might not have the same idea about what makes a good reward. Sometimes we see owners who pet and hug their dogs in delight because they did something right. But the dogs look like they would rather be anywhere else. They lean away from their owners and turn their heads away as if they were thinking, "Gosh, leave me alone!" This type of "reward" is not effective at all since it's unlikely to encourage the dog to repeat the behavior. Instead, it has the opposite effect.

What does your dog like? Make a list of your dog's top ten favorite rewards. Remember that this should be from the dog's perspective – not yours. In other words, include rewards that you would prefer the dog not to have but she nevertheless loves: hunting rabbits, digging sandwiches out of your backpack, jumping up and kissing your neighbor on the nose, etc. You should also include those things you find more acceptable (albeit still from the dog's perspective): chasing a ball, playing with a toy, eating hot dogs, fetching an object, tracking, being chased or whatever it might be. Think about whether it's possible to use the rewards you don't want the dog to do in a controlled manner. Maybe put sandwiches in your bag?

Then try to rank the items on your list in an approximate order. What does your dog think is the most fun thing of all? Second best? Now you have a list that you can use. When you are going to teach the dog something she finds extremely difficult, use the top (of the accepted) rewards. Simpler exercises don't often require the maximum reward – the dog still thinks it's worthwhile to work for a lower "payment". The dog might also reject certain rewards in certain situations. For instance she might not want dry dog food when she's just eaten, but a little canned cat food might

still get her attention. The surrounding environment can similarly affect the dog. In other words, the list can change, but it still provides a good indication of what rewards your dog likes best.

Different Rewards – Different Effects

It's not just how much the dog likes the reward that matters when it comes to learning. Different rewards have different effects on the behavior that was just rewarded. Sitting and watching game plop down in front of her is often very stressful for the dog. The increased stress level might lead to whining, which is a deadly sin in the world of field trials in most countries. How do you want your dog to behave? What emotion should she exhibit? Depending on your answers, you can decide on how you want to reward your dog. If you want your dog to be attentive but calm, food and petting might be the right reward. If you want speed and keenness, a ball might just do the trick.

For those who have a dog who loves to be touched – do it! Find different ways to touch your dog, depending on what emotion you want the dog to exhibit in the behavior you are rewarding. Lena's Rottweiler Dacke likes to stand between her knees while she scratches his rump. He snorts and grunts and hops on his back legs. The scratching makes him energetic and high-spirited. It's a reward that Lena uses when she wants Dacke to tackle a more challenging exercise. However, if they are working on heelwork, when he is to be calmer, she lightly strokes her fingers along his side or gives him a treat. He responds with two wags of his tail, calm and collected. Think about how you would like your dog to perform a particular exercise and reward her in such a way that you reinforce the correct behavior.

Reward Markers

No matter what reward we chose to use we almost always use a reward marker to mark it before giving the dog her reward. We usually use a clicker or just a word like "yes". When we say "reward" or "click" we thus mean "mark and reward" the behavior.

Play

We are big fans of using play as a form of reward. Games provide endless variety. As we mentioned before, choose wisely how you play based on what you are trying to teach the dog. How do you play with your dog? Does she like to be chased? Do you usually roll around in the grass together? Is your dog ball-crazy?

A dog we know thinks it's insanely fun when his owner walks like a spider with one hand towards him, slowly, creeping at first and then – attack! Another loves to (calmly and with care) be dragged in the grass, lying on his side, hanging onto his toy in a tug-of-war. A third loves to jump straight up and down again and again. You can weave different basic skills into your play that will be useful when you are teaching the dog different exercises later on. Quickly running to and away from you, turning, sitting down quickly, taking an object, holding it and releasing it, are all examples of skills you can teach through play. Nothing creates a better sense of togetherness. Play with your dog and you'll see how much your relationship improves.

Treats and Food

If you have a food-motivated dog, treats and food are some of the easiest rewards to use. The advantage of using an edible reward is that it's quick and easy. A lot of play can wear the dog out and environmental rewards are trickier. Having treats in your pocket or hand makes it easy to do a lot of repetitions in a short period of time. We like using our dogs' regular food as a reward. Why should everything in the food bowl be free? Most often they receive their meals in the bowl, but even then they need to make contact with us and wait for a cue to get the chance to eat it.

Spaniel and retriever breeds are often said to have a "will to please", that is to say a desire to please their handlers. We would rather say that they often have a "will to eat" or "will to have fun", and we want to use that as much as possible in our training.

> **But ...**
> *... won't my dog become fat from all the treats I give her as a reward? No, not if you:*
> · *Reduce the dog's food on days you have given her a lot of treats.*
> · *Use the dog's food as a reward.*
> · *Give the dog healthy treats (that are not full of sugar, fat or salt).*
> · *Vary the kind and amount (no one feels good from eating too much of just one kind).*
>   *Try small amounts of new kinds to see how your dog likes them.*

Petting, Touching and Verbal Praise

It's sometimes easy for clicker trainers like us to forget about social rewards. It's a little shortsighted since the only rewards that are allowed in the majority of competition events are social: petting, touching and verbal praise. During field trials, rewards are even more restricted, since we are supposed to remain silent and not touch the dog. We think it's a good idea to use social rewards during training, but we use them most often in combination with other rewards.

We have thus far never encountered a dog that is always willing to work for petting and praise alone. On the other hand, we have seen dogs that work for petting and praise in combination with the use of aversives if the dog doesn't do what she's supposed to. We doubt, however, that it's the social reward that is maintaining the behavior, but rather the desire to avoid the aversive, as well as being allowed to keep working. You can tell whether or not the reward is effective by looking at whether the dog wants to repeat the rewarded behavior. Verbal praise and encouragement can be used as support signals or as "keep going signals" to let the dog know she's on the right path. For example, we might initially use it when the dog is hunting when we notice that the dog has gotten the scent of the object. Remember not to overuse it to the extent it becomes nagging, or a crutch that prevents the dog from performing the exercise without your verbal support.

We started this chapter with a description of a dog that appeared to think that her owner was clingy and awful. It's not entirely uncommon that the same dog in another situation, maybe at home on the sofa, wants to cuddle up and be cosy with her person. Try to recreate something the dog likes at home in a training situation. Later in this chapter, we will also discuss how you can teach the dog to appreciate social rewards. You can play social games with your dogs, such as pushing and shoving each other.

Study how your dog reacts to being touched. The majority of dogs seem to be calmer when their chests are stroked and some get a little excited when they are stroked on the sides of their bodies. Some like it when you nuzzle their ears while others duck when you scratch them on the head. Not all dogs might appreciate the classic "pats on the shoulder" – you know when people pat their dogs on the side of the body, like "pat, pat, pat". Does your dog like that? She might, but regardless, pay attention to what happens when you do it.

Lamp Posts and Lakes

Since a reward is anything that your dog is prepared to work for, you can use the environment as a reward. If your dog likes to sniff, you can teach her a cue/reward "go and sniff."

Likewise, you can use lamp posts, other people, friendly dogs, swimming in lakes, etc. as rewards. You can use anything your dog wants or likes to do that you approve of as a reward! Doesn't that offer fantastic opportunities for learning?

When you use the environment as a reward, you might need some degree of control of the dog, possibly by using a leash or a long lead, so that you – if need be – can interrupt the dog if she tries to reward herself. Interrupt the dog by putting a treat against her nose and allowing her to chew on the treat while you calmly lead her away from the reward. You can also reward your dog abundantly when she spontaneously breaks away from the reward, for instance when she stops sniffing and looks up at you again. The latter can also help a dog that is easily distracted to ignore the distraction and instead want to be with you.

Think about the effects that environmental rewards have on your dog's behavior. Certain rewards, such as playing with other dogs, can wind your dog up too much. What emotion do you want your dog to have while you are training?

For working spaniels or retrievers, the work – searching, fetching and carrying – is often a reward in itself. We naturally use this when training, such as getting the dog to fetch a marked retrieve that has fallen after she heeled for a few meters first. (A marked retrieve means that the dog sees an object fall and notices where it lands. Walking at heel means that the dog walks beside you, but her gaze is directed towards the area where she will be working).

Go and Sniff and Come Back

Lena's cocker spaniel Totte's favorite thing in the world is sniffing. Previously, Totte was consumed in scent-rich environments and it wasn't easy to get his attention. Lena decided to take control of the scents and use sniffing as a reward instead.

The goal of the exercise is to have the dog sniff on cue, as a reward after she has performed another behavior you requested. When she has sniffed for several seconds, she should then voluntarily return so you can keep working. When you start teaching the dog this activity, remember to do it in a place where you aren't likely to find too interesting scents. The lawn in your backyard is a good place to start.

Do the exercise as follows:

1. Put the dog on a leash. Allow her to wander and sniff at the end of the leash. Click after several seconds of sniffing. The majority of dogs will turn when they hear the click and then you can reward them with something really good. If your dog doesn't turn to you, walk up to her and put the treat under her nose. You can start adding the cue "go and sniff" when the dog starts sniffing.

2. Repeat the step above until you see that the dog consciously goes to sniff. Maybe she will stop sniffing as if to say, "Where's my reward?" Then you of course click and give her a grand reward. Now you change the focus

from rewarding the dog for sniffing to voluntarily interrupting her sniffing. You shift from clicking when the dog sniffs on cue to when she stops sniffing of her own accord. The goal of the exercise is to click and reward the dog when she interrupts herself.

3. Once the dog understands what this game is about, proceed to increasingly difficult environments. When you come to a spot where you notice your dog is eager to sniff, have her first do a little exercise with you, for example look at you and maybe heel for a step or two, before rewarding her by saying "go and sniff". If the dog doesn't interrupt her sniffing in the more challenging environment, click for the sniffing and go up and reward her with treats.

4. A key success factor is that you have really good rewards that the dog values more than being able to sniff. Therefore, don't start training in an environment with too many challenging scents. It may initially be difficult to compete with the scent of a deer, but after a while it could be the other way around so that the dog chooses not to sniff and just wants to be with you when you play this game. This means a value shift has taken place and the dog thinks it's more worthwhile to be with you than to do something else – just the way you want it.

Easily Motivated Dogs

It's a delight to train an easily motivated dog if your whole training philosophy is based on rewards. We want to congratulate you if you can pick and choose rewards and have a dog that is happy to do almost anything for a brief tug-of-war or for a piece of dry food.

The only thing you might consider is not giving out rewards too generously. There are still certain rewards that are at the top of your dog's list – don't waste them. Use them when

Diesel

the dog has done something especially good, maybe when you've had a breakthrough with a difficult exercise or when you want her to put forth her best effort.

Difficult-to-motivate Dogs

Sometimes the dogs attending our courses do not want to play. Thankfully, the saving grace is most dogs still like food and can be rewarded with something edible. The real challenge is when the dog doesn't want to eat (more than maybe a few pieces of liverwurst once a week) or play. Then we really have to do some brainstorming with the dog's owner.

Before we begin experimenting with trying to get the dog going, we always try to find out if the dog might be sick. Does she have an illness? She might have sore muscles or joints? If there are no such indications, we ask the owner to think about whether the dog ever plays and makes mischief. If so, when does she do so and how?

A German Shepherd we know, who had been mistreated in his previous home, initially had no desire to play with his new owner. She thought about it and realized that the dog gleefully chased the leaves that swirled around the streets in the fall. She brought bags full of leaves to their first training session! Later on in the training, she was exchanging the leaves for various toys, because the dog had eventually figured out they could have fun together.

There are obviously some cases that are difficult to solve, such as the dog who only plays for a few seconds or just stands there looking at us while we twitch around. Our experience is that the dogs that are specifically bred for work almost always enjoy playing, but sometimes it can be a bit difficult with the non-working breeds. For the few

dogs that we've encountered who did not respond to any reward, the first step tends to be a trip to the vet and then to a physical therapist. In such cases, there has almost always been something wrong with the dog. Sore throat, back pain, stomach problems, thyroid problems, and muscle pain are a few of the reasons that the dogs haven't been interested in anything we could think of as a reward and thus hard to train. Most often, the problem can be treated. When we see the dog again, she has a totally different energy and is interested in most of our suggestions.

Teaching a Dog to Like a Reward

We are seldom satisfied by rewarding the dog in one single way – for instance, only with treats. We want to be able to use as many different kinds of rewards as possible. This is because different kinds of rewards help us achieve, as we mentioned before, different effects. Play, for example, can teach the dog a lot of basic field trial skills. That's why we make the effort – if necessary – to teach the dog to like different forms of rewards. "What?" You might be thinking. Can you really teach a dog to like a reward she initially turns her nose up at?

> ### But ...
> ... if hunting in itself is a reward, we don't need anything else, right? In the end, work is an excellent reward for most dogs, but we initially need other rewards to teach the various tasks we want the dog to perform. Even during more advanced training, we want to be able to reward the dog in various ways to regulate her activity level and because it's extremely impractical if work is the only form of reward.

Yes, it's entirely possible! If the dog only likes a single kind of treat and you have control over it, you can teach the dog to like other prospective rewards. Take a dog that isn't so

2. Then take out a rope toy and start playing with it by yourself. As soon as the dog shows interest in the toy, give the cue "go ahead" and allow her to run to the bowl with the hot dog.

3. Gradually make the criteria more difficult (in other words, increase what the dog has to do to earn her reward) so the dog starts chasing the toy, trying to grab it, biting it, getting a firm hold, pulling and so on.

Don't be surprised if something magical happens then: suddenly the dog is obsessed with tug-of-war and doesn't want to release the toy when you cue "go ahead". However, it's not hocus pocus. Just as we saw in the exercise "Sniff and come back", there has been a value shift and the toy is now worth more to the dog than the hot dog.[2]

If your dog doesn't like to be petted while she is working, you can reward her with something she likes more after you pet her. For example, stroke the dog along her side or on the chest and then (or initially at the same time) give her a treat. You can also use the same approach if you have a dog that loves to play but isn't so interested in treats. Give her a treat and as a reward for taking the treat, then let her play. We have encountered dogs that at first were entirely unsinterested in treats that eventually became treat crazy. This technique also works with dogs that normally respond to treats but are sometimes too blocked or excited to take them. This might occur during field trial training if the dog would rather go out and retrieve than eat dry food.

At the same time as we spend a lot of time working on rewards, we also use the dog's natural preferences. Lena's food crazy spaniel Totte has the exact speed and intensity she's after when he runs to her while retrieving, even though

interested in tug-of-war (on the assumption that the dog is medically cleared) but loves hot dogs. (A prerequisite for being able to do this exercise is that the dog knows the cue "go ahead", which we will describe later on in this chapter). Then do the following:

1. Put a few bits of hot dog in a bowl a bit in front of the dog (without saying "stay" or "no" to the dog. She must voluntarily choose not to take the hot dog). If she tries to take the hot dog, put the bowl further away.

---

[2] This is known as Premack's principle. A more probable behavior reinforces a less probable behavior. Gradually, the initially less probable behavior becomes more probable.

the reward consists of food (which is often seen as being calmer than play). Giving him a ball or rope toy as a reward isn't always as effective, so she uses food instead.

Coach Says

If you want to compete in field trials, teach your dog a quiet and discreet form of reward to use during competitions. During retriever field trials, you are not allowed to touch the dog too much or at all. In some countries no one is likely to say anything about an extremely quick scratch on the ear. You can also teach the dog a low voiced whispered word of praise, such as a short "yes" or just a smile. When you're training, have every fifth reward be something that would be appropriate during a competition. Make sure that the dog really sees praise as a reward – teach it if necessary! Also remember to get to know the regulations in your country before teaching the dog a discreet reward to use during competitions.

Points of Success

In our training, we want to know that we have a point of success to return to if everything goes down the drain. A point of success is a situation where we know that the dog can successfully perform a certain behavior, so we have a chance to reward her. This will increase self confidence for both the dog and the handler.

For us, at a minimum, the dog should take at least one kind of treat. The second step is that the dog should make contact with us to receive a reward. However, the point of success we return to doesn't always have to be so basic. If we have spent a lot of time training delivery to hand and the dog suddenly drops the object on the ground, the point of success might be repeating the hand target (the dog puts her nose in our palm) a few times without the object and reward the dog accordingly. Then we'll try it with the object again. You can

read more about this in the chapter "Delivery to Hand".

If we encounter a situation where the dog is blocked and doesn't take the reward, we will take a step back in our training or wait until the dog is relaxed enough to take the reward. Elsa's golden retriever Diesel can become so blocked during marked retrieves in water (right when she sees the bird fall) that she won't take dry food. In Elsa's experience, when she sends Diesel out it is difficult to get the dog's attention while she is working. Her willingness to take dry food is an indicator of her attention and stress levels. Elsa does not let her work until she is calm enough to be able to take the treats and swallow them.

Get to know your dog so well that you in any situation can identify an appropriate point of success to return to if necessary. The more difficult the situation, the more basic the point of success you must return to. We always start our training sessions with a point of success and then make the session increasingly difficult.

Rewards First – Then Rules

Do you have a dog that throws herself at both you and the toy, almost knocking you over and drawing blood? Or do you have a dog that prefers to steal the treat bag out of your pocket and then swallow the entire thing whole? In both cases, it might be time to implement some rules about how and when the dog receives her reward. The alternative might be expensive and painful …

We want a dog that doesn't look twice when we train with our hands and pockets full of treats. We want to be able to have the toy hanging out of our pocket without the dog going after it. We teach the dog impulse control through reverse luring. In return for ignoring the treat or toy in our hand, the dog receives another treat as a reward. Read more about reverse luring in the chapter "Taking and holding". We also teach the dog that she is allowed to take the toy when we give the cue "take it".

Go Ahead!

The goal of this exercise is to teach the dog that she is only allowed to take what she wants after we have cued "go ahead". We have different methods to teach the dog "go ahead" for treats and "take it" for toys, but you can also teach both cues in the same way. We do the following steps to teach the dog the cue "go ahead":

1. Put a few treats in a bowl.
2. Lower the bowl to the floor. If the dog moves towards the bowl, lift it up. (Remain quiet. Don't say "no" or "stay"; what's important is the dog's voluntarily choice to leave the treat alone).
3. When the bowl is on the floor and the dog is just about to start to go towards it, cue "go ahead" (without using hand signals, we want the dog to react only to the verbal cue).
4. Switch between rewarding the dog for waiting without going to the bowl with treats in your hand and rewarding her with "go ahead".
5. As the dog improves, you can wait a little longer before you cue "go ahead". If the dog tries to take the treat out of the bowl before this, just lift the bowl up and repeat the exercise.

If you have a puppy, you can do a version of this exercise by holding the dog between your legs and pushing the bowl in front of you along the floor. Hold the puppy if she tries to get away and once she has calmed down, release her and cue "go ahead". Don't battle with the dog. If she finds sitting between your legs unpleasant, give her a reward first and then push the bowl away. We will use this more later on to teach the dog directional retrieves.

Take It!

This is how to teach the dog to take a toy only on cue (the prerequisite is that the dog is genuinely interested in the toy, otherwise you have to teach that first):

1. Cue "take it" just as the dog picks up the toy a few times.
2. When you have taken the toy back from the dog, wait until she sits (later you can proceed when she is still, but at the beginning it's easier for you to see if the dog is sitting than if she is just standing still). The first few times you can reward the dog with a treat when she remains sitting.
3. Carefully show the dog the toy. If the dog gets up, hide the toy behind your back and wait until the dog sits down again. If the dog stays sitting, cue "take it" and start playing. If the dog doesn't take the toy, try it again. If it still doesn't work, drop the rules for a while and just play with the dog a little until she really wants the toy again.
4. Then show the dog the toy for a longer period of time before you cue "take it", so you eventually can put the toy on the ground in front of the dog and she won't pick it up until you give the cue. Remember that the dog should react and take the toy on your cue, not because you wave the toy at her.

Dogs with a lot of energy might need these kinds of rules. But there are also dogs that are a little more cautious. They usually need to be encouraged to break all of the rules. The more they throw themselves at us to get their reward, the better. They are more than welcome to celebrate in triumph when they have grabbed the toy and would prefer not to give it back to us. Then we know that we have successfully developed an effective reward system.

Rewards While Hunting

The ultimate reward for most gun dogs is naturally being able to hunt, that is to say doing what they were bred to do. As we mentioned previously, we can use hunting as a reward in itself. Most often, we need other kinds of rewards apart from allowing the dog to work during the learning phase of various exercises. However, there are also situations where we want to use rewards other than work even when we are doing more advanced training. In this book we describe a lot of basic exercises that require a variety of easy to manage rewards. Some dogs are not sufficiently motivated by hunting so they need other kinds of rewards. In that case, we continue to reward the dog with whatever encourages her to work. The benefits of having several different rewards during field trial training are, in other words, enormous. We can teach and refine different skills, regulate the dog's activity level and as a bonus, we'll have a dog that thinks it's really fun to work with us.

Summary

- A reward is anything a dog is willing to work for.
- Rewards first – then rules!
- You can reward the dog in a variety of ways: various types of play, treats, social rewards, work, environmental rewards, and so on.
- Different rewards have different effects on the behavior the dog is to perform.
- You can teach the dog to like different rewards.
- Identify your points of success.

Sam

Play - the Ultimate Reward

In the previous chapter, we said that the more rewards we have, the better. We want to emphasize the importance of play since it offers so many possibilities. Moreover, we start most of our training sessions with play.

We want to have a dog that both immerses herself in play and plays with us in all environments, so this is where we begin our training process both with puppies and with older dogs. Play is, quite simply, an unbeatable form of reward that most dogs love (or learn to love) and it's an effective and structured way for the dog to burn off her energy. Moreover, it can set the right pace and energy level for the exercises we are teaching and it strengthens our relationship with the dog.

But it doesn't end there. We jokingly said that we really could have settled for writing just this one chapter because almost all of the skills we are going to describe in this book start with play. Using play, we teach the dog the basics of holding, releasing, staying, sitting, performing marked retrieves, hunting, transporting between activities, being calm, and so on. You'll first encounter these playful exercises in the majority of chapters under subheads such as "Play to Inspire Taking and Holding" and "Play to Inspire Steadiness".

Coach Says
Teach your dog to play in all environments: at home, in the woods, and on the street to make it easier to teach the dog to perform other behaviors in the same environments.

Study Your Dog

The first thing we usually do is to figure out what games the dog likes and takes to easily and which games she finds more difficult. A common mistake that we dog trainers tend to make is thinking, "My last dog was never interested in balls, but my new dog sure will be." Then we embark on the mission "Love your ball" when the dog in front of us is already ball-crazy but actually needs to work on tug-of-war.

Play with your dog both with and without objects. See what happens when you roll a ball, drag a rag on a long rope behind you, offer a tug toy, or tease the dog with some light play-wrestling. What does your dog seem to like? We want our dogs to think that playing with us is the best thing in the world. It is best to start out using the dog's favorite form of play, because this is the most effective way to get her going. After the dog is engaged we can spend more energy training the dog to play in the ways she is not as interested in.

Getting Started with Tug Games

Most dogs start practicing tug-of-war as puppies. They play tug with their littermates, pulling on ears, tails and blankets. Some dogs are more cautious than others and it might take a little while to get them going with tug-of-war. Others bite down on the toy immediately and pull back with everything they have. The easiest way to get the dog going is to use a soft, bite friendly toy, such as a sheepskin or an old, thick sock attached to a long rope. Drag the toy after you and have the dog chase it. Remember to always be dragging the toy away from the dog. We have never encountered a dog that likes having a toy pushed into her mouth. That can actually be an effective way to make her hate her toy, or even refuse to have anything in her mouth at all.

Coach Says
When you play tug of war with your dog, take care not to violently jerk the dog from side to side as you can hurt her back. Have the dog pull straight back and follow her movements.

Some dogs think that games of chase are much more fun than tug games and it may take the dog a while to take the toy from you. The following exercises are a lot easier if the dog really gets going and tugs, but even after you have gotten the dog to really get into tug of war, chase games can also be a good addition to your bag of rewards. Don't stop using chase games when the dog has learned to tug, use both.

If the dog isn't interested in the toy, you can "talk" to the toy, throw it in the air, and make it exciting by pretending that the dog isn't allowed to have it. You can also play keep away with a friend and throw the toy back and forth without letting the dog get a hold of it. Don't talk to the dog while you're doing it, but focus entirely on the toy. When the dog seems interested, you can stop throwing the toy and instead drag it away from the dog so she will try to join the game. Some dogs can even be motivated by another type of competition. If the dog has to sit and watch while you play with a friend's dog she might be more intent on joining in and playing.

Always end the training session when the dog is still interested in playing, not when she has lost interest. The latter will teach the dog it doesn't pay to stay engaged.

Don't give up! It can take time, but keep trying. Think about when the dog is most energetic – when she's just woken up, when you come home from work, when you are going for a walk, and so on – and take the opportunity to introduce the toy at that moment so the dog will be easier to motivate.

But ...
... you can't play tug with a retriever, or the dog will chew the game to pieces! No, no! Let us kill that myth once and for all. The opposite is true – the dog will develop a better hold by playing tug and the dog understands the difference between a tug toy and a bird.

Playing is Something We Do Together

When you've trained your dog to enjoy different games, it's time to introduce some structure to your play. We want the dog to always play with us (not by herself with the toy), to come back with the toy, and to release the toy on cue.

Coach Says

Have fun with your dog and take your time when you reward her. It's important that you are also engaged in the game. The dog will notice immediately if you are bored.

Does your dog run around triumphantly with her toy when she "wins"? Do you chase after her as you become more and more irritated? The dog probably thinks it's a really fun game, but you are not as amused. You can solve this problem in a couple of ways. We want to teach the dog to release the toy when we want it, and we also want to teach the dog that it always pays off to play together with us.

Running after a toy that has been thrown is the same as fetching and bringing it back immediately. When we are sure we can always get the toy back spontaneously, or when we request it, we can also use the formerly irritating chase game as a reward. We give the dog permission to run away with the object, pretend to chase after her and when the game is over, ask the dog to bring the toy back or wait until she spontaneously returns. The signal that it is time to stop playing is either to stop chasing her and stand still, to give a recall cue, or hold out our hand (which we previously taught the dog to put the object in).

Teaching the dog to play with us even though she has her own toy might initially seem a little tricky, but it's well worth investing time in it. Start with two identical tug toys that the dog likes equally well. Have the dog start playing with one of them. Then let it go and start playing with the other. Encourage the dog to play with you instead of the old toy. When the dog starts playing with you and the new toy, play intensively for a few minutes before you drop the toy and start playing with the first one. Once again encourage the dog to switch toys and start playing with you instead.[3]

Mio picks up the toy that Åsa introduces.

Mio plays intensively.

Åsa ignores the old toy and starts playing with the new one. Mio switches to the new toy.

By encourage we mean enthusiastically proclaim your excitement (towards the toy you are playing with), drag the toy along the ground and make the toy interesting in other ways. Don't say, "leave it" or anything else that draws attention to the toy the dog is playing with, but focus fully on playing with the new toy. Have a lot of fun with your toy and be engrossed in your own play. If the dog wants to carry the other toy somewhere else, practice indoors or on a fenced-in lawn to contain the dog, or put the dog on a harness and long line.

The On and Off Game

Dogs must be trained to have on and off switches. Some dogs are calm by nature and they won't need much training for this, but the majority of dogs need to learn how to go from on to off. The "On and Off Game"[4] is an excellent way to teach the dog a signal to calm down. You can also use this method to teach the dog to release an object on cue:

1. Put a leash and collar or a harness on your dog.

2. Get her playing for 20-30 seconds.

3. When you stop playing, take your dog by the collar and release the toy. It's important that you release the toy immediately since the dog will hold on to the toy even more if she sees that you also want it.

4. Calmly hold the dog by the collar so she can't lie down and chew on the toy. Make sure that you are calm and quiet when you do this. You should hold the dog only as much as is necessary to keep her from lying down, but not to the point that it is unpleasant (you shouldn't be lifting the dog by the collar but rather have a loose hold).

[3] We borrowed this exercise from Susan Garett, www.clickerdogs.com. Check out her YouTube videos showing how she does it.

[4] We borrowed this game from Eva Bodfäldt, author of the book "Follow me – a deal with your dog"

Maria gets Nellie excited by playing.

After playing for a moment, Maria releases the toy and holds Nellie by the collar.

Nellie calms down and releases the toy. Then it's time to start playing again!

5. When your dog has calmed down and released the toy, you can start playing again. You can also reward the release with a treat and then start playing again. In time, you'll notice that the dog relaxes and releases the toy as soon as you take her collar.

Getting the Toy Back

Eventually you'll need a cue to get the dog to release the toy, but prior to this there are a few different ways to get the toy back. Either you put a treat against the dog's nose until she releases the toy, after which you give her the treat. Or you hold the dog by the collar until she releases the toy, as we described in the "On and Off Game" above. The third option is to just steal the toy from the dog when she has a looser hold. Stealing the toy like this will be useful when training later on, because you teach the dog to keep a firm hold as the toy might just disappear. The last alternative is probably only usable at the early stages of training before the dog has learnt to keep hold of the object. You can read more about how to teach the dog to release on cue in the chapter "Delivery to Hand".

Coach Says

Do you get irritated when your dog bites your hands when you are playing tug? Try tying a long rope on the toy so the dog's mouth is further away from your hands. Make sure whatever is on the end of the rope is extremely bite-friendly and that the rope isn't bite-friendly at all. If the dog still bites your hands, stop playing when she bites and then start again when the dog is a little calmer. Present the toy to the dog so she takes it the way you want her to take it.

Learning and Play

As we mentioned earlier, you will notice that when we start teaching something new we almost always start with using play as a resource. Play draws on a lot of the basic skills we want to teach: When you are playing with the dog and hide the toy behind your back, the dog will look at you to get the toy again (focus). The dog takes the toy and wins when her hold is distinct and engaged (taking). The dog brings the toy to you and immediately gets it back as a reward (delivery to hand) and so on and so forth.

Starting all teaching with play is a straightforward and fun way to foster a strong relationship between you and your dog. If we could look into the minds of our dogs, we would want them to both feel and think that training is like a really fun party. Fortunately we don't need to look into our dog's mind to see if they are happy and having fun – their body language is usually a good indicator.

Inappropriate Play

Is play always a good thing? No, there is also such a thing as inappropriate play. Examples of inappropriate play are when you rough-house so fiercely with the dog that you knock her over. Typical displacement activities – things an animal does as a result of too much stress – are a dog humping her handler's leg, starting to chew on the handler's arms and hands, or starting to bark hysterically. Dogs can become slightly afraid of their handlers when they play, so get to know your dog and her temperament. Many people think that a rough free-for-all is the way you have to play, but there are other options. Inappropriate play can also occur when the dog is excited before and/or after an exercise where the dog needs to be calm and focused. A quiet game where the dog is allowed to chew on her favorite ball or where you push each other around lazily might be the best game for your particular dog. Try many different types of play to discover which is the most appropriate level for your dog in a given situation.

Play with Distraction

Since play is such an important part of our training, we want the dog to be able to play with us in any environment. We also want her to be able to ignore other distractions in the immediate surroundings. Being able to play with you wherever you are, regardless of what else is happening is a good foundation to teach the dog to remain focused in the face of distractions. For example, it is desirable that the dog

is able to heel when dummies are falling to the right and left or while other dogs are working around her.

Just like anything else we teach the dog, it is best to start with an easier challenge and then increase the level of distraction. Start with simple distractions in an environment the dog is familiar with – at home in the backyard or in the kitchen. As the dog is able to deal with more and more distractions, gradually introduce more challenging environments. The better the dog becomes at playing while ignoring the distraction, the more challenging the environment can be.

A simple distraction game involves two equally desirable tug toys where the dog is allowed to play with one of them.

1. Hold the toy with one hand and play with your dog.

2. When the dog starts to pull and is into the game, carefully take out the other toy. As opposed to the exercise we described before, you should not pretend to play with the new toy. Just let it sit in your other hand while you keep playing with the dog with the first toy.

3. After a while, start gradually moving the new toy more and if the dog manages to keep playing, wave it around more and more. If your dog releases the first toy, remove the distraction toy and start playing with the first toy again and make the exercise a little easier. If the dog finds it difficult, start with a toy that she finds less desirable than the first one.

4. Successively introduce a higher value toy. You can also have a helper manage the distraction toy. Remind your helper not to make the distraction too difficult to begin with.

Every chapter in this book contains several concrete descriptions of how you can use play to train your dog to ignore distractions. You'll find sections such as "Focus with Distractions", "Holding with Distractions", and so on. These playful exercises lay the groundwork for your dog to gradually be able to perform behaviors such as taking, holding, fetching, walking at heel, coming, and staying during flushes in all possible environments with all possible distractions.

Summary

- Play allows you to train almost all the basic skills needed in gun dog training.
- Find out what kinds of games your particular dog likes.
- Find as many different ways as possible to play with your dog.
- If your dog is able to play in various environments, she is more likely to be able to perform other tasks in the same environments.

Focus

We want our dogs to follow and check in with us without us having to nag, which is so incredibly boring. Having the dog look at us is moreover the foundation of almost everything she has to do and learn, so contact and focus are among the first things we start teaching her.

The dog must be able to look at you when you say her name, but things are a lot easier if you don't have to cue the behavior all the time. In the beginning, it might feel like it takes an eternity for the dog to look at you, especially in distraction rich environments. But if you begin in an easy environment and make sure you have your dog make contact with you before anything else happens, she will soon do so of her own accord in every environment. Avoid clicking your tongue, stamping your foot or anything else to get the dog's attention. Otherwise the dog won't learn to spontaneously make contact with you, but instead will learn that you will nag her to get her to do so. A lot of dogs actively seek contact with their humans. Use this; when the dog spontaneously makes eye contact in different situations, praise her or click and give her a reward.

Coach Says

Always start your training session by having your dog make contact with you, so you know that she is in the right frame of mind and wants to work. Do the same thing when you take the dog out of the car or go through a door. Wait, calmly and silently, until she makes contact with you before letting her out. Then you can start your walk or training.

Play to Inspire Focus

When we say contact or focus, we mean that the dog should look us in the eye. We preferably start teaching this using play.

1. Get the dog going so she becomes engaged in the game.
2. Steal the toy from the dog. Quickly hide it behind your back and wait for the dog to look at you. If the dog tries to run behind your back to take the toy, try hiding it under your arm or inside your sweater so the dog can't get to it.

3. When the dog looks at you, take out the toy and start playing again.

A good approach with a puppy or small dog might be to sit on the ground and play so it's a little easier for the dog to look you in the eyes. In the beginning, it's enough if the dog just casts a quick glance towards us. Later we increase the level of difficulty so the dog must make eye contact for the toy to come out again.

It might be difficult to steal the toy from a dog that is used to playing tug games. That's exactly the way we want it! Eventually even inexperienced dogs will learn to get a better hold on the toy (otherwise it might just disappear!). When it's no longer possible to steal the toy from the dog, it's time to teach her to release the toy when we ask for it. Teaching the dog to hold on to the object for dear life will be extremely useful later on during your gun dog training. The dog should place great value on holding on to an object. It therefore doesn't matter if you weren't able to steal the toy from the dog in the previous exercise. Either you can say, "thank you" (if the dog can release the object on cue) or you can place a treat against the dog's nose so she releases the object. Then hide the toy and reward the dog when she makes contact with you.

Pitfall

We can't stress this enough: Don't try to entice the dog, wait until she spontaneously makes contact with you. This might initially take some time, but if you shorten the leash and wait, the dog will make contact sooner or later.

Follow the Handler – Play Simon Says

Besides looking at us when we stand still, we want the dog to look at us and follow us when we move. When the dog stands in front of you, faces you, and focuses on you, try

backing away a little bit. Click and reward the dog if she follows you and continues to look you in the eye. Then make the task a little more difficult by backing away more quickly or slowly and by turning in different directions. Reward the dog when she continues to focus on you. It might be beneficial to vary your rewards by sometimes giving her treats and other times play. When the dog easily follows you, back up, turn and walk forward with the dog next to you. In more distracting environments, you might need to go back to having the dog follow you when you back away.

Go to various places and teach the dog to make contact, both on and off leash (once you've reached that point). The goal is for the dog to follow you regardless of what's happening in the surrounding environment. When the dog is on leash, it can be easy to forget to work on having the dog following you and instead direct the dog with the leash. Rather, try to forget the leash and teach the dog to follow you with a loose leash. If it's hard to forget the leash, tie it around your waist or to your belt. If we stop, we want the dog to stop before the leash is taut. You can start teaching the dog by having her close to you and rewarding her for looking at you:

1. Take a step forward and stop.
2. Reward the dog when she stops and makes eye contact with you.
3. Try taking a step to the side and reward the dog when she stops. If the leash is taut, stop and wait until the dog makes contact with you or turn and walk in the other direction. Reward the dog when she makes contact with you and then try stopping again.
4. Advance the training so the dog can follow you when you run five steps forward, turn to the right, go two steps and then stop with the leash still loose.

5. This can be beneficial to train during your walks, even when the dog is off leash. Click when the dog makes eye contact with you and toss her a treat. Then continue the walk and reward the dog the next time she makes contact with you.

Focus with Distractions

This is an extremely simple but brilliant distraction exercise with endless possibilities:

1. Preferably start by sitting on the floor with the dog in front of you. Hide a few treats in one hand and hold them so the dog can get to your hand. If it's too difficult, you can hold the hand with the treats still at your side. Just ignore your dog if she tries to get at the treats by licking your hand. Stay totally quiet!

2. As soon as your dog takes her nose away from your hand, click and give her a reward. Preferably reward the dog with the other hand (the one that doesn't have treats). After several repetitions, wait until the dog removes her nose from your hand and looks up.

3. Maybe next time the dog might look up at you a bit longer before you click, and after she has tried that, maybe she will look you in the eye. Sometimes the dog's glance might be very quick, so be ready with the clicker!

4. Keep practicing until the dog doesn't show any interest in your hand but looks you in the eye instead. Then you can try different positions with the hand holding the treat: high, low, in front of you, behind you. While you're doing this, reward the dog when she makes eye contact. You can also try opening your palm so the treat is visible.

Focus during Training Sessions

When you are in the middle of a training session, don't let your dog walk away and investigate the environment

...m maintains eye contact even ...ough Jenny is enticing him with ...eats.

several yards away and then come back and receive a treat for making contact. Because then you are teaching the dog that it's okay to go off on her own and then come back to continue training. Instead, keep the training sessions short so the dog works with you without wandering away. In a more challenging environment, you might initially keep the training sessions to ten seconds or even less. You might also put a leash on the dog and keep the leash in your hand and hold it gently if the dog tries to wander away. Keep in mind that the dog might go off because she really does need a break. In that case, you've been training for too long. Allow the dog to rest a little bit and then continue training. Make sure that you are the one to interrupt the training next time, before the dog loses focus.

Everyday Focus

Teaching the dog to focus is a lifestyle! We reward our dogs for making contact every day, as often as we can. This might be while we go for a walk and the dog stops and makes contact with us or comes up beside us and looks at us. Another example would be our dog spotting another

dog and making contact with us (instead of running up to the other dog) or when we go through the door and the dog looks at us for permission before she is allowed to go out. In other words, we are teaching the dog that it is worthwhile to keep an eye on us and to seek contact with us.

If your dog isn't used to making contact with you, make it easy for the dog at first. If you've never trained her to make contact at the door, the dog will hardly be able to look at you for several minutes before you go out. Start the training at the dog's level. The "Play to Inspire Focus" exercise, described earlier, teaches your dog to make contact with you more often, even in other situations. You must always be prepared to give your dog a reward!

Summary

- Reward your dog when she spontaneously makes contact with you.
- Teach the dog that it's worthwhile to keep an eye on you – regardless of what's happening in the surrounding area.

Elsa and Ludde

The Road to Learning

When we are going to teach the dog a behavior, we always follow the same path. We call it the road to learning.[5] We follow this path throughout all of our training and it helps us progress in a structured manner. If the training doesn't go as planned, we just make a U-turn and go back a bit before moving forward again.

5 Egtvedt & Køste, Lydnadsträning i teori och praktik, 2008.

The road to learning consists of a number of checkpoints, where we first determine the goal, then make a plan, and finally start training. In our training, we start with an offered behavior to which we then add a cue. Over time, we also start adding distractions while training a particular behavior until we can finally combine it with other behaviors and increase the dog's mental stamina by not rewarding every instance of the behavior.

Goal Setting

Before we start training, we should always set our goals. These should be as specific as possible to help facilitate the training. What should the behavior look like? In which situations is the dog to perform the behavior? We also consider the types of rewards we want to use and the activity level and demeanor we want the dog to exhibit in her behavior.

If we use a marked retrieve as an example, our goal is for the dog to run out at full speed, take the object with a firm but gentle hold and then return straight to us at full speed and put the object in our hand. The dog should be able to do this in the forest and in a meadow, in a marsh and in water, and when there are other dogs and people nearby. The dog should be quiet and still beside us, looking towards the area where the mark will fall. The dog's body should be tense, but not to the point where she's shaking and almost whining. Nor should the dog sit there too relaxed; she should be engaged in what's happening around her.

This is a clear and concrete goal. However, we aren't quite ready to start training yet. First we want to break down the various parts of a marked retrieve: sitting still and silently next to the handler, remembering where the mark fell,

running out to the object, picking it up, returning with it and delivering it. When we have broken down the various components of a behavior, we identify the criteria and objective for each part, that is to say we make a plan for each of the small steps that make up the entire behavior.

Make a Training Plan

A training plan is made up of the steps that we are planning to take on our way towards accomplishing our overall goal. For delivery to hand, we start by teaching the dog to touch her nose to our hand (hand target). First she should do this without an object and later with an object, so that the dog learns she should always deliver the retrieved object to our hand. In this case, the first step in the training plan looks like this:

Goal:

- The dog distinctly presses her nose into your hand as quickly as she can when she sees your hand. The dog is quiet and focused on the task for the entire session.

Training plan:

1. The dog sniffs your hand when it's offered two inches from the dog's nose. Reward!
2. The dog lightly presses her nose into your hand when it's offered two inches from her nose. Reward!
3. The dog presses her nose hard into your hand when it's offered two inches away from her nose. Reward!
4. The dog presses her nose hard into your hand when it's offered four inches away. Reward!
5. Offer your hand eight inches away. Reward! ... and so on.

When writing down your training plan, leave enough space between each step so you can add more details as needed.

Animal trainer Bob Bailey says, "be a splitter, not a lumper". We think this is a good phrase to keep in the back of your mind when making a training plan. Quite simply, it's better to break the behavior into many small steps than to have a few larger steps. If the training progresses faster than you thought, you can always skip steps. A training plan is a dynamic document that you constantly assess and change as necessary. As this process becomes more natural, you can easily make a plan on the fly if the behavior you are training isn't too complicated.

When we make a training plan, we should also consider how we are going to achieve the behavior. Are we going to shape it? Are we going to use any kind of aid? If so, how are we going to eventually fade out this aid? There is nothing wrong with using aids; we just have to have a plan for how to remove them. Remember though, that it often takes less time to teach many behaviors without aids than it does to

teach them with aids and then having to gradually remove those aids. One example is the down, which we can most often capture when the dog spontaneously lays down.

We should also consider the dog's skills and natural behaviors. If something is particularly easy for the dog, we should definitely use it during training. If a dog easily takes an object, we can skip the step that involves showing interest in the object and immediately reward the dog when she takes the object. If we are going to teach the dog to spin and we know that she spontaneously spins to the right, we should start by teaching her to spin to the right. It's silly to make things more difficult than they need to be.

Coach Says
You can find a training plan template on our webpage www.retrievingforalloccasions.com.

Shape the Behavior

Once we have a training plan, it's time to start training. We always start with developing a behavior voluntarily, without a cue, according to our training plan. Often we do it by shaping the behavior, which means we gradually get the dog to perform the behavior we want. We can also alter the environment to make it easier for the dog to perform the desired behavior or use some kind of target. An example of altering the environment might be allowing the dog to run on a straight path to teach her to go straight out while running to a blind. (Running to a blind involves sending the dog straight out away from you to a certain area. When she's in the right area, you blow your hunt whistle to cue the dog to start searching. When the dog finds the object, she brings it back to you). Removing distractions is another way to correct the environment, for instance moving further away from other dogs at the beginning of our training and then moving closer. When using a target, we might first teach the dog to search for and step on a mouse pad. Then we place the mouse pad further away and gradually move it so the dog can run straight out even when the mouse pad isn't there.

When we start training, we always want to have everything working in our favor. If our goal is that the dog should be calm when she performs the behavior, we don't train when she is hyperactive. We might start with a walk or sit and relax for a minute and then we start training.

Coach Says

Don't wait too long to add a cue! As soon as the behavior appears approximately the way you want it, you should start giving a cue. Then you can switch between training the behavior voluntarily — and refining the details — and training on cue.

Add the Cue

When the dog performs the behavior as we want it and can do it time after time, we can start adding a cue to the behavior. You can read more about that process in the chapter "Do What I Say". In short, we start by giving the cue when the dog performs the behavior and we know that she will perform the entire behavior correctly. When training marked retrieves, for instance, this would be when we have seen the dog run out, fetch the object, and bring it straight back several times. At first, we say "fetch" at the exact moment the dog takes the object. Then we give the cue earlier and earlier until we finally give the cue to the dog when we want her to perform the behavior.

Proof the Behavior

The most important element of learning is training the dog to perform a behavior even when there are distractions present – this is called proofing. It's great if the dog can perform a behavior at home where she is calm and quiet, but the behavior isn't that useful if the dog can't do it anywhere else. Distraction training means that we generalize the dog's knowledge so that she can perform the behavior regardless of what else is happening around her.

When the dog is able to offer a behavior voluntarily while we are standing in our usual training position, we can start to gradually alter the environment. We might sit down, stamp on the ground, or move to a new spot. When we add distractions, we might need to go back a bit in the training plan in order for the dog to perform the behavior. Don't be afraid to do so! Just because a dog can do something at home doesn't mean she is able to do it in a new environment.

We're not just using distraction training with offered behaviors, but also behaviors on cue. The recall is a clear example of when we use distraction training on both the voluntarily offered and the cued behavior throughout the dog's entire life. We reward the dog when she voluntarily ignores a distraction and comes to us (even when not being called) as well as when she comes to us when we call her away from the distraction.

Variable Schedule of Rewards

When a dog can perform a behavior on cue, it's time to start working on a variable schedule of rewards. Using a variable schedule isn't about removing rewards entirely, but rather about varying how and when you offer them as well as how long the dog needs to work before she gets what she wants. The goal is that the dog will always know that working will pay off, even if she doesn't know exactly when the reward will come. For instance, when walking at heel, sometimes we reward the dog after the first step, and sometimes after the fifth, and eventually after 50, 100, 300, and so on.

Variable reward schedules are extremely important in building the dog's mental stamina. We also use it when we start to connect the different components into a whole. If we see that there is a weak link, we can work on it separately as well as reward the dog when she performs it during the overall training.

A frequent "clicker ailment" is that the handler rewards the dog too often, without daring to push the dog and make the task more difficult. In order to connect several parts and have longer training sessions with the dog, we have to introduce variable schedules of rewards somewhat early. If the dog is used to getting a reward every fifth second, it makes it difficult for her to get through an entire field trial without a reward.

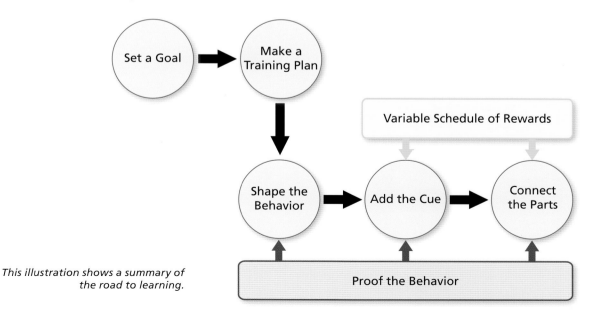

This illustration shows a summary of the road to learning.

At the other end of the spectrum, another "clicker ailment" is the handler rewarding the dog too seldom, above all at the beginning of training and if the handler is a beginner with clicker training. Remember to continually adjust your training plan after your session and keep a record so you can see exactly how the training is progressing.

There are a few rules of thumb that are helpful when determining the right amount of rewards. A few signs that you are rewarding the dog too often:

- The dog is correct 99 percent of the time.
- The dog expects her reward in a specific place and becomes frustrated when she doesn't get it.

A few signs that you are not rewarding the dog enough:

- The dog loses concentration and walks away.
- The dog looks miserable (crouching, putting her tail between her legs, etc.).
- The dog often makes mistakes.

Connect the Parts

When we have taught the dog all of the different parts, we can begin putting the entire behavioral sequence together. We can later connect all of the different behaviors together into a competition program or field trial. We previously wrote about distraction training at every step, but remember this also needs to be done with the entire behavioral sequence.

We often use forward chaining or temporary chaining[6] to increase the dog's mental stamina to do things she can already do well; the dog doesn't know when the reward is coming, but she knows that the reward will come sometime. When we put retrieving and marks together, we believe back chaining is more effective, which means we always end in the same way and instead add components at the beginning. It can be difficult to understand when you read about it and we've even had a few participants in our courses refer to it as "the back chaining mess", but don't let that scare you. You will soon become an expert in back chaining.

---

[6] The informal expression for this is chain. However, the technical definition of a chain is a series of behaviors in a fixed order. What we refer to when we say chain is the technical definition for behavioral sequences. We have chosen to keep the term chain because it is easier to understand.

Repeat after us:

34

1234

555 1234

202 555 1234

Did you notice how it got easier every time you got closer to the end of the chain? What we're doing is learning each part individually. Then we put all the pieces together and start from the end. First we repeat the last pair of digits. Then we add the next to last, and continue with the last two. In this way, we link the pieces of the chain together. We give the dog a reward at the same place in the chain – after the last part.

Coach Says
Remember that if the chain is long, the reward must also be worth-while; the more challenging the chain, the better the reward.

Sooner or later the dog will test you to see if there is an easier way to get a reward. During retrieving, for example, she might try placing the object at your feet instead of in your hand. If you ask the dog to pick up the object again and then put it in your hand, you are teaching the dog an entirely different chain, which you don't want. That's why it's important to interrupt the chain as soon as something goes wrong. The easiest way to do this is to just hide the reward and call the dog, or by removing the object that the dog released. If it's a chain you have completed many times in the past, you can try completing the entire sequence one more time. If that still doesn't work, you need to start again with back chaining or spending more time on the individual parts that aren't working before you reintroduce it into the sequence.

The biggest advantage of back chaining is that the chain is extremely stable since each new link reinforces the previous one. That means that when the dog does something correctly, being able to continue the chain is a reward in itself as she is one step closer to receiving her ultimate reward. Every cue in the chain thus has a double function and becomes the glue that holds it together.

When you want to put long chains together, it can be advantageous to break them up into smaller segments and then put them back together in different configurations. You can back chain the last three parts of the chain and then connect them back together with the two first parts that the dog had mastered previously. You can also create overlapping chains that you then put together.

Learning All the Time

The road to learning describes how we teach the dog things during our planned training sessions. But of course, the dog is learning all the time, not just when we've decided to train. In our daily interactions with the dog, we obviously don't compose training plans for every item the dog is to learn, but we still keep this in mind.

One example is when we are to go out for a walk. We want our dog to sit quietly and calmly on the doormat while we get our things together and get ready. That's why we reward the dog when she seeks out the doormat. Then we reward her for sitting and finally we reward her for remaining sitting for longer and longer periods. Next we add the cue, "Wanna go for a walk?" which means, "Now we are going out, so it's time for you to sit on the mat and wait". A good distraction is to run in and out of the hall to get things you forgot in the other room while the dog patiently waits on the mat. When the dog is able to ignore you, it's time to introduce a variable schedule of rewards. Finally, when there is no other way to reward the dog, we open the door and go out – exactly what the dog wants. In other words, the dog will receive a reward for sitting quietly every day for the rest of her life!

Train, Prevent, Interrupt

As we wrote previously, clicker training is part of our everyday lives as we establish ground rules for how we want to integrate the dog into the family. As the Swedish gun dog trainer Sten Christoffersson puts it, "I want to give my dog good habits from the beginning". That's what we want too! That's why we train the dog to do the things we want, but when we don't have the time or energy to train actively, we make sure we prevent the dog from learning unwanted behaviours. If that still doesn't work and the dog does something we don't want, we interrupt the behavior in a neutral way. In short, we always follow the strategy: Train. Prevent. Interrupt.

A typical example you might see in a home with a dog that loves to carry objects is the dog who might bring you a dress shoe or go to a corner and chew on it. We start by training the dog to leave the shoes alone, such as by standing by the shoe rack and rewarding the dog when she looks in another direction. We also give the dog other toys that she can carry around and enthusiastically praise her when she takes them instead. As we progress and make the training slightly more advanced, we can leave the shoes beside the toys and praise the dog when she takes the toys instead of the shoes. The first few times we do this, we place the shoes far enough away that we are sure the dog will make the right choice. When we don't have time to train, we can put baby gates or chicken wire in front of the shoe rack or just put the shoes in the closet. If the dog still manages to get a shoe and happily runs away with it, we calmly go after the dog and give her a treat in exchange for the shoe.

We have taught our dogs that it's okay to carry things that are on the floor, but that they should leave things that are on tables and shelves alone. That means that shoes on the floor might be brought to us while we are enjoying our breakfast, but shoes on the shoe rack are off limits. When we started training, we first made sure that there weren't any delicate shoes lying around and when necessary, we put chicken wire in front of the shoe rack. The shoe stealing usually subsides on its own as the dog learns what behaviors pay off the most. You yourself choose how you want to spend your energy: training or preventing and training something else. If we want to be left alone while we eat breakfast without being presented with a lot of objects, we can either make sure that there aren't a lot of things left out or we ask the dog to go and lay in her crate during that time. We should be cautious in encouraging dogs that have a hard time relaxing and prefer pacing back and forth to actively search for objects when we're not training. In the long term, it can become extremely irritating. At the same time, it's a balancing act since in all of our training, especially in gun dog training, we want the dog's first instinct to be to come to us as soon as she has something in her mouth. It's a behavior we want to encourage sufficiently in our daily interactions.

You should also consider how this training can affect other skills and behaviors you are working on. It's counterproductive to teach the dog to stay steady when a bird flies up if we allow our spaniel to run after a ball before we give her the "take it" cue (we should wait until the ball lands). During field trials, a spaniel is to stop as soon as she flushes the game but in the ball game we just described, the dog runs after it instead. Another example is other family members permitting the dog to do things that you don't, such as running away with an object instead of delivering it to your hand. Decide what's important to you and your dog, but always be conscious that what your dog learns can have consequences for other behaviors you want to teach her.

Summary

- Plan your training, train and then evaluate your progress after each session.
- Make sure you use distraction training with every behavior, both offered and on cue.
- Learning occurs all the time so you have to have a general strategy for everything you want the dog to learn: Train. Prevent. Interrupt.

Tassla

Taking and Holding

We want quick and accurate deliveries, which is why we must teach our dogs the correct way to pick up an object. After picking up the dummy, we want the dog to return to us at lightning speed. This means we have to teach the dog to get a firm but gentle hold on the retrieved object from the beginning so she doesn't have to set it down to get a better hold.

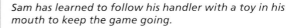
Sam has learned to follow his handler with a toy in his mouth to keep the game going.

A lot of spaniels and retrievers have a loose grip despite the fact that they love to carry things. So, we need to teach them to keep a firm hold on the dummy at all times.

Play to Inspire Taking and Holding

We begin teaching our dogs how to take an object with the help of playful exercises. Start with a long, soft toy, such as a braided rope.

1. Start playing with the dog and back away from her so she follows you with the toy in her mouth. Hold the toy and keep playing with the dog while you continue to back up.

2. Release the toy a little bit (keep backing up) and if the dog maintains a strong grip, grab the toy again and continue playing. In the beginning, seconds matter, so be quick to start pulling at the toy again.

3. In the end, you should be able to let go of the toy entirely and grab hold of it again without the dog changing or loosening her grip. We want the dog to come after us with the toy because she wants to continue playing with us.

4. When the dog has a good grip and puts her weight into pulling the toy, we reward this by allowing the dog to win the toy. Sometimes we tease the dog a little when she wins, and sometimes we step back directly so that she comes after us with the toy in her mouth, and we can start playing all over again.

If the dog stops playing and starts shaking the toy, or if she lays down and chews on it, carefully take the toy and start again, that is, get the dog riled up with play until she gets a good grip on the toy again. In the next round, make it a little easier by not letting go of the object entirely, but rather, keep a loose hold on it, and back even further away from the dog so that she follows you. It will be harder for the dog to lie down if she keeps moving. Several successful repetitions in a row will teach the dog that we want her to hold the toy firmly. The next step is making the task more difficult by standing still. Teaching the dog to hold an object while being close to us is the basis of all gun dog training. By using play to inspire taking and holding, we are also teaching the dog the basics of delivery to hand and the recall.

Shaping the Pick Up

The majority of spaniels and retrievers love to have things in their mouths. However, if you have a dog that doesn't want to hold things, you can click and reward the dog with a treat when she shows interest in the retrieve object, for opening her mouth and finally picking up the object. However, these exercises are a bit more demanding of your technical abilities as a trainer. In the worst case scenario, you might click when the dog releases or spits out the object instead of when she holds it. Clicking for interest in and holding on to dummies works well too, but we believe that teaching through play encourages a better and more stable hold. Therefore, we

always start with play before we experiment with clicking and giving the dog treats. Play also helps to spark the dog's interest in the object so she actually enjoys holding it. First, we get the dog going with play so she takes the toy and holds it. Then we try this with a dummy. We present the dummy to the dog in a calm manner so she doesn't start playing with it immediately. But if the dog is entirely disinterested in the dummy we might have to start playing a little to make her take the object. If the dog runs away with the dummy, starts shaking it or chewing on it, we return to working with toys first and then calmly introduce the dummy again, and teach the dog to follow us with the dummy in her mouth.

Release at the Click

When we use the clicker to train the taking and holding exercises, we want the dog to release the object quickly when she hears the click. This way, we avoid reinforcing unwanted behaviors between the click and the reward, such as the dog running away with the object or starting to chew on it. To teach the dog to release an object at the sound of a click: Start with an object that she's not particularly interested in keeping. Give her the object, click and wait for her to release the object spontaneously, after which you offer ample rewards. If your dog doesn't release the object while you wait, try using the "Let's play together!" exercise (described in the chapter "Play –the Ultimate Reward") and click at the exact moment when she releases the object to pick up the other toy. In the beginning, we click just as the dog lets go of the object, and later on we click just before she lets go of it. Eventually the dog will learn that the click means, "release".

Holding Different Objects

Different objects require different techniques for holding and carrying. Remember to train with as many objects as possible – small, large, hard and soft dummies – and also other objects such as branches, forks, shoes and plastic lids. Anything you can think of that can help boost the dog's understanding of holding and carrying.

Some dogs are not fond of objects that smell of other dogs. During field trials, your dog has to hold game and dummies that don't have your scent on it, so borrow objects that others have used and teach your dog to hold them as well.

Taking in the Middle of the Object

When the dog takes the dummy, we want her to pick it up in the middle. She shouldn't take the dummy as if it was a cigar since she might drop it. If your dog immediately takes the dummy in the middle, you don't need to spend extra time working on this. Just pay attention if your dog starts holding it sloppily, in which case you will need to go back and work on the pick-up again.

Coach Says

In the beginning, you might want to prevent your dog from picking up the dummy by the string by simply removing the string. After several successful repetitions, you can reattach the string and reward the dog only when she takes the dummy in the middle.

In the beginning, we introduce the dummy in a way that makes it easy for the dog to hold it correctly. Later on we make it more difficult so the dog has to choose to take it in the middle in order to receive her reward. If your dog hesitates at all and isn't interested in taking the dummy, you should most certainly avoid starting to teach her a proper pick-up. The risk is that you will reinforce the dog's hesitation. Instead, you should go back to work on using play to encourage the dog to take the object so it becomes an activity she enjoys.

Coach Says

If you want to see how your dog reacts to a dummy that doesn't have your scent on it, ask a friend to place one of his or her dummies in the woods for your dog to find.

Another training technique is to use plastic bottles partially filled with water. They require the dog to learn how to get a firm and balanced grip; otherwise she can't carry the bottle. Start with a half-filled bottle. When your dog's performance improves, you can vary the amount of water in the bottle. Eventually, it shouldn't matter if the bottle is empty, partially or totally full – the dog should be able to carry it. You can also purchase dummies with three sections that serve the same function as a bottle.

The dog must also learn how to pick up game correctly. When the dog has a little more experience with game, she will most often learn how to balance it properly in her mouth. Otherwise she won't be able to carry it. If the dog often goes for the wings, you might need to secure them with a rubber band a few times so she can only pick the bird up by the middle.

But ...

... it doesn't work to have treats nearby when I am practicing retrieving, because my dog just spits the dummy out. In fact, that's what most dogs do in the beginning. But if we take the opportunity to teach the dog that it pays off to keep the object, even when she knows you have treats, you get a dog that really knows what she is doing.

Taking from the Ground

At first, we let the dog take the object out of our hand for the simple reason it allows us to have the most control over the object and how the dog takes it. When the dog takes the object correctly, we try lowering it further and further towards the ground until we finally set it down. But so far we haven't given a take cue because we want the dog to pick up the object correctly of her own accord.

To make it easier for the dog in the beginning, we start with holding the object with both hands, one on each end. Some dogs immediately pick up the object from the ground, so we won't spend too much time on it here, but if the dog finds it difficult we need to take several steps back. For instance, we can set the object on our feet, so it's elevated a little and is easier for the dog to pick up. We can also place the object between our feet to hold it in place until the dog takes it the way we want her to. Another technique is to hold the object with one hand while it's still on the ground. We loosen our grip little by little, until we are just holding it with one finger and finally let go entirely. Experiment to see what works best for you and your dog.

If the dog starts to hold the object by the end again, we pick up the object and make it a little easier for the dog. If necessary, we let the dog take it from our hands a few times. Then we put the object on the ground again.

Ready, Set, Go!

To really make the dog want to take the object, we can get her going a little by holding her by the collar and saying, "Ready, set, go!" excitedly and then release her towards the object. We can also compete with the dog and run with her towards the object. If the dog doesn't get ahead of us, we grab the object and tease her a bit before trying again. However, we have to be extremely careful not to make the dog feel uncomfortable and become fearful that we are going to steal the object. If that's the case, it might be time to stop the game or let the dog win almost every time to boost her confidence and make her excited to play the game.

> ### Coach Says
> *When training, work on one thing at a time! When you are training your dog to take the object, click and reward her for taking it. Allow the dog to release the object at the click and don't worry about the delivery to hand. You can work on that later on and then connect it to the pick-up.*

Taking the Object with Distractions

To get the dog to take the object and immediately look up at us, we first practice the exercise while standing a short distance away and then introduce distractions before we increase the distance.

"Merry Go Round" [7]

The goal of this exercise is to get the dog to turn back to us as soon as she takes the object even when distractions are present:

1. Put your dog on your left side and hold the dummy in your right hand at the same height as the dog's nose.
2. Spin to the right and have the dog chase the dummy and grab it.

---

[7] We've borrowed this exercise from Eva Bodfäldt, www.evabodfaldt.com.

3. When the dog takes the dummy, let go of it and back away from the dog so she follows you.

4. Click and reward the dog when she immediately turns towards you.

5. Do the same thing again, but just as the dog grabs the object, have your helper create a minor distraction, such as saying, "Hello." In the beginning, what we want is to have the dog look back within a second after the distraction, then that she only glances at it and eventually turns towards you right away without even acknowledging the distraction.

If it becomes too challenging and your dog goes to check out the distraction, silently bring the dog back and make a new, easier attempt. Vary the distraction (increasing or reducing the difficulty) so that the dog is successful most of the time. Remember that success is the main way that will teach the dog what we want her to learn.

Pitfall

If the dog wants to run away with the object, go back to the basic exercise where you play with the dog and back away from her so she wants to follow you and continue the game. If necessary, use a leash to keep her close by.

If the dog becomes too excited when she chases after the dummy, wait to give it to her until she's calm. Have the dog take the dummy from you when you are standing still or when she has offered a sit. Then try turning away from your dog slowly and have her take the dummy while you are still moving. When she can take the object from your hand even when there are distractions, experiment by doing the same thing with the dummy on the ground. If it's too advanced and your dog doesn't perform well, make it easier and try again. If the dog's holds become sloppier and sloppier, remove the distractions and practice taking the object from the ground again.

Yodler takes the dummy that Pär gives him and immediately looks up at Pär.

When Pär backs away, Yodler follows after him with the dummy in his mouth.

Even when there are distractions, Yodler is able to keep holding the dummy while looking up at Pär.

Take the First One!

When the dog is able to pick something up, we also want her to take the first object she finds, without wondering if there is something else to find. The goal is to prevent the dog from looking for more items when she has game or other objects in her mouth.

1. Start with two identical objects that the dog likes to pick up.
2. Set them a few yards apart and position yourself and your dog close to one of them.
3. Wait until the dog spontaneously grabs the closest object and turns toward you. Click and reward the dog.
4. Then move the objects closer and closer together until they are finally right next to each other.
5. As the dog masters the task, you can add more items of varying levels of attractiveness to your dog and move yourself further away from the pile of objects.

If the dog takes the wrong item or starts to pick and choose, call her to you and then place the objects further apart before trying again. Remember to increase the level of difficulty one step at a time; either more items or longer distances.

Hold on for Dear Life

When the dog spontaneously brings us something, such as a toy, we don't want her to release it when we try to take it. Instead, we want her to keep the object even if we pull on it – just like we want her to keep the dummy or game until we ask her to drop it in our hand.

Since the dog is already used to us poking at the objects she has in her mouth and she knows to hold on to the object even when we pull on it, this task is often easy to accomplish.

When the dog brings us a toy, we carefully touch it and if she keeps holding on to it, we can either say "thank you" and reward her, or allow her to keep the toy, praising and petting her. If the dog releases the toy, we snatch it away, teasing her gently before giving it back to her. Then we try poking at the toy again, but only to the extent that the dog is able to keep the object. Gradually, we make it more difficult by grabbing more and more of the toy before we say "thank you" or allowing the dog to keep the toy. In the end, we will be able to grasp the toy firmly, without being able to pull it out of the dog's mouth.

This exercise teaches the dog to actively hold the object, and reduces the risk that she'll drop or lose it.

Elsa asks Diesel to fetch a ball.

Diesel picks a ball and brings it to Elsa.

Holding with Distractions – Reverse Luring

Does your dog drop the object from her mouth as soon as you take treats out of your pocket? It's easy to assume that treats don't work in this situation and that it's time to put them away. But that assumption is wrong, and you won't teach your dog to hold on to the object that way. We want the dog to learn that it's worthwhile to hold the object in spite of the distraction of the treats. Furthermore, if she holds the object, she will be rewarded. We call this "reverse luring" because we pretend that we are trying to "entice" or lure the dog to drop the object. We want the dog to think, "Ha! You're trying to trick me. I'm definitely not letting go".

Reverse luring can be used in any training as an initial controlled distraction. The easiest way is often to start with poses that require the dog to stay still, such as sitting. When the dog sits, show her treats in your open palm. If the dog remains where she is, reward her while she is sitting. If the dog gets up or tries to take the treats, close your hand and wait for her to sit down again. You shouldn't say anything at all – just wait. The fact that you close your hand (and by doing so withhold the dog's reward), plus then rewarding her while she remains sitting, sends the dog important messages about what's worthwhile and what's not.

When the sit works, you can do exactly the same thing with taking and holding:

1. Get your dog going by playing with a toy.
2. Once the dog has a good hold, show her the treats.
3. If the dog keeps a hold of the toy, say "thank you" and reward the dog (if she's able to let go on cue, otherwise click and reward the dog so that she releases the toy at the click). If the dog releases the toy before your cue or click, close your hand holding the treats and then start playing with the dog again. Be quiet and be sure not to say "no" or something similar if the dog releases the toy.

In the beginning, the dog only needs to hold the toy for a short while – it might only be a split second the first time. Then gradually extend the time and move the treat closer and closer to the dog. Do the exact same thing when the dog sits with the object in her mouth.

When Rooibos sits, Mary shows him a treat. If he ignores it he will be rewarded.

If Rooibos stretches out his nose or gets up, Mary closes her hand.

Reverse luring can be used again later by increasing the level of distraction, such as dropping treats on the ground. Start by dropping the treat behind you, near your foot, so you can put your foot on it if the dog attempts to take it. Click and reward the dog when she keeps the toy even when there is a tempting treat lying on the ground. As the dog becomes more skilled, drop the treats closer to her. Don't make it too hard at first, but gradually increase the difficulty. The biggest challenge for the handler tends to be remaining completely silent during the exercise. If you feel the need to say "no", clear your throat, or stop your dog, you've made it too difficult. We control the treats, and the dog learns to control herself. Most dogs will master this exercise after a while. A fun complementary exercise is to throw the treats closer and closer to the dog. By the end, you should be able to throw an entire fistful of treats at the dog's feet without her going for them.

Another way to "distract" the dog is to play with other toys or have some of your friends try to make the dog lose concentration. But remember that the dog should succeed almost every time.

Reverse luring can easily become a kind of crutch in the sense that the dog won't perform the behavior you want without it. Make sure that you wean off of reverse luring as quickly as you can. You do this by varying the exercise so that sometimes you use your hand a little bit, sometimes not at all, and sometimes work with other distractions instead.

Coach Says
Four out of five successful repetitions is a good rule of thumb to determine when it's time to increase the level of distraction. If the dog makes mistakes more often than that, you should reduce the distraction and try again.

Holding while Sitting
Puppies often believe that it's simply not possible to keep something in their mouths while they sit down. Most often they will drop the object. Regardless of whether you have a puppy or an adult dog, it's a good idea to train her to hold an object both when she sits down and while she remains sitting. This becomes yet another way to teach the dog to hold the object until you say "thank you."

Sam

There are two ways to teach the dog to sit down with something in her mouth. Either we teach a very good sit cue or we work with a voluntary sit:

1. Begin by reinforcing offered sits when your dog is in front of you.
2. Give your dog the toy when she sits down. At this point, use a slightly smaller toy that is easy for your dog to hold, but not one that is her most prized possession (while being sufficiently valuable so that your dog still wants to hold it).
3. Click while the dog sits and holds the toy (your dog is allowed to release the toy when you click). Reward your dog while she remains sitting.
4. Repeat a few more times with a voluntarily offered sit.
5. Then give your dog the toy before she has sat down and wait until she sits voluntarily.
6. Click and reward the dog when she holds the toy while she sits down. If she drops it before the click, make it a little easier once again and repeat the exercise with the dog offering sitting down without the toy, and then give the dog the toy at the moment she begins to move to sit down.

If your dog has successfully mastered the sit cue there is another way to teach your dog to sit with an object in her mouth: You can test it by saying "sit" when the dog has something in her mouth. If she then drops the toy, just pick it up and give it back to her again, or allow her to take it from the ground. When she once again has the toy in her mouth, try saying "sit" and reward the dog when she sits and keeps the item. If she still drops the toy, start with the voluntary sit as we described earlier.

So far you've been training with the dog in front of you, but the dog should be able to sit both in front of you and by your side with the toy in her mouth. The first few times you train your dog to hold the toy as she sits at your side, you can cue her to sit, stand next to her (so that she ends up on your left) and give her the toy. Click while the dog is holding the object and reward her while she's still sitting.

Also try poking at the object when the dog has it in her mouth. At first, poke gently and then with increasing intensity. Click and reward the dog when she maintains a firm hold – that is, when the object doesn't move when you poke at it.

Then gradually increase the time so the dog can remain sitting longer with the toy in her mouth. If you want to proof the behavior, you can gradually begin to move farther and farther away from her so that she remains sitting at a distance with the toy in her mouth. Proofing means that we teach the dog to do more than is necessary, for instance, we train her with more severe distractions than are likely to occur during a field trial. Proofing will make it easier for your dog to perform properly no matter what happens around you. When the dog can remain sitting at a distance with the toy in her mouth, try other objects and eventually even game.

Chewing and Hard Mouths

By splitting the training into small increments we most often get solid taking and holding behaviors. If you experience problems with chewing or that your dog grabs too hard, becoming "hard mouthed", you must go back in your training. Most often, problems occur when you are moving at too high a speed or when your dog's arousal level is too high. That is, if the dog has a tendency to chew, don't train when the dog is

wound up. Instead, wait until she is calm and focused. Then we put the dog in increasingly more challenging situations, but make sure that she doesn't become stressed. The majority of dogs hold objects correctly when moving slower, but can start chewing when the pace increases. Some dogs, however, will hold the object solidly when moving at a higher pace but chew when moving slowly. Here you need to try different approaches and see what works best for your dog.

We try to teach the dog to hold without chewing through the tug-of-war games we described at the beginning of the chapter. If that doesn't work, we try introducing the object when the dog is calm and use reverse luring to see if she can keep a firm hold then. Sometimes an external reward in the form of a bowl of treats helps because the dog will be so focused on the food bowl that she will keep a firm hold. Place a bowl next to you and give the dog the object. Click and say "go ahead" if the dog holds the object with a firm grip, without chewing. We are talking about seconds or even split seconds. The first few times you should say "go ahead" almost before she has time to notice that she has something in her mouth. Then gradually extend the time.

Sometimes the dog only chews on certain items. Start by practicing with the objects the dog doesn't chew on or bite too hard and reward her a few times. Then introduce more challenging objects and allow the dog to hold them for only a moment. Then gradually increase the amount of time the dog is holding the object and have her start by taking the object from the ground. Begin by putting your dog on a leash and having her walk next to you with the object in her mouth. Then slowly increase your pace. If the dog starts to chew, try walking a little faster. If that still doesn't work, take the object from her and try again. You might have to go back to playing the game we described before.

Diesel

Another exercise is to click the instant the dog takes the object, almost before she has time to lift it off the ground. For this to work the dog must first have learned to release the toy as you click, otherwise there's a risk that she will manage to begin chewing after the click. When you are certain she will release at the click, do the following:

1. Put the object and the dog in front of you.
2. Click the instant the dog picks up the object.
3. Gradually allow the dog to lift the object more and more.
4. When the dog has mastered this, you can increase the pace of the exercise by throwing treats so the dog can run after them to gobble them up, then come back at a slightly higher speed towards the object. If the dog then begins to chew again, wait until she has calmed down a bit and give her the rewards beside you instead of throwing the treats.

This exercise requires precise timing from you as a handler. You have to click just as the dog takes the object, but before she has time to throw back her head and start chewing. In other words, you need to practice your timing before you attempt this kind of exercise.

Coach Says

An example of how to practice your timing is to throw a pen in the air and then click precisely when it's at the top of the arch. You can also practice your timing in front of the TV: Click every time the newscaster says "now" or every time the chef on a cooking show puts a ladle into a pot. If you have a child around, he or she might enjoy playing a shaping game. You train each other to perform different activities, such as standing on a chair, turning on the light or spinning around. The person holding the clicker decides what the "student" should do, but remains silent.

Game

As mentioned previously, spaniels and retrievers are used for hunting small game such as birds and rabbits. Some dogs spontaneously take and hold game immediately, while other dogs' interest for game needs to be worked on.

With most dogs, you need to maintain their interest in game by regularly allowing them to carry it. It's enough to have the dog carry the game while walking next to you, so you can do other exercises with dummies in the meantime. For those who are not interested in competing in field trials, it's of course great to just practice retrieving for fun without using game.

Game should be handled with respect. When you take game from the dog, lay it gently on the ground and don't throw it. Remember to show consideration for your fellow humans when training in areas frequented by others who might not be used to game. A pile of dead birds right next to a bike path may be an unpleasant surprise for passersby.

Getting Your Dog Used to Game

There are many ways to introduce your dog to game. The easiest way to do it is when your dog is a puppy, and then continue to regularly expose her to game. But most people we meet during retrieving courses have dogs that are a few years old and have never carried game before. In that case, it may take the dog some time to get used to it.

The first time, you can just introduce the game and see what the dog does with it. Have the dog sniff it a bit, lay it on the ground and let her investigate. If the dog starts to bite and lick the game, remove it. If you can, take the game out into a wooded area, show it to the dog and then give her a chance to familiarize herself with it. If the dog takes the game right

away, praise her and encourage her to carry it. Most spaniels and retrievers will become excited in this situation if you talk to them and scratch them on the rump. If the dog is really hesitant about game, try stuffing it in a sock, thus allowing her to get used to the smell and the weight. When the dog seizes the sock with the bird in it without hesitation, you can try taking the game out. Alternatively, cut holes in the sock so feathers stick out a little here and there. When the holes are so large that there are mostly feathers and not much sock, you can remove it completely.

There are also dummies with feathers and rabbit skins and you can of course attach feathers to any object the dog is prone to taking. Use your imagination and don't be afraid to experiment.

Taking Game

Some dogs will already be so used to game that they take it immediately while others still might be hesitant. If your dog still appears hesitant, continue trying out different ways to get the dog used to the game.

When we try to teach the dog to pick up game, we don't click when the dog shows interest in the game if she's still suspicious, because she might become even less inclined to take the game. We often become a bit stiff if we just wait for the dog to show interest in the game and our body language or manner might be interpreted as negative and discourage the dog from taking the game at all. However, later during training, when the dog happily takes the game, we can click and reward the dog for a correct grip.

Initially, to get the dog to take the game, we do the same as we would with taking a dummy:

1. Keep the dog on your left side and the game in your right hand.
2. Spin around to the right and keep the game away from the dog while you turn so that the dog follows the game and eventually grabs it.
3. When the dog takes it, back away and praise her for continuing to hold on to the game.

If the dog is too excited when she takes it or bites too hard, don't introduce the game until the dog is calm (a still tail or voluntary sitting are good signs) and move calmly yourself. Slowly move the game away from the dog so she doesn't build up too much speed before she takes it.

Coach Says
Put some hand sanitizer in your training bag so you can wash your hands after handling game. Not washing your hands after handling the game is obviously not dangerous, but you may feel better if your hands are clean.

tower over the game; the dog should grab it immediately without thinking about it. If the dog takes the game after you've thrown it, you should immediately back away from the dog and praise her.

Happy about Game!

Another way to encourage the dog's love of taking and holding game is to introduce it in a situation where the dog displays the desirable behaviors we want in situations where she is to carry game. Bring out the game when you know your dog is really happy (without being hysterical). Lena's cocker spaniel Totte was initially interested in the game, but he didn't really want to take it. After trying the exercise mentioned above a few times, Lena instead began to give Totte game when she came home after being away for several hours. When Lena comes home, Totte is always very excited and when he's really excited he enjoys carrying something. He carries gloves and hats, keys and shoes – whatever he can find and preferably something his owner gives him. One day Lena came home with a crow in her hand. Totte gently took the crow and proudly strutted around with it, going back and forth between Lena and her husband. Both praised him, scratched his rump and showed him how proud they were. After doing this a few times, they were able to introduce game in other situations and Totte seemed to have overcome his initial skepticism and took the game with greater confidence.

> ## Pitfall
> *Dogs don't like to have things pushed into their mouths. Never force a toy/bird/dummy/object into your dog's mouth! Instead, move the object away from the dog so that she voluntarily grabs*

If the dog still doesn't take the game, try to spark her interest by pretending to be overly interested in the game yourself while ignoring the dog. Turn away from the dog, hold the game up in the air, quickly show it to the dog and then lift it up again. The message should be, "What a nice bird I have here! Too bad it's not for you!" but in a teasing and friendly way. You can also "talk" to the game (look over your shoulder first to make sure no non-dog person is watching …) or play a game of "keep away" with a friend without letting the dog get the game. Keep the training sessions short and stop when the dog is the most interested.

When the dog shows interest in the game, lower it, and yank it away from the dog again. You can also try letting the game touch the ground a little. If the dog does not seize it instantly, pick it up again and continue keeping the game away from her. We don't want to give the dog the chance to stand and

Carrying Game

To get the dog accustomed to game and to carry it properly, it's good to have her carry the game while walking beside you. (If your dog hasn't mastered walking at heel really well, you can have her on a leash during this exercise, and encourage her to follow you). In particular, small birds can be difficult to carry properly and in that case, the dog must first learn this lesson while moving at a slow pace.

When the dog happily grabs the game out of your hand and carries it while she walks beside you, you can try allowing her to take the game directly from the ground. When you've gotten this far, the dog usually likes to pick up game on marked retrieves, but may still be a little hesitant when freely hunting a larger area or with certain kinds of game. What usually happens is that the dog runs out and takes the game, but on the way back realizes that she has something in her mouth and spits it out before she has given it to you. Spend a lot of time teaching the dog to carry game beside you before you start throwing it.

Walking with Game

If you want to see if your dog will spontaneously grab the game, try placing it in a wooded area without her seeing it. Then take the dog for a walk. Walk normally and ignore whatever the dog does. If the dog picks up the game, praise her heavily and reward. If she walks past the game, practice more on taking the game from your hand and carrying it at your side.

Pitfall

If you have a dog that doesn't automatically go after game, be careful of trying to get your dog to take the object by shouting encouragement and praise – it can easily turn into nagging. In the worst case scenario, the dog will feel pressured and become even more skeptical. Focus on training the dog's interest in the game instead.

Work with Different Kinds of Game

Various types of game smell different and dogs tend to prefer some over others. Remember to train with different kinds of game, both in size and species.

Fowl, such as duck and pheasant, tend to be easier to train the dogs to carry, while geese can be a bit trickier because of their size. Wood pigeon can be difficult for an untrained dog as its feathers easily come off in the dog's mouth, and it can thus be uncomfortable to carry. Preferably start with another kind of game, such as partridge or duck.

Partridge, duck, geese, pheasant, rabbit and hare are common kinds of game used for retrievers in the UK. Snipe and woodcock are occasionally shot amongst other game and generous hosts may also provide grouse. Spaniels in the UK retrieve the same kinds of game, with the exception of geese.

The types of game used in US field trials depend on the state laws. Various species of upland game birds such as woodcock, grouse and quail, are usually hunted.

In some countries there are field trials using cold game, i.e. game that has been shot prior to the trial, whereas in some countries only warm game, i.e. game that is shot during the field trial, is used. Check the field trial rules in your country to see what you need to focus your training on.

Game is best preserved in the freezer. You can use it both frozen and thawed. The advantage of using frozen game is that it keeps longer. Take out the game, practice taking it and then put it back in the freezer. Make sure to practice with thawed game too because the smell differs from frozen game, and it's also a little different to carry. You can usually thaw and refreeze game a few times before it spoils. Roll the game in newspaper so it dries out a little. Don't forget to tell your family which shelves in the freezer they should avoid taking meat from for Sunday dinner!

Coach Says

Avoid giving the dog a "hold" cue. Instead, teach her to hold the object until you say "thank you". If you say, "hold" during a trial, you're telling the judge that your dog usually drops the game ...

Undesirable Game Handling

If the dog starts chewing on the game, bites too hard or starts rolling on it, remove the game and start to practice having the dog take the game again with more control, as described earlier in this chapter. This will increase the value of picking up the game, so the dog is no longer interested in rolling on or chewing it. If you have practiced taking the game and want to allow the dog to pick the game off the ground but

are not entirely sure she will be successful, you can always put the dog on a leash. This way, you can either prevent the dog from rolling on the game by carefully holding on to the leash or by calmly reining her in. Then take the game and try the holding exercise again. Naturally, you remain silent when you interrupt the dog. Sometimes dogs roll because they may find wild game appealing to rub on, so you might want to try with different kinds of game. Once the dog is able to take different kinds game, you can reintroduce the more appealing game.

Bitches can behave differently when they are in heat. They might start doing things with the game that they've never done before. In such cases, it might be a good idea to take a break from training with game for a few weeks. In some countries bitches in heat are not allowed to compete at field trials, whereas in others they are allowed to. In the US they are run last, but check the regulations of your country to see what applies to you and your dog.

Challenge

Can your dog hold the dummy and turn to you when:
- *A helper claps her hands?*
- *There is another dummy on the ground?*
- *A helper holds out a piece of ham?*
- *There is a hamburger on the ground?*

Sub-goals – Taking and Holding	Completed
Take an object from your hand	
Pick up an object from the ground	
Hold an object when sitting beside you and in front of you	
Hold an object when you bend down, put your hand under the object, and poke at the object	
Hold an object while moving	
Hold an object while sitting	
Hold different kinds of objects	
Hold an object despite distractions (for example, treats in the vicinity, several objects to choose between or other people in the area)	

Summary

- Teach the dog to hold the object and turn towards you despite distractions.
- Teach the dog to carry various kinds of game and objects by your side – both on and off leash.
- Teach the dog to keep the object in her mouth, despite distractions, until you say "Thank you".

Love

Delivery to Hand

Delivery to hand is one of the most important skills we can teach our dogs when it comes to retrieving. As soon as the dog finds game, she should pick it up and come straight back to us at full speed without caring about what else there might be to find. A lot of dogs spontaneously run after and pick up objects. But bringing back those extremely interesting discoveries isn't always as much fun.

Delivery to hand refers to the entire behavioral sequence from the moment the dog takes the object to when she turns around, comes back and puts the object in our hand. Giving up an object isn't always a dog's favorite thing to do, so the behavior needs to be trained. Most important of all is to reward the dog massively when she delivers the object, and to train with a lot of different distractions.

Play to Inspire Delivery to Hand

This game teaches the dog to quickly take an object, run toward us with it and release it. Start with two identical toys and get the dog playing with one of them, just as you did in "Play is Something We do Together". Instead of letting go of the object the dog is playing with, become passive with the object to encourage the dog to switch to the other toy. Say "yes" and start playing with the other toy exactly when the dog switches. Repeat this until the dog changes toys as soon as you say "yes". Now you can start throwing the toy a little bit away from you. When the dog takes the toy, say "yes" and offer the other toy so the dog will spit out the toy she just took and start playing with you instead. Gradually throw the toy further away. Later on, you can have the

Totte keeps ahold of the toy despite the tempting treat in Lena's hand.

If he releases the toy, Lena closes her hand.

dog run a bit further towards you before you say "yes" and switch to the other toy. Finally, the dog should be in front of you before you reward her. Then you can start combining this with delivery to hand, but even at later stages in your training you can come back to this game to work on holding and running back to you at high speed. You can also try a different version of this game by throwing different kinds of objects, dummies and birds. It's a good exercise to use to teach the dog to run straight back to you with anything she finds.

Previously we've described how we use play to begin training the dog to take an object. We similarly use play to train delivery to hand and to foster the dog's desire to be near us when she has an object.[8] Do the following:

1. Get the dog playing.
2. When she has a really good hold on the toy, present your open palm with a treat (reverse luring).
3. If the dog maintains her hold for a split second while you offer your hand with the treat, say "thank you" or click and when the dog then releases the object, give her the treat she just ignored. If the dog lets go before you've said "thank you" or clicked, close your hand and start playing again.
4. Gradually increase the amount of time you hold your hand open before you say "thank you".

Delivery to Hand in Everyday Life

In our daily interactions with the dog, we also try to come up with ways to encourage and reward the dog when she comes to us or wants to be near us when holding something in her mouth. The dog should always feel comfortable being around us when holding an object. We offer petting and scratching when the dog brings her – and our own – things and never

---

[8] We borrowed this game from Siv Svendsen, www.amokk.no.

engage in a power struggle when she has something in her mouth. If we want the object the dog is carrying, we exchange it for something yummy she really loves. We often give the object back to the dog once we have gotten it.

Hand Targeting

Besides making the dog comfortable with bringing us an object, we naturally also have several exercises to teach delivery to hand. In gun dog training, we use the hand target to teach the dog to put objects in our hand. We think that the hand target is the most useful target. The dog puts her nose in our hands, with or without the object in her mouth. The hand target also results in a quiet, effective recall where the dog runs all the way to us (so we can grab her collar). We can also "move" the dog, begin teaching her tricks like weaving between our legs, or put her head voluntarily into the collar by following our hand. This is how you can teach the hand target:

1. Start by hiding both of your hands behind your back.
2. Stretch out one hand and hold your palm about two inches from your dog's nose.
3. Click when your dog curiously puts her nose forward to investigate your hand. Make sure that the dog is actively touching your palm and not you touching the dog's nose – she won't learn anything that way. Reward your dog for touching your empty palm using your other hand.
4. When your dog eats the treat, you should have your target hand behind your back. Take it out again when the dog is ready to repeat the exercise.
5. Then try holding your hand further and further away from your dog's nose so that she has to move to reach your hand. If your dog just sits there and looks at you, you've

made the exercise too difficult. Hide your hand behind your back again and begin closer to the dog during the next repetition.

We want the dog to press her nose forcefully into our hand. It helps the dog to really deliver the object to our hand and not "happen" to drop it right in front of us. It also looks good at a field trial – the delivery becomes distinct. As soon as the dog understands the exercise above, teach her to touch your hand harder by not clicking when the nose touch is too weak. In that way, you can gradually teach the dog to press harder into your hand.

When the dog can give your hand a hard tap, teach her to keep her nose against your hand for several seconds. Do the same as above. Don't click for short taps and extend the duration gradually so the dog performs the exercise correctly several times. At the same time, she learns to keep her nose there for a longer period of time. Teach your dog to keep her nose in place for five to teen seconds.

When the dog understands that she should press her nose in your hand, you can start to vary the exercise. Use different hand positions: high, low, in front, behind, between your legs, and so on. Move your hand backwards a bit so the dog has to chase it. Remember to vary which hand the dog taps so that she can target both hands equally well.

Hand Targeting with Objects

Do the following exercise to fluently move from hand target training without objects to hand target training with objects:

1. Reward the hand target a few times.
2. Then give the dog the object, alternatively let her pick it up from the ground, offer your hand and let the dog touch

it with the object in her mouth. Click and give the dog a reward. If that doesn't work, try playing a little with the dog. Allow her to win the object and then introduce the hand target.

3. You can also back away from the dog as you're playing with her. Drop the object and continue to back away when you introduce your hand target. Click and reward the dog when she puts her nose (with the object) against your hand.

4. When the dog pushes the object in your hand as soon as you introduce it, you can start replacing the click with a "thank you".

If the dog ignores your hand, you can work more on the hand target and perhaps use a less enticing object. It's easier to get a good retrieve if the dog is calm and doesn't enjoy "a party for one" with the object. Try to be close to the dog when doing this exercise. Organize it in the same way as you did when you were only training the hand target so the dog recognizes the concept. There's a good chance the dog will touch your hand even when holding an object. You might also need to make it enticing for the dog to touch your hand. In that case, you should go back to the previous exercise and offer the dog more and better rewards when she presses her nose against your palm without an object. Upon seeing your hand, you want the dog to throw herself towards it as if touching it were the best thing that could happen.

In this situation, don't reward the dog if she drops the object and touches your hand without the object. You don't want the dog to drop the object as soon as she sees your hand. Instead you want the dog to wait to release the object until you say "thank you" or click. Take your hand away and let the dog take the object again. You can either pick up the

When Sam drops the dummy too early, there is no reward. Instead, Catharina tries again.

object and give it to the dog, or just wait until the dog picks up the object by herself. Then introduce the hand target a little closer to the dog so the dog only "happens" to brush against your hand with the object. Click and reward.

Pitfall
Remember to keep your hand still so the dog will seek out your hand instead of you reaching towards the dog and the object.

Remain silent until your dog has pressed the object into your hand. If you feel the need to encourage or lure the dog to keep a hold on the object, you've made the exercise too difficult. If you've previously taught the dog to touch her nose against your hand without an object (as in the exercise we described above), it's not going to be that difficult to increase how long your dog should hold the object before you say "thank you". But don't make it too hard in the beginning – you've already raised the level of difficulty by adding an object. We therefore need to reduce our expectation when it comes to the duration – in other words, we need to reduce the time. Then we can successively extend it again.

Drop on Cue
We want even the most enthusiastic participant in tug games to immediately drop the object when we say "thank you". At this point, your dog is likely to drop the object when you click or after targeting your hand. If the dog still hasn't learned to drop at the click or in your hand, you can use the "On and Off Game" we described previously in the chapter "Play – the Ultimate Reward". When we want to end the game, we take the dog by the collar and let go of the toy. When the dog drops the toy, we say "thank you" and give her a treat.

Another good way to start teaching the "thank you" cue is to say the cue at the exact moment the dog spontaneously drops the object and then reward her with a treat. Eventually you can also use the introductory exercise described in this chapter, playing with the dog and showing her a treat in your open hand. Then say "thank you" when the dog has a good grip on the object.

In the beginning, you need to play it by ear. If you aren't completely sure of your "thank you" cue, don't say it when the dog is hyperactive, but wait until she's playing calmly. It is easy to destroy a "thank you" cue by repeating it too many times when the dog won't let go of the object anyway. Avoid prying the object out of the dog's mouth. If the dog maintains a firm grip and really wants to keep the object, she will bite down even harder if you show interest in the object by starting to squabble with the dog over it.

Coach Says
Praise and pet your dog when she brings you an object, even if it's your phone. It should always be nice to be near you with an object (and you can put the phone out of harm's way for next time). Crouch down and pet the dog in her favorite spot and talk lovingly to her while she's holding the object. This way you build value in being close to you with the object.

Delivery-to-Hand Games
When the dog enjoys pressing the object against your palm, you can start putting your hand in different positions so the dog has to search for it, just as we did in the exercise for hand targeting without objects. Even with an object in her mouth, you could let the dog target your right hand followed by your left hand to get her reward. The result of this exercise is often that the dog learns to have a better hold

on the object. When the dog has released the object, throw it so she can fetch it again. If you are using a tug toy, you can first play with the dog a bit, and then hold out your hand so the dog delivers the toy in it, throw the toy, get it back, play a bit more and so on. Vary the direction you throw the toy and the rewards you offer – sometimes you give the dog a treat, and sometimes you throw the toy.

Resource Guarding

Resource guarding means that the dog wants to keep an object or other resources for herself and defends them against other dogs and people. The dog might run away with the object and/or growl when we approach. If your dog resource guards, it's extra important to never engage in a struggle with the dog over items. The dog growls at us in this situation because she doesn't trust us, because she believes we are going to take the object. If we then take the object, we prove the dog right; she can't trust us. Instead, we want to reward the dog for bringing us the object.

If the dog goes under the table with her objects and growls when we walk by, we should just walk by again and throw the dog something extremely tasty. Then we keep walking by the table and throwing treats to the dog until she stops growling.

If you have children and a resource-guarding dog, never allow the kids to take objects from the dog. Leave the dog alone when she has a chew toy until you've trained her to allow the kids to be able to take things from her (if you want them to be able to do so).

Teach the dog that you can also be useful to her, even if there is an item that she would prefer to keep for herself. Lena has taught her dogs that she will help them pull the marrow out of a bone if they bring it to her. When the dogs have chewed on the bone for a while, they will bring it to her with a plaintive look. Together they get out the marrow furthest in the bone and then the dog may take the bone again and go on her merry way. The only thing you need to watch out for is that it really, really hurts to have a large marrowbone dropped on your foot …

Another way to get the dog to stop guarding objects is to give her so many objects that she can't possibly guard all of them. If the dog guards bones, spread 20-30 bones on the floor. If she gathers several of them and puts them in her crate, just remove them (when the dog has left the crate to get more of them) and put them back on the floor again. The most important thing is to never allow the dog to gather all of the bones. That way, you provide your dog with endless resources and she doesn't need to guard them anymore.

Trading Objects

If the dog is extremely possessive and doesn't want to approach you at all with the object, you'll have to work a little harder. Start by having the dog on leash and train your hand target both with and without objects. You can then combine it with trading objects with the dog off leash or on a long line, depending on how far she runs. Get a hold of two identical objects and do the following:

1. Give the dog one of the objects.

2. When the dog comes close to you, throw the other object (it's likely the dog will exchange the object).

3. Pick up the object the dog dropped.

4. The next time the dog approaches you, throw the object again.

5. Then continue in the same manner so the dog gets closer and closer to you with the object and can finally begin to put it in your hand.

If the dog has a really large mouth, you might need three identical objects. According to the Guinness Book of World Records, a Golden Retriever in the United States currently holds the record for holding five tennis balls in his mouth …

Dead End

A long and narrow room, such as a hall, is the ideal space for this game:

1. Sit several yards from the wall and throw a toy against the wall.

2. When the dog runs after the toy and takes it, she is likely to run away with it, away from you. But you're sitting so

that she must pass close to you (it's the only escape route due to the narrow space).

3. As soon as she passes you, click and offer the most desirable reward possible.

4. Show your delight when the dog brings the object to you, even if that might not have been her initial intent.

5. If you have a really possessive dog, you can more or less put the reward under the dog's nose so that she can't avoid it.

6. Repeat the exercise several times and start backing further and further away, preferably into another room if possible.

Coach Says

Be creative with games and exercises if your dog wants to keep everything for herself. There is an endless variety of these kinds of games:

- *Give the dog a really, really enticing reward when she does something right.*
- *Never try to get your dog to come to you by coaxing her – then she learns not to come unless you coax and beg.*
- *Break up the training into small, small steps.*
- *Start training with lower value objects so you will have the greatest chance of success.*

Delivery with Distractions

When the dog understands that she should deliver the object to hand, we start introducing various distractions. It might be someone saying "hi", falling dummies, dummies to jump straight over, or treats in a bowl. At this point we can introduce distractions at three different stages: when the dog is on her way to the object, when the dog takes the object, and when the dog is on her way back with the object. The goal is for the dog to come straight back regardless of what else is going on. Often dogs are most easily distracted when they are coming back with the object, but some dogs are also easily distracted on the way out, so remember to train both.

A common problem is that the dog runs to people standing next to you to show them their object or to figure out what they are doing there. During field trials, both shooters and throwers – those who throw the dummies or game for the dogs to fetch – can pose a challenge. Make sure to do distraction training with "strange" people in the woods and teach the dog that she should always come straight back to you regardless of who else is nearby.

At close distances, it's easier to influence the dog and teach her what we want her to do. That's why we train delivery to hand with distractions at close proximity. Once that works, we increase the distance. We always start with simple distractions and then make it progressively more difficult.

Straight Back to Us

If your dog always runs straight back to you with the object, you'll avoid having problems with the dog exchanging objects or searching elsewhere with the object still in her mouth. We can't overemphasize the importance of making

it worthwhile for the dog to come back to you with the object! Make it extremely enjoyable for the dog to do what you want her to do. Or as animal trainer Bob Bailey puts it: "You have to make it worthwhile for the animal to participate in your silly little games". If you encounter problems later on in your training, the solution is often to make deliveries more worthwhile, by offering really enticing rewards while training.

To teach a dog not to exchange objects, you can have the dog fetch a dummy:

1. When the dog is on the way out, place another dummy several yards in front and to the side of you so the dog has to run by it on the way back.
2. Then move the distraction dummy closer and closer to the dog's path so that in the end she has to jump over it.
3. If the dog tries to take the distraction dummy, quickly pick it up without saying anything and then try again. If the dog still manages to take the dummy, just calmly take it back from the dog and repeat the exercise above with the object a little closer to you.

Speed

We want the dog to gallop towards us with the object, if it's not too heavy of course. If the dog really likes her reward, the speed will come almost entirely on its own. If the dog is a little calmer, you might need to work specifically on speed. Train when the dog is most energetic and do a number of quick repetitions.

You can use a helper and have your dog run from the helper to you without an object. Then the helper gives the dog the object just before she runs away. If the dog finds it unpleasant

to be held by someone or doesn't want to take something from another person, you can work on that separately first.

There are a lot of different kinds of speed games that involve the dog running both with and without objects. Figure out what works best with your dog. The majority of dogs like chasing their person. Do the following:

1. Ask a helper to hold your dog.
2. Run away a bit.
3. Stop and turn towards your dog.
4. When you stop, your helper releases the dog, preferably when she pulls towards you and wants to get away.
5. When the dog starts running towards you, turn and run away again.
6. When she manages to catch up with you, take out an enjoyable reward.

You can also do this exercise without a helper:

1. Hold your dog's collar and throw a meatball.
2. Release the dog and at the same time start running in another direction.
3. Before your dog has eaten the meatball, stop and turn back towards her so you are standing still when the dog sees you.
4. The dog will likely run towards you. Reward her by throwing a meatball in the other direction at the same time as you run away again.
5. Eventually you can allow the dog to run right up to you, exactly as she does when she's going to give you the object, before you reward her.

If you want to reward the dog when she is at top speed, you can click when the dog is at her fastest on her way toward you and then throw a toy behind you. Think about the timing. It's easy to click too late – when the dog has already put on the brakes to stop next to you.

A word of warning in connection with speed training: If you allow your dog to approach you at full speed and launch herself at a toy hanging by your side, you must let go of the toy at the same moment the dog touches it (you can attach a long cord to the toy). Otherwise the dog might get a whiplash injury. Also make sure the dog is sufficiently warmed up before you do this kind of speed exercise.

Various Deliveries

Deliveries can either be performed in front of you or on your left side. Most often it's easier for you to take the game if the dog delivers it in front of you. Then you can use both hands to take the game, especially if it's large. Unfortunately it's a myth that you stay dry during water work if you take the delivery in front. You will get wet regardless of where you receive the delivery. If your deliveries aren't conducted smoothly, the judges can deduct points during a field trial. Most problems we have encountered are associated with side deliveries. We therefore recommend taking deliveries in front.

This book is about field trial retrieving, but since we often receive questions about field trial retrieving versus obedience trial retrieving we'd like to touch on this briefly. One of the exercises in obedience is a retrieve. You can usually choose where you want to receive deliveries there too, in front or at the side, but check the rules in your country to see how you need to train them. The dog learns where she should deliver objects depending on the situation. If we are in an obedience competition stance we want to receive the delivery at our side (according to Swedish obedience rules). If we offer the hand target we want to have the object in our hand, and if we don't do anything at all, we want the dog to just come to us and sit down or stand in front of us, keeping the object in her mouth until we ask for it.

The dog must also be able to perform deliveries to hand when she has retrieved from the water. Read more about how to work on that in the chapter "Water Work".

Delivery is Not Always the End

Having the game delivered to your hand doesn't mean the work is done. During a trial, you either have to put the game on the ground, in your game bag, or give it to a judge and then ask your dog to sit by your side. If the dog is extremely interested in the game or the object, you need to spend some extra time training the dog to give the object to someone else. You can also put the game on the ground and send the dog out again, without allowing her to take the object.

To teach the dog to ignore the game after giving it to you, do the following:

1. Ask a helper to stand close to you.
2. Wait until your dog sits in front of you or beside you and reward her.
3. Reach towards your helper with the object in your hand.
4. Reward the dog when she remains sitting.
5. The first few times, just reach a little way towards your helper with the object before rewarding the dog.
6. Later you can move the object closer and closer to your helper, so he or she eventually can take it.
7. If the dog jumps or gets up, conceal the object behind your back again and wait until she sits down. Start with an object your dog finds mildly amusing, and then move onto more interesting items.

Since we want the dog to do this on her own accord later on in the training, we don't usually add a cue here. Just stretching out our hand while holding an object is a cue for the dog to remain sitting. If your dog really wants the object and jumps and wiggles around, hold the object above the dog's head and let her jump to her heart's content. When she's worn herself out and has all four feet back on the ground, reward her with a treat or even with the object.

You can use the same approach when you want to be able to set the object on the ground without the dog taking it. Put the object down and ask the dog to assume a sit by your side, if she's trained to do so. Otherwise, you can start by asking the dog to perform another exercise while the object is on the ground, such as a hand target or walking with you away from the object. If the dog tries to take the object, just calmly pick it up and try again.

Sub-goals – Delivery to Hand	Completed
Hand target	
Deliver the object in your hand	
Release on cue	
Longer distances	
With distractions (for example, a thrower who stands nearby, several objects on the ground, or a loud audience)	
Run straight out of the water while holding the object without shaking off the water (see the chapter "Water Work")	

Challenge

Does your dog run in a straight line to you with an object even if there is a family enjoying a picnic on her path?

Snoddas

Summary

- Teach the dog that it's a positive and safe experience to be near you with an object.
- Introduce a lot of different kinds of distractions in your training so the dog still runs straight to you as soon as she has something in her mouth.
- Delivery to hand is the solution to a lot of problems. Make it extremely worthwhile for your dog to come to you and deliver items to avoid having her try to exchange objects or keep hunting while holding an object in her mouth.
- If you were only going to work on one aspect of gun dog training, you should work on delivery to hand!

Do What I Say!

It's so much fun to have a clicker wise dog that offers behaviors left, right and center! But naturally, it's important that the dog knows how to do as we say – meaning that she's able to both understand our cues and perform them in all possible situations and environments.

Anders

When the dog is able to do all of this, we say that we have stimulus control. A stimulus is everything that you – or in this case, your dog – can see, hear, feel, taste and smell. In dog training we often use audible stimuli, i.e. signals that the dog hears, such as verbal cues and whistles. But our body language also gives the dog cues: we cast with our hands, turn ourselves towards an object as a signal to the dog to run and fetch it, position ourselves in a certain way when we want the dog to come in to our side, and so on. Most often, the environment in which we find ourselves when we give a cue can also be a strong, influencing stimulus.

Stimulus control means that if we say "sit" the dog sits. But it also means that if we say "sit" the dog doesn't lay down. And if we say "down" the dog doesn't sit. It also means that the dog doesn't sit without hearing the "sit" cue.

Which Cues Do You Use?

Do the kitchen carpet and the fridge have to be part of the cue for the dog to sit when you give the cue "sit"? Hmm, that can certainly be a bit awkward … We often hear students exclaim, "But she knows it at home!" when the dog suddenly doesn't do what the handler cues her to do out on the training field. "Exactly," we reply. "She can do it there because you have trained her there, on the carpet in front of the fridge. But have you trained her to do it on a lawn full of scents, with other dogs playing nearby?"

The solution is training and then training some more. Think about the environments where it's most important that the dog can perform the behavior on cue. First train in an environment with minor distractions and then ramp up the difficulty so the dog is able to perform the behavior anywhere. And then proof the behavior: Teach the dog to perform the behavior in all kinds of strange environments where you will most likely never need it but is still challenging for the dog, such as in a large shopping center.

As Few Aids as Possible

In clicker training, we want to use as few aids as possible so we don't have to wean the dog off them later on. Of course you can use aids, but you need to be conscious of what cue or cues let the dog know to perform the behavior. You also need to have a plan for how to eventually remove these aids. Sometimes using an aid can be a better way to get started rather than having a frustrated dog and handler.

Luring the dog, with a treat for example, is an extremely common aid. You might teach the dog to sit by holding a hand with a treat over her head. Most dogs will sit to be able to reach the treat. Initially, what the dog learns is to follow a hand with treats, not to sit. But if you repeat the exercise enough times as you're saying "sit", sooner or later the dog will learn to sit with the aid of these two cues. If you don't want the hand to be part of the cue, then you'll have to work to remove it.

ica shapes Vill step by step
'l he finally spins all the
 around.

Jessica lures Vill to spin
using treats.

For many behaviors, it's entirely unnecessary to use aids. Sitting is a typical example since all dogs will spontaneously sit and then we can reward that. We choose to begin our training with as few aids as possible.

Other aids might be your body position, touching the dog, correcting the environment, hand signals, or repeating the cue several times. Sometimes it might be a good idea to keep aids as a cue, such as a hand signal for the dog to lie down when we don't have the chance to say "down", but for the most part we want the dog to be able to perform the behavior solely on our verbal cue.

The Cue Ladder

When do we add a cue to a behavior? As soon as the voluntary behavior starts to look the way we want it and the dog does it effortlessly.[9] When the dog takes her reward, swallows it and then immediately offers the behavior again, it's time to add the cue.

When you teach the dog to perform a behavior on cue, follow the steps of the cue ladder. Do the following:

1. Say the cue at the same time as the dog offers the behavior.
2. Say the cue right before the dog offers the behavior.
3. Test your cue – say the cue before the dog has started to think about performing the behavior.
4. Only reward if your dog performs the behavior when you've given the cue, not otherwise. Teach her to wait for your cue.
5. Say nonsense words – don't reward the dog if she performs the behavior. Then say the real cue and reward. Mix in other cues the dog knows so that she learns to differentiate between the different cues.

---

[9] Egtvedt & Køste, Lydnadsträning i teori och praktik, 2008.

Initially, the dog might be a little startled when you suddenly say something, so start out by giving the cue when the dog has almost completed the behavior. If your dog stops and looks at you when you say the cue, wait a bit and see if the dog still performs the behavior.

In step 2, it might look like the dog has performed the behavior on cue, but the dog is really just performing the behavior because she has done so several times in a row and gotten treats for it. Don't make the exercise too difficult too quickly.

When you get to step 3, give the dog several seconds to think in the beginning. Five seconds might feel like an eternity, but your dog will respond faster and faster. Here you need to be sensitive so you say the cue when you believe your dog is really going to respond. If you've just started training recalls, you shouldn't yell "come" when the dog runs after the neighbor's cat. You need to hold your tongue and go and get the dog from underneath the nearest tree instead. It would be ideal if you could make the dog believe that she simply can't do anything else than the correct behavior when she hears the cue, and that comes from not having the chance to make a mistake and still receive a reward.

Do What I Say When I Say It

Now the real fun begins! Up until now the dog has received a reward every time she has performed the behavior and we have given the cue when the dog performs the behavior or when we know she will do it. Now we're going to begin to teach the dog to perform the behavior only when we want her to (step 4). Say the cue when your dog stands and looks at you. If the dog performs the behavior, for instance sitting down, without you saying anything, don't reward her. If she gets up again, wait for a minute before you say the cue and then reward her for sitting. Now you can start switching between rewarding the dog with treats and saying the cue when she waits. When the dog is able to stand and wait for the right cue, you can add in other cues the dog has mastered (step 5). If you want you can also say a nonsense word. If we give another cue, we of course want the dog to perform the requested behavior and not something else.

To be successful during trials and competitions, we need to be sure that the dog learns how to switch between voluntary behavior and behavior on cue, so she understands whether

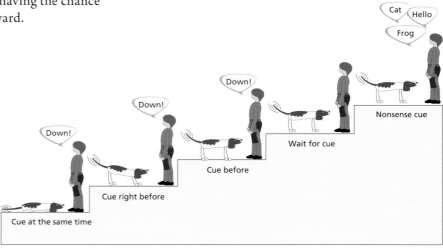

The cue ladder provides a model for our approach to teaching the dog to do what we want when we want.

or not she is supposed to wait for a cue. During step 4, you have to be careful that the dog only performs the behavior on your cue. It's impossible for the dog to understand cue training if she's sometimes supposed to listen and other times receives a reward for coming up with something else voluntarily. This means that if you are training sit on cue, it should only pay off to sit on cue. If you are training a voluntary spinning behavior, only voluntary spinning should pay off. Accordingly, it doesn't pay for the dog to add a voluntary spin when you are training sit on cue.

Generalize This

In order to teach the dog to perform a behavior in the same way, both voluntarily and on cue, regardless of the environment or distractions, we start adding minor distractions at an early stage. We call this generalizing the behavior. When the dog has understood what she's supposed to do, we can change things in the environment. That might be how we stand, where we offer the reward, the surface we are standing on, sounds, weather, or the location. Make the task a little easier when you introduce a new distraction so the dog has a little extra time to think, even if she can perform the behavior immediately without distractions. The more distraction training you do, the sooner the dog will be able to perform the behavior anywhere. You can use generalization training with both voluntary behaviors and behaviors on cue.

As a consequence, you can be on different steps of the cue ladder in different environments. At home, you might be on step 3, where you have started saying the cue for the dog to sit. But when you come to a meadow full of game scents, the task becomes too difficult so you begin by working with the voluntary offered behavior and work your way up to giving the cue at the same time as the dog performs the behavior (step 1 cue training). Remember that a cue is not the final goal. We want the dog to be able to voluntarily offer the behavior in case we want to refine a detail, use the behavior in another situation, or simply because we just want our dog to be good at offering a lot of behaviors.

If Your Dog Doesn't Listen

Sometimes it feels as if the dog doesn't listen to your cue, or at the very least doesn't do what you had in mind when you gave the cue. At those times, you need to have a well thought out strategy for what you should and shouldn't do. There can be many reasons why the dog doesn't do what you say. Maybe the dog truly didn't hear you or maybe she was occupied with something else. The dog isn't trying to provoke you or assume leadership, which are explanations we sometimes hear. Most often, the dog hasn't sufficiently learned the cue or she doesn't see any value in performing the desired behavior the way we planned. We tend to believe the dog has mastered the cue after a few repetitions, but for reliable results the dog must have performed the behavior a great many times in a variety of situations. Five repetitions are not enough; the number is more like 100 or 500. Naturally this varies from dog to dog. It also depends on how accustomed the dog is to learning new cues. The more cues the dog knows, the quicker she usually learns new ones. Remember that repetition is the mother of all learning.

What do we do if the dog doesn't listen to our cue? It depends on how much we've trained that particular cue. If we've just taught it, we'll immediately go back to step 1 and have the dog offer the behavior voluntarily and then move on to giving the cue at the same time the dog performs the behavior. If we've already spent a lot of time training the

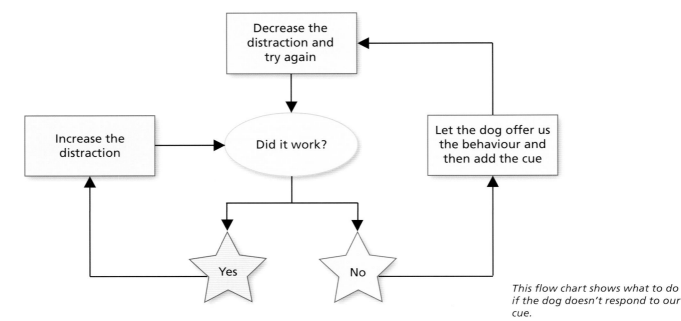

Decrease the distraction and try again

Increase the distraction

Did it work?

Let the dog offer us the behaviour and then add the cue

Yes

No

This flow chart shows what to do if the dog doesn't respond to our cue.

cue in question, we can reduce the distractions (for instance, waiting until the dog looks at us) and then try again. If that works, we can add more difficult distractions (see the flow chart above). Sometimes we also need to think about whether or not our reward is sufficiently valuable. Does the dog think it's worth working for?

What we don't want to do is repeat the cue: "Sit!", "sit!", "sit!", "good!" We want to teach the dog to do it correctly the first time when we say the cue. If the dog still doesn't respond to a cue we've spent a long time training, we might just take a step backwards, say "oops", and try again.

Try out the cue in different environments. If it doesn't work take a step back in your plan and make it a little easier. It's perfectly fine to experiment with the cue a bit because we always have a plan for what to do if something goes wrong.

Fluency

To develop truly reliable and stable behaviors, we work with something called fluency. A fluent behavior is performed with speed and precision every time. You might say that it's in the dog's bones. It's also more resistant to extinction – it "sticks" even if it isn't rewarded. Furthermore, the behavior is easier to generalize to new environments and to combine with other behaviors. It requires little energy for the dog to perform, both mentally and physically, and the dog will remember it even if we haven't worked on the behavior in a long time. It's also easier to have stimulus control with fluent behaviors. However, fluent behaviors shouldn't be confused with reflexes. A reflex is always an unconscious response and species specific. It can't be taught. But we can teach behaviors so well that they are performed almost as fast as a reflex.

How do we make a behavior fluent? We repeat the behavior many times and progressively make it more difficult. We want to emphasize, however, that it's not a good idea to train fluency only on one behavior at a time because the dog might then fixate on the behavior and find it difficult to offer other behaviors. Switch up your training so you are actively training three or four behaviors at the same time.

Fluency is something we train during one or more training sessions for each behavior, somewhat early in the learning process. Later on we can then focus on having the dog perform the behavior in different environments, at different times, and with different distractions. We don't train more complicated behavior chains, such as long marked and blind retrieves, to fluency, but focus instead on achieving fluency in simpler behaviors such as deliveries and sits.

Challenge
Does your dog sit when you have a bucket on your head and say "sit"? Or when you stand behind a door? Or when you use a high and squeaky voice?

How Does the Dog Know When She is Supposed to Listen?

People often ask if our dogs end up offering behaviors all the time, and if the dog doesn't get confused when sometimes we want her to listen to a cue and other times we want her to offer behaviors voluntarily. Sometimes we handlers probably make it more complicated than it needs to be, because dogs understand quite quickly what leads to rewards. If we give a cue the dog knows that it doesn't pay to offer the behavior voluntarily and she must wait until she hears a cue (step 4 on the cue ladder). If we later want to return to working with the voluntarily offered behavior, we'll reward the dog for something she does spontaneously, for instance,

Jenny and Fjodor

turning her head, looking at us, or sitting down. We often have a certain stance or choose to sit down when we work with voluntary behavior. In other words, our dogs learn to read us and therefore they know whether or not they are expected to offer a behavior.

How do we tell the dog not to offer a large number of different behaviors at every turn? The simple answer is that we don't. We let the dog know what pays off right now. When we take a break from our training and want the dog to be calm, we can use one of our break routines. In everyday situations, we most often ignore the dog when we don't want her to be active and sometimes we reward her for lying down when nothing is happening. However, we make sure to reward her when she's calm, and that she doesn't get wound up by being rewarded. When we train for competitions, we work a lot with stimulus control so that the dog learns to wait for the cue and only do what we ask. Step 4 on the cue ladder therefore almost becomes the most important step for a clicker trained dog because it can sometimes be a bit difficult to wait for a cue.

As you've understood by now, adding a cue to a behavior is not only about naming said behavior; it's about achieving stimulus control. This means that we train the dog to do what we say regardless of the environment, what smells and sounds surround us, and whether we are standing on our heads or on our feet when we give the cue.

Åsa stands in different positions depending on what she's training with Mio.

sel

Summary

- Follow the steps in the cue ladder to reach stimulus control on the dog's behaviors.
- Be sure to teach the dog how to switch between cued behaviors and voluntarily offered behaviors.
- Use aids if necessary, but wean them off as soon as possible and be conscious of which cues the dog is responding to.
- Generalize both voluntarily offered behavior and behavior on cue.

Steadiness

During a field trial, your gun dog must sit and stand like a statue both beside you and at a distance following a stop whistle. She also needs to be able to hold a position while moving – when walking at heel, for example. A lot of things will be going on at the same time – the judge approaches to greet you, shots go off, game flies up and falls, and other dogs are working all around. In other words, there are a lot of temptations to be resisted!

We encounter a lot of situations every day that provide an opportunity to teach the dog to remain steady. One of the first things we teach a puppy is to be able to sit and wait for the cue "go ahead" before she can have her food. When we go on walks, we also work on having the dog sit and then reward her for remaining in sit while we greet someone. Besides these everyday training situations, there are also a number of exercises we can do to teach the dog to stay steady.

Play to Inspire Steadiness

The easiest position to start training steadiness is usually a sit. We teach it by using the "Take It" game we described in the chapter "Rewards". The dog is allowed to play with the toy after she has restrained herself and remained in sit even though she has seen the toy. It's a really fun game that can be taught quickly, especially to puppies. The end goal is for the dog to be able to remain in sit while you wave the toy, throw it on the ground, and run away with it before giving the cue "take it".

Totte remains in sit even though Lena tempts him with a toy.

As a reward for remaining in sit, Lena tells Totte to "take it" and he throws himself at the toy.

Treats

In combination with the "Take It" game to train steadiness, we also use treats to train the dog to remain in sit. Wait until your dog sits, and then click and reward her while she's still sitting. In other words, "click for action, treat for position".[10] If the dog manages to get up, you need to be even quicker with the reward next time. Offer the treat above the dog's head (without allowing the dog to get up) so you reward the dog for keeping her butt planted firmly on the ground.

When your dog is sitting, you can start with reverse luring. It becomes an exercise in self-control for the dog. She isn't allowed to take the reward but must remain in sit in order to receive it. You can then use the same idea with all kinds of distractions: balls, dogs, people, game, and so on. The exercise can be used, for example, to teach the dog that she's only allowed to greet a human friend when all of her paws are on the ground. Start by rewarding the dog for sitting. If she remains in sit when someone approaches, she can either get a reward from you or a "go ahead" to greet. If the dog gets up without permission, the person should turn away until the dog sits again.

---

[10] Bob Bailey, www.behavior1.com.

Pitfall

If your dog gets up and comes to you, don't reward her. Nor shou[ld] you reward her if she reaches towards your hand to take the reward. Wait until she is sitting calmly and still and then reward her. With your other hand, take the treat from your open hand a[nd] give it to the dog. In other words, she isn't allowed to take the trea[t] from your open hand herself. Put a lot of treats in your hand to easily repeat the exercise without having to fumble in your pocke[t] for new ones. Moreover, it reinforces the dog's self-restraint; she isn't allowed in any situation to lunge at the hand with treats.

Steadiness with Distractions

Work on steadiness both with and without distractions. You can come up with your own distractions, such as sitting while the neighbor's cat saunters by or children play soccer. The "Take It" game we mentioned earlier offers endless possibilities: Throw the toy over the dog's head, rub it over the dog's paws, wave it in front of the dog, and so on.

You can also train with distractions that occur during a field trial, such as having the dog remain in sit when the game falls, other dogs are working and judges greet you. The more distractions you can find, the better. Even if a distraction doesn't occur during a trial, you will still encounter challenges you've never thought of during trials (and in everyday life). If you've already trained with a lot of other strange distractions, it will be easier for the dog to perform correctly when she encounters a new distraction.

Teach the dog to remain at your side while both you and your helper throw objects. Sometimes have the dog fetch them and other times have the dog remain in sit while you fetch them. Work is one of the best rewards for a dog trained to hunt. Reward the dog for remaining in sit beside you by throwing a mark and allowing her to fetch it. To manage the dog's expectations, switch between giving the dog a reward from your hand and rewarding her with work.

When you are training with distractions, don't worry about how long the dog remains in sit, reward the dog immediately after the distraction. Later on you can extend the amount of time she is to remain in sit and add distractions to the longer duration. In our experience, dogs quickly learn to recognize distraction games and sit very successfully as long as there are active distractions. A lack of distractions

can pose a challenge, however. Therefore remember to sometimes work without any distractions and just focus on increasing the amount of time.

Coach Says

Use the environment to train steadiness and self-control. If you discover something the dog wants to have or do, wait until she has sat down and then cue "go ahead". As the dog begins to master the task, increase the amount of time she has to wait before you cue "go ahead". This idea transfers over to field trials: Your dog is walking nicely beside you — you send her on a blind retrieve, or your dog is sitting at your side when the shot goes off and the mark falls — you send the dog to retrieve the mark.

Increasing the Duration

When we train a skill that requires more time (such as steadiness) and the dog needs to concentrate, we increase the time by rewarding the dog at random intervals. That way the dog learns that rewards don't always come at the same point in time, but it pays off to wait even if the reward isn't immediate. The rate of reward might look like this: reward after one second, five seconds, two seconds, ten seconds, two seconds, three seconds… If the dog leaves her position and walks towards you, stay calm and wait until she sits down again or say, "sit" and continue the training. Teach your dog to sit at your side and wait for at least ten minutes, have a distraction occur every now and then, but make sure that a lot of time passes without anything happening. If you want to train for a field trial for retrievers in the UK, the dog is required to sit or lie beside you for almost an entire day.

But …

… isn't it easier to just get angry or grab the dog when she tries to run away? At first glance, it might seem easier to correct the dog physically or verbally, but we want to teach the dog what she should do instead of what she shouldn't. By being rewarded for remaining in sit and preventing her from rewarding herself by going off on her own, the dog starts to understand what we want her to do. An example is using marks as a reward for the dog to remain in sit at your side. If the dog jumps the gun, you or your helper can just pick up the object so the dog doesn't get rewarded.

Cues

During field trial training, a whistle is used to tell the dog to stop. After the stop whistle, the dog is to remain on the spot, either standing or sitting. One of the most important things you can teach your gun dog is to stop and stay where she halted. Read more about how to teach this in the chapter "The Stop Whistle".

Decide what cues you want to use to teach the behaviors that require steadiness (sit, stand and down). Some people choose to first say, "sit" and then "stay" or "stop", while others just say, "sit" and let that mean, "remain in sit" until the dog gets some other kind of information. It doesn't matter what version you choose. The main thing is that you are consistent and clear about what the cues mean to you and your dog. You can start to add the cue when the dog can voluntarily remain in sit for a moment. Make sure you give a release cue or interrupt the position that requires steadiness with another cue so the dog learns to remain in sit until she receives another instruction.

Steadiness during Field Trials

The steadiness required during field trials for retrievers means that the dog should be able to sit and walk beside you when the marks fall, and when the guns or judges indicate where you should send the dog. In the novice classes in some countries there is only one dog working at a time, but sooner or later the dog should be able to do the same things while other dogs are working.[11] In the UK, a field trial will take the whole day, so the dog must be able to hold steady for long periods of time. Sometimes the dogs may even work at the same time, for instance each one in her own search area.

An even bigger challenge is the steadiness that is required during field trials for spaniels. In most countries, the dogs are tested with live game even in the novice trials. The dog should be able to stop and stay still when the bird is flushed and after the shot. For spaniels, two dogs might also be hunting at the same time. A spaniel must also remain with you and complete her work with other dogs in the vicinity.

---

[11] Called "honoring" the other dogs in US.

Sub-goals – Steadiness	Completed
Remaining in sit beside you	
Walking at heel (see the chapter "Heelwork")	
Stop and hold position at a distance after a stop whistle (see the chapter "The Stop Whistle")	
During a flush (only spaniels, see the chapter "The Stop Whistle")	
With distractions (for example shots, marks, other dogs working)	

Challenge

Can your dog watch a mark fall, but instead of running for it, lay down when you say "down" and then walk with you in the other direction before she's allowed to retrieve the mark?

If not, reduce the distraction and work on cue comprehension in various environments so the dog really listens to you instead of guessing what she should be doing.

Summary

Reward your dog in position to reinforce the idea that she is to remain in place.

Gradually extend the duration and increase the distractions.

Teach the dog that it pays off to restrain herself.

Stina

Calmness Training

We really require a lot from our dogs when it comes to shifting between being active and being calm during a hunt.[12] On one hand, the dog should be able to lie down and wait in the car or sit quietly and watch while other dogs are working. On the other hand, she should be ready to work at a moment's notice with complete focus on the task at hand. To keep the dog from expending unnecessary energy, we want to teach her to relax and rest when she has a chance.

---

[12] Called "a shoot" in the UK.

In the chapter "Play – the Ultimate Reward", we wrote about the "On and Off Game". That game is also useful with calmness training. If you have played the game a lot, your dog is likely to relax as soon as you grab her collar. You want to further develop this to the point where your dog almost lies down and goes to sleep when there isn't anything going on or when she isn't working. Remember to switch between activity and calm; you can't make an active dog calm just by training calmness. One way or another you have to give your dog an outlet for her energy!

Relax on a Mat

In order to train your dog to relax you can use a mat where you teach her to settle and be calm. Start working on this when you are sitting with your dog on the mat in a peaceful environment. Massage your dog and reward her for being still. When she is still, you can also reward her with a short working session. After working, sit down on the mat again with your dog until she relaxes. Don't allow the dog to work or get off the mat if she isn't calm. Do this training when you have plenty of time and preferably start when your dog is just a puppy.

Coach Says

Train your dog to relax and be calm in as many different environm as possible, but especially in the kinds of environments where you needs to be calm and relaxed. Think about your own mood when y are doing this training. Are you calm?
Irritated? What's your breathing like? You can't expect your dog t be calm and relaxed if your body is tense with impatience and you breathing is short and jagged ...

Is Your Dog Really Calm?

It's easy to believe that a dog that is lying totally still is relaxed, but if we look a little closer, we see that some dogs lie with every muscle in their body tense, ready to go. This is not what we want. We want the dog to really relax. Study your dog! Some dogs lock their gaze on whatever they're anticipating, others start shaking in all or part of their bodies when they are anxiously waiting for something. We don't want this because it can build up stress that might later be vocalized.

What your training plan is going to look like depends entirely on the individual you have in front of you. Some dogs mature slower, and then you need to take your time with training. Some are calm by nature and others are easily wound up. Training a dog to be calm might sound easy, but can be extremely difficult. Start in a calm environment with few distractions and then gradually increase the level of difficulty. One of the most challenging things for a dog that loves to work – who knows how fun it can be to retrieve – is to watch other dogs work. Beginning with that kind of incredibly difficult distraction would make us doomed to fail.

Calmness with Distractions

Work on training for calmness in as many different environments as possible: in the forest, at home in the kitchen, at a friends' houses, in town, on the bus, or at an outdoor café. If you have the opportunity, look for a place where you know a lot of wild animals roam, or go to a game park or a chicken coop. When your dog has had a chance to relieve herself, sit down with the dog and don't allow her to work or do anything else before she's relaxed or has even fallen asleep. This is called habituation and means that the dog gradually becomes used to an environment and no longer reacts to it.

To "just be" is something the dog has to learn. The best way to do this, is to let the dog just be with us in a lot of different situations, without us paying too much attention to her. That way, we teach the dog to relax. Sometimes the dog might need help relaxing, for instance by having her space limited or by being leashed beside us until she falls asleep. We spend a lot of time together with our puppies, but teach them as soon as possible that it's okay if we leave without them being able to come with us. At first, we are of course only gone for a few moments at a time, but later on we extend the time more and more.

We always pay attention to the dog's level of anticipation and emotional state during our training. The dog is never allowed to work if she is too wound up. Instead, we always switch back and forth between activity and calmness. During a training session, we might sit down and take it easy for a long while and then only do one single exercise. It might be that we lay out a small hunting area while the dog watches us and then sit down with the dog and have a cup of coffee. (Holding an area means that the dog should search for an object in a small hunting area). When the dog has relaxed and stopped looking at the hunting area, we stand up calmly, take the dog with us and allow her to work. Then we might take another break. If your dog exhibits too much anticipation when looking at the hunting area, you can't expect any major relaxation at the beginning. You can watch for small signs, that the dog is able to look somewhere else than the hunting area or becomes quiet. To create the right amount of anticipation for work you can also try laying out two areas with game or dummies. If the dog is fixated in one direction, you can turn around and send her in the other direction once she is calm. If the dog won't calm down before you start working, sit down on the mat or interrupt your training and take a walk. Try again later when the dog is calmer.

You also have to teach the dog to sit quietly and watch while other dogs are working. If the dog starts to whine, turn around and walk away so the other dogs are out of her sight. Stand as far away as necessary for the dog to be able to calmly sit and watch or lie down and sleep at your feet. Calmly reward the dog by petting her or giving her treats when she is quiet. It requires a good deal of energy to just sit still and wait, a lot more than it takes to run out and search for game.

The Backpack

When your puppy is small, it can be good to teach her to sit quietly between your legs while you stand or sit behind her, almost like a backpack.[13] In stressful situations, you can put your dog between your legs, stroke her chest, and help her relax. You can of course teach this to older dogs, but then you might need to reward the dog more and shape the behavior of coming into this position between your legs. If you have an adult dog, it can be difficult to physically hold her in place. You risk ending up in a struggle with your dog. With a small puppy, you can just carefully lift her into the right position and gently hold her there until she has calmed down. Don't let the dog wiggle loose; we want to teach her that fun things can happen when she relaxes, not that she can get away whenever she feels like it.

13 We've borrowed this exercise from Eva Bodfäldt, author of "Follow Me – A Deal with Your Dog".

Wait in the Car

Start off with short training sessions when you want the dog to learn to be alone. Begin by leaving your dog alone in the car. Leave her with a tasty marrowbone the first few times so she has something to occupy herself with. In the beginning, leave the dog after you've exercised her and she's a little tired so there's a greater chance she'll stay calm. When the dog has gotten used to staying calm in the car, you can start leaving her without the marrowbone. Go back to the dog and reward her now and then when she's quiet. If she makes a noise, try waiting until she quiets down before you go back. The majority of dogs will quiet down after a while. If the dog starts to panic after being left alone, avoid leaving her for so long that she has a chance to panic. Only leave the dog when you think she'll be quiet and return before she starts whining.

Put a bowl of treats next to the car so your training buddies who walk by can help reward the dog. It helps the dog to accept passersby instead of barking at them and guarding the car.

The dog will often be excited to ride in the car since it usually leads to something fun. Take her with you when you go to the store for impromptu relaxation training in the car when nothing is happening at all. Naturally, remember that a dog in the car and warm weather are a bad combination.

All Tied Up

You use the same approach to teach your dog to stay calm while being tied up. Start with short training sessions and reward the dog when she stays sitting or lying. If she starts digging or biting on the leash, calmly walk back and interrupt the behavior. Wait until she sits or lies calmly, reward her and then try leaving her again.

Gudrun with friends

Calmness during Field Trials

During field trials, the dog isn't only tested on steadiness, but also on her ability to wait calmly beside you for her turn. The dog needs to remain quiet and focused on the task at hand.

Summary

- Use every opportunity that presents itself to train calmness.
- Don't let the dog work if she makes a noise or is too excited.
- Remember that you should also be calm when training calmness with the dog.
- Remember to switch between being active and being calm. The dog also needs an outlet for her energy.

Pitfall

Don't allow the dog to work when she's too excited or when she whines, or she will learn that such behaviors lead to something fun. Instead, we want to teach the dog that she must be calm and quiet before she's allowed to work.

Challenge

Can your dog lie down and fall asleep beside a soccer field where children are playing a game?

Sub-goals – Calmness Training	Completed
Relax on a mat	
Lay at your feet when you sit down	
Sit and wait while tied up	
With distractions (for example, while other dogs are working, shots, or an audience)	

A Spotlight on Behavior

You have probably noticed that there are several recurring themes in our training that appear in chapter after chapter. One thing you've no doubt picked up on is that we never, neither physically nor verbally, correct the dog in a way that she might perceive as unpleasant. Instead, we shine the spotlight on the correct behaviors.

We focus heavily on organizing the exercises so the dog succeeds. Then we can reward her for doing the right thing. We work with what is known as positive reinforcement. Don't think about positive in the everyday sense but rather in terms of mathematics. Positive means plus (+), which means we add something. Positive reinforcement thus means that we add something we know the dog wants. For example, you say "sit". The dog sits. You give her a ball.

Setting up the training so the dog gets it right and we get to reinforce the behaviors we're looking for is one of the guiding principles of our training. But what do we do if the dog does something wrong? Well, not much really. We withhold the reward we intended to give the dog for the correct behavior and we also prevent her from rewarding herself, for example by maintaining control of the reward or leashing the dog. This is called negative punishment. Again, think in mathematical terms. Negative means minus (−), which means we take away the reward. This is a type of punishment in that the dog has been cheated out of her sweet. For example: You say "sit". The dog continues standing, staring at you. You don't give her the ball you intended to give her for sitting.

Joy or Frustration

We want the dog to look forward to the reward and be really happy about it – and feel a little disappointed and frustrated if she doesn't get it. The dose of frustration and disappointment should never be so great that the dog gives up and stops working. Instead, we want her to be enthusiastic about trying again. A little frustration is necessary to make progress with training, but there should always be a great deal more joy than frustration!

When the dog does something undesirable, we can also use extinction, which means we ignore the dog's incorrect behaviors. We don't see extinction as particularly useful for field trial training, but there are situations we encounter in daily life where it's applicable. For example, a dog that shows off her tricks to get a treat when we are eating: We ignore her and continue to eat.

> **But ...**
> ... aren't the dog's instincts too strong for clicker training to be effec[t] in field trial training? Well, a gun dog that's let loose will likely try a lot of things she finds fun, which we might not find equally amu[s] First and foremost, we make working with us and doing what we w[ant] high-value activities. Moreover, we can always control the dog by us[ing] a leash or long line. We also try to control distractions as much as possible, by for example using a helper to pick up a thrown dumm[y] that the dog isn't supposed to take. We also break all behaviors do[wn] into small steps so the dog learns what she's supposed to do. When the dog knows what to do, she will also work at a distance despite [her] strong instincts. We teach the dog that she needs to listen to us to [be] able to do the activities she loves the most!

Ludde

The Clicker and Offered Behaviors

We always use reward markers in our training. Most often we use a clicker, but it might also be a particular word, a whistle, a sound or something else that tells the dog, "What you are doing now is exactly right and you will get a reward for it". You might have heard the whistle during a dolphin show. The whistle means, "That vault was excellent, come here and get a fish". In field trial training, however, we use the whistle as a cue and not as a reward marker.

The final goal of our training is that the dog voluntarily offers behaviors. Almost all learning begins with the dog offering a behavior voluntarily, without being lured or for that matter threatened. Learning occurs more quickly and the behavior will be more reliable and stable, if the dog determines how and when to do it. The dog will also be more engaged this way. The dog will think training is fun and you can skip using unnecessary aids. We can also use voluntarily offered behavior if we want to reteach or further develop a behavior, such as shaping a crawl from a down.

Coach Says

If you are going to teach your dog a word to use as a reward marker, pick a word that you don't often use, but that's easy to say and remember. Lena says "chic", while Elsa says "hat" to Diesel and "click" to her other Golden Retriever Ludde.

And this, dear reader, is clicker training! It's not as much about the little box called a clicker as it is a training philosophy that comes from behavioral psychology and the laws of learning.

Crime and Punishment

As you can see in the illustration on the next page, there are other perspectives and ways of working. The main approach then is to find mistakes that can be punished instead of desired behaviors that can be rewarded. This method is called positive punishment and is associated with feelings of fear and insecurity in the dog. This method also uses negative reinforcement that is associated with a sense of relief coming from avoidance or escape from something unpleasant. One example of this is the forced retrieve. The trainer pinches the dog's ear until the dog takes the dummy, thereby escaping from the pain of the ear pinch (negative reinforcement). Another example is a swift leash jerk when the dog pulls, which causes the dog to stop pulling on the leash (positive punishment). According to both proven experience and research, these training methods also work.

Why? Because!

Once we had a student who had used correction based training with her dogs for several years. Then she attended a clicker training course and radically changed her training methods as a result. One day she commented, "Earlier I was always in a bad mood when I was training. I was angry at my dog during almost every training session. Now I'm almost always happy and I laugh every time we train."

Sometimes it can be difficult to change an established dog training method. We usually say that getting the right perspective is a good start. Try catching your dog being good and make sure to reward her!

Challenge

During your next walk, take a minute when you are totally silent (no cues and no hand signals). Then reward everything the dog does right. How many rewards does she get in a minute? What is a good behavior, in your opinion? It might be eye contact, a loose leash or the dog just standing still watching a deer instead of running after it.

Jargon

Within clicker training, there is a tendency to use a lot of jargon – scientific terms which sometimes are hard to comprehend. The advantage of all of these terms is that they have clear definitions and that we can have discussions regarding how they're being used.

Almost all dog training occurs through something that is called operant conditioning. Operant behaviors are all behaviors the dog can choose to perform, or not. This applies to

	Positive = adding something	Negative = removing something
Reinforcement = behavior increases	Positive reinforcement Add something the dog wants Feeling: Joy	Negative reinforcement Remove something the dog doesn't want Feeling: Relief
Punishment = behavior decreases	Positive punishment Add something the dog doesn't want Feeling: Fear	Negative punishment Remove something the the dog wants Feeling: Frustration
Extinction The behavior doesn't have a connected consequence ("doesn't work") and therefore disappears.		

The illustration shows the basic principles of operant learning and the emotions associated with the four consequences.

clicker training as well as other kinds of training methods. Operant conditioning means a behavior is followed by a consequence – a reward or a punishment. The consequence affects what happens the next time; for example, receiving a really good reward for performing a behavior increases the likelihood that the dog will repeat the same behavior. Likewise, a well timed punishment reduces the likelihood that the behavior will be repeated. The terms we have previously described, positive and negative reinforcement and positive and negative punishment, are the cornerstones of all operant learning. The learning process is the same for all species, animals as well as humans.

In addition to operant conditioning, there is something that is a bit more difficult to control: namely, classical conditioning. Classical conditioning relates to emotions and reflexes, that is, all behaviors the dog does not have control over. These behaviors can include blinking, salivation and knee jerks in humans.

Classical conditioning means emotions and reflexes are paired with various stimuli. A stimulus can be anything: a word, a sound, an object or a smell. If we say to you: "Imagine you are biting into a lemon." What happens in your mouth then? Most likely you will begin to salivate. This is a clear example of classical conditioning. The word "lemon" elicits an internal reflex. Had we, however, said "lemon" to someone who doesn't know what the word "lemon" means, no such salivation reflex would be elicited. Another example of classical conditioning is when the hunter takes out his gun before the hunt and his gun dog starts to get excited. A dog that has never hunted probably won't react at all. There are some behaviors, such as "sit", that the dog has mastered so well they're almost inherent and automatic.

However, it's still an operant behavior. The dog can still choose not to sit. So even if the behavior is extremely well learnt, it's not a reflex.

When we train, we mostly work with operant learning, but emotions and the classical conditioning process are always in the background. Sometimes we choose to work with classical conditioning, for example when dealing with fearful dogs. A more detailed description of such training is unfortunately outside the purview of this book. If you want to read more about it, we recommend the book "Click to Calm" by Emma Parsons.

A Scientific Misinterpretation

Research has provided us with valuable information about our animals – how they learn and act in different situations. But sometimes the interpretation of this research can go wrong. We think it's interesting that one of the most prevailing theories about dog training stems from a misunderstanding. We are talking about the dominance theory.

In the 1920s, Norwegian psychologist Thorleif Schelderup-Ebbe studied his chickens and found his hens were organized according to a certain order when they had limited food. There was a chicken pecking at everyone else, the next in line pecked on all but the first, the third pecked on all but the first two and so on, with the exception of the wretched hen who didn't peck on anyone but got pecked by everyone else. The concept of the pecking order was born. Animal scientists around the world jumped on the idea of studying the social organization of animals. Since the term "pecking order" alluded to birds, the term "hierarchy" was used instead. Animals high in the social hierarchy were seen to be dominant and those further down submissive.[14]

After several decades of research that in various ways confirmed the dominance theory, it began to be sharply questioned in the 1960s. It was then this misinterpretation came into the light. The criticism was that almost all of the studies had been done on captive animals (including wolves) or animals that for various reasons had limited resources, thereby making the hierarchy more visible. It was therefore easy to believe hierarchy was the most important social structure.

But ethologist and researcher Per Jensen says: "Because it is relatively easy to study dominance in groups with

[14] Jensen, 1983, Den missuppfattade dominansen ("The misunderstood dominance"). Published in Hundsport and HundMagazinet (nr 1-2 2003).

Ingela and Snoddas

limited access to resources, many other factors in the pack dynamic have been overlooked. The ranking is indeed a repellent factor – it helps to keep enough space between individuals to keep aggression at bay. One presumably recognizes there must be even stronger and more important attracting factors. Otherwise, animals would not live in packs."[15] Jensen's point is that dominance has very little meaning in the everyday functioning of the pack and how individuals interact with each other. Other social relationships are much more important.

From having believed that animals organize themselves based primarily on this aggressive system of dominance, research has instead discovered that the relationships of pack animals rather seem to be friendly and even affectionate![16] Jensen also argues that we have bred the domestic dog so much we can't willy-nilly compare it to wolves.[17] The concept of dominance in the relationship between dogs and humans is therefore probably entirely meaningless; there is no research showing that the concept is transferable to a relationship between different species.[18]

We think it's time for a paradigm shift in the world of dog people. It's time to question the prevailing order and seriously break the norms linked to dominance and aggression in the relationship between dogs and humans. Clicker training does just that. As we said in the introduction, it's simply ethical and fun dog training. It's also smart and effective training that leads to good results.

Love and Friendship

Training your dog in the positive and playful manner offered by clicker training creates a feeling of togetherness. But everything you do with your dog where you're in some sort of contact and where there aren't any aversives involved for the dog strengthens your bond. We want to have a loving and friendly relationship with our dogs. They're part of our family and therefore also an important part of our everyday lives. They come with us everywhere it's possible to bring a dog, they spend time with our families and friends, they relax on the couch with us, and so on. But we are the ones who decide what the dog may and may not do. All of this helps us to have confident, trusting and responsive dogs.

---

[15] Jensen, 1983, Den missuppfattade dominansen. Published in Hundsport och HundMagazinet (nr 1-2 2003).
[16] Miklosi, 2007, Dog Behaviour, Evolution and Cognition.
[17] Jensen, 2010, lecture at Adventure Dog Conference.
[18] Miklosi, 2007, Dog Behaviour, Evolution and Cognition.

Totte

You first and foremost build a strong relationship with your dog by spending your everyday life together, but also during your training sessions.

Leadership and Boundaries

In dog training the concept of leadership is much debated. Depending on how we interpret it, it can be good or bad. We sometimes think that the term "bad leadership" is used as an excuse for poor or nonexistent training. We never tell our students they have "bad leadership" because this does not provide any information about what should be changed. In the true clicker spirit, we focus instead on the concrete actions we can take to improve the situation: better timing, better rewards, more frequent rewards, or easier exercises.

This does not mean that we don't set boundaries in our training. We have many rules for how our training should work, but we don't believe that the dog is working to make us happy or that she knows what is right and wrong. The dog simply does what is worthwhile, and it's up to us to organize the training so that the dog chooses to do what we want. For us, the concept of leadership is something positive in the sense that we lead our dog down the right track: take care of her, worry about her, and teach her what she needs to be able to do in our world. Leadership is an obligation that is earned, not a right to be demanded.

Summary

- Clicker training is about:
  - » Rewarding correct behaviors and preventing the dog from rewarding herself.
  - » The dog voluntarily offering different behaviors and us using as few aids as possible.
  - » Using a reward marker that tells the dog, "You did the right thing and you'll soon get a reward".
- The laws of learning are the same for all species, humans as well as dogs. We all do what pays off.

Isac and Breeze

Recall

"Come!" Your dog stops dead in her tracks, turns in the air and runs straight to you as fast as she can. That's how we'd like all of our recalls to look. This is partly to give the dog greater freedom, and partly because sometimes your dog's life can depend on her coming when called.

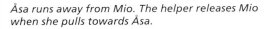
Åsa runs away from Mio. The helper releases Mio when she pulls towards Åsa.

The results are generally better the earlier you start training, but you can also improve the recall with older dogs. Once again, walks are an excellent opportunity to train. Reward the dog every time she voluntarily comes to you so she learns it's worthwhile to keep tabs on you.

"My dog never comes to me voluntarily when we're on walks", some people say. Reward your dog when she looks at you, which hopefully she does on occasion, or when she just stops and stands still. If you have a puppy, you should start training at home in a safe environment. When the puppy spontaneously comes to you, say your recall word and give her lots of rewards when she comes right up to you.

Play to Inspire Recall

We inspire recall through play by setting up various speedfilled exercises. One of the first exercises we do is the chase recall. In short, you get the dog to chase and catch up with you:

1. Ask a helper to hold your dog while you walk or run away. You might choose to just quickly show the dog you have a toy or a treat.

2. When you've walked a bit away, turn towards your dog and stand still while your helper releases the dog.

3. When your dog runs towards you at full speed, give your recall cue and reward the dog when she reaches you.

Once you've done this a few times you can start using the exercise when you are on walks, that is, you call your dog when she spontaneously runs towards you. Later, you can try calling the dog when she isn't occupied with something else. Then try your recall cue in progressively more difficult situations. Try to do a number of recalls on every walk and the more difficult the recall, the better the reward. Go to places where the dog can be off leash, or possibly on a long long line, so you can train a lot.

When the Battle is Lost

Once you start using your recall cue it's important not to "water down" the signal. Avoid calling the dog in situations where she won't listen. In that case, it's better to go and get your dog (or possibly put a long long line on her so she can't run off). It can also be useful to continue rewarding the dog when she spontaneously comes to you even after she has already mastered the recall. Call to the dog when she is on her way to you since you can then be sure the recall will be a success!

The Best Reward

As with all other learning, it's important you consider your rewards. On one of our recall courses a student asked, "Can you serve your dog dinner when she comes when called on

Elsa and Diesel

walks?" Of course! The owner put the dog's dinner (her raw food that she loved) in a jar with a lid in a backpack. When the dog came when called, she cheered, took off her backpack, invited the dog to help her open the backpack and then let her pounce on the food. After the owner continued this training and gave the dog both this and other rewards several times, the dog now comes when called even when a deer or a moose runs across the path in front of her.

The Whistle

The most common signal for the recall consists of several shorter signals. This is also frequently combined with holding your arms straight out at your sides, which also acts as a visual cue.

You can use any kind of whistle of course, but it can be advantageous to buy tuned whistles because you can then easily buy new ones when you misplace the old ones … The Acme 210.5 and 211.5 are whistles commonly used during spaniel and retriever trials. Since a spaniel works close to her handler, a slightly lighter whistle (210.5) or a silent whistle is often used, since it's more discreet and not as disruptive. A silent whistle or a supersonic pipe emits a sound that humans can't hear, but the dog can hear it. It's often possible to set it to make a small sound so we can hear how we are blowing into it.

Use Your Hand

It's a good idea to combine recalls with the hand target that we described in the chapter "Delivery to Hand". When the dog is headed towards you, put your hand out so the dog can aim at it. The hand target means the dog will come all the way to you so you can put a leash on her if necessary.

If you want the dog to go away from you to do a new recall with the hand target, you can either throw a treat or use a helper to hold the dog while you run away. Stop and call the dog at the same time as your helper releases her. Then reward the dog when she comes to you and puts her nose against your hand.

Coach Says

If your dog jumps away when you try to put the leash on her after having called her, work separately on taking her collar and rewarding her for it. Teach the dog that it's fun when you quickly grab her collar because then she gets really good rewards. You can then start combining the recall with the hand target and grabbing her collar before you reward her.

You can also have the dog run between you and your helper's hand targets or between family members' hands. Do the following:

1. Start with having your helper near the dog. The helper holds out his or her hand, then clicks and rewards the dog when she taps the hand.
2. Hold out your hand, click and reward the dog when she taps your hand.
3. Then it's your helper's turn to click and reward the dog when she taps his or her hand.
4. Then repeat the entire sequence again so the dog goes back and forth between the two of you.
5. As the dog runs between your hands, you can start adding the recall cue. Do it initially as the dog runs towards your hand, then exactly when the dog starts to turn around to head towards your helper, and finally when the dog has eaten the treat offered by your helper.

The person, whomever the dog just left, should become passive and ignore the dog while waiting for her to run to the next person. At the same time, the person the dog should go to next should hold his or her hand so the dog can easily see it the first few times, in order for her to understand what the game is all about.

Recall with Distractions

In our opinion, a big part of the recall involves the dog learning to ignore distractions – in other words, choosing you over whatever distraction is present. We start with an easy distraction and then make it harder and harder. We take the same approach no matter what the distraction. First we reward the dog when she voluntarily ignores the distraction, then we add the cue when the dog is on her way back from the distraction, then we add the cue when the dog is heading towards the distraction, and finally we add the cue once the dog has busied herself with the distraction.

Voluntarily Ignoring a Distraction

The very first thing we do in the recall training is to teach the dog to voluntarily ignore a distraction. Start by rewarding the dog for looking at you. Then allow her to go up to a person who has a treat (not the dog's very favorite) in his or her hand (say "go ahead" if necessary, but try to be quiet and let your helper lure the dog to come instead). The helper doesn't give the treat to the dog but keeps his or her hand closed and allows the dog to investigate. When the dog removes her muzzle from the hand, even if only an inch, click and reward her. The dog need not turn toward you the first few times. Gradually increase the level of difficulty so the dog removes her nose completely and turns towards you.

> **But ...**
> ... we can't allow the dog to approach every kind of distraction! N[e]
> and that's also the end goal. It's at the first stages of our training
> that the dog is allowed to go up to the distraction. If you train wit[h]
> a lot of different distractions, the dog will learn that it's always
> worthwhile to come when you call, both when she's close to and fa[r]
> away from something enticing.

Soon the dog won't bother to go up to the person because she knows the reward comes from you. Reward the dog for staying with you and increase the distractions. Ask your helper to make a little noise, talk to the dog (though we don't think saying the dog's name or "come" is fair), playing with a ball, clap his or her hands – any kind of distraction you might come up with. Continue the exercise using new distractions until your dog voluntarily ignores them as well. Remember; Don't make the distractions too difficult too quickly, because we always want the dog to succeed most of the time. If the dog falls for the distraction we just make it a little easier the next time. We want the dog to turn around halfway on her way to the helper (that's exactly what we want our recall to look like, the dog turning around before she reaches the distraction). Therefore, we make sure the dog can turn around from fairly simple distractions before we make them harder. We are careful not to let the dog create a behavior chain that always involves running towards the helper and then back to us. If the dog runs the entire way several times in a row, make the distraction a little easier so the dog is able to turn around at the halfway point.

Coach Says

Vary the rewards you are using a lot so the dog doesn't just get the same old dry food every time she comes. Sometimes it's dry food, sometimes a ball. Next time you might allow her to hunt a small area, and then pull out a tug toy. The dog should never know what kind of reward she'll receive, just that she will receive one.

Away From the Distraction

When the dog voluntarily has chosen not to care about the distraction and is heading back to you, give your recall cue.

Repeat this several times with different kinds of distractions so the dog really connects the behavior of running towards you with your recall cue. Then move onto the next step.

Towards the Distraction

When the dog starts to turn back to you before she reaches the distraction, you can say the cue as the dog is headed for the distraction. The first few times, give the cue almost immediately after the dog has left you, perhaps just a few steps. Give your dog ample rewards when she listens. If she doesn't listen, have your helper quickly remove the distraction. The helper should then become passive and completely ignore the dog. Quietly go and get your dog and complete a successful repetition of the previous step, that is call the dog when she is on her way to you from the distraction. As the dog becomes more proficient, wait longer and longer so the dog gets closer to the distraction before you give the recall cue. Finally you should be able to call the dog when she's only a few inches from the distraction.

Ada is allowed to investigate Emma's hand, where treats are concealed.

When Ada removes her nose, her handler Tinna clicks and rewards her.

Finally, the handler calls Ada before she has reached Emma.

The Triangle

A distraction exercise we like to do at this stage in the recall training is the Triangle. You need at least one helper and preferably two. If you only have one, we suggest putting a harness and leash on the dog. Start by doing several easy recalls you know the dog can do and reward her properly. Then do the following:

1. Form a triangle where you stand in one corner, your helper stands with the dog in the other corner, and you throw the ball into the third. If you have a third helper, he or she should be near the place where the ball lands.

2. When you have thrown the ball and it has landed and is lying still, call the dog. The dog should be about as far from you as she is from the ball. (Initially it can be good to have the dog a little closer to you than to the ball).

3. When you know the dog won't hesitate before choosing to run straight to you instead of running for the ball, give your cue when the ball is in the air. Your helper, who's holding the leash, should release the dog as soon as he or she feels the slightest pull towards you.

4. The next step is throwing the ball at the same time as you call the dog. Now you can also start moving the dog and the helper so they come closer and closer to you, to finally end up right next to you. Then your helper can step aside entirely: now you are the one handling both the dog and the ball.

5. Throw the ball again, with the dog beside you, preferably without a stay cue. As soon as the dog runs after the ball, give your cue. If you've trained your dog that she's never allowed to leave you without a cue, tell her "go ahead" first so she doesn't need to break any rules.

After this first exercise you can slowly increase the level of difficulty. Slowly means that the dog succeeds four out of five times before you make it more challenging. The next step is calling the dog after she has run only a few yards towards the ball, then a third of the way, then half, then two thirds, and finally the trial by fire: Calling the dog right before she is going to catch the ball.

There are four things to keep in mind while doing this exercise:

1. Give the dog an extra generous reward every time she succeeds following an increase in the level of difficulty.

2. Randomly allow the dog to run up to the ball and take it. Otherwise you run the risk of the dog becoming hesitant about taking the ball.

3. Take periodic breaks. This is a demanding exercise for the dog and you might not get through all of the steps in the

Diesel

same day. It all depends on what your foundation looks like. We have several students who have moved from the easiest step to the most challenging at an impressive rate.

4. Never say "no" or do anything to prevent the dog from taking the ball if the dog fails. Just take it easy and start the exercise again.

Coach Says

Do a lot of successful recalls every day. Every success goes into your dog's archive and makes your recall cue stronger and stronger. Quite simply, we want to brainwash the dog to believe the only thing she can do when she hears the recall cue is run to you.

Occupied By the Distraction

When the dog has mastered the recall when running towards the distraction, it's time for the advanced lesson. The biggest challenge of all is calling the dog once she has reached the distraction and is occupied with it, such as greeting your helper or playing with another dog. Start by trying to call the dog when you think she will choose to come. Initially, this will probably be after she has checked out the distraction, but as your dog gets better at the recall you can call her earlier and earlier.

The following is a simple way of training the recall when the dog is already occupied with a distraction:

1. Throw a few boring treats on the ground and allow the dog to search for them.

2. When you notice the dog sniffs a little less and looks up at you, give your recall cue and reward her amply for coming.

3. If that doesn't work, repeat a few simple recalls and then try again.

4. Later give your recall cue even earlier, before your dog is done sniffing. However, be sure to have several successful repetitions.

In the beginning, you should be standing quite close to the dog, but increase the distance as the dog gets better at the recall. You can also throw treats into two different areas. Allow the dog to search one of the areas, call her and reward her with a "go ahead" to look in the other area.

The exercise we just described is the first exercise before being able to do more advanced training with more challenging distractions, such as calling a dog in from work. When a dog starts to think hunting is incredibly exciting, she becomes more difficult to recall. Hopefully we don't need to call a working dog that often, but sometimes it's necessary. For example, the dog might be hunting the wrong area or something happens that means you have to suddenly send her in another direction. Training is therefore necessary so you can be sure the dog will come even while she's working.

Start easy. Either call the dog at the exact moment she starts hunting before she has really gotten into the work, or allow the dog to hunt a little bit first and when she starts to tire and is hunting a little less intensely, try giving your recall cue.

Don't call your dog unless you are 99 percent sure she will come. Some dogs enjoy hunting so much they are entirely immersed in it and it's almost impossible to call them in the beginning. Then you need to find a way to make the distraction less difficult. You can try making the dog sit, pretending to put something exciting in the forest and send the dog to hunt in an empty area. It will likely be easier to call the dog since there isn't anything to find. Study your dog and see what works best – success is the most important factor in your training.

> ## Pitfall
> *Don't call the dog again if she doesn't respond the first time. The dog will only learn that she doesn't need to come immediately. Instead, calmly go and get her and try again.*

Remember not to call the dog from work too often. Particularly in hunting, we want the dog to work independently and not stop and check with us to ask: "Aren't you going to call me?" That isn't to say that we wait to do this kind of recall training. We do it occasionally, but the bulk of our training is focused on recalls in other situations so the dog will have an automatic response to the recall cue. That increases the chance the recall cue will be successful even when the dog is doing what she enjoys most. In summary, there are six steps to recall training with various distractions:

1. When the dog voluntarily (without a cue) heads away from the distraction.
2. On cue when the dog is headed away from the distraction.
3. On cue when the dog is headed towards the distraction (call early).
4. On cue right before the dog reaches the distraction.
5. On cue when the dog reaches the distraction.
6. On cue when the dog is occupied with the distraction.

Sub-goals – Recall	Completed
Voluntarily run towards you (during walks)	
Voluntarily run from your helper (who is holding the dog's collar) to you	
While working and with distractions (such as helpers with treats, tossed objects, game, and according to the six steps)	
Out of the water and through the water (see the chapter "Water Work")	

Summary

- Reward the dog when she spontaneously comes to you during walks (you can even add the hand target).
- Do a lot of successful recalls and give the dog ample rewards. Think brainwashing!
- Don't call the dog when you know it's a lost cause and she won't respond.
- Train with as many kinds of distractions as you can think of.

Challenge

Write down a distraction your dog can be called off from now. Write down another one that you think the dog will be able to ignore in a week, and then write down the most challenging distraction you can think of. Then work on those distractions during the week. At the end of the week, check what you wrote down. Can the dog now ignore the distraction of the week? Good job! Now increase the distractions, until you can finally call your dog from the most challenging distraction you wrote down.

Wilma and Rooibos

The Stop Whistle

When you blow a stop whistle, the dog should stop immediately, either sitting or standing, and make contact with you as if to ask, "What do you want?". For spaniels sometimes it's enough that they stop without looking at you. What's important is that the dog is under control for the work to come. The stop whistle is the only brake you have during the hunt! This makes it very important, so train it well with as many distractions as you can.

The goal of the stop whistle should be for the dog to stop – and preferably sit – at the signal even if a rabbit runs right in front of her nose. But we start by teaching the stop whistle with simple distractions and then proceed to more difficult challenges.

Play to Inspire Quick Stops

The advantage of teaching the stop whistle through play is that the dog learns to sit quickly and when her arousal level is high. Play hard with the dog and then steal the toy. As soon as the dog sits, reward her by starting to play again. When you're confident that the dog will sit whenever the toy disappears, blow a stop whistle when the dog sits and then start playing again.

The Whistle

The most common stop whistles are either one long or one short signal. Some people use a short whistle for standing and a long whistle for sitting. Stop whistles are also combined with a hand signal, most often a hand held up in the air, similar to the stop signal used by police.

Offering the Sit

If the dog has difficulties offering sit during play, we start by training the dog to offer a sit in calmer situations. Don't lure the dog to sit, bend forward or do anything else – just wait for the dog to sit on her own accord, click and reward. Stand close to the dog at the beginning so you manage to reward her before she gets up again. Conclude with a release cue so the dog knows that she may get up. When the dog has sat several times and you are sure she will offer the sit, you can start adding the stop whistle. If the dog gets up before you reach out to reward her, you can wait to give the dog the treat until she sits back down again (even if you clicked while she sat). Next time, be even quicker when rewarding her. You can allow the dog to get up after the click, but in our experience this is a great way to reinforce steadiness if you're careful to reward while the dog is sitting. As the dog gets better at sitting still, you can train the dog in progressively more difficult situations. However, increase the level of difficulty cautiously so your dog rarely makes mistakes. You can also click and reward the dog when she stops voluntarily in the woods and makes contact with you. In the beginning, you can use reverse luring to get her to stand still until you get there. Once you've done that a number of times, you can try to add the stop whistle when the dog stops to see if she will sit.

Stopping When You Back Away from the Dog

When the dog can sit in front of you, start backing away from her slowly so she'll follow you and then reward her when she sits down from being on the move. Progressively move backwards faster and faster. When the dog can offer a sit from fast walking, you can start to teach the dog the stop whistle and the hand signal, by first blowing the whistle at the same time as your dog offers the sit. Then whistle increasingly earlier and finally blow the whistle before the dog even contemplates sitting.

When adding the cue, it's important that you blow the stop whistle only if you are reasonably sure your dog will sit. Avoid "watering down" the signal by blowing several times if the dog doesn't sit down immediately. Instead make the environment a little easier, wait for the dog to offer a sit, and then add the whistle again.

Vary your rewards so your dog sometimes gets a treat, sometimes a ball and sometimes perhaps a little game of tug. Use active rewards so the dog eagerly anticipates the stop whistle. Be sure to put the reward behind the dog so she doesn't move towards you when you blow the whistle (you want the dog to stay in place). That may mean you throw the reward behind your dog, or you run up to the dog and play with her behind the spot where she was just sitting.

Pitfall
Remember to also reward the stop whistle even after the dog has mastered it so she will be happy and expectant when hearing the signal. During trials, you might need to use the whistle a lot and then it's important the dog enjoys it.

Stopping on the Way from You
When the dog has turned away from you, for instance in the woods, you can try out your stop whistle. Blow when the dog is pretty close and only partially facing away from you. If your dog stops and sits, click and reward her. If the dog doesn't stop and sit, spend more time training on the stop whistle while backing away from your dog or when the dog is closer to you in the woods.

Another way to teach the dog to stop is to "throw the dog away". We do that by luring the dog with a ball.

1. Take the ball in your hand and pretend to throw it.
2. Allow the dog to run after "the ball".
3. When the dog realizes there isn't a ball and turns to you, blow your stop whistle and throw the ball as a reward.
4. Later on, you can also try blowing your stop whistle just before the dog turns to you.

If you are a spaniel owner, however, you might want to think twice before you do the exercise above since the steadiness might be affected. You can reinforce steadiness and sitting by teaching puppies they are to stop and sit when they see anything go up in the air, whether it's a ball or a bird.

Coach Says
It's up to you whether the dog should stand or sit. Most often it's better to have the dog sit since that makes it easier to keep the dog in place after the stop whistle. If you successfully start with sitting, you can easily work on standing by rewarding the dog when she's at a further distance when she turns and looks at you before she manages to sit. If your dog is easily excited, you might want to train her to sit down at the stop whistle so she has a chance to calm down before she starts working again.

Stopping While Heading towards the Distraction

Stopping on her way towards the distraction becomes more difficult the closer the dog gets to it. That's why we start training with easy distractions at a fair distance. We gradually move from training at home in the kitchen, where the dog can ignore a thrown treat and offer a sit, to an acute situation where a rabbit is bouncing away just a yard in front of the dog. This involves two kinds of training: stopping at the stop whistle and also the distraction itself becoming a cue to stop. Read more about this in the section "Flushed Game Means Stop".

You can work with the initial distractions in the following way:

1. In a controlled manner, throw a treat behind you and blow the stop whistle.
2. If your dog responds, reward her.
3. If the dog doesn't respond, just pick up the treat calmly and try again with an easier distraction or no distraction at all.

When you need slightly more challenging distractions, you can ask a friend for help. Have your friend act like he or she is having fun and maybe make some noise. Once the dog has taken a few steps towards your friend, blow the stop whistle. If the dog doesn't stop, you can either choose an easier distraction or train the stop whistle without any distractions. If the dog goes all the way to your helper, he or she should just ignore the dog. Later on, have your helper offer increasingly more challenging distractions, such as dragging a toy along the ground, throwing a ball or luring the dog with really tasty treats. If the dog runs ahead despite hearing the stop whistle, your helper should just pick up the distraction so the dog can't get to it.

But ...

... what do I do if my dog loses interest in the stop whistle and becomes worse and worse at responding to it? First and foremost, you need to ask if your rewards really are good enough. This is a difficult challenge for the dog so she must find it worthwhile to do as you say – bring out the dog's absolute favorite rewards. Also, try to take a step back in your training and work on teaching the dog to respond to the whistle in an easier environment for a while. Then carefully move forward again.

Stopping on the Way towards You

Stopping on the way towards you is usually more difficult than stopping on the way from you because the dog is keen to run all the way up to you to receive her reward. You can start by setting a bowl behind the dog. When the dog looks at you, cue "go ahead" and your dog gets to take her reward. Once you've done this a few times, start to call the dog, and once she's coming towards you, cue "go ahead". After a few such repetitions, blow the stop whistle, and then (when the dog has stopped) cue "go ahead". Gradually, you can begin to try this without the food bowl. Think about your reward placement so the reward ends up behind the dog and not between you and the dog. If the dog has a reward behind her, she'll stop more quickly without taking any steps towards you.

Sometimes the dog will slow down when coming towards you because she knows you intend to stop her. Therefore intersperse stop training with recalls without stops and reward your dog for running all the way to you at full speed. It can be useful to reward recalls by throwing a toy behind you, so the dog can run at full speed past you to take it. Don't blow the stop signal if the dog is running slowly. Instead, do the exercise again and either blow the stop signal when the dog runs fast or just reward her for running fast on a plain recall.

Now you can also take the opportunity to train push backs, i.e. casting the dog away from you when the dog is facing you at a distance. Simply cue "back" instead of "go ahead" when the dog is supposed to turn around and run to her reward. The advantage here is that you can gradually phase out the reward the dog has seen you put out and instead do a push back to a reward she didn't know about. When this works, you know the dog isn't dependent on having the reward behind her to stop, and your "back" cue also works with hidden rewards. Read more about this in the chapter "Blind Retrieves".

Use your imagination when you train the dog to stop. There is a variety of different approaches and we have described only a few. If you are creative and find new, unexpected variations, your dog will get really good at stopping at your whistle.

Coach Says
To teach the dog to stop both when she's running away from you and when she's coming towards you, you can use a large target, such as a car mat. Have the dog run onto the carpet and blow the stop whistle once the dog is on the mat. Vary the distance and direction between you and the mat as well as between the mat and the dog. Gradually work on fading the target.

a "throws" Ada away and 's the stop whistle at the time as Ada stops.

Ada stops when she hears the stop whistle.

Flushed Game Means Stop

For spaniels, a flying bird means that the dog should stop and then perhaps sit. The dog has then finished hunting and flushing and the hunter will shoot the game before the dog is allowed to work again. This can also be a useful everyday skill. Then you know your dog won't retrieve unless asked to do so and that she won't run after live game.

123

To teach the dog that a flushed bird means stop, it's important the dog has mastered both steadiness and the stop whistle in somewhat challenging situations. When you begin training your dog to stop as soon as she sees a flying bird, repeat a few steadiness exercises first and then some stop whistle exercises. Then have the dog walk on your left side. Throw an object with your right hand and blow the stop whistle. Reward the dog when she sits. If she doesn't sit down, rehearse the stop whistle a few more times without the object. As your training progresses you can start trying out a variety of objects and also work with the dog off leash. Do this first by your side, and then a short distance away, until the dog sits down as soon as you throw a ball in the air.

Stop Games

With a puppy we want to do things right from the beginning. You can do this exercise[19] as soon as you bring your puppy home:

1. Sit on the floor with your legs out in a V-shape. Put the puppy between your legs and hold her with your hands around her chest.
2. Roll a ball a bit in front of you.
3. If the puppy wants to run after it, keep a gentle hold around her chest. As soon as she quietens down, let her go. Preferably tell her "yes" or "go ahead".

[19] We've borrowed this exercise from Sten Christoffersson, www.naturredaktionen.se.

When the dog can resist running after the ball, you can add a sit before she gets a "go ahead". If she sits from the beginning, allow her to do so. To make it more difficult later on, you can have the dog stand first and then wait for a sit.

As soon as you and the dog are on the same page, make the exercise more and more difficult. For example, you can throw the ball further, remove your hands from the puppy's chest, stand up, move outside to more difficult environments, and so on. Train your family members to avoid throwing objects when playing with the dog. If they absolutely want to, they need to do it the way we just described. This is how you gently brainwash your dog to believe anything that flies or is thrown away means she must sit. There can be disadvantages with this approach if you want to do any other kind of training besides gun dog retrieving. In obedience training, there are several occasions where we really want to be able to reward the dog with a ball flying over her head, such as when the dog should be sent away at full speed. If you want to do this in the future, it's a good idea to teach the dog that if you don't say anything, she should sit down as soon as you throw something, but she's allowed to run if you throw something and cue "go ahead". Be careful to enforce the rules; the dog is never allowed to run without permission.

Increase the Challenge

When your dog is able to sit while you throw an object, begin to create more challenging situations. One approach is to put a rope over a tree branch. Attach a dummy or a rag to one end, and then you or your helper can pull on the other end so the dummy flies up into the air. You can also use a long riding whip with a rope at the end. Tie an object or a rag to the rope. Another method is to tie a floppy toy to a long line and have a helper hold the furthest end of the

Lena carefully holds Tassla at the same time as she throws the ball.

Tassla sits when she sees the ball fly away.

When the ball is still and Tassla sits, she receives permission to run and fetch the ball.

line. (We suggest using a tracking line). Put the dog one yard from the toy. Then use the following training plan:

1. Blow the stop whistle while the toy is completely still.

2. Blow the stop whistle. Just as the dog sits (or stops if you want the dog to stand at the stop whistle) your helper pulls on the line so the toy jumps forward a bit.

3. Blow the stop whistle as your helper pulls on the line.

4. Blow the stop whistle just after your helper pulls on the line.

5. Don't blow the stop whistle at all, testing whether your dog will sit from just the cue of the toy being "flushed". (If the dog doesn't sit, you need to be fast and blow a stop whistle).

Give the dog plenty of rewards after each success, especially when the dog succeeds at a new, more difficult task. When your dog has passed the above four steps, start over again, but this time both you and your dog should be moving forward. When you approach the toy, follow the same training plan as before but start with number two. Remember that every time you do the exercise, you should start with a task the dog mastered during your last training session. Make it more and more difficult regarding the environment and your helper's position. The toy could be hidden in tall grass and the helper positioned in a way so the dog doesn't associate him or her with a particular exercise. We simply want to surprise the dog as much as possible.

If you don't have a helper, you can buy a "bolting rabbit", an object that is attached to a long rubber cord. You can tighten up the rubber cord and then draw the cord back to trigger it so it sends the object flying. It requires a certain synchronicity, so we recommend having a helper the first few times.

Lena pulls on the line.

When Tassla sees the object fly up, she sits down.

Lena rewards Tassla while she is sitting.

There are even automatic "bird launchers" that allow the handler to trigger it to throw an object with a remote control. If you have access to homing pigeons you can use the same principle with remote controlled cages.

The Stop Whistle during Field Trials

During field trials, you need a stop whistle to be able to halt the dog and give her further directions. For spaniels, the stop whistle also serves as a brake when a bird is flushed or when other game, such as rabbits, run away. Spaniels need a stop whistle in all stakes, except in water trials in some countries, while it usually only becomes important for retrievers in the advanced stakes. In the UK, however, the stop whistle is important in all stakes.

But ...

... what do I do if I can't get mad at my dog for running after a rabbit? Begin by calling the dog if you think she will respond and reward the dog if she comes. If the recall doesn't work, calmly retrieve the dog or remain where you are until the dog comes back on her own. Then you can put a harness and a long long line on the dog for a while, so you can stop her by stepping carefully on the long line if necessary. Then you can really focus the training on how the dog should behave when a bird flies up. Remove the long line only when you are absolutely sure the dog is steady.

Challenge
Can you stop your dog when she spies a ball your helper has just thrown?

Sub-goals – The Stop Whistle	Completed
Stop in front of you (sitting or standing)	
Stop at a distance	
Voluntarily offered stop in the woods	
Stop when you back away from the dog	
Stop while running away from you	
Stop while running towards a distraction	
Stop while running towards you	
Steadiness. Stay after the stop whistle	
With distractions (for example, when running towards a helper, when the dog is looking for something, or when game is flushed)	
In water	
Stopping when game has been flushed (spaniel)	

Summary

- Train with distractions, distractions and more distractions! Often the stop whistle works well if there aren't any distractions nearby or when the dog has a lot of energy.
- Reward the stop whistle often. Most importantly, you want the dog to eagerly anticipate it.
- Teach your spaniel to stop when seeing a flushed bird.

Controlling the Madness

Most people who start with clicker training are immediately delighted with it. They are amazed at how quickly they can teach new behaviors as well as how much fun both dog and handler are having along the way. Initially though, when you first start training, you may experience a period of confusion. You will have questions, such as how do I do that, what do the various signals mean, and what rules are needed to optimize the training?

Sometimes clicker training might seem a little boundless, but we want to emphasize that it's more about how the individual trainer puts this way of training into practice. Our training is based on a foundation of rules and frameworks, a basic training system, which makes training effective and fun. It allows us to maintain control of the madness.[20]

Most people find a training system that works for them, but several years later they might discover that they did something inconsistently. Remarkably, the dog has still understood. One set of rules might work amazingly well with one dog but not with another, and that's when things need to be reconsidered.

Our training system is based on rules or signals, both when training voluntarily offered behaviors and behaviors on cue. The rules and signals have to do with release cues, how we start and finish the training, our transports and our rules regarding play and breaks.

You can start training your dog as early as you like since you can always adjust the degree of difficulty based on your dog's ability. Even during the first few days, when you bring home your new puppy, you can start with simple exercises such as the basics of play, focus, steadiness, recall, holding, carrying and releasing objects. But keep your training sessions short.

Day-to-day

Most of a dog's day consists of time we don't consider "training time", but leisure time (even though dogs continue to learn whenever they are awake). When we are sitting on the sofa watching TV, we don't want a dog that whirls around or shows off her tricks. We want our dog to lie down and go to sleep, so we simply ignore the dog when she's trying out

---

[20] Swedish dog trainer Fanny Gott coined the phrase "controlling the madness", www.fannygott.com.

Totte

all her tricks and reward her when she sits and eventually lies down. If your dog is really active, you might need to put her leash on the first few times to help her calm down and be still. Soon the dog will learn it pays to lie down and rest when we are on the couch. And as she learns this, you can gradually reduce the rewards for lying down. Daily training is about reinforcing what we want our dogs to do and making sure that they don't learn erroneous behaviors.

We begin teaching our signals from day one, that for example offering behaviors will be rewarded and it pays to lie down and sleep when nothing happens. Since we want the dog to offer behaviors during training, we must teach her which behaviors are desirable in other situations. When we are sitting at the kitchen table, it pays to go and lie down or politely ask for food by staying calm and silent under the table while we eat. When we pick up the treats and sit down on the floor, offering different behaviors will pay off well.

We use a lot of environmental cues to let the dog know what we want. It's easier for dogs to learn environmental cues than verbal cues. Whose dog doesn't run to the door when the leash is taken out, or whose dog doesn't stand at attention when the refrigerator door is opened? The dog has clearly learnt the behavior that leads to rewards in these particular situations.

Training System
During the day, there are a great many environmental cues that tell the dog what we expect. There are also a lot of environmental cues in training – dummies, the training bag, the forest clearing where we usually train, and so on. During training, we spend extra time teaching cues that will make it easier for us to achieve our goals. Many beginners to clicker training worry about doing something wrong. Don't.

One of the most important things is working towards having a shaping savvy dog, who offers a lot of behaviors. You can hone the details later. We have refined our training system, but still discover things that surprise us. The most important thing to know is that everything we do has consequences. But to begin with, we want to say this: Keep going! It's better to experiment than to leave things the way they are.

Now we will try to describe our training system a little more concretely. It's not particularly unique. A lot of clicker trainers use this approach, with a few differences.

Voluntarily Offered Behavior
The dog is most often in front of us when we work with voluntarily offered behavior. But some of the voluntarily offered behaviors we desire are supposed to occur when the dog is close beside us: walking at heel, coming into heel position, being steady, as well as in various situations where the dog starts by running away from us, for instance during a blind retrieve. We usually keep the amount of time spent training voluntarily offered behaviors at our side quite short. Mostly, this is when we make the switch from a front-facing position to a side position. Otherwise, most behaviors in the side position will be on cue.

> But ...
> ... doesn't clicker training place stress on the dog? Maybe. It probably would be stressful if we were constantly training very active behaviors and only did fast-paced training sessions without any rules or limits. But if we teach the dog what we expect and vary our training, the dog will learn to be both active and passive. And if we adjust our criteria based on the dog's ability, it won't be a stressful experience.

Transitions between Voluntarily Offered Behavior and Cued Behavior

When we switch between training with voluntarily offered behavior and cued behavior, we'll take a small play break to mark the transition or just turn around and change positions and type of training simultaneously. The signal for us to start with cued-based training is simply that we give a cue. If we then want to switch to voluntarily offered behaviors we play and immediately start clicking for a movement to emphasize that we are working on voluntary behaviors now. Does it seem difficult? The funny thing is that the dogs will quickly learn what we're doing. It's us humans who tend to overthink things and believe they are more difficult than they actually are.

Steadiness

When working with voluntarily offered behaviors there are three behaviors that all require the dog to be steady, and therefore we have some kind of release cue from them. These behaviors are the sit, the stand, and the down. When the dog lies down on her own, we click, walk up to her and bend down to reward her while she's still in position, stand up straight again, and release her. In other words, the dog is not allowed to get up until we give her a release cue (we use the cue "free"). Another alternative is to throw a treat on the ground and cue "go ahead". We can also "lure" the dog out of the position, that is to say allow her to gnaw on the treat she received as a reward while we move the hand holding the treat so that the dog follows. If the dog gets up after the click, we need to be a little quicker next time so we manage to reward her while she's still in the desired position. Feeding the dog while she remains steady sends the message, "Stay here until you receive a new instruction." It's extremely useful in instances when you want your dog to do something at a distance away from you. We have the dog sit, lie, or stand where we want her to be (without giving a cue!) and feed her in that position a few times before we walk to the place where we intend to be. After that we release the dog with a "free" cue. We work on that independently with the dog next to us before increasing the distance. Such a start cue isn't always necessary – turning towards the dog can be a signal that it's time to do something else, such as sit at a distance.

Release Cues

We allow the dog to release her position by using the following:

- "Free" means "That's right, come out of your position. Come over here and we'll keep working." We say "free" after the click and reward or in place of the click. The dog will then come to us to keep working or to get her reward.

- "Go ahead" means "Run and get your external reward". External rewards can be a food bowl, a toy, a thrown ball, being able to greet another dog, or being allowed to run to something else the dog thinks is a reward. Cue "go ahead" either after the click or instead of it.

- "Take it" means "Go ahead and take the toy" we are holding in our hands or throwing.

- "Go" tells the dog "Get going and start working". Most often this means the dog runs towards an object we just set out. In such situations, however, it might be equally effective to remain silent or to restrain the dog by the collar and let go when she pulls on the collar and wants to run. "Go" is a cue that we also use to tell the dog the training has begun before we've added the real cue in situations where the dog knows the direction in which we are going to work.

- The click means "That was exactly right and the treat is on its way". We try to give the dog the reward as soon as possible after the click. The click ends the behavior with the exception of sit, stand, and down, where we use "free" (see above).

Transports[21]

During training sessions, we often need to move from one place to another, for instance from the location where we are playing to the training site. Have you seen your dog try to do a billion other things – pull on the leash, sniff, greet another dog, or sneak a toy – during such a transport? It's obviously very easy to become irritated in such a situation! We really don't want to have such disturbances during our training sessions, so there are a few different ways to transport the dog.

If the dog hasn't mastered an off-leash follow or walking at heel to the place where we are going to start or end our work, we should attach the dog to ourselves like a magnet, either a toy magnet or a treat magnet. If you have a small dog, you might even carry her.

The idea behind transports is that we're always attached to the dog, which makes it easier to stay in the training zone.

The dog is allowed to chew on a treat in our hand or play with a tug toy while we move. Good transports make training more effective and conserve energy. Sometimes we allow the dog to transport herself with a "free" from the crate or from the blanket to where we will start the training session. But first we have to have played crate games. [22]

Transports like toy and treat magnets should primarily be used during training before the dog has mastered walking at heel. When it's time for a field trial, the dog must be able to walk beside us and if we stop and wait she must calmly sit or lie beside us until we start moving again. We work on having the dog walk beside us and being calm separately before combining them.

Ending a Training Session

When the day's training session has come to an end, we say, "now we're done" and throw several treats on the ground or just say, "go play" and continue to walk. Afterwards, the dog should be free to do as she pleases, if we are at home or in the woods. If the environment doesn't allow the dog

---

[21] We've borrowed this expression from Eva Bertilsson's and Emelie Johnson Vegh's book "Agility right from the start".

[22] If you want to learn more about crate games, search for it on YouTube.

Mary transports Rooibos in various ways: holding his collar, offering treats, offering toys, and carrying him.

since she might think you are still training while you are actually taking a break. Think about what break routines work best for you and your dog. The easiest thing to do might be to hold the dog by the collar or sit down together with her and hold her still. Crate games are also a great alternative. You can ask the dog to go in the crate or lie on her blanket and wait there until it's time to start training again. You can of course even teach her to "take a break" or whatever cue you want to communicate, "Lay down where you are standing right now and take it easy." Make sure the dog sees the break as something positive; it shouldn't be a punishment to take a break. You could also reward her for taking it easy and relaxing.

Can I Train Too Much?

A common question is, "How much training can I do with my dog?" Our answer is: "It depends." With a small puppy, you might have three to four one-minute sessions per day. With an older dog, you might be able to have ten two to five-minute sessions over the span of an hour. But in the long term, it depends entirely on your dog, how much she can handle, how accustomed she is to training, and how much she enjoys her rewards. We try to vary the training, in terms of behaviors, pace and rewards.

We have a few rules of thumb that we always follow:

- Keep the training sessions short! It's a lot better to have ten one minute sessions with breaks that allow you to assess how things are going rather than have a single ten minute session, where neither you nor the dog is able to concentrate the entire time. Use an egg timer or count out a number of treats in your hand before you start so you know when it's time to stop. Breaks are important for

to do whatever she wants, we transport her with the help of a game, treat magnet, tug transport, or walk at heel to an appropriate place to take a break, which is most often a blanket, crate, or car.

Break Routines

Initially, we'll most often use extremely intense, short training sessions. Since we want the dog to offer a wide range of behaviors, we must teach her early on when to take it easy and not offer behaviors during a training session. If you want to discuss something with a training partner, give the dog a break and have your conversation without trying to train while you chit chat. Both you and the dog need to be in the training zone for your training to go well. If you start talking to your partner and forget your dog, there's a risk she'll either get bored, walk away or offer a great many good behaviors that you fail to reward. It also prevents your dog from becoming frustrated and start barking at you the dog to be able recover before the next session, and to allow her new knowledge to sink in. It also gives you a chance to evaluate how well the training is going and if you need to change anything. If we have a short training session one day, and then work on the same thing the next day, we will see more progress than if we have a single, longer session. The dog simply sleeps on it!

- Vary the rewards! We also find different ways to deliver the treats; sometimes the dog may take them out of our hands, sometimes she gets to chase them, and sometimes she gets to catch them. One good way to vary the rewards is to take out five treats, and when they are gone take a play break. During the play break, sometimes we also add a social reward like petting or praise.

- Be flexible and read your dog's signs! If the dog is unsuccessful after two attempts, we have to adjust our criteria, otherwise the dog won't learn what we intend for her to learn. If we lower our criteria a few times, we can soon raise them again. Reading the dog's signs means that we are conscious of the dog's activity level, engagement and mood throughout the training session. We adjust the training according to the dog's mood on that particular day.

- You don't have to end with success. It can be nice to end on a high note so, if things are going really well, you might want to end the session a little earlier than planned. If things are going poorly and the dog starts to get tired, it's better to take a break than to keep trying for success. Otherwise, we'll have to lower the criteria so we know the dog will be successful. As long as we have good break routines, it's not a punishment for the dog to stop training. Instead, it helps reenergize the dog so the next session goes better.

Of course, sometimes we have long training days with our dogs, such as when we are taking a class, competing, or if we go and train together with friends for a few hours. But even under those circumstances we make sure to keep our sessions short and take frequent breaks. The longer we keep training, the shorter the session. An appropriate length for a training session is often one to five minutes, followed by a short break to allow both the dog and handler to maintain maximum focus. The break can entail a game or a rest on the blanket. The total training session might be ten minutes, but it should be interspersed with playing before the dog gets to rest on her bed.

Of course, we also have sessions that focus on endurance. Read more about that in the chapter "The Road to Field Trials". In this chapter, "Controlling the Madness", we describe how to refine exercises and learn new skills and then it's preferable to keep sessions short.

When is The Best Time to Train?

Hold your training sessions at a time that works for you. Maybe a breakfast session works best for your schedule, or maybe an evening session. Or why not in the middle of the day, or all three? We often train while we are on walks. We always have some kind of reward with us, most often treats or a toy. It's a good opportunity to reward desirable behaviors: a loose leash, stopping and looking at the neighbor's cat instead of chasing it, and walking politely at our side. How much we reward different behaviors depends on the dog's skill level. If the dog is eight years old and used to walking on leash, we might not reward her for walking on leash more than once a month. But if we have a small puppy, we would reward her for walking on leash a lot. After a little while maybe we'll have a short training session. It could be anything: holding an area, retrieves, or steadiness exercises. When we're done, we might go a little further and then after a while sit down on a tree stump and work on being calm.

Training during walks is extremely efficient for a number of reasons. First and foremost, the dog learns to perform behaviors in a variety of environments. In addition, we get natural breaks before our next training session. The dog will also check on us more even when she's off leash and spontaneously come back to us to see if there's anything fun going on. We take the opportunity to reward her when she comes back. It provides a good foundation for recalls and understanding of following us.

Who's in Charge of Training?

It's our responsibility to make sure that our dogs choose to train with us. When the dog is young, or when she's "new" to us (you can train this with an older dog just as well), we spend a lot of time teaching her it pays off to stay and train with us. That doesn't mean we beg our dogs to come join us or coddle them. Rather the opposite really. We want the dogs to beg us. If they could use words, we'd want them to say, "Please train me right now. Please!"

If the dog wants the rewards she has to seek contact or offer the desired behavior. We want the dog to say, "Now I'm ready. Now we can train". This is because we want to be able to start training without having to convince the dog to come and join us every time. Initially we can do this by limiting the dog's opportunity to do something else, for instance by having her on leash. When she seeks contact, we start the training session, ideally with play. Once our training is more advanced, it's still important to keep working on

this. Focus and the dog's willingness to work with us are the basis of all additional training. There are dogs who need to be reminded of this throughout their entire lives, especially if they are very extroverted.

There's no point in starting a training session if the dog is focused on something else. In the worst case, this can destroy what we've previously taught the dog. If we always entice the dog to come to us and nag her until she does what we want, we are communicating to her that she doesn't need to keep track of us and that we'll let her know when something is going on anyway. At the same time, she'll also learn that nothing fun comes from doing what we ask. The dog might even end up thinking all training is boring. Instead, gauge the training to meet the level where your dog is today. Even if all of the other dogs you see seem to be able to do a lot more, you must adjust your training to match your dog's ability. The dog isn't trying to intentionally frustrate you by not listening to you or not responding to your cues. She just hasn't properly learnt what it is we want her to do. She might be able to perform an exercise at home, where we have spent a lot of time training, but she isn't able to do the same thing when we introduce a new environment. Then we have to start over again in the new environment and make things a little easier for the dog and then gradually increase the level of difficulty again.

Distraction Training

We think training the dog to ignore distractions, also called "proofing", is a lot of fun! It's also extremely useful, which is why there are sections on training with distractions in almost every chapter of this book. The goal of distraction training is that the dog gets a look on her face as if she's thinking, "I know you're trying to trick me, but I'm not

going to go for it. I know what I'm going to do". Then she walks by the distraction, and offers the desired behavior. We actively arrange as many distractions as we can come up with in terms of environments, noises, training positions, movements, reward placements, and so on. Below you'll find several suggestions on distractions.

- Environment – the woods, the kitchen, the shopping center, the soccer field, the beach.
- Noise – hoot like an owl, knock on the wall, say nonsense words such as "cucumber" and "parking spot", sing a song.
- Training position – stand up, sit on the ground, lie on the floor, stand on a chair, stand behind a gate, have a bucket over your head.
- Movement – jump on the spot, wave your arms, swing back and forth, clap your hands, move your shoulders in different directions.
- Reward placement – put toys on the ground, hold treats in your open hand, throw a toy, pretend to throw a ball with a ball launcher (it acts as an extension of your arm, allowing you to throw the ball much further), rub a toy over the dog's body, wave a toy frantically.
- Weather – sun, darkness, rain, snow, fog.
- Helper – playing with a toy, pointing towards where you are going, standing very close, making strange noises, wearing a large, noisy rain jacket, speaking loudly, clapping, laughing.

External Rewards

Teaching your dog to work for an external reward – one she has seen you place on the ground or one placed at a distance – is extremely useful. It's nice to not always have the treat on us (we might need to use our hands for something else).

Additionally, it teaches the dog self-control so she doesn't run after something interesting when we don't want her to.

In the beginning, the dog finds this extremely difficult since in the dog's world, it's completely illogical to refrain from doing something fun (the reward) and do something else prior to receiving the reward. We want to teach the dog self-control or Doggy Zen, as it's sometimes called. The idea behind it is to abstain from something now (in this life) to receive something better later (in the next life).

When we put out an external reward, we want to avoid saying "no" or stopping the dog from taking it. The goal is, as we mentioned before, to teach the dog self-control. Since it's intended to be a fun reward, we don't want there to be any negative associations with it.

Instead, we start by teaching the dog how to behave when she's around external rewards:

1. Reward the dog when she offers a sit. Give her several treats for staying in the sit.

2. Put a treat in a bowl. Place the bowl on the floor in front of the dog.

3. If you succeed, that is to say if the dog successfully controls herself and remains in sit, cue "go ahead". If the dog looks like she's getting up to go to the bowl before getting the release cue, immediately pick the bowl up. It's likely you might not even manage to put the bowl down all the way. The dog might get up when the bowl is halfway to the floor. Then just lift the bowl again and wait until the dog sits. Then try again.

4. Sometimes you might reward the dog with a treat from your hand for remaining in sit, that is to say before you've come all the way down to the floor with the bowl. Then try setting the bowl down again.

5. Gradually make the exercise more difficult so the dog must do more and more before she's allowed to go to the bowl. Maybe look you in the eyes, follow you several steps away from the bowl, or offer several other behaviors. But don't make it too difficult too quickly. Remember to remain silent during the entire exercise, except when you reward or cue "go ahead". No clearing your throat or saying "no"!

When you try the exercise where the dog follows you away from the bowl, it can be useful to have a helper "save" the bowl if the dog tries to be sneaky. If you don't have a helper handy, you can use a (loose) leash as you start to walk away from the bowl. In the worst case scenario, you can prevent the dog from rewarding herself before you give her permission by holding her back on the leash. It's not the end of the world if the dog gets the reward despite being on leash, but next time use a shorter leash to prevent your dog from doing the same thing again. Try to remain neutral and still when you cue "go ahead" so you are sure that the dog is only reacting to your verbal cue and not your body language. You'll be glad you did so later on in the training process.

Summary

- Think through your training system. Write down what you do and what you want to do so you later can discuss it with your training buddies.

- Think about:
  - » Break routines.
  - » Transports between where you take a break and where you train.
  - » Release cues.
  - » How to transition between voluntarily offered behaviors and cued behaviors.

Elsa and Ludde

Holding an Area

Dogs live in the world of scents. They use their noses more or less all the time. Holding an area is all about the dog using her nose. We want to tell her: "Now is the time to use your nose as much as you can. You should stay in this area until you find something."

Holding an area is a part of directional retrieves. We send the dog to an area where we know there is one or more objects we want her to find. In the beginning, the area is just a few yards in diameter, but when we put it together with longer directional retrieves, the dog's hunt area will automatically expand. In this chapter, we describe how we teach the dog to hunt in a small area on cue. You can read more about how we send the dog to the area where she's to hunt in the chapter "Blind Retrieves".

Play to Inspire Holding an Area

You can use kibble during your walks to train your dog to hold an area. Bring a little of the dog's food when you are going out and have the dog hunt for it. We only want to train the hunt whistle at first and it's more effective if the dog is hunting for treats since we then don't have to work with the delivery to hand. If you still want the dog to hunt for an object but you know the dog hasn't mastered the delivery, click and reward as soon as the dog has found the object. Don't worry about whether or not she releases the object. If the dog wants to run away with the object, keep her on leash and do a lot of extra training on deliveries.

The Whistle

The most common hunt whistle is a rolling sound: "Tutuuu, tutuuu, tutuuu". Some people blow the hunt whistle only when they want the dog to start hunting, while others choose to blow it as long as the dog is in the right area or repeat the whistle now and then. Decide what works best for you and your dog.

Teaching the Whistle

Do the following to teach the dog the hunt whistle:

1. Hold the dog by the collar. Throw several treats on the ground close to her so she can see them. Release her collar and once she starts looking for the treats, blow the hunt whistle. Repeat this step several times in various environments before you move on to the next step.
2. Have the dog sit, put several treats on the ground next to or behind her (so she still sees them), and blow the hunt whistle. If the dog doesn't start hunting, repeat the first step a few more times. You can also start adding a hand signal if you want to be able to direct her to hold an area. (Read more on that later on in the section "Holding an Area in Different Directions").

Linnéa and Daisy

3. Have the dog sit, hide one of her favorite small objects well in the grass next to her, and blow the hunt whistle.

4. Have the dog sit, hide treats or an object near her so she can't see them (although the dog should see that you are hiding something), blow the stop whistle and wait for her to make contact with you, and then blow the hunt whistle.

5. Have the dog sit, hide the object or the treat right beside her, walk a bit away, blow the stop whistle so the dog makes contact, and blow the hunt signal.

6. Hide several treats without the dog seeing, have her near the hunt area, blow the stop whistle so she makes contact (even if she's already looking at you, which will give you another success with stop whistle training), then blow the hunt whistle. If the dog doesn't start hunting, repeat the second step a few more times.

7. When your dog knows how to go out in a straight line on a blind retrieve, hide treats or an object so the dog can't see it. Send her out on a retrieve. When the dog is in the right area, blow the stop whistle and then the hunt whistle.

In the beginning we blow the hunt whistle when the dog's nose "is on" and later we blow the whistle for the dog to activate her nose. It's usually easy to see or hear when the dog has begun using her nose. First, her nose moves while "sniffing" and secondly, you can often hear a little clucking or deeper sniffing sound that means the dog is really using its fine tuned scent instrument. Some dogs may be wary of or accustomed to waiting for permission and therefore won't start looking for the treats on their own. If necessary, you can cue "go ahead" on a few occasions to have the dog start hunting. But try to fade that cue as soon as possible and instead throw the treats once the dog has already started to put her nose to the ground.

The illustration demonstrates how to teach the hunt whistle with a directional signal. If you don't want to use a directional signal when the dog is holding an area, just skip it. Remember to increase the distance between you and the dog, not between the dog and the hunt area.

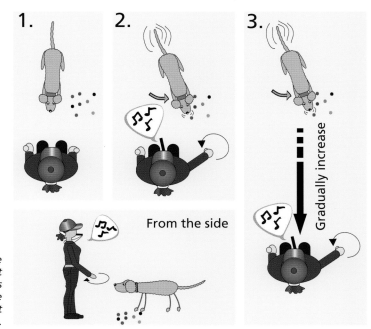

Hiding the Object

You can hide anything you want when you teach the dog to look for an object. However, the first few times it's a good idea to hide something you know the dog is interested in. Once the dog knows what this exercise is about, there is an endless number of objects you can use. The greater variety of objects you use, the more proficient the dog becomes. You'll be glad you trained her with all kinds of strange objects the next time you lose your car keys or phone in the forest.

But ...

... we can't allow the dog to hunt for treats, then she'll do that during field trials instead of hunting game! This might be the case if your dog's only allowed to hunt for treats and doesn't have any interest in objects, so remember to vary what the dog hunts for (treats, balls, game) and do a lot of distraction training.

Try to use as small an object as possible. This is partly because it's easy to hide, and partly because there are fewer scents for the dog to hunt for. This teaches the dog to really follow the scent. We find that it's good to use small stuffed animals when training the dog to hold an area. You can also cut up one of the dog's favorite toys and place a tiny piece of it in the hunt area. Teaching the dog to hunt for small pieces is a good way to proof your training.

Pitfall

It's easy to accidentally increase the distance between the dog and the area too early. When the dog hears the hunt whistle she should always start hunting around her feet and stay in a small area. Therefore don't increase the distance between the dog and the designated hunt area before you're able to send the dog there, blow the stop whistle and then blow the hunt whistle. Instead, start by having the dog sit near or in the hunt area and increase the distance between you and the dog.

Hide the objects so they aren't visible, but at first, always let the dog see when you hide them. We don't want the dog to hunt with her eyes, but rather she should always use her nose to find the object. Initially, you can let the dog watch as you put out the objects, so she knows that there is something to look for, but not exactly where. Tear up a little grass and put it on the object or hide it under some moss. In the end, you can also bury the objects or try hiding them at different heights. The dog might be a little confused the first time the object isn't on the ground and may appear to think, "Well, something smells here. But there isn't anything on the ground ...". Then the dog starts hunting overhead instead.

If the dog doesn't hunt for the object, you should first and foremost increase the dog's interest in it. Use the object to play with the dog, get her to play tug with it and throw it a few times so she gets to retrieve it. You can then take a break from playing and put the object behind a tussock and cue your dog "go ahead". When you hide the object, rub it on the ground in a couple of different places in the hunt area (about a yard in diameter) so the scent is spread out a bit. This teaches the dog to ignore scent traces where there's nothing, and instead find the spot where the scent is the strongest and where the object is actually located. You can also ask a helper to put out objects on occasion so the dog will take objects that don't have your scent on them.

Should I Blow the Stop Whistle before the Hunt Whistle?

It's a matter of taste if you want the dog to stop and make contact before starting to hunt. But if we want to be able to direct the hunt to the right or left in the hunt area, we need to make contact with the dog first. If we see that the dog "stumbles" over the hunt area, we usually blow the hunt whistle immediately. However, if we want to direct the dog in a particular direction first, we blow the stop signal first and the hunt whistle after the dog has made contact with us.

Coach Says

Work on the stop whistle separately. When the dog has mastered both the hunt whistle and the stop whistle, you can start combining them by blowing the hunt whistle as a reward for the dog halting at the stop whistle. Be careful to vary the rewards and tasks after the stop whistle. You want the dog to make contact with you when you blow the stop whistle rather than putting her nose to the ground and beginning to hunt instead.

Holding an Area in Different Directions

When you have blown the stop whistle, it can be useful to have the dog hunt in a particular direction (see the illustration earlier in this chapter). You can do this by working on the steps we mentioned earlier in the chapter. However, think about which side of the dog you put the treats, and point so the dog hunts there. To teach the dog to look to the right, position her in front of you with her nose towards you. Put treats to the right of the dog (from your perspective), blow the hunt whistle and signal the dog to hunt there with your right hand. Then do the same to the left, that is, put treats to the left of the dog (again, from your perspective) and signal her to hunt there with your left hand. Teach the dog the right and left signals at the same time and spend an equal amount of time training both. Then gradually increase the distance between you and the dog. The dog should still be close to the designated hunt area. If you do this at a distance before the dog is sure that the hand signal and hunt whistle mean she should hunt around her feet, there is a risk she will instead come to you and look beside you (since you pointed there).

Holding an Area with Distractions

Once the dog has learned what holding an area involves, she will probably think it's great fun and be able to hunt even if there are distractions present. You should still do distraction training when teaching the dog to hold an area. Sometimes there will be more than one object in an area. It's important the dog comes to you immediately after she has found one of them, and not keep hunting with an object in her mouth. You should therefore try to put several objects in the area and have the dog fetch them one at a time. If you encounter problems with the dog exchanging objects or continuing to hunt with one in her mouth, we recommend training more on "Straight Back to Us" in the chapter "Delivery to Hand" and "Take the First One!" in the chapter "Taking and Holding". Make sure the dog continues to hunt if another dog walks by, if a shot goes off, or a mark falls in the distance.

Emma trains Musse to hold an area.

Sub-goals – Holding an Area	Completed
Hunt in a small area near you	
Fetch and deliver objects	
Hunt in a small area at a distance	
Being cast to the correct area and start hunting	
With distractions (such as shots, a helper playing with a toy, or other dogs nearby)	

Challenge

If you blow the hunt whistle when the dog sees there isn't anything to find, such as on the living room floor or on concrete, will the dog activate her nose and start hunting? If she does, throw a treat on the ground as a reward.

Summary

- Teach the dog to activate her nose and start hunting as soon as she hears the hunt whistle.
- Use small objects and hide them properly so the dog really has to try to find them.

Heelwork

During the hunt, your dog should be able to walk beside you off leash at the same time as she concentrates on the action out in the field. Moreover, the dog should be ready – at any moment – to run out and work on your cue.

While walking at heel, a retriever should walk with her head at about her handler's knee level and look forward. Heelwork for spaniels is not as strict as it is for retrievers. A retriever is usually positioned close to you on your left side (those who hunt and shoot with their left hand have the dog on their right side), while for spaniels it's sufficient if the dog stays around your feet. We recommend that you also teach your spaniel how to walk at heel, which is a useful skill both in day-to-day life and at field trials.

From the time the dog is a small puppy, we teach her that our left side is the best place to be. Sitting, standing, walking and running on our left side are things the dog should want to do. We reward the dog with praise, treats, games, petting and caresses when she spontaneously comes up to us on our left side. Sometimes we continue walking while we reward the dog with treats so that she's moving while eating her treats. This way, as soon as the treats are gone, the dog is already in the correct position for the next repetition and we can soon give her another reward. Accordingly, the training flows a little smoother without the dog performing a lot of other behaviors we don't want at that moment.

Elsa rewards Ludde when he spontaneously comes up beside her.

Play to Inspire Heel Position

It can be useful to reward the dog with play by presenting a toy on our left side and spinning around to the right while playing with the dog. This teaches the dog to follow us even when we turn.

We take the opportunity to reward the dog on walks when she spontaneously seeks out our left side, both when on and off leash. Even if we, at a later stage in our training, want the dog to look forward while walking at heel, we'll reward her when she looks at us and spontaneously comes up close beside us. Then we take the opportunity to reward her for continuing to walk beside us. We also try to reward her when she casts a glance forward. This is particularly applicable to dogs that have been training a lot of obedience heelwork and thus have learnt to keep their eyes glued on their handler's face. Then we try to be quick to put the reward right in front of the dog's nose so she doesn't have time to look up at us after the click. As our training becomes more advanced and the dog looks forward, we can strategically place the reward a bit behind our backs to make the dog anticipate the reward appearing from that direction. There's still so much excitement to entice her forward.

If you know that your dog likes to run to a particular location on your walks, you can use that as a reward. In the beginning, it may be a good idea to have a leash on your dog so she doesn't take off when you don't want her to. When the dog walks calmly by your side and controls herself, give your "go ahead" cue so she can go where she wants. Walk very short distances the first few times, maybe just a few steps. Then, you can gradually extend the distance.

Make the whole thing into a fun game. Challenge the dog to follow you on your left side. Start by rewarding the dog when she's in the correct position beside you, preferably a bit too far back as opposed to a bit too far ahead. The first few times you can stand beside your dog, then you can start moving in different directions, a few steps at a time. Reward the dog when she comes close beside you. Then make the game more challenging so the dog follows you when you try to sneak away, when you try to run away, and when you walk at a normal pace.

When the dog seeks the correct position beside you as soon as you begin to move, you can add the cue. It might be a light tap on your thigh or a verbal cue such as "here", "with me", or something else that works for you. The cue for obedience heelwork is most often your competition position (a very straight body posture) and the "heel" cue, so choose something different if you also want to participate in obedience trials.

Sense and Sensibility

It's important to use both sense and sensibility when you start teaching your dog to walk at heel, especially if you also want to compete in obedience; It's sometimes easy to fall into the trap of rewarding overly energetic and engaged heelwork in a hunting context. Ultimately, we want the dog to be able to walk long distances beside us. She won't make it if she's too excited. Therefore we want to create a feeling of calm so the dog can rest and catch her breath before the next task. In the beginning we thus train heeling when the dog is calm and isn't highly anticipating work. Walks are an excellent opportunity to train, either when the dog has had a chance to burn off some steam or at the end of the walk when we're on our way home. The dog should be able to walk beside us in calm situations before we move onto more stressful environments.

Anders and Rasmus

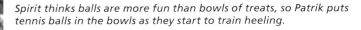

The heelwork requirements in different stakes vary in different countries. In the novice stake for retrievers the requirements for heeling are usually not so stringent, but the dog should be able to walk near your side without you having to nag too much. In the more advanced stakes, your dog should flow with your movements without you having to focus on her. You should instead be able to fully concentrate on the trial task and trust the dog to follow you. We want our dog to move fluidly and work on that regardless of whether we aim to start field trials or not.

Heelwork with Distractions

To ensure the dog masters heeling, it's important she maintains her position despite distractions. Remember to add the distractions in small increments so your dog succeeds as often as possible. Later on, you can vary the rewards so you sometimes reward the dog by allowing her to work. For example, if your dog is walking at heel when a dummy falls, allow her to fetch it.

We like to train heelwork by putting out two food bowls 20-30 yards apart (see illustration).[23] The dog should know that there is something in the bowls.

1. Walk back and forth between the bowls and reward the dog with the cue "back" when your dog is in the correct position and looks forward.
2. If your dog ends up ahead of you, turn all the way around to the right (so the dog has to go the long way around you) and walk towards the food bowl that was previously behind you.
3. If there are too many turns and too few rewards, you need to make it easier so your dog can succeed. Stop and take only half a step before you send her towards the bowl in front of you. You can also reward the dog with treats out of your hand a few times and then start walking and sending her to the bowl as a reward.

In the beginning, the dog should just find the correct position by your side, without walking longer distances. Usually, the dog is in the best position right at the beginning (from a halt) or right when you turned around from one of the food bowls. Send the dog as soon as she gets into the right position. If you are training by yourself, you can have a leash on the dog in this situation, so she can't run to the bowl before you cue "back". You can also have a helper pick up the bowl if the dog runs off too soon.

When you have started training blind retrieves, meaning the dog can run straight out from you to retrieve an object,

23 We borrowed this exercise from Eva Bodfäldt, www.evabodfaldt.com.

say "back" instead of "go ahead" when you want the dog to go to the bowl. Read more about this in the chapter "Blind Retrieves".

When your dog always assumes the correct position, start adding more distractions, and then extend the amount of time the dog should walk at heel. You can, for example, have a helper lift one of the bowls a little and talk to the dog. If the dog falls forward, i.e. ends up too far ahead of you, just turn and continue toward the food bowl behind you. At first, keep the dog in position for just half a step and then reward her with the cue "back".

Coach Says

Train heeling at different paces: quick, normal, and slow. You can also try changing your pace on occasion to see if the dog is attentive. Reward the dog when she maintains her position.

When you have made significant progress and the dog thinks it's fun to fetch dummies and game, you can add a little heeling before each new activity in order to get some extra training. This helps develop the dog's endurance and teaches her to follow you, since you are the source of all things fun. It will serve you well in your ongoing training, and it's a must during field trials since you will move between the various tasks.

We strongly recommend your distraction training includes walking behind a person. This person should preferably have a broomstick over his or her shoulder, if you don't have a gun handy. During field trials, you often walk behind the shooter and then it's good if your dog heels with you and not with the shooter.

Pitfall

Remember not to repeat your heel cue over and over again if your dog doesn't listen. Patting yourself on the thigh is also a cue. It should be a light pat even during competitions, so don't start to drum harder and harder to get the dog to listen. If your dog doesn't respond to the cue, go back and train with her offering to heel, then add the cue again.

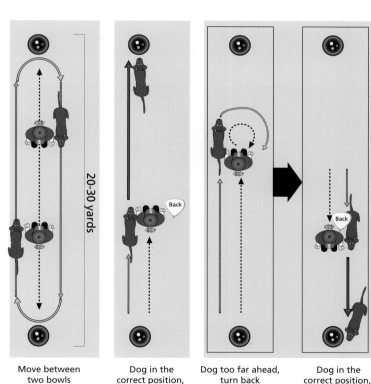

Move between two bowls | Dog in the correct position, reward | Dog too far ahead, turn back | Dog in the correct position, reward

20-30 yards

The illustration shows how you can use food bowls to teach your dog to walk at heel despite distractions.

154

If during training the dog pulls ahead and ends up next to the shooter instead, turn around and walk the other way, or stop and wait until the dog assumes the correct position again. The only way for the dog to move forward is to walk beside you. If you are careful to be consistent throughout all of your training, your dog's heeling will be excellent. This is good to keep in mind even if you have a spaniel, even though the position isn't as precise for spaniels. If you allow the dog to work when she walks ahead of you she will learn that she should walk in that position. Just stopping or turning around and allowing the dog to figure out what

she is supposed to do looks much better than scolding the dog. During a field trial, you can't turn around but you can change your pace to see if your dog is paying attention.

If you want to make the exercise more difficult, start by walking side by side with the shooter (with the dog at your side). Then the shooter begins walking much faster so he or she walks away from you. Who does the dog walk with then? You or the shooter? If the dog doesn't stay where you had intended, train in the same way as when the shooter walked in front of you.

Getting into Heel Position

Heel position means the dog sits on your left side. For the dog to get into heel position (sit beside you) when she's in front of us, we teach her to make a U-turn to our side. You can train the dog to get into heel position and to walk beside you in parallel. Before the dog knows how to get into the position, you can either place yourself beside your dog or have her come up to your side while you walk and then begin exercises that require the dog to be in heel position. It's easiest to teach the dog to get into position from being in front of you. You can either shape the behavior without a target or you can first teach the dog to stand with her front paws on a target, such as an eight times eight inch piece of wood. It's good if the target is around two inches high, so it's clear to the dog whether she's standing on it or not. The initial advantage of using a target is that the dog's front legs will end up in the correct place and you can place yourself in the correct position in relation to your dog.

Ingela and Snoddas

Using a Target to Teach the Heel Position

Do the following to teach the dog a target:

1. Put the target on the ground. Click and reward the dog as soon as she approaches the target, sniffs it, puts first one and then finally two paws on it.

2. Reward the dog for staying on the target and even do a little reverse luring to get her to understand that she should remain there.

3. Finish by rewarding the dog in a way that gets her off the target or by giving a release cue so the dog knows she may come off of the target.

4. When the dog easily steps up on the target, position yourself so the target is on your left side. In other words, the target should be placed so that when the dog steps up on the target and pivots toward your side, she'll end up in the correct position.

Then proceed as follows:

1. Stand in front of the dog, face to face, and wait until she moves a hind paw a little bit. In the beginning, it doesn't matter which hind paw, but just be on the lookout for the slightest movement. Since the dog eventually should pivot to your left side, you may want to pay attention to the left hind paw, which should move towards the right hind paw.

2. If your dog remains still, you might need to start by rewarding her for shifting her weight.

3. When the dog has taken a step, move so you end up facing each other again, and wait for the next movement. Always move counterclockwise and let your dog pivot towards your left.

4. Gradually make it more difficult so you soon stand still and the dog takes a step, two steps, three steps, and so on with her hind legs before she gets her reward. If you stand still, the dog will eventually move all the way to your left.

5. When the dog turns all the way to your left, you can start moving to the right around the target so your dog follows you on your left.

6. Now position yourself next to the target and not in front of it – that's where you're going to be in the end.

In the beginning we don't worry about the fact that the dog should sit by our side but focus only on the hind movements. Allow the dog to move to your left side and reward her while she's standing.

Diesel gets into heel position after delivering the dummy.

Elin and Cleo

Fading the Target

When the dog turns to your side as soon as you set out the target, it's time to fade it.

1. Do a few repetitions with the target when you are standing still next to it the entire time.
2. When the dog has come to your side, click and reward her there.
3. Then throw a treat in front of you so the dog gets off the target.
4. While your dog is looking for her treat, lift up the target, without the dog noticing it, and remain standing in exactly the same place. The only difference now is that the target is gone.
5. If you are lucky, your dog will immediately pivot her hindquarters into the right position. If she doesn't, wait for the smallest posterior movement and reward that.
6. Then put the target back, do two repetitions with the target and then one without.
7. Gradually do more and more repetitions without the target.

Sitting at Your Side

To get your dog to sit at your side, do the following:

1. Have the dog offer a couple of sits in front of you, reward those.
2. Stand next to the dog and get her to stand up using a treat.
3. Most likely the dog will sit next to you rather soon, click and reward.
4. If the dog wants to turn around and sit in front of you instead, you can do this exercise with a wall to the dog's left the first few times.
5. When the dog sits down, take a step forward so she follows you, and then wait until she sits again.
6. When you've repeated the sit a few times you can start putting it together with the pivot to your side. Have the dog pivot to your side and wait a bit, and the dog will most likely sit. Click and reward.

You must also train the dog to come into the correct position from the right and from the back, as depicted in the illustration to the right.

Sit When You Stop

When your dog is walking at heel and you stop, she should automatically sit without you having to say anything. Start with the dog sitting at your side and then reward her, take a step forward so that she follows and wait until she sits down at your side again. Do this at different paces and in different directions, so that the dog is able to sit beside you regardless of situation. You can also have the dog sit beside you and take a step forward. Then, call the dog to your left side and reward her when she sits down (see illustration).

Be sure the dog sits down square to you. If she often falls out to your left, avoid rewarding her with your right hand and start training next to a wall or a low ledge so that you can get straight sits. Then you can gradually fade the ledge by having your dog sit next to it, then without it, then next to it, and so on.

Obedience Heelwork and Gun Dog Heelwork

Heelwork during field trials differs from obedience heeling mainly because the dog doesn't look at you during gun dog heelwork. During obedience heelwork, the dog should look up at your face the whole time. During field trials, the dog is to walk beside you and look forward to see where the game falls so she can retrieve it. You can teach your dog the difference between heelwork in the two contexts, even at the same time, if you are careful with what signals you are using. The dog will soon learn to connect a short cut lawn

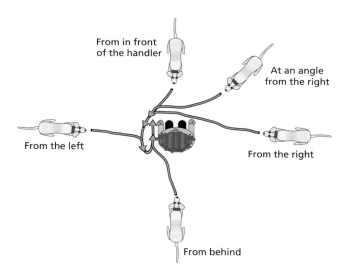

The dog should be able to get into heel position regardless of which direction she comes from.

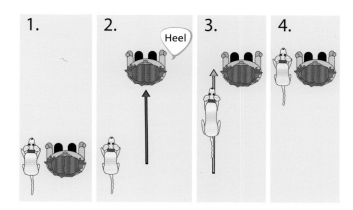

This way you can teach the dog to both sit when you stop and to get into heel position from behind. Have the dog sit, take a step forward, and recall her. Reward the dog when she sits down.

and a handler in competition position (very straight and formal) with obedience heelwork. Similarly, the dog learns to connect a more relaxed handler and a forest environment with gun dog heelwork. We also use different cues in conjunction with the various types of heeling.

Coach Says

Teach the dog to follow your left leg both when walking at heel and when you turn on the spot. It will be useful for example if you suddenly have to turn around to send the dog in the other direction. Also work on training the dog to remain sitting when you start on your right leg so that you can move that leg when you direct the dog for a blind retrieve without the dog dashing off. If the dog knows she should follow your left leg and stay when you move your right leg, you use it during heeling so the dog pauses a little every time you move your right leg forward. That way your dog doesn't end up in front of you as easily.[24]

Ingela and Cesar working on gun dog heeling.

At first it may be helpful to properly distinguish between the environments where you train obedience heelwork and gun dog heelwork. When the dog has learnt the difference between the different types of heelwork, we want her to be ready to do gun dog heelwork on the lawn and obedience heelwork in the forest. As a way to proof and distraction train the two types of heelwork as much as possible. The first few times, the dog might find it a bit difficult to know which one applies. Lower your criteria if it gets too challenging or when you enter new environments. You should also pay attention to where your dog is looking. That way, the dog will soon learn to master the difference between the two kinds of heelwork.

Ingela and Cesar working on obedience heeling.

[24] We borrowed this exercise from Philippa Williams www.dogsforlife.co.uk.

Sub-goals – Heelwork	Completed
Get into heel position from the front, right, left, and behind	
Walk in the proper position and look straight forward	
All angles and paces	
Longer distances	
Different surfaces	
With distractions (such as shots, walking behind the shooter, or falling marks)	

Challenge

Can your dog heel behind "a shooter" who is playing with a ball, and then throws the ball into the woods while you continue to walk by?

Summary

- Train heeling with many different distractions so the dog really masters the skill.
- Walk at heel towards fun things, that way your dog will enjoy heelwork. However, pay attention to the dog's energy levels while walking at heel so she doesn't become too excited.

Christina with Etta, Game and Solo

Problem Solving

Have you gotten stuck in your training? Pulled your hair and prayed to a higher power? Tried "everything" but nothing works? Contemplated whether you should stop with dog training and start collecting stamps instead? Relax, don't worry, we've all been there. When it happens to us, we bring out our toolbox.

To help diagnose the problem, at the top of our toolbox we have a question sheet with four questions. These questions will help us figure out if our timing is right, what criteria we are setting, if the rate of rewards is sufficient and if the quality of the rewards is sufficient. And somewhere in the answers to those questions we will find the problem – and that means the solution is close at hand.

Timing – What Are We Rewarding?

We get what we reward, which unfortunately is not always the same as getting what we wanted to reward. One example is when we accidentally send the dog to retrieve a mark just when she's about to run in. What is being rewarded then is not sitting there and waiting but rather getting up.

Criteria – What Do We Want the Dog to Do in Order to Get Her Reward?

The criterion we set is what we want the dog to do to get her reward. We make training plans where we achieve the final goal step by step. Here we would like to add a word of warning to those who are new to clicker training. Beware of setting your criteria too high and making your training too difficult. It's a problem we see a lot of. "This isn't so hard, she will be able to do it," the handler says. It usually ends with a frustrated dog and a frustrated handler. And zero learning. Instead, it's good to be able to return to a point of success. Later on, when some skill has been acquired in this way of training, it's common to fall into the rut of just repeating the same basic stuff instead. All of a sudden everyone becomes a bunch of neurotic perfectionists …

Moderation is actually the best. But how do we know when things are just about right? When is it time to make things easier or more difficult? A good rule of thumb is usually that four out of five repetitions should be successful before you move on to a more difficult task. We call it the 80 percent rule.[25] When the dog is correct more than 80 percent of the time, we raise our criterion. If, on the other hand, the dog is correct three out of five times, we should stay on the same level or make it easier. If the dog is never or correct less than two times, we have probably moved too fast, and we should take a step back in our training instead.

---

[25] Bob Bailey, www.behavior1.com.

Totte

Pitfall

A common mistake many handlers make when it comes to learning is lumping together too many parts of a skill and training them simultaneously. Break the skill down into small steps that you teach separately before putting them all together. Work on one thing at a time. Then the entire behavior will be more robust and reliable. What they say is true: no chain is stronger than its weakest link.

Rate – Are We Rewarding Too Often or Too Seldom?

Are you the stingy type? Well, then your dog might learn more slowly and you might not make any progress in your training. Every reward provides the dog with information about what's right. But neither is it good to be indiscriminately generous. If we reward the dog for everything at random, we'll run into trouble with being consistent with our set criteria. This doesn't apply when the dog is learning something new – then it's almost impossible to be too generous. In that case, rewarding the dog is great, because it tells her she's on the right track. It also builds value in being able to keep working and for the very behavior we are training. In addition, it's less likely the behavior will be interrupted by distractions. But a high frequency of rewards should not be confused with simply feeding the dog. Generally, we think beginners tend to reward too little and those who are a little further in their training too often. Both the set criteria and the rate of rewards must be flexible. As soon as we increase the level of difficulty, such as adding noise or changing environments, we might need to increase the rate of information (in other words the rewards) for a while and then reduce it again.

The Quality of Reinforcement – Are Your Rewards Good Enough?

It's so easy to keep using the same old hot dogs and the same old ball day in and day out. But then one day we're out of

hot dogs and we take pieces of pancake with us when we go out to train. And suddenly everything runs like clockwork. The dog makes breakthrough after breakthrough. "Finally a reward worth working for", the dog seems to think. High quality rewards can do the trick, but is it possible to have a reward that is too good? Yes, in a sense. There are dogs that completely lose their minds in anticipation of a certain reward. They start barking, whining, nibbling on their owners and lose all self control. That is rarely something we want to encourage.

If there's a reward you want to use in your training, but it makes the dog too crazy, you simply start by teaching the dog how to behave around that particular reward. If the

Elsa and Ludde

dog, for example, finds it difficult to work when there is a ball on the ground, you can start by rewarding her for not trying to take the ball. You can either reward the dog with treats from your hand or you can reward her with the cue "go ahead" to allow her to take the ball. Then you make the task progressively more difficult so your dog must look at you, walk with you a bit, perform a trick, and so on before she gets "go ahead" for the ball. This exercise comes with a small caveat: The idea isn't for you to say "no" to the dog or to nag her. If you feel you must say "no" or if it just slips out, make the exercise a little easier.

TCRQ – Timing, Criteria, Rate, and Quality

Timing, criteria, rate of rewards, quality of reinforcement, or TCRQ[26] as we call them, work together, as you have noticed. The rate of rewards and what criteria you set often overlap. High quality rewards sometimes mean you can significantly raise your criteria. Really good timing combined with a really good reward can help the dog understand on the first attempt.

Nature and Nurture

Some dogs are, as we mentioned previously, easier to reward than others. Dogs are partly affected by their genetic make-up (their genetics) and partly by the environment where they grew up. This also affects what solutions work in your training. Some dogs are excited by a cloth being quickly pulled along the ground, while others get going with a tug game. Try to make use of your dog's nature instead of working against it.

Relationships and Basic Needs

If we don't find the solution in TCRQ, we need to consider whether there might be other things in your dog's environment that need to change. If the dog is to be able to engage in training with us, her basic needs must be met. Does the dog have an outlet for her energy? Does she get enough sleep and relaxation? What other forms of entertainment does she have? Is the dog allowed to bite and gnaw? Does she have outlets for her breed-specific traits? Does she have adequate and nutritious food? Or does she perhaps get too much food? If the dog is overweight she's not likely going to want to run too much, and thus, might not be as interested in the reward. Is her overall health good? Does she get the warm ups and cool downs she needs? If the dog is tense, maybe she needs a massage. The dog needs to have an outlet for both her physical and mental energy, i.e. gymnastics for both body and brain. Clicker training in itself provides a lot of mental exercise, but if the dog has any of the problems described above, we might need to start with simple things like just letting her look for treats on the ground. Hunting and field trials are stressful for a dog and she needs to be in good shape to compete. When the dog is full grown, it's a good idea to supplement your training of various skills with cardiovascular exercise, such as swimming, jogging or running next to you while you ride a bike.

The relationship between the handler and the dog also affects the training. By making sure the dog is feeling safe in everyday life, and by making training enjoyable for the dog, we build a good relationship. If the handler puts excessive pressure on the dog, or previously trained with physical or verbal corrections, the dog may not find it fun to train together. Therefore, problem solving might also mean we look at the overall relationship between dog and handler.

---

[26] Egtvedt & Køste, Lydnadsträning i teori och praktik, 2008.

It doesn't work so well to teach the dog something in a fun way if the rest of the dog's day consists of physical and verbal corrections. Then the handler needs to rethink his or her relationship with the dog. It's about choosing a way of working with the dog or to some extent actually choosing a lifestyle!

If That Still Doesn't Work ...

The solution may not always be so simple. Sometimes it requires several changes. If you've turned yourself upside down in your attempts to be creative, but neither you nor your friends can understand what's wrong, then it might be time to think about whether there's something wrong with the dog. If the dog is sick or in pain, medical treatment is the only solution. It may also be that the dog is genetically more limited in her capacity to work than we as handlers would like. This is quite important to keep in mind when choosing a dog, and we should always keep it in mind when we train. We can't hold high ambitions for trials if they are beyond our dog's ability.

Summary

When we get stuck, we use the acronym TCRQ to solve our problem:

1. Timing – what is it we wish to reward?
2. Criteria – what do we want the dog to do to receive a reward?
3. Rate – are we rewarding the dog too often or too seldom?
4. Quality – are our rewards good enough?

The dog's basic needs must be met for training to be successful.

Tassla

Introduction to Gunfire

For gun dogs, the sound of gunfire is synonymous with something extremely enjoyable: Wohoo! Where did the game fall? Where did it go? Where should I run? But shots aren't just about the gun shot itself, but also about the dog having the skills of sitting and waiting for instructions. Therefore, shots shouldn't be too much fun or the dog might run in or start whining, thus being eliminated from the field trial.

We want the dog to have a moderate amount of expectation when it comes to the shot. She should be interested, but not so wound up that she whines. Neither should she be afraid of gunfire.

A dummy launcher and ear protection are good investments that make it easy for you to accustom your dog to shots. A dummy launcher is a device that you load with a blank cartridge and that launches a special dummy. To just train shots, use it without the dummy. Remember you need to have permission from the gamekeeper or landowner to shoot with a dummy launcher and to keep your distance from residential areas when you shoot so you don't scare anyone. Check with your local office for laws on shooting.

During field trials, the dog must be able to sit still beside you and to walk beside you even when shots are going off, and game or dummies are falling close by. Keep a leash on your dog at first if you think she might run in (i.e. leave your side without permission) when she hears the shot. Reward the dog when she remains beside you. Once the dog is accustomed to gunshots, you can shoot in one direction and then allow the dog to work in the opposite direction to teach her not to lock onto the direction in which the shot was fired.

Looking Ahead

Teach the dog to look ahead or at the thrower instead of at the shooter after the shot, so the dog doesn't miss the mark. In the beginning you can shoot and then the thrower "quacks" before she throws the mark (i.e. the thrower makes an odd noise, bangs something, or quacks like a duck to catch the dog's attention). Gradually your thrower can hide more and more until he or she is no longer visible and the dog

Ingela

still looks ahead or, even better, in the direction of the gun after the shot has gone off. To begin with, we shoot first and then throw, but in reality it's the opposite: first comes the throw, and then the shot. If you want to work on this without shooting, you can ask your helper to throw the mark, and then clap her hands together hard, so it almost sounds like a shot. If you train alone, you can of course throw the dummy yourself, and then clap your hands together.

When the dog sits at our side, we want the shot to be a signal to remain there, calm and attentive. If the dog is out and working when a shot is fired, the dog should keep working even after the shot. For spaniels, shots are almost always associated with a bird flying up, which then becomes an additional signal for the dog to sit and remain in place.

Pitfall

Once the dog is accustomed to gunfire, remember to spend a lot of time training steadiness after a shot so you don't always allow the dog to work after hearing a shot. It's extremely easy for your dog to become too excited by the shot and possibly even run in as she hears gunfire. To balance the dog's anticipation, you can sometimes end your training session with a shot and then go home.

Gun Wariness

Some dogs find shots unpleasant. Gun shy and gun wary are not the same thing. Gun wary means the dog thinks that gunfire is a little unpleasant, but we can often work with this and overcome it. Gun shyness can, however, be so severe that the dog flees in panic or becomes paralyzed in fear, and it may not be possible to address through training. We will now focus on gun wariness. If your dog is gun shy we recommend you contact an experienced trainer to see if the problem can be solved.

Some signs of gun wariness can be the dog startling, looking concerned, crouching, and lowering her tail, barking, growling, or starting to sniff excessively to disconnect herself from the unpleasant experience. Sometimes stress responses don't manifest until a while after the shots, such as panting, walking around uneasily, and having difficulty concentrating.

By being attentive to your dog's reactions, you can soon teach her to associate gunfire with pleasant things. If you have a shooting range nearby, you can accustom your dog to gunfire by walking near it with your dog when they are shooting. Start doing this when the dog is a puppy. Remember to stay far enough away from the shooting range so that the dog won't be at risk of being scared. Try to ignore the shots and walk as you normally would – if you react to the shots, you might transfer your fear to the dog. Do your usual training, reward the dog for coming to you, do some tricks, or send her out to look for a toy. If you have friends who have dogs that are accustomed to gunfire, you can go for walks with them when there is shooting, preferably with the dogs off leash, so your dog will learn that the shots are not something to be afraid of.

Once you have a good idea of how your dog will react in the vicinity of the shooting range and she is able to remain calm, you can be more specific in your training. Ask a friend to shoot as far away as necessary so the dog won't become afraid. Reward the dog when the shot goes off. The rewards can be anything: treats, playing, looking for dummies, and so on. You can also do an enjoyable activity while the shots are fired. For example, play a fun game or have the dog search for her favorite tasty treats. The goal is that your dog should look expectant instead of uncomfortable or fearful when the shot goes off. The shooter can then begin to walk closer until he or she is eventually only a few feet away. If the dog appears to be gun wary, increase the distance until the dog becomes calm again. Don't increase the difficulty too quickly but instead sometimes have the shots go off nearby and sometimes far away, just as you would when extending the duration of different steadiness exercises.

By having the shooter move (while you and the dog are stationary), the place where you and your dog are standing should hopefully become safe and enjoyable. The dog doesn't need to move closer to the scariness but the scariness comes closer for a moment, and then disappears again.

Changing the dog's emotional response to gunfire may take some time, but don't give up. Make sure to have really good rewards and avoid situations where the dog becomes so affected she won't take treats or play with you.

Sub-goals – Introduction to Gunfire	Completed
Being calm during gunfire	
Steadiness while sitting by your side	
Steadiness while walking at heel	

Challenge
Can your dog sit off leash beside you, see the shooter, hear the shot, and then turn with you and walk in the other direction?

But ...
... I can't play with the dog when the shot goes off, because then her associations will be all wrong! You can most certainly play! If the dog is gun wary, it's great if she can learn to connect gunfire with something fun. If the dog is accustomed to shots and is expectant when hearing gunfire, it's important that the dog is engaged in the activity you have chosen for her to be engaged in. That is, sometimes playing with you instead of running after the shot, sometimes sitting still at your side, and sometimes running after a mark.

Summary
- Make sure your dog has the right associations when hearing a shot – calmness and attentiveness.
- If your dog is gun wary, make sure you are far enough away so the dog doesn't become frightened when she hears the shot. Gradually work closer and closer and reward the dog when she hears the shots.

Field Trials for Retrievers

The rules and regulations for retriever field trials vary between countries, but in general they are divided into field trials and working tests. The difference between them is usually that the field trials are during a hunt and the working tests are simulated hunts using dummies or cold game.

The different tasks in a retriever field trial are marked retrieves, where both the dog and handler see the game fall and blind retrieves, when the handler knows where the game has fallen and directs the dog into the area. In some countries, sweeping up is also included, when neither the handler nor the dog know exactly where the game is (the handler knows the approximate area). The dog should be able to work both on land and in the water.

In addition to the hunt related tasks, a retriever needs to be able to wait calmly while other dogs are working and walk beside her handler while other dogs are walking, when shots go off, and when game falls. The dog should be steady and quiet the entire time she is working and not leave the handler's side without permission. The handler directs the dog using verbal cues, hand signals, and a whistle.

United States

In the United States, there are field trials and hunt tests. American trials are set by judges in controlled environments, which are meant to simulate an actual hunting experience. Dogs are run individually on exactly the same test pattern. There are several different clubs in the United States that organize field trials and each has its own rules and regulations. The following applies to the American Kennel Club (AKC). For the complete regulations, visit www.akc.org.

Hunt Tests

AKC has three classes: junior, senior, and master.

The junior class is the entry level for the hunt test. The dogs are allowed to wear a collar and leash. Your dog should walk nicely on leash to the spot where the judges have instructed you to go. When you're ready to begin, you signal the judges.

The throwers, who are positioned in the field, will throw and shoot a bird for your dog to mark. When the bird has fallen, the judges will tell you to release your dog to go find the bird. When your dog has found the bird, she should deliver it to your hand in the previously designated area. Your dog is required to retrieve four birds, two on land and two from water, and she will be graded on this. The judges look at marking, style, perseverance and trainability. Dogs in the junior level are not competing against each other but instead scored against a standard. There is a set passing score, and after four passes you'll receive an AKC certificate and you can add the letters JH (for Junior Hunter) to your dog's registered name. Your dog has to be at least six months old to enter.

The intermediate level in AKC hunt test is the senior class. Here your dog will be working off leash and without a collar. You'll walk up to the designated starting point where your dog will sit quietly with you until the judges indicate that it's time to begin. Your dog will now do a double retrieve (mark two birds) and deliver each bird to hand. There is a double retrieve on land and one from water. Your dog also needs to "honor" another dog's retrieve, which means that she'll be required to sit and watch another dog on the line perform her retrieve. The senior level also includes blind retrieves. This means a bird is placed out of the dog's line of sight. The spot will be marked for you as a handler. You and your dog now get to find the bird together as a team. The dog will be tested on two blind retrieves, one on land and one in water. As at the junior level there is a set passing score and your dog needs to pass four times to receive the certificate and get to add SH (for Senior Hunter) to her registered name.

The most advanced level is the master class. Here your dog needs to be an accomplished retriever, being able to do multiple marked retrieves on land, water or both, blind retrieves at all times, and honor other dogs as in the senior level. In addition, your dog should be able to perform a walk up where she walks next to you while a bird is shot and then sits beside you until the judges tell you to release her. A master level dog is expected to make fewer mistakes, demonstrate a better memory, a higher degree of obedience, and better hunting skills. The master test has to include at least five hunting situations with multiple marks both on land and in water.

After having achieved a SH title your dog needs to pass five master tests, and if you don't have the SH title, you need to pass six tests in order to earn the MH certificate and title.

Field Trials

Field trials are used to see how the breeding and training of the retriever breeds are developing. These trials are designed to be more difficult than hunt tests. If nothing else the dog has to cover a lot more ground, making retrieves over 300-600 yards. Field trials have different classes for professional and amateur handlers. Unlike in the hunt tests, the dogs are judged against one another in field trials.

Your dog will be judged firstly on natural abilities (memory, intelligence, attention, nose, courage, perseverance and style) and secondly on trained abilities (steadiness, control and delivery). The judges will look at how straight a line your dog works on during the retrieve, if she needs to be directed to find the bird, and her general style. Your dog will also be asked to honor (watch another dog work) during the trial. At the end of each series, the judges will decide on which dogs they want to try further, and they will continue to do this until they have decided on the placing order of the dogs.

The titles you can work for in the discipline are Amateur Field Champion (AFC) and/or Field Champion (FC). In order to earn the AFC designation, your dog has to win a National Championship Stake (handled by an amateur, see the AKC handbook for further information on the regulations for this), or win 15 points with at least one win of five points or better in certain specified classes (for example Owner Handler All-age). To earn the FC title you dog needs to win a National Championship Stake or win ten points, in for example Open All-Age.[27]

---

[27] http://www.peakperformancetraining.info/AKCHuntTests.html.

United Kingdom

In the UK, the primary organization for official field trials is the Kennel Club. There are field trials, Gundog Working Tests, and Working Gundog Certificates. The field trials are the official trials and therefore the more important competition. For the complete field trial regulations, visit www.thekennelclub.org.uk.

Field Trials

Field trials are held in the shooting season – usually from August to the end of January. A trial takes a full day, and some trials are run over two or three consecutive days.

Field trials can be done in two ways: Firstly they can be walked up where the handlers and dogs walk in a long line and the game flies up ahead or as they pass is shot, or secondly they can be driven where the guns and competitors stand still while the game is driven over them and shot. The distances aren't as great as at the US trials. They are usually not greater than 250 yards, but there is no upper limit.

While the dogs and their handlers wait for their turn, they walk in a group behind the line with the dogs on leash. This is called the Gallery – with the Chief Steward – and there will be someone carrying a red flag to indicate where the group is. When it's time for your turn in line, you will be directed by the Chief Steward to which place to take and then remove the leash when instructed to do so by the judge. The dogs must be prepared to wait. It's extremely important the dogs remain quiet and steady even when they are not working.

Your dog will be judged on her marking ability, natural game finding ability, control, drive and style, being quiet, her retrieve and delivery as well as nose and quickness in gathering up the game. You'll first be judged by one pair of judges, and if you're successful then go on to a second round with a second pair of judges. There isn't a set minimum number of retrieves in order to win a trial, but in general there's a minimum of five retrieves for a Novice Trial and six for an Open. It's not possible to say what kind of retrieve you'll encounter since it's all "live" shooting.

There are three stakes: Novice, All Age and Open. In order to be allowed to start in the Open Stake you must have won a Novice trial. It's in the Open Stakes you can get your Field Trail Champion title (FTCH). To be awarded the title you either have to win first place in two different Open Stake trials (one two day stake with 24 dogs and one with at least twelve dogs, so in total either two two day open stakes or a two day and a one day open stake), or be placed first in the yearly international retriever championship. You also have to gain a Drive and a Water Certifcate to gain the FTCH title. There is also an unofficial Field Trial Winner (FTW) title that states the dog has won a field trial.

Gundog Working Test (GWT)

A working test is an unofficial competition intended to simulate a shoot (in the US called a hunt) and thereby assess a retriever's working ability. During a working test, live game is not shot and dummies are used instead. Working tests can be run any time during the year and are most often only open to the arranging club's members.

A working test consists of four to six exercises, each of which is worth a maximum of 20 points. Sometimes the assessment is based on how long it takes for a team to complete a task. The winner is the one who receives the most points. If two dogs receive the same number of points, the tie is broken by holding a run off where the dogs perform various tasks until a winner can be determined.

Your dog's dummy finding ability, speed and directness of the retrieve will be judged. The judges are looking for good marking ability, quick pick ups, fast returns, natural nose, quietness, control, drive, and style.

There are four classes in the Working Test: Unclassified, Puppy, Novice and Open.

Working Gundog Certificate (WGC)

This certificate's role is to provide proof that a dog and handler team is qualified to work on an actual shoot. The WGC is not a competition, but there are criteria your dog will be measured against. The Kennel Club awards the certificate and will list the tasks that were completed on the day. You can get a WGC on game or dummies.

Your dog's control, obedience, temperament, hunting, and retrieving are all being assessed during simulated shooting field exercises. There will be shoot assessors observing all participants throughout the day.

Handlers and dogs walk together to the starting point with the dogs off leash and under control, and a simulated drive with dogs assessed both in the beating line and waiting at pegs. The dog will be assessed when hunting for seen and unseen dummies after the drive, fetching a marked retrieve from water and a marked retrieve from over an obstacle as well as in a steadiness exercise where dogs are left together while handlers collect decoys.

The WGC is open to all Kennel Club registered gundogs and their handlers.

Other Countries

Some countries also have official field trials that only use cold game. Sweden, for example, has two kinds of official tests, field trial that involves a hunt and field trial where cold game is used. Sweden also has an unofficial working test that uses dummies.

For the specific rules in your country, contact your local Kennel Club or Gun Dog Club.

Field Trials for Spaniels

The purpose of a spaniel field trial is to show the performance of a properly trained spaniel in the field. If anything the dogs should work even more perfectly since it's a trial situation and not an everyday shooting. The rules for spaniel field trials vary between different countries, but the basic principles are the same: The dog should hunt and flush game so the game can be shot and then, when cued by the handler, the dog should bring the game to the handler. In other words, the dog needs to be properly trained since she will encounter major challenges.

During a spaniel field trial, the dog is assessed on her willingness to cooperate, desire to hunt, and ability to retrieve, but also her ability to remain calm and quiet. Some practice trials use dummies rather than live game.

Spaniels' most important tasks happen before the shot, during fieldwork, when the dog systematically hunts and flushes game (in contrast to retrievers, who start working after the shot). However, spaniel field trials also involve retrieving, most often in the form of marked retrieves. The handler should therefore be able to direct the dog to the correct area to retrieve game she didn't see fall. During blind retrieves, the dog is sent to a particular area to find and bring back the game. The dog should be able to perform these tasks both on land and in the water. To be able to cover large amounts of ground, sometimes several dogs work in pairs next to each other at the same time, also known as braces.

Steadiness is also an extremely important part of spaniel training. During field work, the dog must stop and stay perfectly still when the game is flushed. The dog is also required to remain silent. The spaniel should be able to walk near her handler while other dogs are working and game is shot and falls. Handlers direct spaniels, as they do with retrievers, using cues, hand signals, and whistles. Some of the things the judges will look at are scenting ability, how the dog uses the wind, her steadiness, and proof of a soft mouth. Your dog will be scored on game finding ability, steadiness, style, and retrieving.

United States

Many different clubs organize field trials in the United States, but the rules discussed here apply to the American Kennel Club (AKC).

The field trial stakes are breed specific, but there are also stakes that allow more than one breed to take part. Dogs compete in a series and at the end of each series, the judges decide which dogs they want to see again.

If your dog is to be able to receive an award, she must compete in all land series and if there are any water tests, she needs to run in those too. Both officiating judges must also have judged your dog if she's going to be placed and/or receive an Award of Merit.

In all stakes, the shots will be fired over your dog and she might be worked up and down wind, and also in water.

At a spaniel field trial the following are the official stakes: Puppy, Novice, Limited, Open All-Age, Qualified Open All-Age, and Amateur All-Age.

For an English Springer Spaniel, a Cocker Spaniel, or an English Cocker Spaniel to become a Field Champion in the

US, she must win either a National Championship Stake, two Open All-Age Stakes, two Qualified Open All-Age Stakes, or one of each. Alternatively, she must win either an Open All-Age Stake or Qualified Open All-Age Stake plus ten championship points, which she earns for a second, third, or fourth place in Open All-Age Stake or Qualified Open-All Age Stake with at least ten starting dogs.

To become an Amateur Field Champion the dog must win a National Amateur Championship Stake, two Amateur All-Age Stakes, or an Amateur All-Age Stake plus ten championship points.

Before an English Springer Spaniel, Cocker Spaniel, or English Cocker Spaniel can become a Field or Amateur Field Champion or win a title, the dog must have shown she can retrieve game from water after swimming. The water test is one or two bird retrieves. The dog will be asked to retrieve cold game, thrown at gunshot, after a swim. Water tests can be held as separate events or in conjunction with field trials.

United Kingdom

There are both Kennel Club sanctioned and non-sanctioned field trials in the UK, and also separate trials for amateurs.

The trials are all run during a hunt with live game, unless it's a water test where cold game might be used occasionally.

The dogs compete in runs, corresponding to series in the US. At the end of each run, the judges will decide which dogs they want to see again. At the end of the day, the judges agree on a winner of the field trial (if there is a dog that is a worthy winner, otherwise there might be no winner at all).

An Open stake is where you can qualify towards the title of Field Trial Champion (FT Ch) and towards being allowed to enter into the Championships or Champion Stake for your breed. There are All Age Stakes open to all dogs of a specific breed without age restriction, Novice Stakes and Puppy Stakes.

Cocker Spaniels can earn the title Field Trial Champion if they place first in the Cocker Spaniel Championship or win two first awards in open stakes. English Springer Spaniels can get the title by placing first in the English Springer Spaniel Championship or by winning two first awards in open stakes. Before a dog of either breed can be awarded the title Field Trial Champion, she must also receive a Water Certificate. A water test can either be a separate trial or part of a field trial.

Mini

Blind Retrieves

During a blind retrieve the dog should run straight forward until you blow the stop whistle followed by the hunt whistle, or just the hunt whistle. After stopping the dog, you should be able to direct or "cast" the dog to the right, left, or back. During trials, the judge indicates the location of the game and you decide how you want to direct the dog there. During spaniel trials, the handler is allowed to direct the dog if she flushed game that was shot but couldn't see the area of the fall.

184

There are a lot of different ways to teach blind retrieves, such as shaping, using visual stimuli, food bowls, objects, and targets. We like to combine several of these elements.

Play to Inspire Blind Retrieves

We start shaping the dog to run straight out from us by clicking and rewarding when the dog points her nose ahead, takes a step forward, takes off galloping forward, and finally gallops straight out. Make sure the reward appears in front of the dog so she doesn't have turn to you to receive it. The first few times you might need to throw the treat or ball over the dog's head when she looks ahead and click just as she spots the reward. When your dog begins to run further and further ahead of you, a ball launcher can be a great help.

In order to do a little preparatory training for blind retrieves to the right and left, we can point to the right or left when the dog stops and makes contact during a walk, to indicate which direction we are going to walk. At that time, it can be a good idea to point the dog in the direction you think she wants to go. When the dog moves in the right direction, we can either reward her by throwing a ball, running up to her with a treat, or just continuing in that direction while naturally verbally praising her.

Coach Says

You can start with exercises to train blind retrieves when the dog is a puppy. Sit on the floor with the dog between your legs. Scoot a bowl with a few treats in it along the floor and hold the puppy until she sits calmly looking at the bowl. Release the puppy and cue "back". Later on, you can add a hand signal, so the dog looks towards the bowl when you point at it.

We often bring one or two toys on walks and use them to train blind retrieves by "accidentally" dropping them and then directing the dog to fetch them. We only do this when we know that the dog has mastered deliveries. Initially the dog gets to see us drop the object, and as she becomes better at blind retrieves we drop the object without her seeing it.

Casting without Delivery

To avoid having to deal with deliveries and retrieves and only train casting, we can initially direct the dog to targets or food bowls.

It can be useful to train with an extremely large target, such as a bath mat, so the dog can clearly see it. The important thing now is not for the dog to stand on the target, but that she runs towards it. You can also use a stick or an upright plastic bottle that she can clearly see. Begin to teach the dog

Elsa and Diesel

to go to the target at short distances. Click for looking at the target, moving towards it and eventually stepping on it or touching it with her nose.

Once the dog understands what to do, you can increase her desire for the target by keeping a light hold on her collar until you feel that she really wants to go to it. It should feel like releasing a taut rubber band.

As the dog improves at this exercise, you can gradually increase the distance. Switch between rewarding the dog on or near the target and having her come back to you to get her reward.

Spaniels

While hunting, spaniels should work within the gun range, a maximum of 20 yards from the handler. However, during a blind retrieve or to fetch injured game, the dog is allowed to go outside the area. Blind retrieves are usually placed not more than 20-50 yards from the handler. Adapt the exercises in this chapter according to the distances that apply to spaniels.

Casting with Bowls

The advantage of using bowls is that the dog gets her reward immediately when she arrives at the goal. Treat bowls often foster a very strong desire to run out, but you can also use targets or objects if the dog likes that better. Depending on which signal you want to train, place the bowls on opposite sides of the dog. It's easiest to start with lining, meaning that the dog runs straight out from your left side. To begin teaching the dog to run a line using food bowls, do the following:[28]

---

28 We have borrowed this exercise from Eva Bodfäldt, www.evabodfaldt.com.

1. Keep the dog on your left side. Have your helper set the food bowl down one to two yards away (and lift it up should the dog run in).

2. When the dog looks at the food bowl, cue "go ahead". If necessary, your helper can show the dog that there is something tasty in the bowl.

3. If the dog leaves immediately when you cue "go ahead", start cueing "back" followed by "go ahead". When you notice that the dog responds to "back", stop giving the "go ahead" cue.

4. When the dog responds immediately and solely to your "back" cue, add the hand signal. Hold out your hand and send the dog when she looks straight at the bowl (in the direction of the hand).

5. Increase the distraction (i.e. having your helper do something fun). Reward the dog with a "back" when she stays.

6. The next step is signal control. Now we want to teach the dog to only run out when we cue "back", and not, for example, when we say "cucumber". Say a nonsense word and reward the dog with "back" or a treat from your hand if she remains sitting beside you. She should also be able to sit and wait beside you before you give the cue.

Tinna shows Speed the bowl.

Emma cues "go ahead" when Speed looks at the bowl.

Once you've gotten this far, you can make the training more advanced in a few different ways. Preferably train all of the different steps in parallel:

- Increase the distance. Retrievers should eventually be able to go 50-100 yards straight out (in the US sometimes even 300 yards or more). For spaniels, 40-50 yards is sufficient (spaniels can obviously go further, but usually it's not necessary).
- Practice having the dog go straight over obstacles in her path, such as a stonewall or fallen trees. Start near the obstacle and then back further and further away from it.
- In the same way, the dog should be able to swim straight over water and go straight into water (i.e. not start running back and forth on the shore).

Be sure to cast the dog when she looks at the bowl, before she has time to look at you. Usually, we train the dogs to focus on us and look at us to gain permission to do something, but now we want her to look straight ahead instead. The first few times you train with the food bowl, you might want to cast the dog precisely when your helper sets the bowl down. Then you can wait a little longer before you cast the dog, but not so long that she has time to look at you.

Be silent except for the casting cue, "go ahead" and praise. If something goes wrong, ask your helper to lift up the bowl or allow the dog to take the rewards anyway. It's not the end of the world if the dog manages to take the reward once or twice. It's better than getting angry with her. Prior to the next repetition, simplify the exercise to set the dog up for success.

Vary how you set out the bowl. Sometimes the dog must sit and watch when you put it on the ground, and other times she can walk with you (on your left side on or off leash, depending on how far you have come with your heelwork). If you have the dog with you remember to put the bowl down when the dog is walking properly so that the dog gets to move forward in the exercise as a reward.

> ## Coach Says
> Make sure that your dog is sitting straight by your side, otherwise she will run on a crooked line during blind retrieves. Initially, you can cue the dog to sit, put yourself in the correct position next to her and ask your helper to move the bowl, so that it's straight in front of you. You can then work separately on training the dog to come in quickly and sit straight at your side.

Casting with Objects

When we know the dog has mastered deliveries and she enjoys running straight out to a bowl or target, we begin to replace these with objects. We use toys or dummies that the dog gets to run and fetch. Then we alternate between sometimes sending the dog to a target or a food bowl and sometimes to an object. Don't train for several months with only food bowls. Instead start weaving other objects into your training at quite an early stage. We follow the same steps with objects that we previously outlined with food bowl casting. However, if we did a good job with the

Vendela teaches Olle push backs by placing the bowl behind him.

food bowls or target training, the dog already has a good understanding that the cue means to run straight out. In that case, we might be able to skip some of the steps. If the dog's deliveries start to get sloppy, we stop training casting with objects and return to training with the target or bowl and work on deliveries separately.

Combining Casting with the Stop Whistle

Once you've begun training the dog to respond to the stop whistle, you can combine it with casting exercises to a target or food bowl. Stand with the dog next to you. Put the whistle in your mouth, so you have it ready. Send the dog and when she has eaten the rewards in the bowl, blow your stop whistle and reward the dog for making contact with you (or for sitting, depending on your chosen stop whistle behavior). Keep in mind the dog should stay at the bowl, not move towards you. It's a good idea to reward the dog behind the bowl, either by giving a treat, throwing a ball or running over and playing with her.

If you know you can send the dog to the food bowl from 20 yards away, but the stop whistle works only five yards away, you can either keep training on the stop signal separately or put something messy in the food bowl, such as cream cheese, so it takes the dog some time to eat it. While the dog is eating, move closer, close enough that the stop signal will work when the dog has finished eating. By "sneaking" closer while the dog eats and combining that with working on the stop whistle and then gradually increasing the distance, your dog will respond to the stop whistle at greater and greater distances. The bowl thus also becomes a kind of target where the dog learns to stay.

Pitfall
Remember to keep the hand you signal with steady so you don't distract the dog just as she's about to run out. Place your hand slightly in front of your dog at her eye level so she has a clear line towards where she's going. Have the whistle ready in your mouth as soon as you send the dog.

Keep in mind that the dog must run straight ahead with her nose held high and not start searching until you blow the hunt whistle. If you switch to hidden bowls too early, i.e. the bowls the dog didn't see you put out, or if the dog doesn't find the bowls right away but instead starts searching for them, you may run into trouble with the dog running with her nose low to the ground. If you notice that the dog puts her nose down, do a couple of repetitions when you are absolutely sure the dog knows where the bowl is and will run straight to it.

In reality, we will not get completely straight lines and right angles, but at short distances, we make sure the dog will go perfectly straight in order to get her to go as straight as possible later when the distances increase. The dog should run straight, even over obstacles such as stonewalls, streams and trails.

To make it easier on yourself, you can put out bowls next to different landmarks, so you can see where to send the dog. In open spaces you can use bamboo sticks with red or green post-it notes. You can also train yourself to identify landmarks in open areas. This can be quite difficult and requires a lot of practice.

Coach Says
A tube of cream cheese is an excellent reward to smear in the bowls or have in your pocket on walks.

Right, Left and Back

When we cast the dog to the right and left it's always our right and left that counts (see illustration on next page).

Blind Retrieves

The dog has her nose pointed towards us so she can both see and hear which direction we want to send her in. If the terrain is overgrown and challenging, it's good to have trained with just the verbal cue so you can direct the dog even when she can't see you – and you might not see the dog. During field trials, you are allowed to move around much more and make more sweeping gestures than during obedience competitions and the judge will indicate if you've moved too much. When you signal to the right or left, start with an upright hand and then indicate the right or left. You can even take a step in that direction at the same time making your signal even clearer. The push back signal is easiest to do with one hand above your head and then you move your hand towards the dog and spread out your fingers as you give your verbal cue. The advantage of doing it with one hand is that you can teach the dog to turn to the right or left depending on which hand you direct her with and hence you get more precision in the retrieve. Practice without the dog, perhaps in front of a mirror, so you can find signals that feel comfortable for you and are clear to the dog. You can use whatever verbal cues you want. We think it's easier to say "right" and "left", but we also know handlers who say "away" and "lost", or "get on" and "get out".

Coach Says

When you start to put a stop whistle together with blind retrieve make sure to signal the stop with the same hand you use to sen the dog. If you are sending the dog to the right after the stop whistle, put up your right hand when you blow the stop whistle That way you are prepared for the blind retrieve and don't need switch hands before you can send the dog.

To teach the dog the signal to go to the right, put the bowl to the right of the dog (from your perspective). Then, stand in front of your dog, a few yards from her, and cast the dog to the right with a hand signal, and cue "go ahead". When the dog takes off immediately on the hand signal and "go ahead", you can start to cue "right" followed by "go ahead" and eventually a hand signal and your verbal cue to go right will be enough. Do the same thing to teach the signal you use to direct the dog to go to the left.

The push back cue tells the dog "turn back and run away from the handler". You can teach the dog the signal by placing the bowl behind the dog, so the dog is sitting between you and the bowl. This is often the trickiest signal to teach because the dog must remove her focus from the bowl and face you before you cast her.

When you work on the push back cue, it may be helpful to have a helper set the bowl down for you. When you cast your dog your helper can move the bowl slightly the first few times so the dog understands where to go. Start with short distances, only one to two yards the first few times. Then gradually extend the range, so your retriever is able run 50-100 yards to the right, left, or back. For spaniels, game doesn't usually fall further away from them than

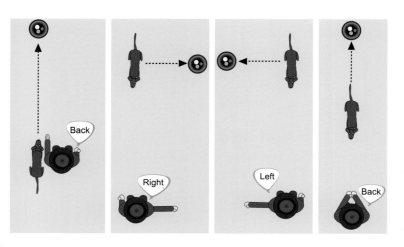

The illustration shows how you can teach the dog to run straight out from your side to the right, left and further back (backwards from the dog's perspective since she is facing you). When you are going to line the dog from a heel position, you are facing the same direction, but when you are going to cast the dog to the right, left or further back, the dog is facing you.

maybe 20-50 yards. If the distance is more remote, often the handler is allowed to walk forward a bit with the dog.

We like to train the various directions in parallel, so the dog doesn't learn to always go in the same direction. When the dog has mastered the casting signals with targets or bowls and also has mastered the delivery, we do the same thing with objects. Simply place an object, such as a toy or a dummy, in the same way as you did the bowl. At first, you might need to repeat deliveries a few times.

Coach Says
It's good to be able to direct the dog to the right or left, but straight lines are more important because the dog will then be able to find the correct destination without having to be redirected.

Once the dog has mastered the stop whistle, an extremely effective training method to teach the casting signals is to set out three to five bowls in a row, with 10-20 yards between them to start with. It's important the dog responds to the stop whistle so she doesn't run to the next bowl before you cue "go ahead". The first few times you do this, you can choose to put a reward only in the first bowl and leave the second bowl empty. If the dog doesn't listen to your stop whistle after the first bowl, she won't be rewarded if she continues to the second bowl. To train the left signal, position yourself according to the illustration below and send the dog. While the dog enjoys her reward, move so you end up

in front of her again and are ready for the next repetition. You can do the same thing with the right and back signals.

Coach Says
Remember to reduce the distance somewhat or show the dog there is something to run to every time you switch to a new environment until the dog has properly learned blind retrieves.

Increasing the Distance
Remember to begin increasing the distance quite early in your training so you don't get into a rut by always training at the same distance. Putting out cones or poles is a good way to mark your training range.

1. Put out several poles in a straight line with 20 yards between them.
2. Place an object or a bowl of treats at the farthest pole.
3. Have the dog sit between the farthest pole and the next pole.
4. Stand near the next pole and cast the dog back.

The illustration shows how you can train multiple casting signals in a row. Start by casting the dog to the left. After each repetition, move so you are once again opposite the dog and thus have a perpendicular line to the next bowl.

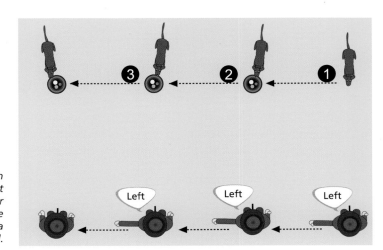

When this works, vary between one of these difficulties at a time:

- The distance between the dog and the farthest pole.
- The distance between you and the pole.
- Distractions.

When you add distractions, you may need to reduce the distance again. You can also have the dog sit between you and the farthest pole, do a recall, stop her and then cast her back out again. If you want to do the same thing with the left and right signals, you can put out more poles, such as a grid with nine poles, or rotate the whole exercise 90 degrees to cast the dog to the right or left to the same area as before.[29]

Blind Retrieves during Field Trials

For retrievers, blind retrieves become more and more important as they progress up to higher stakes. In some countries blind retrieves aren't a part of the field trial or hunt test for Novice and Junior Stakes. In the open stakes and advanced stakes the retrieve distances increase greatly, and there are higher demands on accuracy. You need to be able to cast the dog in all directions: back, right, left, and further back as well as coming forward hunting. We refer to the regulations in your country for more information.

For spaniels, blind retrieves are not as important, but if needed the handler should be able to cast the dog during field trials. We think, however, that blind retrieves are fun and also a good exercise to teach the dog to pay attention to your signals. So, we spend both time and energy on teaching our dogs – even spaniels – to master the blind retrieve.

For more information on blind retrieves at field trials, check the rules and regulations in your country

[29] We have borrowed this exercise from Philippa Williams, www.dogsforlife.co.uk.

Support Cues

If necessary, you can support your dog by repeating your cue or "yes" to indicate that she's on the right path. It's especially useful for your dog to understand support cues at greater distances or if there is an obstacle in her path. Be careful so you don't start to nag, however. Use them in moderation to provide support only when necessary. You are allowed to use support cues during field trials, so we don't need to make the task harder than it already is for the dog should she lose focus or hesitate. If you discover that your dog becomes totally dependent on your support cues, take a step back in your training and work on more visible lines so the dog becomes reliable at running out straight.

Catharina and Sam

Blind Retrieves

The end goal is that the dog should be able to go out on blind retrieves, in other words that the dog goes where we ask her to, even if she doesn't know if there's anything there. When the dog is confident with bowls and objects she knows are there, you can start working with bowls or objects that the dog hasn't seen in advance. Make the transition gradual. For instance, you might let the dog see you put out a bowl and then go for a little walk before casting the dog to the bowl. You can also send the dog to a bowl she saw you put out and then have the dog come back to you while a helper fills the bowl with treats out of the dog's sight. Then, cast the dog to the same bowl again.

Do longer casts with bowls and objects the dog knows about (50-100 yards for retrievers, shorter for spaniels). In the beginning, make blind retrieves much shorter, maybe 10-20 yards, so the dog quickly gets rewarded for trusting your signal and running out.

You can also try to cast the dog out into "nothing", as in the game described at the beginning of this chapter, and reward the dog by throwing a treat or a ball over her head. Be sure the dog is facing ahead the whole time so she doesn't turn around to check where the reward is coming from.

If the dog doesn't run out, you have made it too difficult. Find a pleasant way to interrupt the exercise and make it easier the next time. Spend even more time working on long memory retrieves and cast the dog on a blind retrieve in conjunction with the memory retrieves you've been practicing. You can also use the wind to your advantage so that the dog gets to catch the scent of the object when she has only gone a short distance. The dog will then probably run all the way. Sometimes you can take a chance and see if you can cast the dog again, but absolutely don't make a habit of it.

Memory Marks

You can also teach the dog to run out on a blind retrieve by throwing a mark and waiting a moment before you cast the dog or by casting her from an entirely different direction. The first few times the dog depends most on what she just saw, but as you wait longer to send the dog the memory of the mark begins to fade. In this case, we don't want the dog to depend too much on sight (then it becomes a mark) but we take advantage of the attraction that sight has. When the dog isn't allowed to retrieve a mark at once, the exercise turns into a memory retrieve.

It's often very easy for dogs to learn to go to a specific spot. We will use this in the next exercise.

1. Ask a helper to throw a mark in an area.
2. While the dog is running back to you, your helper should sneak another dummy into the same area (as we described with food bowls before).
3. Send the dog on a straight line back to the area where she just was. Because the dog has just been there, she will find the area and have an easier time running out.

Start with a fairly short range (10-20 yards) and then increase the distance gradually. Remember to change the destination often, so the dog doesn't become fixated on just going to a specific spot.

The following exercises are perhaps a bit on the difficult side, but we start by describing the basics. These exercises are both fun and useful.

Working Through the Area of the Fall

The purpose of this exercise is to teach the dog to run through an area that she's previously found interesting (see illustration below).[30]

1. Have the dog accompany you when you set out an object.
2. Place yourselves about 20 yards away.
3. Throw a mark that lands five yards from you and the dog, between you and the object that you just laid out.
4. Have the dog retrieve the mark.
5. Then cast the dog back out to retrieve the first object.

There's a risk that the dog will start searching in the previous area of the fall. If this happens, call the dog, walk a little closer and send her out again. Alternatively, you can ask your helper to pick up the object to show the dog where it is.

One way to make the exercise easier is to throw the mark diagonally to the left and have the dog retrieve it and then cast the dog 90 degrees to the right.

To make this exercise more and more difficult, simply increase the distances. This exercise is primarily intended for retrievers but spaniels can also benefit from it.

Using the Area of the Fall for Blind Retrieves

This exercise helps us train blind retrieves in an area the dog already knows.[31] The purpose is to get the dog used to going where we point without searching in the previous area of the fall (see illustration on next page):

1. Set an object out so the dog sees it.
2. Walk 20 yards away from the object, turn 90 degrees to the right and walk 20 more yards.
3. Now imagine that you and the dog, the object, and the spot where you made the 90-degree turn form a triangle. Stand facing the 90-degree corner, so the object lays diagonally to your left.

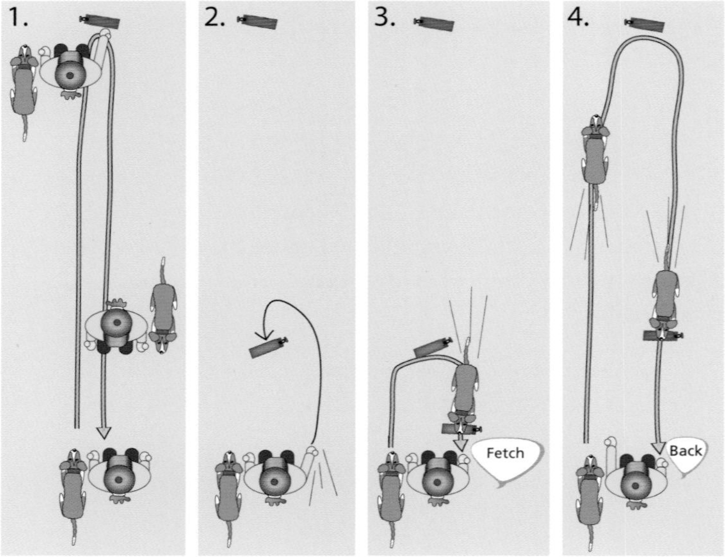

---

30 & 31 We borrowed this exercise from Katarina Eriksson, www.kopparhult.se.

The illustration shows how you can teach the dog to work through the previous area of the fall.

4. Throw a mark to the corner. Have the dog retrieve the mark.

5. Cast the dog to the area of the fall again, blow the stop whistle and send the dog to the left to the first object.

Scent Trails

If you go straight to the bowl or the dummy, and then take the same route back, you leave a scent trail the dog can make use of. This is great at first, but eventually you need to fade this so the dog can run on pristine ground, with no scent to help her. Walk, therefore, in a bow to put the bowl out or the dummy and take the same route back (see illustration below). Cast the dog so she runs somewhere you didn't walk. Make sure the wind is blowing away from the area where you want the dog to run.

The illustration shows how you can use a previous area of the fall for memory retrieves.

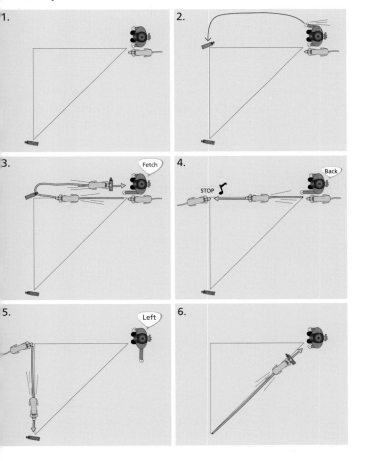

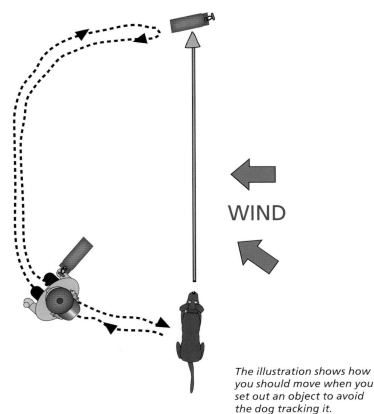

The illustration shows how you should move when you set out an object to avoid the dog tracking it.

Wind in Real Life

When we train blind retrieves, we try to cast the dog as straight as possible, which means the dog runs the most direct route to the dummy and almost stumbles on it when we blow the hunt whistle. In reality, the wind will play a large role (see illustration below). If there are strong crosswinds, it might be a good idea to send your dog at an angle away from the dummy, with a tailwind, so the dog can catch the scent when she's even with the dummy. If we send the dog straight out or at an angle so she ends up on the wrong side of the dummy relative to the wind, the dog will have a hard time finding the dummy when we blow the hunt whistle.

Putting It All Together

When you've gotten started with training blind retrieves, heelwork and holding an area, there are endless possibilities for using bowls to combine them. Put two bowls out, send the dog to one of them, blow the stop whistle (when the dog has finished eating) and send the dog to the next bowl, and so on. Gradually, you can replace a bowl with a dummy, so you might have three bowls and a dummy laid out. The chain eventually becomes "back" – reward – stop whistle – reward. We can choose between going up to the dog to reward her and casting her to the next bowl or dummy as a reward.

There is also a lot you can do with four bowls in a square (see illustration on the next page). You can bring in a little heelwork and cast the dog out to bowl number one in front of you as a reward, then blow the stop whistle and cast the dog to the left to bowl two. While the dog is eating, move so the dog ends up between you and bowl three. Then cast the dog to bowl three. When the dog has finished eating call her to you, then cast her in a line to bowl four and blow the hunt whistle so she can find the dummy and deliver it to you.

You can also combine food bowls and targets. The advantage of using targets here is that you can more easily build chains and teach the dog to work for longer periods of time before she gets her reward.

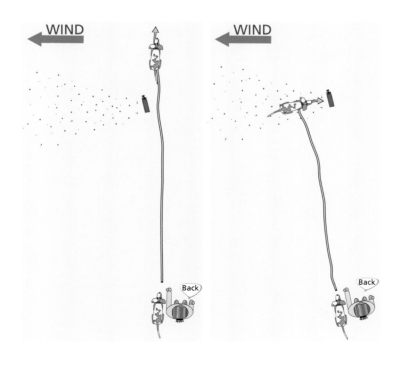

The illustration shows how the wind can affect scents. Keep the direction of the wind in mind when you cast the dog so that she actually has a chance to catch the object's scent.

Remember to occasionally place the bowls so the dog also gets to work on changes in terrain, for example crossing a stream, shifting from field to forest, or crossing a path out of a marsh. We want the dog to learn to go straight when we send her regardless of the terrain.

The illustrations on the following pages provide some suggestions for how to set up your training. Vary the distances and the level of difficulty to suit you and your dog.

Gradually, you can start casting the dog out to "nothing", blow the stop whistle, and cast the dog to the right or left to find a food bowl with a reward or a dummy to retrieve to you.

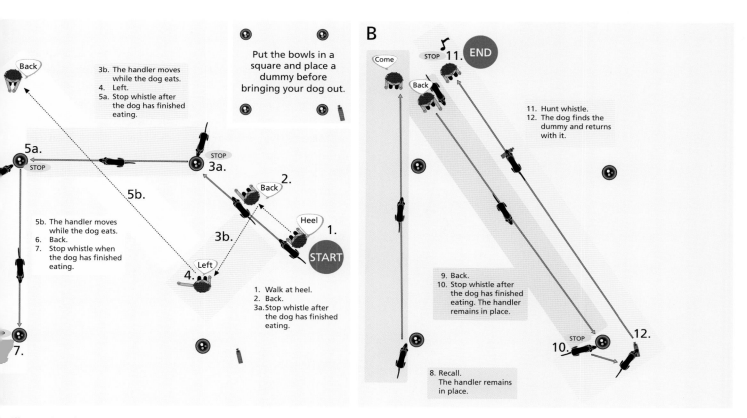

Put the bowls in a square and place a dummy before bringing your dog out.

3b. The handler moves while the dog eats.
4. Left.
5a. Stop whistle after the dog has finished eating.

5b. The handler moves while the dog eats.
6. Back.
7. Stop whistle when the dog has finished eating.

1. Walk at heel.
2. Back.
3a. Stop whistle after the dog has finished eating.

B

11. Hunt whistle.
12. The dog finds the dummy and returns with it.

9. Back.
10. Stop whistle after the dog has finished eating. The handler remains in place.

8. Recall. The handler remains in place.

e illustration shows a suggested training plan once the dog has learned the basics of casting. Start th the dog at point 1. After the cast, the handler remains in place and sends the dog further out. ter cast 2 the handler moves to point 4 to make the next cast.

Blind Retrieves

The illustration shows how you can use three bowls to train the recall, heelwork, casting, and the stop whistle.

1. Walk at heel towards the bowl.
2. Cast the dog to the bowl.
3. Blow the stop whistle when the dog has finished eating.
4. Walk at heel towards the next bowl.
5. Cast the dog to the bowl.
6. Blow the stop whistle when the dog has finished eating.
7. Move and then call the dog.
8. Cast the dog to the bowl.
9. Blow the stop whistle when the dog has finished eating.
10. Go up to the dog and reward the stop whistle.

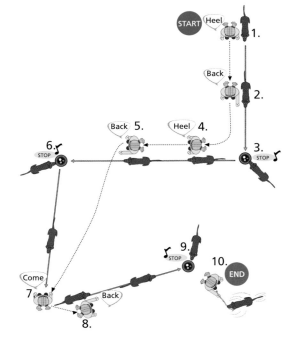

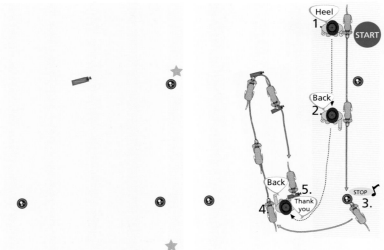

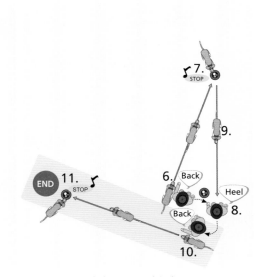

Challenge: Walking at heel near bowls

The illustration shows how you can use three bowls and a dummy to train heelwork, cast out, and the stop whistle.

1. Walk at heel past the first bowl.
2. Cast the dog to the next bowl.
3. Blow the stop whistle when the dog has finished eating, at the same time, go up to your dog.
4. Cast the dog on a straight line to the dummy.
5. Receive the dummy.
6. Cast the dog to the bowl.
7. Blow the stop whistle when the dog has finished eating.
8. Call the dog.
9. Call the dog.
10. Cast the dog to the last bowl.
11. Blow the stop whistle when the dog has finished eating.

Challenge: Working near water

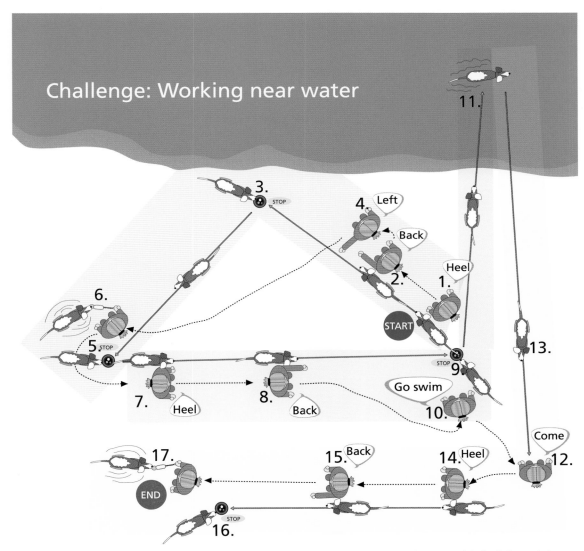

The illustration shows how you can use four bowls to train heelwork, casting, the stop whistle, left, and the recall.

1. Walk at heel towards the bowl.

2. Cast the dog to the bowl.

3. Blow the stop whistle when the dog has finished eating.

4. Cast the dog to the left to the next bowl.

5. Blow the stop whistle when the dog has finished eating.

6. Go up to the dog and reward the stop whistle.

7. Walk at heel to the next bowl.

8. Cast the dog to the bowl.

9. Blow the stop whistle when the dog has finished eating.

10. Go up to the dog and give her permission to go swimming.

11. The dog swims.

12. & 13. Call the dog.

14. Walk at heel towards the bowl.

15. Cast the dog to the bowl.

16. Blow the stop whistle when the dog has finished eating.

17. Go up to the dog and reward the stop whistle.

The Clock

Using bowls, targets, or objects, you can do the classic "Clock" exercise.[32] (see illustration below). Put the dog in the middle and set out three bowls at 3, 9 and 12 o'clock. Then position yourself at 6 o'clock. From here you can then send the dog in any direction and let her finish her treat, change your position and send the dog again or call her. Then have the dog sit in the middle and send her again.

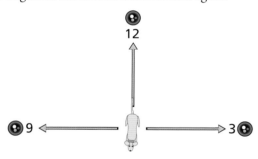

The illustrations show how to set up "the Clock" using bowls.

Blind Retrieves with Distractions

To ensure your dog has mastered blind retrieves, you need to incorporate distraction training. The exercises we described earlier under "Memory Marks" are just a start. Other ways to incorporate distraction training are to have a helper distract the dog on her run out by saying "hello", clapping, or playing with a ball. You can also throw out a mark or a ball along the line the dog is to run. Praise the dog for taking note of where the mark or ball fell and then turn back towards the

line. Cast the dog and as a reward for a straight run out, you can either give her a reward or allow her to look for the ball or mark.

Reduce the distance between the distraction and the line the dog is to run more and more until you are sure the dog will always run straight, even if something else is happening on the side of what. We praise the dog for noticing where the object lands because we always want her to keep track of where things end up. Then it's important for us to be able to cast the dog where we want, and that she doesn't go to the mark. See the illustration below for several suggestions of distraction training.

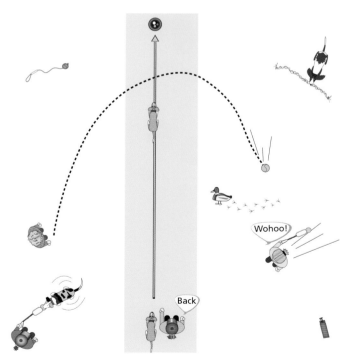

The illustration shows how to cast the dog on a straight line with various distractions. Start with a single distraction and then make it progressively more difficult.

---

[32] We borrowed this exercise from Sten Christoffersson, www.naturredaktionen.se.

Challenge

Set out four bowls 30 yards apart in a square with a fence or stonewall running diagonally through the square (see illustration). Start at the bottom left bowl with walking at heel. Send the dog straight out to the upper left bowl. Blow the stop whistle. Send the dog to the right over the stonewall to the upper right bowl. Blow the stop whistle. Go up to your dog and send her to the bowl that was the previous lower left bowl (where you started – in other words, the dog must run past the lower right bowl on the way). Blow the stop whistle, move so you are standing at what was the previous top left bowl, and send the dog left to the last bowl (see illustration below).

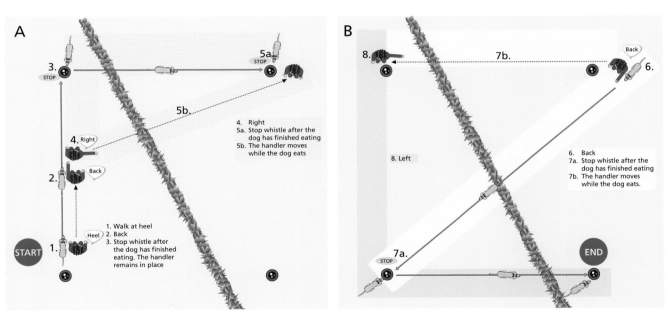

A

3. STOP

5a. STOP

5b.

4. Right

2. Back

4. Right
5a. Stop whistle after the dog has finished eating
5b. The handler moves while the dog eats

Heel

START 1.

1. Walk at heel
2. Back
3. Stop whistle after the dog has finished eating. The handler remains in place

B

8. Left

7b.

Back
6.

8. Left

6. Back
7a. Stop whistle after the dog has finished eating
7b. The handler moves while the dog eats.

7a. STOP

END

The illustration shows a casting challenge you can try with your dog.

Sub-goals – Blind Retrieves	Completed
Straight out from your side	
Focus in the direction of the hand	
Right, left, push back	
Longer distances	
Different types of terrain	
Over obstacles (walls, tree trunks, streams, paths)	
Retrieve and deliver objects	
In water	
With distractions (such as passing by other objects, other dogs, or a strong wind)	

Summary

- Train the casting signals using bowls or targets you set out in different ways in relation to the dog.
- Using food bowls, you can vary and train the dog to follow the various casting signals, the recall, walk heel and hold an area.
- Teach the dog to go straight over obstacles such as stonewalls, streams, trails, and fallen trees.
- Teach the dog to go straight in the direction you are pointing through different kinds of terrain: meadow forests, grass, and clear-cut areas.

Hunting

While hunting the dog works more independently from her handler than during her other work. It's also what differs the most between spaniels and retrievers. Spaniels hunt to flush game so the shooter can shoot it while retrievers hunt to retrieve after the shot, i.e. sweeping up. The spaniel's most important work is prior to the shot, even if they also perform simple retrieves and preferably can be trained to perform all the various skills involved.

Retrievers should independently hunt a large area in front of the handler and retrieve whatever game they find. During that time, the handler remains at the starting point. Spaniels are to cover the ground in front of and to the side of the handler in a zigzag or figure eight pattern while they slowly move forward (also known as quartering). Since hunting is different for retrievers and spaniels, we'll introduce what is required for each breed and then conclude by describing what they have in common.

Play to Inspire Hunting

However, the first thing we do with both spaniels and retrievers is to use a variety of ways to encourage them to follow scents of objects, both indoors and on walks. If you've previously trained the dog to hold an area using objects, she's likely already somewhat interested in following scents and finding objects. You then already have good basis for more advanced hunting.

1. Hide one of the dog's favorite toys in a wooded area (without the dog's knowledge). Leave the toy partially covered, for instance under a bit of moss, but so the dog can still easily catch its scent.

2. Take the dog for a regular "walk in the woods", in other words give the dog her release cue and let her run around as usual (this exercise can also be done with the dog on leash).

3. When you see that the dog has caught the scent, wait until she finds the toy, or if necessary show interest yourself, and gently encourage the dog, "What have you found? Do you have something there?"

4. When the dog finds the toy, give her a lot of praise and then start playing with her.

5. You can gradually start to wait a bit when the dog finds the toy so she picks it up and brings it to you (depending on how far your dog has come with the delivery training).

You can gradually increase the distance between yourself and the hidden toy. This is particularly applicable to retrievers. With a spaniel, you shouldn't allow the dog to quarter more than five to ten yards away from you. You can also start putting out several objects. When the dog has found the first one, brought it to you and you've had a few moments of play, you can continue your walk and the dog can find another object.

Hunting For Retrievers – Sweeping Up

In some countries sweeping up is a part of the field trial for the retrievers, whereas in other countries it isn't, instead it can be done after the trial, outside the competition, or after the hunt is completed. Retrievers work in an area that can be from approximately 50x50 yards to 100x100 yards in front of the handler. During some trials, the judge assigns an area, for example "from the birch to the stonewall", where you are to keep the dog. You are allowed to move around a little bit, which can be a smart way to get the dog to feel confident to hunt in a new area, but if you go too far the judge will let you know.

The dog should preferably sweep up an area close to you first and then work her way out since that is the most efficient way to find the objects. If you walk in a line with other handlers and shooters, you will know when you can move the line forward since there won't be any game left to find there.

Hunting Using Visual Stimuli

One way to teach the dog to hunt is to use a visual stimulus, in other words letting the dog see someone place the object she should find:

1. Have your dog sit, ask a helper to hold her, or tie her up, whichever works best. The point is that the dog sees that something is being placed in the area. Have a helper plant the dummy or do it yourself. If necessary, you or your helper can make noise and stomp around in the hunt area to make the dog really interested.

2. Then cue the dog "go ahead" to start hunting.

3. If additional visual stimuli are necessary for the dog to go out and hunt, get her going with the object, run away with it and put it on the ground. Then send the dog out immediately.

4. When you know the dog will run out and hunt, you can start to cue "go find it – go ahead" and finally just "go find it" so it's the only cue for the behavior.

Judge Låtta points out the hunt area for Ingela and Snoddas.

You should do this both on a ground full of scents from both people and dogs as well as on pristine ground without any scents (meaning that nobody – human or dog – has been moving around there). To prevent the dog from tracking the object, that is to say walk with her nose in the footsteps of those who planted the object, you can either train on scent rich ground or walk away a few yards before throwing the object so there isn't a scent trail leading to it. We do, after all, want the dog to hunt, that is to say systematically run back and forth in the area looking for objects.

As soon as possible, we want to reduce the stimuli so the dog is able to hunt an area even when she hasn't seen anything being laid out. Initially the dog probably won't use her nose so much because she sees the object, but as soon as you start to hide the object the dog will become all the more dependent on her nose. In the beginning it's a good idea to just place out one object so the dog learns to look thoroughly in order to find it. In addition, you avoid having the dog accidently find something should she continue to hunt with an object in her mouth. If you or your helper have covered a lot of ground in the hunt area, or planted objects, the dog may become more interested in running there instead of coming in with the first object she finds. Pay attention to how your dog reacts. If you notice a tendency for her to keep hunting with the object in her mouth or if she lets go of it to check out the other spots, you need to make your training easier. You should also spend more time training deliveries so the dog turns back to you as soon as she has something in her mouth.

Coach Says
When you use stimuli to get the dog to go out, you should make the area a little bigger and more challenging than when you don't use stimuli in order to get the maximum benefit. Try to fade the stimuli as quickly as possible.

Increase the Distance and Reduce the Stimulus

Now we have worked on hunting using a visual stimulus for a while, but during trials, no such stimulus exists. Instead, we have to get the dog to go out and hunt without a visual stimulus. We must also expand the hunt area so the dog looks elsewhere than in our immediate vicinity. A good way to reduce the stimulus and increase the size of the hunt area is to use the same area several times: first place the objects using visual stimuli and then without. In this way, we exploit the fact that the dog has already been far out in that area and has discovered there are things to find there.

Ellen watches while Jeanethe places an object in the hunt area.

We begin by doing the following:[33]

1. Have a helper walk around the hunt area and place one or two dummies in predetermined locations (mark them with trail-marking ribbons) so the dog sees it. Preferably set the dummies out over a large area, 50 to 100 yards deep. Have your helper leave his or her scent all over the area by walking back and forth so that the dog is unable to track her way to the objects. If you don't have a helper, you can do this yourself, but you have to leave the dog at a place where she's still able to see what you are doing. Send the dog to hunt. If she easily retrieves both dummies, proceed to the next step, otherwise repeat this first step again. Leave the trail-marking ribbons for the next time so that you can place the dummies in the same place again.

2. Next time (preferably the day after) your helper can place the dummies in the same spots, but without the dog seeing it this time. Send the dog out to hunt. If the dog easily retrieves both dummies, proceed to the next step. Otherwise repeat the previous step again.

3. Place dummies in new locations in the same area out of the dog's sight and send the dog to hunt. Then try standing on different sides of the area and send the dog to the same area. When you get to a new area, you can go through all three steps again. You can occasionally experiment to see if the dog plunges right in without a visual stimulus (that is, starting with the last step). If that's the case, you can remove the visual stimulus completely.

Using the Wind

Think about the wind already during your first hunting exercises. Depending on how the wind blows, the dog will have an easier or more difficult time catching a scent. Gradually the dog will learn how to use the wind, but in the beginning you have to set up the exercise so that she can more easily take advantage of the wind. Understanding the effect of wind is an entire science. Following a few simple rules of thumb will still go a long way. A strong wind or no wind at all makes things difficult for the dog. Scents are also affected by how hilly the terrain is and how dry or wet the ground is. If the ground is dry, the scent will blow away a lot more easily. In addition, a moderately strong wind can blow almost all the scent far away from the object the dog is to find. This might confuse an inexperienced dog, but after a while she'll learn to follow the scent to find the object. Observe your dog: What kind of wind and terrain does she find easiest or most challenging?

Once the dog has started to hunt well in favorable wind conditions, send the dog out to hunt in slightly more challenging conditions. The easiest condition for the dog

to hunt in is a moderate headwind, since all of the scent is then blowing towards the dog. The most difficult condition is if there is a downwind or crosswind and she is on the wrong side of the game or the object she's looking for.

Teaching Independent Hunting

If your dog stops and looks at you while she's hunting, don't look at her or encourage her to keep working. Wait and see what she does. Hopefully, she'll get back to work. Then you can either reward your dog by calling her or by ensuring that she soon finds something by either getting lucky and finding something that is already laid out or if you throw out a new object without her seeing it. You shouldn't encourage the dog in this situation because we want her to learn to hunt independently. If you encourage the dog every time she stops and looks at you, she will seek more and more support from you.

If the dog comes back to you, sits down, and doesn't return to work voluntarily, you can try walking out with the dog and encouraging her to continue, but only once. We don't want to do this again if the problem isn't resolved immediately, because then the dog learns to turn to us for support. You can also try to walk a few yards further into the hunt area, without saying anything to the dog. Keep looking out towards the hunt area and see if the dog starts hunting again. This of course can also become a crutch, so be careful not to overuse it. If that doesn't work, you have to make things a little easier for the dog next time. Spend more time working on fostering your dog's interest in objects so she really wants to find the objects. Use visual stimuli while hunting so the dog will venture out several times. Then try to successively fade the stimulus again.

Elsa's dog Diesel enjoyed and was somewhat experienced in sweeping up. Elsa then wanted to expand Diesel's sweeping up by adding more items and consequently developing her endurance. She would happily retrieve one or two dummies, but then she came back empty handed (i.e. without objects). Elsa would then stand and study the hunt area. The first time Diesel came all the way in and sat down beside Elsa. "Okay then", Elsa said. "Let's go home." The second time Diesel understood that it paid to continue – otherwise the fun would end. We wouldn't have used this approach with a dog that didn't have a real urge to sweep up. But it can work well on a dog that loves to work and will get fired up instead of dejected by not being allowed to get back to work.

Coach Says

Plan your dummy placement so the dog will actually learn what you intended. Should she take the dummies closest to you first? Then place the majority of the dummies close to you and just a few further out. Do you want the dog to learn to use the wind? Send the dog so she finds the dummies when she's really using the wind. When you are training the dog to hunt, you can make the task trickier and trickier with just a few well hidden dummies. As a result, hunting during competition will be easier for the dog, as there is quite a lot of game to be found but the dog will be used to really having to work during the hunt. Training = difficult and competition = easy!

Always send the dog when she's looking out into the hunt area (but is still responsive to you) and not when she's looking at you. You can also "point out" the area to the dog, i.e. show her which area you want her to hunt, when she is a little more experienced.

The dog should always hunt in front of the handler. In the beginning we make sure there is never anything to find behind us. If the dog goes the wrong way, we'll call her or use our turn signal. As the dog becomes more proficient, we can make a distraction exercise of it:

1. First, we have the dog (or a friend's dog if we want to make the exercise even more difficult) retrieve a mark behind us (meaning we stand so the hunt area is to our back).
2. Then we turn around and send out the dog to hunt again. If the dog seeks out the area behind us where the previous mark was located, we call the dog or use our turn signal.

Hunting Close and at Distance
If you want, you can teach the dog different signals for when she should hunt close to you and when she should hunt much further out. It's not usually that difficult to get the dog to hunt close to you. By contrast, at first it can be tricky to get the dog to go really far out. You can start doing it using a visual stimulus and then gradually removing the stimulus. Bring the dog far out into the area and show her that you put something out there. Then return to the starting point with the dog and send her out. You can also leave the dog at the starting point after having first shown her the object and then walk into the area and set out the object. Once you've done this a few times, you can try sending the dog out without using visual stimulus.

Hunting for Spaniels – Quartering and Flushing
Spaniels should cover a piece of ground in a zigzag pattern, starting by going straight out from the handler's side, coming back just in front of the handler and then immediately going out to the other side (referred to as quartering). The handler is constantly moving slowly forward and thus the

Molly points out the hunt area for Nike.

Molly sends Nike out to sweep up.

Nike sweeps up.

dog is hunting an area about 30 yards wide. The size of the hunt area depends on the type of terrain. Spaniels should be able to quarter through open fields, but they are also sent into dense undergrowth. In a dense cover the dog's side to side movements should be shorter, so that the dog constantly maintains a good contact with the handler. In open terrain, the dog's zigzags should be longer. That means the dog usually works only a few yards in front of the handler. The dog shouldn't be more than 15 yards to the side of the handler so he or she is able to shoot flushed game. Spaniel hunting is done with a shotgun, which has a maximum range of about 20 yards.

Anyone who has watched a spaniel running free in the woods has probably seen that the dog naturally moves in a zigzag pattern or something that resembles figure eights, back and forth. This hunting pattern differs slightly between the spaniel breeds. Cockers tend to hunt in eights or circles while Springers usually make straighter lines. While hunting, the spaniel's natural pattern will be used. Of course, that doesn't mean this behavior doesn't need to be trained, but we use the dog's innate hunting patterns as much as possible. A good hunting pattern often develops naturally as the dog matures and gains experience. We spend most of our training time teaching the dog to stay close to us and to use her nose rather than only her legs. Initially, we never train the dog to quarter more than five to ten yards away from us, because we want to teach the dog to work close to us. It is much more difficult to train a dog to quarter closer to us if the dog has already learned to go far out.

The Whistle

It's good to be able to use a turn whistle when a spaniel is quartering. The turn whistle is often one or two short blasts. Retrievers can also benefit from having a turn signal to keep them within the hunt area, but for retrievers this is most often a verbal cue.

Ability to Follow

The dog and handler have much closer contact when spaniels are quartering than when retrievers are sweeping up. Spaniels should stay closer to their handlers and follow them; if the handler changes direction, the dog should follow. We want to foster the dog's ability to follow so that she constantly checks on what we are doing and learns to see us as the source of all things fun. At the same time, an ability to follow means much more than that the dog should be aware of what her handler is doing. It's rather a state – the relationship you've built with your dog that is always with you: at home, away from home, inside, outside, and on every kind of occasion. You offer food, love, security, play – you control all the resources.

Not only should the dog be convinced that you always throw the best parties, it's important to never let her have

Coffee

the chance to partake in other festivities such as chasing game. A skilled trainer will ensure that the dog won't get the chance to run after game until she has mastered the stop whistle and recall perfectly. Training the dog's ability to follow is in other words not just a series of exercises that you can just pull out when you need the dog to be compliant; it's a relationship that should be built from the time the dog is a puppy. But of course there are still exercises you can do that will enhance the dog's ability to follow as a gun dog, focusing on hunting. One is that the dog and handler initially hunt together. Place some treats on the ground when the dog isn't looking. Walk along with the dog until you reach the treats and point them out. Show your keen interest in the treats by enthusiastically proclaiming how tasty they look while the dog eats them.

Then turn the other way and bring your dog to the next treat stash a little further away. Zigzag forward in this fashion. When the dog knows the exercise, swap out the treats for a ball or another toy, and immerse yourself in these "discoveries" by playing enthusiastically with your dog. Since we want the dog to begin using her nose as quickly as possible, pretty soon you can place treats and balls so they are not immediately visible. You can also start to stay back a bit when the dog is hunting and not accompany her so far out, but instead allow her go out and quarter by herself. When she has gobbled down the treats on one side, you should clearly turn the other way, show interest in the treat stash on the other side, and take a few steps towards it. This will teach the dog to follow your body language and go where your body is pointing.

Pointing or walking in a certain direction should tell the dog "hunt there". You can also start to add a turn whistle. Blow

the whistle at the same time the dog turns back towards you and reward the dog by allowing her to run to the treats on your other side. Gradually you can work towards blowing the whistle before the dog has started to turn. While developing the dog's ability to follow, we are paving the way for the dog to hunt close to us. We train the dog to run moderately long, evenly spaced lines to cover as much ground as possible. A spaniel must always keep within shooting range. If the dog is a little too excited or tense, the dog will pull out, making the distance too long. It can therefore be a good idea to train the dog with shorter distances, in other words train the dog to quarter within about five yards. If the dog gets preoccupied while hunting and tries to take large turns instead of tight

Catharina and Sam

immediate turns, try turning her with the turn whistle, or halt her with the stop whistle. However, you shouldn't use the whistle every time the dog is to turn. The dog must learn to maintain the correct distance on her own.

If the turns still become bigger and bigger, you need to take a step back in your training and practice at close distance again. Organize the hunt so that the next few times the dog will find something just a few yards from you.

Coach Says

When you start training your spaniel to quarter, she has probably not yet entirely mastered the stop whistle and the recall. The best case scenario is if the different skills can be allowed to develop at the same time. But then it's incredibly important that you train the dog to hunt in such a way that your dog doesn't accidentally flush game and chase it! Walk over the training ground where you plan to work with the dog initially on leash or in a harness and long line. Or train in pockets of cover where you're sure there aren't any hares lurking about.

Dry Hunting

When the dog is able to go out and find treats or objects that she hasn't seen you throw out, it's time to let some of the runs be empty, meaning there aren't any treats or objects placed out (known as dry hunting). Remember to reward the dog for working well in the areas you ask her to dry hunt. If the dog goes out too many times without finding anything, there's a risk the dog will become bored and lose her desire to go out and hunt. For a lot of spaniels, especially if they are from working breeds, hunting is a self reinforcing behavior even if they don't find anything. Observe your dog to see how she reacts and adjust your training accordingly.

The Wind Matters

Spaniel hunt is slightly different, depending on the direction of the wind and what the terrain looks like. In a headwind, the dog should systematically hunt the area from left to right. In a downwind, the dog should start hunting 20 yards from the handler and then quarter towards him or her. In a crosswind or diagonal headwind, the dog should follow the wind and hunt diagonally towards the handler's path (se illustration below).

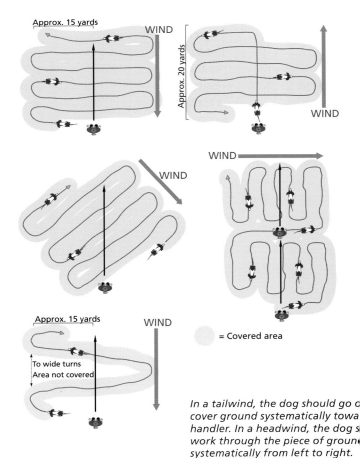

= Covered area

In a tailwind, the dog should go a cover ground systematically towa handler. In a headwind, the dog s work through the piece of groun systematically from left to right.

There aren't any wind conditions you can't hunt in. All hunting patterns are correct as long as they cover the ground and don't miss any game. We choose how we want the dog to hunt by situating ourselves in relation to the wind and then sending the dog. If the dog, for example, should hunt in a thicket at the water's edge, we want her to hunt in a crosswind so we don't have to go into the bushes or into the water.

Above all, we want the dog to turn against the wind and not make a "U-turn" and turn with the wind (also known as back-casting). Frequently dogs will learn this with experience, but be sure to organize your hunting so that initially it will be easier for the dog to turn in the right direction. Dogs from working breeds often have good hunting patterns because it's a trait that has been bred over a long period of time. Genetics combined with experience help the dog learn what a good hunting pattern looks like.

Flushing Game

Flushing is something that "just happens" when the dog encounters game. At first, you should of course only allow your dog to flush game in a controlled manner. Flushing birds is something that many regard as one of the biggest challenges in the spaniel hunt since the dog should sit or stand motionless at the same time as the bird flies up.

This requires training in self control. We want a bird flying up to serve as a cue for the dog to stop. We prefer not to use any additional signals but we also teach the dog the stop whistle.

When the dog responds to the stop whistle in any situation and she has been trained to remain steady with simulated exercises using everything from toys to game birds, we allow the dog to flush game while hunting. As soon as the game runs or flies away, we blow the stop whistle to halt the dog. If we've previously trained the dog to spontaneously sit when the object flies away in staged situations, we use that to our advantage. It's ideal if the dog sits spontaneously, but that can be difficult. That's why we always blow the stop whistle for extra assurance in the beginning. If it doesn't work, end the training session, and train more on flying birds and the stop whistle in staged situations. As always in our training, progress entails taking small steps with a lot of successes. Obviously we don't go immediately from throwing a ball to allowing the dog to flush a rabbit.

To reinforce steadiness even more, it can be a good idea not to let the dog retrieve game the first few times something is shot in front of the dog. Instead, reward her for staying, go for a walk, and then let the dog find and retrieve the game while hunting.

Introducing the dog to hunting live game requires good planning and a solid foundation, which means the dog is both obedient and has the right mindset. It's almost a given that the dog will be excited in this situation, and if she was already really worked up, all of a sudden all notions of steadiness might be gone and your dog might just run in. It's really easy for a handler to become over eager and introduce the dog to game flying up too early, before the dog is ready to handle it. Consult with an experienced instructor when you are going to start teaching your spaniel to flush game.

Commonalities

Now we've gone through the differences between hunting for retrievers and hunting for spaniels. We will turn to the similarities and the areas you need to focus on with both breeds. These include training them not to swap game or dummies, being able to hunt in a variety of terrain, and endurance.

Coach Says

During our daily walks, we try to encourage our dogs to make contact with us as if to ask, "Where are we going?". This can be one way to teach independent dogs that it's worthwhile to keep an eye on us. Hunting requires a balance between allowing the dog to hunt independently and having her listen to you as soon as you ask her to. With some dogs, it might even be a good idea to reward them for voluntarily making contact with you while hunting. This is probably most applicable to spaniels unless you have an extremely independent retriever. Preferably, retrievers shouldn't ask their handlers any questions at all while hunting.

No Swapping

Game should be delivered as quickly and effectively as possible. It's extremely ineffective if the dog swaps game and we thus want to teach the dog to run straight to us as soon as she has found something. When the dog has started to enjoy finding things and has learned that there is more than one object to discover, she might start to continue to hunt with an object in her mouth. If you think your dog will do this, spend even more time training deliveries until the dog immediately turns and runs to you when she has found the first dummy. Before the dog can do this, you can only work on hunting with just one dummy, or with the dog on leash so you can reward her for finding the dummy at the same time as you can prevent her from continuing to hunt.

If you've trained the dog not to swap game and have sent her out to hunt, but see that the dog is going to continue to run with what she has found instead of coming to you, quickly blow your recall whistle. This might possibly serve as a reminder for the dog to come in immediately, and the next time you send your dog out she will pick up the object and come straight back to you. If she doesn't, take a step back in your training.

The Hunt Area as a Distraction

If the dog has seen you or a helper walk around in various places in the hunt area, the dog might want to continue to hunt even more. The biggest distraction for the dog in this case is the knowledge that there are more fun things to find. Therefore take the opportunity to use the hunt area itself as a distraction. You can do this with both spaniels and retrievers, but remember to adjust the distance.

1. Ask your helper to walk around the area or leave the dog in a spot where she can see you walking around. In this

Snoddas

case you don't need to plant any objects, just pretend that you are doing so.

2. Stand with the dog beside you with your back to the hunt area.

3. Place a toy or an object in front of you and the dog and ask the dog to fetch it.

4. Generously reward the dog when she brings the object back to you. If the dog doesn't come back but instead takes off into the hunt area, calmly fetch her and try again, making sure that your dog will really be able to succeed. If the level of distraction is so high that the dog doesn't want to take the object from the ground, try having the dog take it from your hand or just play with it near the hunt area in order to then have the dog pick up the object from the ground again.

5. When the dog comes straight back to you when you are standing with your back to the hunt area, gradually move with the dog closer to the hunt area, and throw the object further and further away. Initially, this will be more of a marked retrieve than hunting, but as the dog becomes more skilled, sneak the object out so the dog doesn't notice, and send the dog out again.

The first time you send the dog out to retrieve an object she hasn't seen you throw, make sure the object is nearby so the dog finds it almost immediately and isn't tempted to run out into the larger hunt area.

If later on in your training you want to make this an even more challenging distraction, you can make noise, stamp on the ground and hit the trees a little at the same time you are pretending to lay out the objects. Then as you become more and more confident the dog will come back even when she's seen someone walking around the hunt area, you can

start setting dummies out (instead of just pretending to do so). Do several repetitions of short range deliveries and then send the dog toward the objects you planted earlier. Make it progressively more difficult by placing out more objects and sending the dog to retrieve them. Remember to generously reward every delivery, because that is the skill you need to practice for the dog to understand the value of bringing the object to you instead of continuing to hunt.

Coach Says

In order to understand how the dog actually sweeps up, it can be useful to use numbered dummies. You can purchase dummies that are already numbered or you can use a fabric pen to number your own. Place the dummies out in numerical order by walking on an imaginary middle path and throwing every other one to the right and left so that all the odd numbers end up on one side and all the even on the other. Then send the dog out to hunt. Remember the order in which the dog brings them back so you can tell immediately if she has missed any. You might discover that your dog has totally missed the area to the right, closest to you. You can work more on this by placing several dummies there and casting the dog diagonally to the right next time.

The Importance of Variety

Introduce as much variety as possible when your dog hunts in terms of objects, terrain, which other dogs and people have been moving around in the area, and so on. Transitions in terrain, such as from a meadow to a wooded area, or a path running through the middle of the area, can lead to the dog limiting the area in which she hunts. Train with a lot of different changes in terrain in all of your work (hunting, marked retrieves, and blind retrieves). Some dogs find it difficult to hunt on pristine ground while others are overwhelmed by the smells in an area where there has been a lot of foot traffic. Train with both so the dog hunts regardless of the area. Remember to wander around the hunt area a bit extra when you place objects or throw them away so the dog can't track them.

Areas with a lot of smells are often the most challenging because there are so many scents to follow. If you run into trouble, lower your criteria and train at short range again. Start with several successful deliveries and reward them generously before you send the dog out again.

Coach Says

To keep the hunt area pristine (i.e. without scents from humans), a ball launcher can be handy. You can either walk along a path in the middle of the area and throw the balls to the sides or walk around the area and throw them towards the center.

Endurance

If the dog has seen something placed out in the area, there is often no problem with getting her to go out the first time. It can, however, be a challenge to send the dog out a second time. To teach the dog to go out again, ensure that the second dummy is a little easier to find as a reward for the dog "daring" to go out again. You can, for example, have a helper stealthily hide a dummy close to where you are working with the dog (without the dog seeing) while the dog is running back with the first object.

The more difficult the hunting and the more dummies the dog has fetched, the better the rewards should be. You can also have one difficult task in one direction and an easier task in the other. When the dog has fetched a few of the dummies from the more difficult side and starts to tire, you can send her to the easier side once or twice instead so you know that the dog will quickly get her reward.

Sometimes you reward every delivery, other times maybe every other, and sometimes you give the dog a huge reward when she has finished hunting or when you are satisfied with what she has brought to you. It can be useful to have trained the dog to work for an external reward even while hunting. Can your dog manage to go out to hunt if she spots a bowl of food nearby? If the dog seems to find it difficult at the beginning, reward her after the first delivery. Then you can have the dog work for progressively longer periods of time before you cue "go ahead".

But ...

*... if the dog relieves herself in the hunt area, I have to correct her
No, don't do that. You might scare the dog and make her less interested in working next time. Just calmly walk and fetch the dog, and then try to figure out why she relieved herself. Hasn't she had a chance to relieve herself beforehand? How many other dogs have weed there previously? Is she tired? Is she motivated? Does she really know what she is supposed to do?*

If it's because many other dogs have weed there, set out a dummy next to a spot where another dog has weed, and reward your dog for picking it up (stand close by in the beginning and have the dog on a leash if necessary). If it's because the dog is too tired, try to work on building her endurance. If this is the first time it happens, you can just wait a little and see what happens. Does the dog start working again? If so, maybe it's enough to just make sure she's had a chance to relieve herself beforehand next time and use even better rewards.

Pace and Concentration

High speed is not the most important part of hunting, but rather the fact that the dog keeps working, follows the scents she picks up, and hunts with a suitable intensity. Dogs that just run tend to forget to activate their noses and therefore do a lot of unnecessary running. Some dogs can also lose themselves in the world of scents, finding the scents more interesting than the objects. If your dog just runs by the objects, stop her from hunting, and build the value of the objects by having the dog retrieve them at short range. Reward the dog generously, play with the objects, and give them to the dog when she is extremely happy.

To increase the dog's concentration, you can hide game or objects under a little moss or tall grass to make the dog work harder. Often you will notice when the dog catches the scent of an object; she will turn sharply, her entire body stiffens, or her tail starts wagging frenetically. Then we want to see that the dog really follows the scent and finds the object instead of continuing to run. Again, this is based on the dog really wanting to find the objects, so if the dog is running because she loves to run and isn't interested in the objects, you need to back up in your training.

The Turn Signal

A turn signal can be an effective way to get the dog back into the hunt area if she ends up outside of it. This is almost a necessity for spaniels, but it can also be useful for retrievers. If a spaniel is quartering stylishly, the turn whistle should be used sparingly. Nor should it be used to prevent the spaniel from going too far out of the hunt area except in exceptional circumstances. If the spaniel goes too far out, go back in your training, and work even more on keeping the dog close. The dogs of handlers who often blow the turn whistle are sometimes too dependent upon them, that is to say they will stop while hunting and "ask" their handler for help. The dog should, however, keep track of the handler so that she will only turn when the handler turns his or her body or starts to walk in a different direction. When the dog is in a dense thicket, or if the dog is very excited, we can use the turn whistle as an additional brake. If we want the dog to search in specific thicket we can control the dog with the turn whistle. Blow it when the dog is heading to the edge of the thicket.

For retrievers, the turn signal should also be used sparingly. You can choose to use a recall signal or a stop whistle, and then cast the dog into the area again, but usually it's easier to have a signal that only means "turn towards me". We avoid using the stop whistle while the dog is hunting or sweeping up because we really don't want the dog to stop and then continue to hunt. Instead, we want the dog to turn around and while on the move continue to hunt the other way (back to us). The recall signal is supposed to mean "come all the way back to me", and the dog doesn't need to do that when hearing the turn signal. She should simply turn around and continue hunting.

When you see that the dog is going to turn while you are on a walk, give your cue ("over here", "turn", whistle) and throw a reward to the dog. Repeat this a number of times and then try giving your cue when the dog wasn't intending to turn.

Rounding a Pole

Another way to teach the dog the turn whistle is to let her go around a pole, such as a plastic post for electric fencing or a weave pole for agility training. Start by shaping the dog to go around the pole. Stand close by at the beginning with the dog at your side and reward each step she takes in the right direction. Preferably place the reward in the direction the dog is to continue, that is, around the pole. When the dog goes around the pole with ease, start to blow your turn whistle (or give your cue) while the dog is going around the pole. Then increase the distance to the pole. Gradually, try using the whistle or saying the cue in situations without a pole. Blow the turn whistle or say the cue when the dog is at a short distance from you and reward the dog when she turns.

Handling Game

During hunting, you will find out for certain if your dog spontaneously takes game or not… You won't always be able to see what the dog is doing, and then it becomes easier for the dog to choose to bypass a piece of game. If the dog ignores a piece of game, bring the dog back, and do extra training with that particular type of game.

Consider asking a helper to stand out in the hunt area to tell you what the dog is doing when you can't see her (this is most relevant for retrievers, you can see spaniels almost all the time except when they are hunting in dense terrain). It's also a great distraction to work on because the judges at retriever trials might walk out into the hunt area to see better

and the dog must be able to continue working regardless. If needed, your helper can entice your dog to take the game a few times, but if the skill doesn't improve, you need to work on taking and carrying instead. You don't want to get stuck where the dog only takes the game if she gets encouraged. Be mindful so that the cheering doesn't become stressful for the dog.

Don't Let the Dog Choose the Game

When you have progressed a bit further with hunting and you have begun to set out several different types of game, remember not to allow the dog to walk away from one piece of game that she doesn't really like and instead pick up something she prefers. We don't want the dog to first pick up what she likes better; we want to teach the dog that she should bring in everything she finds immediately. If the dog is about to leave the game behind, calmly interrupt the exercise by calling her or fetching her. Before you are confident the dog will always take a particular kind of game, you shouldn't use any other type of game in order to prevent the dog from having the chance to ignore it. Work on increasing the dog's interest in game as we described in the chapter "Taking and holding" so that the dog also likes to pick up that kind of game, and then later on use the dog's preferred game as a distraction.

Elsa's dog Diesel preferred ducks to gulls (in some countries gun dogs aren't required to retrieve gulls, and then you don't need to train with that type of game, but the principle is the same if the dog prefers any kind of game to another). As soon as Elsa discovered this, she began to do a lot of extra training with gulls by first building up Diesel's interest so she happily took the gull. Then Elsa had Diesel walk on a leash beside her while carrying the gull. When Diesel had mastered that, Elsa set out the gull in a thicket a few yards away and allowed Diesel to hunt for it. While Diesel was out on her mini hunt, a helper snuck out and planted a duck alongside of the path Diesel would take back. When Diesel returned with the gull, she caught the scent of the duck. Then she had to walk past it and deliver the gull to Elsa. Only then was Diesel allowed to retrieve the duck and then she was generously rewarded for performing this correctly.

Gradually the duck could already be in place when Diesel was heading out to retrieve the gull, but in such a way so that she caught the gull's scent first. If she wanted to go past the gull and retrieve the duck instead, the helper just up lifted up the duck or Elsa gently stopped Diesel with the leash, and tried again, with the duck a little further away.

In the beginning we will do this exercise at a very short range, just a few yards. It's not the distance we want to train, but rather we want to teach the dog to follow up the scent of the first game she finds, not to swap game, and to always come in with the game she has in her mouth first. In the beginning, the game can be slightly visual, but we gradually conceal it more and more so the dog really has to look for it.

Snoddas

Challenge

Is your dog able to find six dummies in an area that is 50x50 yards at the edge of the water with some marshy and wooded areas, where four dogs have just run, and one of them has relieved herself? If you have a spaniel you will naturally move back and forth in order to cover the entire hunt area; a retriever should be ready to cover the entire area herself while the handler remains at the starting point.

Sub-goals – Hunting	Completed
Catch the scent and find the object (dummy, game)	
Retrieve and deliver the object	
Zigzag hunting pattern – quartering (spaniels)	
Larger area (retrievers)	
Various kinds of terrain and obstacles (meadow, woods, swamp, field, in the water, and along the beach)	
Turn signal	
With distractions (for example several dummies, other dogs, or an audience)	

Summary

- Send the dog out when she is looking towards the hunt area.
- Prepare the dog every time you send her and allow her to breathe for a moment beside you before sending her out again (especially retrievers).
- Spend a lot of time training deliveries with distractions in order to avoid problems with the dog swapping dummies or continuing to hunt with a dummy in her mouth.
- Train the dog to hunt in as many different terrains as possible.
- Teach the dog to turn immediately when you blow the turn whistle.
- Teach the dog to quarter in the direction you point (only applicable to spaniels).

Marked Retrieves

The sun is rising and the mist has just faded. A shot is fired. Your dog sits entirely still and watches the game fall. On your cue, the dog runs out to the mark, picks up the game stylishly and neatly, turns to you at the speed of light, and delivers the game precisely to your hand.

A marked retrieve involves the dog sitting, standing, or walking with you and seeing where the game falls (marking) and retrieving it at your cue. This requires a good memory, a desire to hunt, and steadiness. A desire to hunt means that the dog has good endurance and will keep looking for the game until she finds it.

Play to Inspire Marked Retrieves

There are playful ways to train marked retrieves while you are taking walks. When you reward your dog for a successful recall or stop whistle, throw the ball somewhere that poses a challenge; behind a stonewall, up a hill, in high grass or, over a small path. Cue "go ahead" when the object has landed and

is laying still. (If the dog is unable to wait until the object has landed, keep a gentle hold on her collar, and cue "go ahead" when she calms down). The dog should see approximately where the ball has landed, but not the exact location. This will allow the dog to practice her ability to perform marked retrieves at the same time as she gets her reward.

> ### Coach Says
> *Send the dog when she is looking at the object and before she looks at you. Gradually extend the time your dog is looking straight ahead. If the dog looks at you, don't look at her, but instead look out towards the area of the fall. Wait until the dog looks out into the area again before you send her. Next time try sending the dog a bit earlier before she has time to look at you.*

The Retrieve Cue

When the dog has mastered deliveries and you know the dog will bring the object back, you can start adding the retrieve cue. Quite simply, "fetch" means to fetch what you just saw fall as soon as possible. You can choose whatever cue you want. Some people use "yes" and others use "fetch". Some people say the dog's name first, or use only the dog's name. It can be good to say the dog's name if there are a lot of people sending their dogs or you can use distraction training to teach your dog never to run on anyone else's cue.

Elsa has unwittingly trained Diesel that "go ahead" means the same thing as "fetch". If she throws a ball and cues "go ahead", she wants it back as soon as possible. Then she rewards Diesel by throwing the ball again or by replacing it with a treat. We think it's a good approach because then we know that we will get back the objects at once without having to nag the dog to get them. Moreover, this serves as additional "brainwashing" so the dog always comes back to her handler as soon as she has something in her mouth.

Snoddas

The illustration shows how you can back chain a marked retrieve.

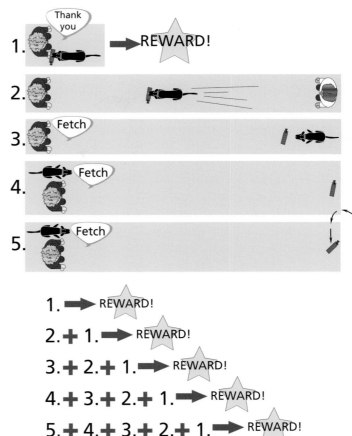

Coach Says

Continue training the delivery until the dog runs at least as fast to you with the object as she does on the outrun. If the dog is able to gallop out to the object, she is able to gallop back as well. Unless the game is very, very large, that is.

Back-chaining Marked Retrieves

When you have all of the parts in place – taking on cue, holding firmly, delivery to hand, remaining steady next to you when the mark falls – you can start back chaining the entire marked retrieve. Remember that no chain is stronger than its weakest link. Generalize all of the parts before you start putting them all together.

Start by repeating the hand target a few times. Then do the following:

1. Give the dog the object and hold out your hand so that the dog delivers it to your hand. Reward.

2. Have a helper hold the dog and stand some distance away. The helper then holds up the object in front of the dog. When the dog takes the object, the helper releases the dog, who then runs straight back to you. Reward. (If the dog thinks it's unpleasant to have someone hold her by the collar or if she doesn't take the object from the helper, you should practice these elements separately before inserting them into the chain. You might also try going straight to the next step.)

3. Put the dog a short distance away and place the object between you and the dog. Cue "fetch" so that your dog takes the object and then delivers it to your hand. Reward.

4. Put the dog in a sit at your side and have your helper set out the object (don't challenge your dog's steadiness too much at first). Cue "fetch" so the dog fetches the object. Reward.

5. Put the dog in a sit at your side and throw the object (or have your helper throw the object). When the dog is calm and focused, cue "fetch". Reward.

Now you have put the parts together into a marked retrieve. Then it's time to add distraction training and perform the marked retrieve in increasingly more difficult situations. Remember that you might need to repeat the back-chaining when you add distractions.

Further Training

In the beginning, you can throw the marks yourself, but also train by having other people throwing and with other people standing next to you or out in the woods. Inexperienced dogs can sometimes look at the thrower instead of the mark and therefore miss seeing the game fall. The dog might also head towards the thrower on her way back to you. Then spend even more time training deliveries and have the thrower gradually move closer and closer to the dog. If the dog goes to the thrower, he or she should turn and ignore the dog, and then you should try again. If you are unsure if the dog will remain sitting when the mark falls, ask a helper to stand close to the mark (or have the dog on a leash) and then he or she can pick up the dummy if the dog goes for it. Do some additional steadiness training until it's perfect.

Straight Over

The dog should try to take the most direct route both on her way out to and in from the mark, that is to say the quickest and most efficient way. This may mean that you need to do some extra training to give the dog the confidence to climb over stonewalls or jump over fences. The dog also needs to learn to go around obstacles that are too high. One time Diesel was to retrieve a mark on the other side of a stonewall. From the place where Elsa and Diesel stood, down the hill from the wall, the wall didn't appear to be too high so Diesel was planning on going straight over. As she approached the wall, she realized it was too high. It was quite obvious that she would have preferred to go over, but she decided to find a better way around instead.

Mark!

When the mark falls, it's important that the dog is attentive and follows the object with her eyes – that is, not looking at the handler or the shooter. It can be useful to teach the dog a "mark" cue that tells the dog to look straight ahead. Start with visible marks. As the dog looks at the mark falling, cue "mark" and send the dog as usual with a fetch cue. Then make the throws and the areas of the fall less and less obvious. Don't let the dog look at you before she goes out on a marked retrieve because we want her to be focused on the hunt area.

Back-chain Challenging Environments and Distance

To teach the dog to find marks on the other side of hills and stonewalls, you might need to back chain the distance so the dog learns to go over obstacles instead of getting "stuck" in front of them.[34] Since the area of the fall looks different from the dog's perspective, it may be helpful to bend down and instead look at things from the same angle as the dog. If the dummy disappears behind a hill, to the dog it might look as if the dummy landed on top of the hill and not on the other side.

Start by throwing a mark in the designated area and having the dog fetch it. Then increase the distance to the area and throw another mark into the same area. Either back up along with the dog or back up when you send the dog. Keep at it with three or four throws to the same area. The next day you can go to the same area and try again with a slightly longer distance from the beginning. Do this in as many different environments as possible so that the dog becomes proficient at both estimating the distance and really focusing on and following the scent until she finds the object.

[34] We borrowed this exercise from Katarina Eriksson, www.kopparhult.se.

An additional challenge for the dog can be estimating the distance in large open fields with no reference points. This requires some experience.

Marked Retrieves with Distractions

At this stage, you have spent a lot of time training deliveries and holding objects as well as steadiness with distractions, which will be extremely useful when it's time to proof the rest of your marked retrieve.

Always have the dog remain in a sit until the mark has landed (possibly have the dog on leash if you don't think she will remain in the sit position or have a helper ready to pick up the dummy). Vary the amount of time the dog must sit beside you after a mark has landed. If the dog gets up when the mark falls, wait for the dog to sit again, and then let her go, or pick up the dummy, throw the mark again, and send the dog while she is still sitting. You can also work on having someone tell you when you can send the dog and having someone tap you on the shoulder when you should send the dog since judges will often do that during field trials.

We also want to teach the dog to be focused on where the mark landed even when other things are happening around us. Have a helper clap, bounce a ball, or walk past just before the mark falls. The majority of dogs are most easily distracted when they are on the way back, as they are fully focused on the area of the fall on the way out. However, you can also try to distract the dog when she is headed to the mark so that you can be confident the dog is fully focused on the task.

Memory marks are on the one hand a way to teach the dog to remember where objects fell even if other things have since happened, and on the other, a way to teach the dog to go out and hunt, even though she didn't just see something land.

1. Throw out a ball or a dummy in sight of the dog.
2. Ask the dog to do something, such as turning around with you, lying down, or running a line in the other direction before you send her on the marked retrieve.

You can also throw a mark and then bring the dog to another place (from where she can still see the area of the fall) and then send her from there instead. In the beginning, do this from a short distance. The longer the distance, the more difficult it is for the dog to relate to the area of the fall.

When we train marked retrieves, i.e. an object that the dog is supposed to retrieve immediately, we will call the dog off if she begins to hunt in a too large area. We want the dog to learn to go to the correct area at once. Memory marks help us develop the dog's ability to perform marked retrieves, but if a lot has happened since the mark was thrown, it becomes more like a memory or blind retrieve, and then we step in and cast the dog in the correct direction. Does that sound contradictory? We send the dog as we do on a marked retrieve if we send her quite soon after she's seen the mark. If a longer period of time goes by, we take it as an opportunity for a little extra casting training.

Marked Retrieves during Field Trials

In the Novice Stakes for retrievers, you will usually only encounter single marks. In Advanced Stakes, however, double and triple marks might occur. For spaniels, marked retrieves during field trials are always in connection with a bird flying up. Double marks are used extremely rarely during field trials for spaniels. Marks can end up both on land and in water, and often the area of the fall is somewhat concealed.

Double and Triple Marks

Since by now you have worked a lot on deliveries, we think that you have the knowledge and experience to start training double and triple marks. Preferably throw the marks far apart from each other at the beginning:

Coach Says

Work on your own ability to identify marks. It's not so easy to remember where they land. It can get a little fuzzy especially with double and triple marks. If you don't know where the dummies are, how can you support your dog?

1. Keep the dog beside you and throw a dummy in front of you.
2. Praise the dog for noting the area of the fall.
3. Then turn around and throw another dummy so you have one dummy in front of you and one behind you (see illustration on next page).
4. Send the dog to retrieve the dummy you threw last. Then the dog must pass by you to get to the first dummy. Therefore, the dog will probably perform correctly (she will come to you without running to the second dummy) and if things go wrong, you can pick up the dummy behind you.
5. When the dog has delivered the first dummy, turn around and send the dog to the remaining dummy.
6. Once this flows smoothly, throw the marks closer together. If things go wrong, quietly and calmly bring the dog back and try again, or better still throw a simple mark you know the dog will successfully retrieve and generously reward the delivery. Then try the double mark again.

Gradually, you can also start experimenting with sending the dog to retrieve the first mark you threw before letting her retrieve the most recent one. It's harder than the other way around, since the mark you threw later is freshest in the dog's memory and thus easier to retrieve.

For double and triple marks, some judges allow the handler to choose which mark the dog is to retrieve first, while others want the dog herself to decide. In any event, you will always benefit from being able to decide which mark the dog should retrieve first, for example if the game was wounded. The judge can sometimes even designate the order in which the marks are to be retrieved to see if the handler is able to determine the order.

Anticipation

Have you ever noticed that your dog seems to believe that some things aren't possible in certain situations? For example, if you sit down on the floor the dog might lie down next to you, even if you cue "sit". That's because the dog easily learns what you usually work on in various situations and can therefore become dependent on certain contexts in order to perform a particular behavior.

Therefore sometimes try giving the cue for a different behavior than the dog expects. When the mark has fallen, you might for example cue "down" instead of "fetch" and reward the dog for the correct behavior. If it gets too difficult, make the marked retrieve or the distraction a bit easier so that the dog will not be so fixated on the marked retrieve that she can't do anything else.

It's important the dog can do this because during a trial or while hunting it may well be that a mark falls in front of you, but at the same time, a wounded bird might be behind you. Then the dog should retrieve the wounded game first to reduce its suffering and because it becomes harder to find the more time that passes. If the dog is completely intent on retrieving the first mark, as she always does when she has seen a mark fall, it may be difficult to get the dog to turn around and run a line in the other direction instead.

Complete the Task

There are two important elements in marked retrieves: that the dog takes note of where the game falls and that she continues to hunt the area until she finds something. You can thus also practice finding and following a scent trail during marked retrieves. Have a helper throw a mark so it's slightly hidden when it falls. Then have your helper drag the game along the ground so it ends up a bit away from the original spot or just pick up the game and move it several yards. The dog should run to the area where she thinks the mark fell, and then hunt to find the game. That exercise can also simulate what happens when a bird is shot and injured. It might land in one spot but then move a bit so the dog doesn't find it at the spot where it landed, but instead finds it somewhere else nearby.

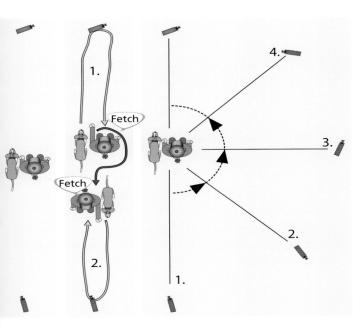

Start training double marks by throwing one dummy in front and one dummy behind you and sending the dog. Then throw the dummies so they gradually end up closer to each other.

Sub-goals – Marked Retrieves	Completed
See where the object falls	
Retrieve and deliver the object	
Longer ranges (spaniels 30-50 yards and retrievers 50-100 yards)	
Different kinds of terrain and obstacles	
In the water (see chapter "Water Work")	
With distractions (for example, a concealed thrower, a shooter standing near you, or running by other game on the way back)	

Challenge

Can your dog watch two marks fall five yards from each other, run out and fetch one of them, deliver it to you, and then run out and fetch the other (without moving towards the second mark with the first dummy in her mouth)?

Summary

- Develop the dog's ability to perform marked retrieves by throwing marks on different kinds of terrain, behind stonewalls, or on the other side of streams and in cover.
- Train the dog to really continue to hunt the area until she finds the mark. If the dog hunts in an area that is incorrect, bring her back to you, and try again.
- If the dog gives up without finding the object, build more value for retrieving the object. Have another dog fetch it or do a couple of simpler marked retrieves and then a more difficult one again.
- A marked retrieve where the dog isn't allowed to retrieve the object immediately becomes more and more like a memory or blind retrieve. Decide if you are going to send the dog as you would on a marked retrieve or direct the dog before sending her.

Water Work

The dog should be able to do almost everything she does on land in the water: hunting, marked retrieves, blind retrieves, as well as responding to the stop whistle, the hunt whistle, and the recall whistle. The dog obviously doesn't need to do a swimming heel, but you have to train heel on marshy ground and at the water's edge. Training the dog not to shake herself off before delivering the game is also a must.

For most dogs, it's natural to shake themselves off when they come up out of the water. But we want the dog to come straight in with the object before shaking herself off because that's the most effective way to get the game to us.

Most inexperienced dogs coming out of the water with an object also put it down on the ground before they shake off. At best, they later remember they had something with them, pick it up, and then come in to the handler. But the mistake has already been made. If the dog puts down wounded game to shake herself off, the game might run away. If the dog shakes herself off with the game in her mouth, she might damage it. Sloppy deliveries also receive deductions during field trials, so you need to teach the dog not to shake off until she has delivered the game to you.

It can be quite difficult to train the dog to work in the water because we can't be as close to the dog as we can on land. It's harder for us to influence the dog when she is swimming than when she is running. In our opinion, it's good to start working on the basics of water work early on. Even with a puppy, you can start getting her used to the water. Train deliveries by the water and do simple casting exercises with bowls over water. Don't wait until everything else is perfect before you start training. It's of course better – and more pleasant – to do water training in the summer, but no matter the season, it's important not to let the dog get too cold.

Recall out of the Water and across the Water

To teach the dog to come all the way in to us, deliver the object, and then shake herself off, we start by teaching the dog to run in to us without objects when she's wet, get a

reward, and then shake herself off on cue.[35] Once she can do that, we introduce the object.

The ideal solution is to find a stream that is two to three yards wide and deep enough to swim in. Then you can be on one side and leave the dog on the other. If you also have a helper, an effective training method is to have the dog run and swim between the two of you. Then you get twice as many repetitions. If you don't have access to a stream, get the dog into the water by throwing a few treats that float. Avoid throwing sticks or things that splash since that might work the dog up too much with the risk that she might start whining. Also, you need to somehow get the object back and if you haven't trained the dog to deliver out of the water yet, she will most likely drop the object before you get it in your hand.

If the dog doesn't want to go into the water at all, start shaping her to get into the water or have her swim together with you and other dogs. Never push the dog to go into the water, or you might make her even more afraid. If you allow your dog to go at her own pace, she will soon discover how much fun the water can be. Then do the following:

1. Repeat the hand target a few times before sending the dog into the water or put her in a sit on the other side of the stream.
2. When the dog is in the water or on the shore on the other side, stand near the edge of the water.
3. Call the dog and hold out your hand target.
4. When the dog touches your hand, reward her with something really good, cue "shake", and reward her for shaking. If the dog shakes before touching your hand, remove the hand, and try again, possibly at a shorter distance.

---

[35] We borrowed this exercise from Eva Bodfäldt, www.evabodfaldt.com.

The disappearing hand makes it clear to the dog that the reward also disappeared. We don't want the dog to be "sorry" about that, but instead just think, "I'll try again and then I'll succeed." For this to work you must first have built up great value for the hand target so the dog thinks it's fun to touch your hand and a little boring when the hand goes away. Otherwise there's no point in removing your hand.

If the dog is so busy playing in the water she doesn't care about your hand target you might need to adjust your training somewhat. For example you can have the dog on a leash, wait until she is ready, and then put out your hand.

Coach Says

You can teach the cue "shake" at home in the shower. When you have bathed the dog, sooner or later she is going to shake herself off. Right when you see she's about to do so, you can cue "shake". You can also gently tickle the dog a little with a finger between the shoulder blades or blow a little bit on her. That usually triggers a reflex that makes the dog shake. You can also take the opportunity to have the dog target your hand and reward her for being able to do it when she's wet.

Avoid rewarding the dog by throwing a toy to her before she has shaken herself off. Then you avoid problems with the dog shaking with the toy in her mouth or putting the toy down. On the other hand, you could definitely reward your dog after she shakes off by throwing a ball on land.

When the dog is able to run out of the water and touch your hand while you are standing on the edge of the water, you can gradually increase the distance so the dog runs farther and farther from the water to you (see illustration on next page). Finally, we want the dog to be able to run at least 50 yards on land to us.

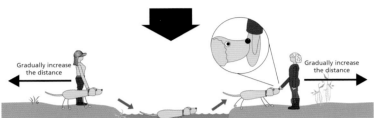

Gradually increase the distance

Gradually increase the distance

The illustration shows how you can start training the dog to go straight into and swim across the water without shaking herself off. First do all this without an object together with a helper and then with an object. You can also train without a helper, for example by using bowls.

Now the dog has probably begun to understand the concept of running up onto land, despite the fact that she is wet, targeting your hand, and then shaking herself off. Then it's time to try the same thing with objects. Either you can put the object in the water and have the dog fetch it, or place it on the other side of a small stream and have the dog swim across the stream, retrieve the object, and then swim back to you. You can also use a helper and send the dog between you and an object. Once you start adding objects you should reduce the distance. Start by standing right beside the water, and then increase the distance again. Sometimes you even have to stand in the water to receive the object, for example if it's shallow, because the dog will then be quite eager to shake herself off. If the dog releases the object before she reaches your hand target, take your hand away, and then try again at a slightly shorter distance.

Teach the dog to get in and out of the water in different kinds of environments: shallow, steep, rocky, and where the dog isn't really able see you or has to run diagonally up from the water to come to you. If the dog shakes herself off too soon, after we make it more difficult, we could try one more time. If it still doesn't work then, we should make the exercise a little easier so the dog succeeds several times before we make it a bit more challenging again.

Coach Says

Since almost everything the dog does on land is also to be done in the water, you need to train all of your whistle signals, cues, and various skills involved in the water as well.

Go Straight into the Water

The dog should preferably go straight into the water, swim straight to the object, retrieve it, swim back, and come up again in the same spot. That is to say she should not start running along the bank before she goes into the water. You might need to help the dog a bit at first by holding her collar, so she goes straight into the water.

When the dog is on her way back with the game, she is allowed to go on land, if she does so smoothly and without dropping the game, although taking the most direct route through the water is preferred. The most important thing during a field trial is that the dog picks up the game as quickly and efficiently as possible. If the dog goes over land, it's important to have worked on deliveries a lot so she actually runs all the way to you without to putting down the game and shaking herself off.

Water Work with Distractions

You should always work on distraction training with the dog close to you before you increase the distance. This is also the case with water; you can influence the dog up close. Examples of good distractions to use next to the water are shots that are fired when the dog is about to enter the water, a boat floating on the water, live waterfowl, and challenging entrances to the water, such as steep banks.

Pitfall

Avoid doing too much training on marked retrieves on open water and marked retrieves with shots, especially with young dogs, since it causes them a lot of stress. Focus instead on calmer activities for instance hunting or running a line, and train separately on shots and water.

Casting and Blind Retrieves in Water

When you work with casting in water, you can use the same training approach as on land. Try putting out bowls on small islands or get really good at throwing things, such as a ball, for the dog as a reward. However, work on deliveries first.

Start practicing the water casting early on, because it's quite difficult. A tip is to find a small pond around which you can place bowls in different places, like in the exercise "The Clock", described in chapter "Blind Retrieves". You can send the dog to the middle of the pond, blow the stop whistle, and then decide if you want to send the dog to the right, left, or back.

Also train the dog to go straight over obstacles, such as small islands in the water. Often, there might only be one island, but it's good if the dog can continue straight over several islands and not start looking on the first island just because that is where she usually looks for objects.

Coach Says

It's important to think of balancing your training and thereby the dog's anticipation. Prepare a small hunting area in the woods and a blind or memory retrieve in the water. When the dog is calm, cast her on the retrieve in the water and then to hunt in the woods. If the dog is too expectant working in the water, just turn around, and send her to hunt in the woods when she is calm.

Water Work during Field Trials

For retrievers water work usually consists of single marks in the Novice Stakes, either in the reeds or in open water. In the Open and Advanced Stakes, there might be both marked retrieves and blind retrieves in water. In some countries a trial can be done without any water work, whereas that is impossible in other countries.

For spaniels, water activities can occur during field trials because any game that is shot should be retrieved even if it falls into the water. If necessary, the handler should also be able to cast the dog in the water. In some countries there are separate water tests where spaniels show their water retrieving ability.

Contact your Gun Dog Club for more information on the regulations in your country.

238

Sub-goals – Water Work	Completed
Run through and swim straight across water	
Run straight down into the water	
Run straight up out of the water (towards the hand target)	
Run through and swim across the water without an object (towards the hand target, shaking off after touching the hand)	
Run through and swim across the water with an object (shaking off after the object has been delivered)	
Stop whistle	
Recall whistle	
Hunt whistle	
Blind retrieves	
Hunting	
Marked retrieves	
With distractions (such as a boat in the water, a thrower standing nearby, or shots)	

Challenge

Can you send your dog on a marked retrieve 30 yards out into the water, when you stand five yards up on land, slightly concealed behind a bush, and receive the game in your hand without the dog shaking herself off?

Summary

- Teach the dog to deliver an object into your hand before shaking herself off.
- Teach the dog to go straight into and swim straight across the water.
- Train all whistle signals and cues in the water.

Elsa ar

The Road to Field Trials

Often we have a goal for our training, such as competing in field trials. To achieve this we must have a number of sub goals. The road to a field trial is paved with basic training skills, building them in stages, and then putting them all together as well as building endurance and developing the right mindset.

Our basic training includes reward management, focus, and development of our training system. We also find it insanely fun – and a great thing to do – to teach the dog a lot of different tricks. Training our dogs to do tricks makes them quick and trainable at the same time as we strengthen our relationship and improve our ability to cooperate. We also teach the dog things we might find useful later on: working at close distance and far away from us, facing us and turn away from us, on different surfaces, and so on. Once our dog loves her rewards and has a good foundation to build on, we can start teaching basic skills or various parts of them, which we then put together to form the entire skill: hunting, marked retrieves, and blind retrieves.

Endurance

We can then combine each individual skill the dog has mastered and put together the entire program or trial. It's not enough just to put together the various skills; we must also build up the dog's endurance. Remember you can start incorporating small chains of behaviors the dog has already mastered early on in the training; this also helps develop your dog's endurance.

Puppies can complete small chains. Even if the dog knows only two or three behaviors, you can ask her to do more than one behavior before rewarding her. It can be for example "sit", hand target, "spin", and then a reward. These need not be things that you will ever use during trials, but only those cued behaviors the dog already has in her repertoire. In our endurance training, we teach the dog there will always be a reward, she just doesn't know exactly when. Keep in mind to only insert behaviors you think the dog will perform correctly into such chains; you are developing the dog's endurance, not refining the details of the performance.

> ### Pitfall
> It's easy to confuse a positive mindset with high energy. In some exercises, we want the dog to be calm and collected while in othe a more explosive mindset is required. But the dog should always radiate happiness and confidence!

When it comes to training, we distinguish between working on details, mindset, and endurance. When we are working on details, we don't want any sloppy executions. They are, however, acceptable when we are doing endurance training, which we will interrupt only if the dog becomes disengaged. When the dog is young, we focus on fostering the right mindset through our training before we start polishing

Janet and Jack

the details or developing endurance. As the dog gets older, training targeted at the dog's mindset and endurance overlap more and more.

Your Responsibility

Do you get angry and irritable when things don't go according to your plan – both during training and at field trials? We do sometimes. But we do everything we can instead to think, "Okay, today I learned something. I just need to go home and think how to train to improve this".

Our most important mission at field trials is to make sure the dog is prepared for them and above all, that she enjoys them! If we create a bad experience for the dog at trials, such as being angry and annoyed when things go poorly, the dog may not want to cooperate in the future. Remember that regardless of the field trial results, you and your dog are winners! Your dog should always leave the field trial with a good feeling. You can work on whatever went wrong at home before your next field trial.

We are the ones responsible for making the training fun and positive. We have to break up the training into manageable steps in a way that challenges the dog but still gives her the chance to constantly succeed. We must also teach the dog how to handle different situations and teach ourselves different methods for preparing the dog to complete her next task. Be sure to support and prepare the dog before the field trial in the same way as you do while training other times so she will feel at home. One tendency we've seen at field trials is for example that the handlers' gestures become increasingly more sweeping as they send the dog out to hunt the more time that goes by. The dog becomes more confused each time because she is not used to it. If you always send your dog with a gentle gesture while training, be sure to also

send her with a gentle gesture at Field Trials. If you find it difficult to control your gestures at Field Trials, you should also train with sweeping gestures in day-to-day situations so the dog gets used to them.

Your mental preparation for the trial is also important. The sports world has come a long way with sport psychology and the same has happened in the world of dogs. The Swedish obedience team wouldn't have won gold at the 2011 World Championships and silver at the 2012 World Championships if they had not had both well prepared dogs and handlers. Think about it: What can distract you before a field trial? Being the first to go? A change of judge? The pouring rain? A well meant comment: "Hope your dog is quiet throughout the trial now. You've been working on it so much!"

243

Henry

Practice Trial

Get together with friends to arrange practice trials as often as possible. The idea is to create a situation that resembles a real field trial as closely as possible. Don't try to run through an entire trial each time, but work on one or two elements and take a break to reward the dog. If you don't want the dog to learn to distinguish between real trials and regular training, you should be careful to train for trials in such a way the dog learns that the reward will always come, just not exactly when. Practice trials give you the opportunity to find out if your rewards are suited for a competition and see if they are effective.

For practice trials, you need to plan in advance who should do what, what the trial itself should look like, and then run one dog at a time. Ask someone to be a judge, another person to be a thrower, and a third to be the shooter. There's nothing wrong with having a slightly rowdy audience as well. The judges greet you and then welcome you to the trial and you start to follow the shooter. The first few times it can be wise to reward the dog for a well performed behavior and take a break already at this point.

Consider which distractions are challenging for you and your dog and introduce them during the practice trials. That gives you an opportunity to teach the dog how to handle them. In some countries the judges for example might have a couple of chairs to sit on, perhaps with a picnic basket next to it. Does the dog also want a snack at that moment or is she able to continue working anyway? A good rule of thumb is that if your training is challenging, field trials will be easy.

Judge Låtta welcomes Ingela and Snoddas to the field trial.

Cooperation – Working Together

One of the things the dog is assessed on during field trials is the dog's willingness to cooperate. Cooperation is not about the dog's blind obedience; rather it should be obvious that you are a team. This means that you do your part and the dog does hers. As we said before you should prepare the dog in the same way for field trials as you do when training. You therefore need to think carefully about the best way to help the dog during trials. Do you need to move between marked retrieves to create the best conditions for the dog to see where the game lands? Will you have the dog sit for a few seconds at your side to catch her breath and be able to focus again after a delivery?

Sometimes field trials don't go as we imagined, and then it's important to have a backup plan. What errors can you allow during the trial? What errors warrant an intervention from you during the trial so that the dog doesn't learn bad habits? In what situations should you keep a cool head and allow your dog to solve the problem herself, and in what situations should you step in and help her? For example, in some trials the judge wants to assess the dog's ability to perform marked retrieves. If the dog completely misses the mark, it may be good that you can direct her to the right area, but then the judge has no chance to see if your dog is a good marking dog or not.

Think about what you will do if the field trial doesn't go as planned. It may be better to receive deductions for extra signals and perhaps being allowed to continue the trial, than to have the dog do something wrong that warrants a score of zero or being eliminated. Sometimes it's also better to intervene in order to prevent the dog from learning things

we don't want her to learn, than to passively stand by and wait for the judge to do something. One example is when the dog has seen multiple marks. If we see that the dog is about to continue to hunt with game in her mouth, we instantly blow the recall whistle. If the dog has run ahead and swapped the game, we should intervene so the dog doesn't learn that it's permissible to swap game. However, we could ask the judge if it's okay that we go out with the dog and have it fetch the game that it put down, before we leave the trial area.

Goals

Training is easier if you have clear goals to work towards. It may be to start competing in field trials or for the dog to be able to walk at heel through town. As we train, we

During field trials, the judge inspects the game the dog has delivered to see that the dog hasn't damaged it.

always have the higher stakes as our goal. Because we are aiming high, we lay a good foundation right from the start and don't allow the dog to be careless with various skills just because she would have succeeded in the lower stakes anyway. This means, for example, that we begin training blind retrieves in water early on, even if they first appear in the more advanced stakes.

We like to break up our goals into performance goals, task specific goals, and emotional goals. Performance goals are long term, such as winning first prize in the Novice Stake. These are goals that motivate us to train, but the closer we get to field trials, the more important it is to focus on emotional and task specific goals because performance goals then only tend to make us stressed and create performance anxiety. We can never control the final results; the judge determines the outcome.

Task specific goals, however, we can always control and they are thus achievable. They deal with small parts of our training. For example if we trained a lot on the hunt whistle, a task specific goal at a field trial would be for the dog to immediately turn on her nose when she hears the hunt whistle.

Emotional goals are related to how both we and the dog feel about our training and field trials. We always want the dog to think that training with us is as good as it gets, the best thing ever. Emotional goals thus always take priority over task specific and performance goals.

Summary

- Start building the dog's endurance as early as possible.
- Prepare the dog for field trials by holding practice trials.
- Find routines that work for you and your dog before starting your dog in a trial.
- Think about your goals for training and competition:
  » What are your long term performance goals?
  » What are task specific goals for the next month?
  » What emotional goals do you have for your training?

Training Plan

Behaviour — Marked retrieve

What does it look like? — The dog sits calmly, quietly, and still at my left side and takes note of where the mark falls. On my cue the dog runs the most direct route, finds the object, takes it, and runs straight back to me to release it on my cue. Later she sits beside me again. If the dog doesn't find the mark at once, she continues to hunt the area until she does.

Sub-goals — Sit beside me, note the area of the fall, run out, hunt for the mark, take the mark, and deliver it to hand.

Distractions to be trained — Gunfire, having an audience, other game/objects nearby, other dogs nearby, the thrower.

Cue — Fetch (stay, thank you).

Date	Criteria	#C/#R	#C/#R	#C/#R	#C/#R
		2/2			
7/6	Take the object while heading towards me, five yards away, deliver to hand.				
	~~Take the object while heading towards me, ten yards away, deliver to hand.~~	4/4			
7/6	Retrieve an object thrown ten yards away.				
		3/4			
10/6	Retrieve an object thrown on the other side of a stonewall.	2/4	4/4		
12/6	Retrieve an object that landed far into a thicket.				
		2/4	4/4		
15/6	Retrieve an object that was thrown by another person, five yards away.				
	Retrieve an object that was thrown by another person, ten yards away.				

#C – number of clicks (=successful repetitions), #R – number of repetitions

Running towards me worked so well that I only di[d]
repetitions before I moved on to throwing the obj[ect]
crossed out step number two on the training plan
The first time I threw the dummy into the thick[et]
proved to be a little too difficult, so she gave up
came back without the dummy. I went and got t[he]
dummy and threw it again.

Water Work

Goal
- Delivery to hand out of the water, approximately 15 yards on land, without shaking off water.
- Memory retrieve through the water, around 30 yards (i.e. she is to retrieve game from a known location, but trust my "back" signal and go back out the entire way).

Execution
I started with a little warm up to really get ready for a lot of successful repetitions. First I repeated the most important step, running up out of the water to my hand target, receiving a reward, and then shaking off.

Once this flowed smoothly without an object, I added a ball that she fetched from a short distance into the water, and then delivered to my hand. After that, I checked that she was spontaneously picking up game on land, and delivering it to my hand (today's game was duck). Then I sent her on a marked retrieve on the other side of the water. As she was returning my helper snuck yet another bird to the same place, to which I then sent her on a line. Again, my helper put the game in the same place and then left the area. After a little break, I sent her to run another line to the same place, and she nailed it!

Step By Step:
- Hand target out of the water while I stood two yards up on shore.
- Hand target out of the water while I stood 15 yards on shore.
- Delivery of the ball out of the water while I stood two yards on shore (the ball was five yards out in the water).
- Delivery of the ball out of the water while I stood ten yards on shore (the ball was five yards out in the water).
- Delivery of the duck on land while I stood five yards away.
- Marked retrieve on the other side of the water, delivery of the duck on land while I stood two yards from the water.
- Being cast a line to the other side of the water, delivery of the duck on land while I stood five yards from the water (to the same area where the mark fell, she hadn't seen the game being placed out).
- Being cast on a line to the other side of the water, delivery of the duck on land while I stood ten yards from the water (the same area as before after a five minute break, she hadn't seen the game being placed out).

Evaluation
So on nine out of ten repetitions, I got exactly what I wanted, stylish deliveries without her shaking off! What we need to keep working on is to really hold the game until I cue "thank you" so she doesn't drop it before I get a good grip on the game (the last repetition she dropped the game a little too early, the others were very good). I intend to do the same as I have done with dummies and other objects.
- Several hand targets with objects in her mouth alternatively to the right and left hand before I cue "thank you".
- Pushing her nose with the object against my hand target until I cue "thank you".

Some Final Words

Now we hope you have a lot of new ideas and are excited to get out and train! Maybe you've even put the book aside while reading to go out and try something new?

We wish you the best in all of your training to come, and who knows, we might see you at a field trial or in one of our classes. We want to send you off to your future training with a few final words:

- Have fun with your dog!
- Have the right focus: Reward everything your dog does right, and think about what she should do – instead of what she shouldn't do!
- Develop as many different kinds of rewards as possible.
- Identify your points of success.
- Make sure to break up your training into many small parts before the dog has to master an entire behavior.
- The most important things to train are: steadiness, deliveries, walking at heel, and running a line. If your dog has mastered these behaviors, you've already come a long way!
- Don't rush but allow your training to take time. Allow the dog to mature and don't stress.

- If you only train one thing with your retriever, work on deliveries! And when you've gotten tired of training that, train them a little more.
- If you only train one thing with your spaniel, train her to be steady to flush. Train steadiness and remaining sitting in all imaginable situations.
- Only allow the dog to work when she is in the right frame of mind – that is to say, calm and focused.
- We encourage you to try different approaches to see what works best for you and your dog. As long as you have fun together, it can't go wrong!

You can download a complete list of sub goals on our website at www.retrievingforalloccasions.com. There you will find a list of all of the book's sub goals in a single document that you can take with you when you are training. You can also download a blank training plan so you can make your own plans for whatever criteria you want to set.

About the Authors

Elsa Blomster has two Golden Retrievers, Diesel and Ludde. She trains and competes in obedience, tracking, rally, and field trials.

Lena Gunnarsson trains and competes in tracking and obedience. She also trains agility, scent work, and field trials with her two Cocker Spaniels, Totte and Tassla.

Elsa has a Master of Science in Supply Chain Management and works as marketing director at an authorized car repair corporation.

Lena is a journalist and an organizational consultant and works with healthcare development with a focus on equality.

Together they run Klickerförlaget Göteborg AB where they give classes in gun dog training using clicker training principles, as well as publish books and organize lectures with selected guest speakers.

Glossary

Blind retrieve: A retrieve where the dog doesn't know where the object is located and only you know in which direction to send the dog. You need to be able to send the dog straight, left, right, and back. We differentiate between blind retrieves, "seen" or memory retrieves. A memory retrieve means the dog has seen where the object is located, but time has passed before she is allowed to retrieve it.

Building value: Generously rewarding the dog for a particular behavior makes it more enjoyable for the dog to perform. The behavior, in simple terms, becomes valuable to the dog.

Capturing a behavior: When the dog spontaneously offers a behavior we want, we take the opportunity to reward it. Sitting is an example of a behavior that is usually extremely easy to capture.

Casting: Refers to the act of sending the dog on a retrieve and then re-directing her at a distance.

Classical conditioning: A theory of learning related to emotions, reflexes and involuntary responses – behaviors the dog is unable to control herself. The dog learns to connect a reflex with a stimulus. Also called respondent or Pavlovian conditioning.

Clickerwise: When the dog has learned that the click means, "you're right" and then offers the same behavior that she just received the click for, and that a lack of click means, "try again or change something".

Clicking: When we write the word "click" we always mean click (or mark the correct behavior in some other way) and reward the dog.

Cold game: Game that is cold when it's retrieved, in other words not recently shot. Sometimes it has also been frozen and

defrosted for the trial or training.

Conditioning: Means the same thing as learning (see Learning).

Contaminated ground: Ground where one or more people and possibly dogs have previously walked and consequently spread a lot of scents.

Criterion: What the dog needs to do in order to get her reward.

Dummy: A cloth bag filled with plastic pellets or sawdust used for training purposes and sometimes during competition to replicate game. Dummies are easier to handle and store than game. They come in a variety of sizes, ranging from 0.05 lbs up to several pounds. The most common weights we use are 0.5, 1, and 1.3 lbs.

External reward: A reward the dog has seen you place somewhere and that she is allowed to run and take when you release her with the cue "go ahead".

Fluency: The behavior is almost automatic and occurs without the dog thinking about it. A fluent behavior also has a very short latency (see Latency) and is performed with speed and precision every time. Fluency can be measured as the number of repetitions of a behavior a dog can perform in a certain time period, such as a minute.

Flushing: When a dog flushes, she hunts the game and drives it from its cover. This can be a bird or other animal, such as a rabbit. When the dog has flushed the game, she stops on the spot to avoid the risk of being hit by a possible shot. Then the dog retrieves the shot game on cue. This only applies to spaniels (as well as pointers, setters and other HPR dogs, but in that case flushing is an undesirable behavior).

Foundation skills: One part of a skill

set. The various foundation skills are then combined into complete skill sets. Køste and Egtvedt (2008) compare the foundation skills with letters that are combined into words (sub goals) and sentences (completed skill sets).

Generalizing or distraction training: We teach the dog to perform the behavior in various environments and in spite of distractions such as toys, people, gunfire, or other dogs.

Hand targeting: The dog puts her nose against the palm of your hand. In other words, your hand is the target.

Holding an area: A small area where the dog hunts for an object or game.

Latency: The time it takes from when the dog has finished her reward until she offers the behavior again.

Learning: Experiences that influence a behavior and thereby changes it. Divided into classical and operant learning (also see Classic conditioning and Operant conditioning).

Warm game: Game that is shot and retrieved during a field trial, a shoot (in Britain), or a hunt (in the US).

Marked retrieve: Both you and the dog know where the object is because you have seen it fall. The most common are single marked retrieves, but in more advanced stakes there are also double and triple marks. A double mark consists of two falling marks before you cast the dog. The dog must retrieve one, bring it back, and then the other one. She shouldn't try to take both of them at the same time or swap from the first one to the second – she has to bring the first object to you first.

Negative punishment: Something the

dog wants disappears, which decreases the likelihood a certain behavior will be repeated. For example, we pick up the mark if the dog runs in.

Negative reinforcement: Something unpleasant disappears, which means the likelihood of a certain behavior being repeated increases. An example is a force fetch, where the handler pinches the dog's ear until she takes the retrieve article. When the dog takes the object, the pain disappears.

Official trial: Results from official field trials are recorded in the official dog register, most often with the Kennel Club.

Operant conditioning: All the behaviors a dog can choose to perform or not. Always followed by a consequence that might be pleasant or unpleasant for the dog.

Positive punishment: Something unpleasant is added which decreases the likelihood a certain behavior will be repeated. For example, the dog pulls on the leash, the handler jerks on the leash and the dog stops pulling.

Positive reinforcement: Something pleasant is added which increases the likelihood a certain behavior will be repeated. For example, the dog sits and we give her a treat or start playing with her.

Proofing: We teach the dog to do more than what is necessary, such as training with more challenging distractions than what are likely to occur during field trials. It makes behaviors easier to perform regardless of what else is happening in the surroundings.

Punishment: Something that decreases the likelihood of a certain behavior.

Quartering: A term used to describe the

pattern a spaniel runs when hunting with her handler.

Reinforcement: Something that increases the likelihood of a certain behavior.

Reinforcing: The dog is rewarded for a particular behavior, which leads to a desire to repeat the behavior. If we intend to reward a behavior, it's important the dog really perceives it as a reward. Otherwise we haven't reinforced the behavior.

Release cue: Refers to the signal that allows the dog to leave her position to continue working with us. We cue "free" when the dog should come out of her crate or when she may get up from a sitting position.

Reliable behavior: We say a behavior is reliable when the dog is correct more than 95 percent of the time.

Reverse luring: The dog controls herself and abstains from something she really wants in order to receive her reward. Often we show the dog a treat in our open palm when she behaves correctly and then close the hand if she tries to take the treat.

Running a line: A specific term relating to walked-up shooting where a dog runs up the line of guns until she hits shot scent, blood scent, or is halted with a stop whistle and instructed to hunt.

Run in: The dog tries to go for a retrieve without you giving her a cue.

Shaping: Gradually building the behavior we want by rewarding the dog for every step in the right direction.

Shaping-wise: Means almost the same as clicker-wise (see Clicker-wise). The dog has learned the rules of the game and is always trying a little more without giving up so that

we can gradually shape new behaviors.

Stimulus control: The dog offers the desired behavior on cue. If you cue "sit", the dog sits and does nothing else, such as lying down. The cue can be a word, a whistle, a hand gesture, or something else in the environment. The cue is anything the dog observes that she has learnt to associate with performing a certain behavior.

Strategic reward placement: We place rewards in a well thought out manner that either reinforces the position the dog is in, facilitates the start of the next repetition, or makes the dog anticipate going in a particular direction.

Sweeping up: A retriever specific work where the dog freely hunts in an area where neither you nor the dog knows where the object is. In some countries this is part of the field trial for retrievers, whereas in others it's something that is done by dogs not under judging any more, or just after a hunt to make sure all game is found.

Target: Quite simply whatever the dog should touch with some part of her body, such as a paw, nose, or butt.

Unofficial trials: The results from unofficial trials are not reported to an official register and are not visible anywhere else besides the organizer's records.

Thank you!

We are especially grateful to Jenny Nyberg, who in addition to creating all of the fantastic illustrations for the book, also acted as editor for the Swedish version of the book. Your questions, suggestions, and comments helped us take the book to new heights!

Thanks to Catharina Fahlberg, Elin Carlsson, Åsa Davidsson, Ingela Hammar, Jan Kallenberg, Jonas Martinsson, Kristina Cederberg, Låtta Bergstrand, Patrik Andersson, Shadi Kajevand, Sten Christoffersson, and Thomas Stokke who have read and commented on our Swedish manuscript based on their knowledge of dog training and field trial training. Thanks also to Philippa Williams, Erica Munro Ferguson, Maxine Furnandiz, Janet Botterill, Shirley Carew, and Sarah Winter for letting us use your knowledge about UK field trials and gun dog training, and to Jenni Dix from "Legacy Canine Behavior and Training", Chris Kitterman and Inga From from "Positive Gun Dogs of Minnesota" for doing the same with a US perspective.

Thanks to Charlotte West for translating the book to English and Emelie Johnson Vegh for your tireless efforts and questions while editing the translation. You've both thereby helped us share the book with a wider audience.

Thanks to Johanna Simonsson and Ludvig Aust for designing our ideas.

Thanks to Ulrika Jannert Kallenberg at "Orda Om" for a thorough and refreshing "hard" proofreading. We would also like to thank Olov Carlsson, Jenny Axelsson, Åsa Davidsson, Låtta Bergstrand, Ulrika Norell and Shirley Carew for proofreading.

Thanks to Per Jensen, at the University of Linköping, for fact checking the chapter "A Spotlight on Behavior" as well as suggestions for literature that made us wiser.

Thanks to our two-legged masters of field trials: Eva Bodfäldt, Thomas Stokke, Philippa Williams, Jeanethe Johansson, Katarina Eriksson, and Catharina Fahlberg. We would also like to extend our appreciation to Cecilie Køste, Morten Egtvedt, Maria Brandel, and Fanny Gott who made us better dog trainers.

Thanks to all our models and photographers.

Thanks to our dear training buddies for putting up with us, laughing with us, celebrating our successes with us, and helping us move on when we are tearing our hair out.

Thanks to all of our students – hundreds of you at this moment – for bringing all of your different dogs and questions to us and challenging us to become better instructors!

Thanks to our two-legged darlings Jonas and Ludvig for supporting us even though we spent most of our vacation buried under our manuscript ... and then continued to indulge us during the months ahead.

Last but definitely not least: thanks to our dogs Dacke, Diesel, Ludde, Tassla, and Totte for everything you have taught us and all of the joy you bring to us everyday!

Love!
Elsa & Lena

WORLD-CLASS SWEDISH COOKING

English translation copyright © 2013 by Skyhorse Publishing, Inc.
First published by Norstedts, Sweden, in 2012, as *Frantzén/Lindeberg* by Björn Frantzén and Daniel Lindeberg. Published by agreement with Norstedts Agency.
Photography: Fredrik Skogkvist
(Photos on pp. 42, 43, 160, 165, 190, 191 by Stefan van der Kwast Gissberg and p. 30 by Torbjörn Jonasson)
Transcription: Göran Lager
Art Direction/Graphic Design: Stefan van der Kwast Gissberg
Illustration: Martin Bergström
Image Processing: Anders Wandin
Prepress: Elanders Fälth & Hässler, Värnamo

www.skyhorsepublishing.com

10 9 8 7 6 5 4 3 2 1

Library of Congress Cataloging-in-Publication Data
Frantzén, Björn.
[Frantzén/Lindeberg. English]
World-class Swedish cooking : artisanal recipes from one of Stockholm's most celebrated restaurants / Björn Frantzén and Daniel Lindeberg ; foreword by Mons Kallentoft.
     pages cm
Includes index.
"First published by Norstedts, Sweden, in 2012, as Frantzén/Lindeberg"--Preliminaries.
ISBN 978-1-62087-735-7 (hardcover : alk. paper) 1. Cooking, Swedish. I. Lindeberg, Daniel. II. Frantzén/Lindeberg (Restaurant : Stockholm, Sweden) III. Title.
TX722.S8F6813 2013
641.59485--dc23
                              2013006015

Printed in China

WORLD-CLASS SWEDISH COOKING

Artisanal Recipes from One of
Stockholm's Most Celebrated Restaurants

BJÖRN FRANTZÉN AND **DANIEL LINDEBERG**

FOREWORD BY
Mons Kallentoft

TRANSLATED BY
Stine Østtveit

Skyhorse Publishing

A surprising gastronomical journey led by the demand for authentic ingredients and sustained by the freedom to fantasize and create.

Daniel Lindeberg

Björn Frantzén

CONTENTS

INTRODUCTION

There lies a vested interest in publishing a book—to have everything we work to do each day in print and available for anyone who is interested. But it occurred to us that this was not the only reason to undertake this project. We realized there were many things we had not really thought out and that we still had so many unanswered questions. The work to write a book over three hundred pages long made us sharpen our focus even more and gave us the opportunity to gain knowledge in order to develop our restaurant even further.

THIS BOOK GAVE US A DEADLINE TO WORK TOWARD. Over a year before the book went to print, we sketched out what we needed to achieve and complete. Before we delivered the manuscript to the publishing house, we went through every statement, fact, assumption, method, and ingredient to make sure the writing was accurate and crystal clear.

The journey of writing this book was absolutely amazing, not only because of the hours spent in the kitchen trying out new recipes—most of which were not served in the restaurant until after publication—but also because we found new challenges, suppliers, and techniques.

Some of our discoveries while working on this book came about through pure exploration and by confirming things we already knew. For instance, we didn't understand why fish seemed to taste so much better when it was matured under ice and was no longer "fresh" in the strict sense of the word. The same was true for our preference to receive live crayfish, lobster, and scallops in our kitchen and to kill them moments before serving. We believed they tasted far better prepared this way, but now we understand why. This understanding, in turn, resulted in our working with our fishermen to teach them how to use the Japanese method of killing fish.

To arrive at this conclusion, we had continuous contact and meetings with some of Europe's sharpest researchers, some of whom combined an interest in the taste and texture of fish and shellfish with their scientific knowledge. Through our observation and their research, we determined when seafood is at its very best for serving; it's all about the fishing methods, killing, draining, temperature, tenderizing, and preparation after it reaches room temperature.

Our cookbook project also increased our contact with the farmers at our two vegetable gardens. After closely following a full growing season, we became more familiar with their work. We came to understand how they work with old flavorful cultivars and fight against industrial sowing. We studied the deep knowledge these farmers hold and grew to appreciate how they developed various methods to create unique ingredients for us. To make full use of our vegetable suppliers, we adjust our menu based on what they deliver; we believe there is no acceptable reason to use unripe raw ingredients that are not at their absolute best in the mere interest of offering the same menu every night. A few years ago we introduced our "*vita menyer*" ("white menus"), which means our guests have no idea what will be served that evening. This gives us considerable freedom to compose dishes in accordance with what is delivered fresh to our kitchen. In one dish, we go as far as to let the gardens decide the flavor, look, texture, depth, and preparation of the dish, and we've even named it accordingly: *Satio Tempestas*, which with a few added words translates to "satisfaction based on season and time of year."

We had achieved such positive results with the fish and shellfish from the cold Nordic seas and the produce from the gardens in Malmköping and Askersund that we were very disappointed when we could not find a Swedish breeder who could deliver the quality we demanded of fowl, pork, veal, and beef. We felt that because our vegetable farmers find the best varieties that are not engineered for high yields and convenient transportation at the expense of taste, we should have the same approach to the meat we use.

As luck would have it, we met a pig farmer at one of our gardens who bred Linderöd pigs, considered the "national pig" of Sweden. We had already experienced the genuine taste of Linderöd pork when we bought a 480-pound (220-kilogram) pig named Clarissa who provided us with her own *lardo di colonnata* for a long time. The Linderöd pork is often said to taste nostalgic, "like pork used to taste"; it has a good fat content that carries a deep and mild meat flavor, with a little hint of the wild.

The same farmer also helped us breed cage-free chickens that are allowed to move freely outdoors and pick and choose whatever they want to eat. Sadly, a fox killed the first brood, but these things happen, and we could never imagine buying chickens of inferior quality to cover our losses. We cook according to season, without compromise, and the chicken season is short. It only lasted for a couple of weeks after the fox had killed all of our matured chickens.

During the year we worked on the book, we also looked for breeders who could deliver the absolute best beef. One who looks will find, and we struck gold in Gotland and in Jämtland with two different kinds of meat. The first is a cross between Simmental and Angus and is bred on spent grains (from beer brewers), and the other is a Swedish mountain cow.

We believe that through our selection and quest for quality, we end up with the ingredients we want. In return, we give back to a small group of enthusiasts who give their all to produce high-quality products the old-fashioned way, with the accompanying hard physical work, low yields, and poor resistance to diseases. These are entrepreneurs who, as strange as it may seem, are propelled not solely by money, but rather by a kind of idealism. And it is no secret that we are extremely dependent on these people. They, in turn, are very dependent on us, as our payment for their products is income that usually goes right back into their business. If more people worked in this way, Swedish farming would be greatly enriched, and the quality of the work would improve along with the status of the industry.

We feel privileged to be able to write a book about our relatively short existence as a restaurant, over three hundred pages about our profession, a job that, to us, means working all hours of the day and night—a job that affects not only our own lives, but also those of our families and friends.

We've divided the book into a few very clear chapters and a few sections that overlap.

There are two reasons why the recipes in this book are not presented in the traditional way. Firstly, we never work with recipes in our kitchen, and secondly, our dishes demand so many

elements and restaurant tools that few people would be able to prepare them in their homes. Just one recipe for one dish would be so specialized and extensive that there would simply not be enough space to list each element in this book.

We have, therefore, opted instead to describe various dishes and share our thoughts behind creating these dishes and menus. With a few exceptions. The ingredients command the cooking process, and every chapter has an introduction explaining our thoughts and philosophy as well as the scientific findings we've researched that enable us to serve the very best.

It is our wish to convey a sense of our work and our flavors, our uncompromising attitude, and our gratitude to all of our colleagues, those in the restaurant as well as our qualified suppliers.

....

Björn Frantzén / Daniel Lindeberg

FOREWORD—THE MAGIC OF THE *NOW*

Gastronomy is the art of the *now* and as such is intimately connected to our human nature.

Man takes his first breath in one moment.

He takes his last in another.

We all share this premise, rich or poor; wise or dumb; brown, white, yellow, or red. Life consists of a long string of *now*s that should be caught, twisted, turned, worried over, and enjoyed.

What happens after a baby takes its first breath?

It cries.

Then, it crawls towards the breast and food, hungry with its entire life and world ahead, in search of nurture for both body and soul.

Later everything changes.

And really, nothing at all.

Look up at the sky and notice that jets paint it white like never before.

Like ants, people keep marching across the entire planet.

We live in a world increasingly populated by people obsessed with trying to catch the present moment, define it, embrace it: adventure junkies adrift in a seemingly infinite universe.

The world is at our feet, and we take it; a playful or quiet moment is our right.

No journey is too long or too short. The jet streams take us around the world to meditate, climb mountains, take mindfulness courses at a spa, and in Singapore, Hong Kong, Tokyo, and Shanghai, flustered Asians look for happiness in a slew of brand-name stores.

We jump from moment to moment.

In a never-ending frenzied dance.

And in this dance, we dance towards the planet's culinary temple.

Nothing wrong with that.

For how many moments are spent in a restaurant visit?

Millions, millions, and millions more.

It can be like this: You're sitting in your living room near Holland Park or Union Square or Circular Quay, and you read in a magazine about how the hottest restaurant on the planet is currently in Stockholm, on a small street in Old Town, and that it is impossible to get a table because the seats are few and the demand is immense.

Six months' wait!

My God!

But something inside you stirs because, deep inside, you know that one night one of those tables will be reserved in your name.

You think about how it will be then.

Your lips smack, you get hungry, you feel the anticipation, and then an email drops in your inbox.

"We have made a reservation . . ."

The flight is booked, the websites are visited, and with your eyes and brain and imagination, you eat your way through the coming evening.

Another email arrives a few days before your visit.

"We want to remind you . . ."

By now you can barely contain yourself, you want to be there, at the restaurant, with your behind safely resting on the sleek chair.

But you need to be patient.

And then, you finally arrive in Stockholm, and maybe your legs are aching after a long flight, and it's unbearably cold and dark here, and there's ice in the air as you find your way to Lilla Nygatan.

But then he stands before you in the dark, the doorman of the restaurant.

Despite the cold.

Despite the fact that he makes a dent in the restaurant's budget that every other restaurant in town finds unnecessary.

And now he opens the door, says "Valkommen," and even if you don't understand what he is saying, you understand what he means. A few steps inside, candles light up the darkness, and the tattooed tough guys in cook's clothing behind the shining counter smile at you, and you know you have arrived, your long wait is over.

But you also know that this is when it will all begin.

When does a life path become just slightly straighter?

Is it in a grandmother's kitchen? Where a small child hangs on his grandmother's legs and helps out as she bakes buns and cakes and tarts and bread and God knows what else? Is it the intoxicating goodness of the scents in such a kitchen that makes the small tot decide to go the restaurant route? That makes him want to be a pastry chef?

Maybe, maybe not.

It could just as easily happen when an eleven-year-old is invited to join a friend's family at the restaurant Rendez-Vous in Apelbergsgatan and experiences the rich revelation of home-made béarnaise sauce. Or when, too soon, he sees his soccer career end because of an injury and wonders: What the hell am I supposed to do now?

The two boys' roads crossed in the kitchen of a restaurant in Sollentuna.

It was decided: one day they would do something together.

Without throwing caution to the wind, however, nothing gets its continuation; without audacity, the world does not widen.

So, Frantzén and Lindeberg were left with a few options: Falsify work certificates to be employed as an apprentice at a two-star restaurant in London with a small space on lovely Charlotte Street?

Why not, when an opportunity for employment presents itself.

Work hard and work long hours for pocket change.

Live like a dog.

Burn your hands and scar your arms.

And every day come back for more and more and more in some sort of methodical, nearly unbearable, purposeful madness.

And later a boat crosses the English Channel.

There, in Paris' seventh arrondissement, at dinky Rue de Varenne, the skin gets even more blisters and the bags under the eyes darken, but what does that matter when you can learn how Alain Passard draws the mystique out of his vegetables, despite a clattering chaos in the kitchen every night?

L'Arpège.

Few names command as much respect among gourmets. Why? Well, there is a standard in Passard's cooking, a direction, and a clear ambition.

Then, it's back home to Stockholm to look for a space; for now, years later, the boys, now young men, will "do something together."

Ultimately, after a long search, the dreamers find a home on a sweet and cozy street in Old Town.

To paraphrase Raymond Carver, the phenomenal writer who portrayed the everyday in literature, there is an abundance of talent in humans, but talent properly utilized is much rarer.

I know that Carver's words are true.

Evidence of utilized talent can be tasted in real life. Where?

At Lilla Nygatan, for instance.

Frantzén/Lindeberg was never supposed to become a gastronomical shrine.

Rather, it was the space that led the decision to go in that direction. "What can we do here?" was the question asked when the contract was signed.

The space had previously been the home of one of Stockholm's most prominent restaurants, and F/L carried the torch in many ways.

In my opinion, there is something extraordinary about allowing one's circumstances to shape something, rather than trying to shape reality based on a specific idea or thought. Call it an exploring curiosity, a childlike openness to existence that few adults can, or dare to, allow themselves.

In the early days of Lilla Nygatan, there was a sense of humor.

It can easily turn out that way when a person is subjected to a challenge that seems overwhelming. How to gather all the possibilities a gastronomically top-tier restaurant requires, how to bring the seemingly endless stretch of various *nows*, into one whole? To a functional, brain- and soul-nurturing, lingering experience?

Where to begin? Continue? How to stop?

It is easy to seek laughter in such situations and the relief that such exhalation offers. You can always count on a laugh, that's for sure.

And so, the guests of F/L could order the "Tour de France," a France-shaped plate with a representative cheese from six stops along the Tour de France, and listen their way through the cheese plate from an iPod's recorded audioguide to the flavors, narrated by Swedish broadcaster Ulf Elfving or actor Stellan Skarsgård.

They could bathe in a cloud of cinnamon smoke.

But day by day, F/L chiseled its own aesthetic, taking control over more and more of those aspects that together make a gastronomical universe, and just as suddenly, there is no longer room for circuses.

"It didn't feel right," is the short explanation.

I think of the restaurant's own vegetable gardens, where beloved—yes, almost adored—vegetables are harvested at their very best.

How many Swedish restaurants have their very own vegetable gardens?

Not many, as far as I know.

F/L has two, painstakingly obtained and maintained at that, given our somewhat hostile climate and in ways limited gastronomical culture.

I can also imagine the owners' great sorrow the day a fox broke in and stole their restaurant's own black chickens. Then it was certainly easy to hold back laughter and feel in the deeper chambers of the heart.

One of the world's most developed culinary areas is San Sebastián in the Basque Country. The doyen in the area is a man by the name of Juan Mari Arzak who has on multiple occasions pointed out to me that he tries to see the world through the eyes of a child. He is seventy years old now, but he still wishes for toys on his birthday.

Eduardo Chillida, one of the twentieth century's greatest sculptors, also lived and worked in San Sebastián.

Chillida argued that art is made up of poetry and construction combined.

What did he mean by this?

I believe it's about gaining enough knowledge, skill, and practical scope that you can allow your intuition to work freely.

Chefs rarely use the word *art*.

But nevertheless.

Vegetables from your own garden. An old cow that belongs to you. A particular scallop for which you searched for such a long time, finally found by a deep-sea diver from Norway.

The knowledge of the exact number of seconds a scallop should be steamed. (Just until it opens.)

Your teacher's sensibilities transformed to certainty somewhere deep inside your own spine.

Your knowledge of the trinity. How two known elements can be complemented by a third for a dramatic effect.

And so the plates of scallops with algae butter and white truffle are carried out in the dining room at Lilla Nygatan. Presented by a brigade aware that eccentricity can elevate a waitressing job to something more. And there sit the guests, about to drop their jaws with every bite of the dish.

It tastes good, but anyone can see that the guests are moved to the depth of their souls.

There is a magic in this moment, they seem to think. A moment's sense of the *now*'s contrast to eternity.

Through structure and poetry, the chefs in the kitchen have created art.

Even if it was never a spoken goal.

Beautifully so.

And worth every hour upon hour upon hour spent on a jet stream.

Gastronomy is the peculiar art of *now*.

Not so remarkable, really.

But how long does the *now* last?

At F/L, the practical management of time comes last, after the immediate needs of the ingredients.

I have been in many of the world's most celebrated kitchens. And in almost every single one, you can find small plastic cans, pots, and flasks with prepared ingredients, ready to be used in the cooking of lunch or dinner. The *mise en place* is extensive, for practical reasons. The chives are chopped, the tartare is cut ahead of time.

But does this taste the best?

Rarely, rarely.

At F/L, almost everything happens in a deliberate *now*, at the absolute last possible moment. The herbs are chopped right before they go on the plate, the crayfish meat is turned into tartare seconds before being served, and the dough for the bread rises on the guest's table, where even the butter is churned *à la minute*.

Now can also mean waiting.

When is a fish best? When it is as fresh as possible?

This is true for some varieties, some parts. But not for others. It takes courage to let a fish fillet mature for two weeks in our culture, just to make it as umami-rich as possible.

The custom of allowing fish to mature is Japanese, from sushi masters and the kaiseki tradition.

F/L looks to the East nowadays.

The menu is *omakase*, the choice of the chef, even though guests can come with requests. But not too many do, and why would they want to?

A true kaiseki meal follows a pattern that's been developed over hundreds of years, a pattern that is not too different from the Western haute cuisine culture, with amuse-bouches, entrées, main courses, desserts, macarons . . . salty, sweet, tart, raw, cooked, soft, runny, crispy, beginning and end . . .

For instance, a kaiseki meal always contains sashimi somewhere early on. And there is, of course, raw fish in the beginning at F/L, with an introduction of, for example, halibut, sliced with the same skill as the Japanese masters.

In the kaiseki tradition there is, contrary to popular belief, a great deal of flexibility for the chef. Almost every listed dish can be exchanged, replaced by whatever the chef of the day finds most satisfying.

But the rice dish, on the other hand, should always be included.

Is there a "holy rice" component to our Western haute cuisine tradition? Is there something that cannot be substituted without completely losing our meal's structure and tradition? The fish dish? The poultry? The meat?

The answer lies in the reason why rice must always go with a kaiseki meal. First and foremost, it is required for the sake of filling up the guest—not only the body, but also the soul. Nothing impresses the Japanese guest more than perfectly made rice, and the dish arrives at the end of the meal when the guest needs to feel fully satisfied.

And that might be the only banal rule we have left for Western gastronomy: The guest should leave the table full. Stomach, soul, and heart.

But at what price do we achieve this perfect fullness?

And who pays the price?

We revisit the crayfish mentioned above.

Let's pretend that it's March today, at this hour, at this second, in this restaurant in Stockholm.

The crayfish has been killed after a life spent in cold seas. It was brought here alive from the east coast to the west coast in the restaurant's own specially designed cages and met its fate in the kitchen at F/L. It died quite happy, the crayfish, less stressed than usual, because it had its own chamber in the cage. Crayfish seem to prefer it that way because, otherwise, they start attacking each other.

Now, what do we do with the recently departed crayfish?

It tastes best raw. This is how it fits our meal pattern, our structure. Chop it into tartare, blend it with vanilla, maybe add a few drops of oil and apple as a contrast?

The guest at Lilla Nygatan chews, taking in the silky smooth, lightly chilled softness of the crayfish tartare, feeling a stirring in his or her soul from the thunderous flavors of the churning, cold seas.

What doesn't the guest know?

Maybe this:

The crayfish he or she is now eating was caught by a fisherman in the stormy Skagerrak fewer than twenty-four hours earlier.

It's a dangerous job.

Deadly dangerous.

Only a few years ago, two fishermen drowned while doing just this. The following night, waiters in Stockholm had to tell their guests: "Sorry, tonight we don't have crayfish."

Think of these fishermen the next time you feel the sweet magic of crayfish in your mouth.

Remember that the last breath that filled their lungs consisted of 40°F water instead of oxygen-rich air.

And that, in a way, they made that sacrifice for you.

For your enjoyment and happiness.

In the cocoon at Lilla Nygatan, all of life's worries have vanished.

You are calm, in every way. You place your platinum card down for payment and shiver a bit at the thought of heading out into the harsh Nordic night. But then again: Is there not something strangely exotic about how those gigantic snowflakes fly toward the ground in swirling circles underneath the streetlights?

And then, after a friendly thank-you and good-bye, you are out on the street.

You are happy.

You feel great.

You got what you came for, and more.

While you walk home through the dark night, under glimmering stars barely visible behind the veil of scattered clouds, you try to place your experience within the contemporary Nordic gastronomic tradition, but you really can't. The meal you just ate stands on its own, here and now, in perfect symmetry with the movement of the world and its inhabitants.

In bed in your hotel room, you may think about how the F/L kitchen is sometimes referred to as an "intelligent kitchen."

But you think that is a paltry description.

For your experience this evening went beyond the conscious intelligence and delved deep into your nameless emotions.

You think of the impossibility of gastronomy in a time of hunger, injustice, and misery, but realize gastronomy is after all a little like literature, art, architecture: a sanctuary for humanity, where we can rest, look ahead, and let ourselves celebrate what we are capable of achieving and who we are.

It's after two in the morning when you finally fall asleep in a hotel room in Stockholm. And perhaps you dream about that first moment when this story began, the story that continued from Holland Park, or Circular Quay, or Union Square, to this moment.

And maybe you dream about your very last moment, the moment you know awaits you in both wakefulness and sleep, as it does for everyone.

And in a dream it will occur to you.

The fragment of recognition that this moment is your last may just be the exact sum of all of your other moments—the love you've experienced; the sights you've seen; the pain you've owned; the caviar, foie gras, chicken, steak, turbot, truffle, crayfish, sardine, horse, perch, car-

rot, potato, and the bread you've tasted, all the things that found themselves in your mouth, traveling through your organism, crawling even deeper through the membranes in your body that no scientist can name and into what is really you.

So you dream.

Later you wake.

And think:

Where am I going next?

And later:

When will the doorman at Lilla Nygatan open the door for me again?

. . . .
Mons Kallentoft

HISTORY

It was an early morning at Edsbacka Krog, a restaurant in Sollentuna, just north of Stockholm, and the park down to Edsviken was a pale gray. The restaurant had one Michelin star in 1992, but now it was 1998, and Björn came striding into the kitchen with his knives, followed by Daniel. They both had expectations, a certain cockiness, and great ambitions.

Christer Lingström's Edsbacka was a highly regarded place to work for a young chef. Those who worked there could hold their heads a little higher.

Björn was immediately placed in the hot kitchen, Daniel in the cold as a pastry chef—both felt like they were chopped liver, but their relatively short apprenticeships at starred restaurants abroad had provided them with a great deal to contribute to Edsbacka.

EDSBACKA KROG

Soon, this would become the first restaurant in the country to get two Michelin stars, but by then, both Björn and Daniel had already left Edsbacka's kitchen. "Christer Lingström was great at creating a joyful workplace. It was fun to work there. We've carried the joy of working with us ever since."

"I had no idea what this entailed, so I just took a risk . . ."

It was not love at first sight when Björn and Daniel met at Edsbacka Krog in 1998. But Daniel lived in Traneberg and Björn at Kungsholmen, and Edsbacka was situated "far out" in Sollentuna (about ten miles north of Stockholm) so they started to walk together to and from work and began to spend a lot of time together. After work, they cooled down with kebabs and pinball, and they started talking about food, mostly to clear their heads and relax.

Björn had worked at Edsbacka once before to get training and experience. Back then, he'd worked in the kitchen for free.

"The cooking school I attended did not teach even the most basic skills. When Fredrik Pettersson, one of the head chefs at Edsbacka, asked me to make a béarnaise and sent me down to the basement to get tarragon, I didn't even know what tarragon looked like. Daring became my strength those first years. Right after graduation, I traveled to England and got a job at a starred restaurant in London. I had spiked my résumé with work experience from a starred restaurant in Sweden, but I didn't say anything about the fact that I had worked for free. The consequence of this white lie was that I was immediately placed by the stove in the hot kitchen. One of the first things I was asked to make was scallops. I had no idea what this entailed, so I just took a risk and started frying them carefully all over, sort of like how you would fry meatballs. The master chef came running over and screamed, 'What the hell are you doing?' I put on a casual face and answered quickly that this is how we would fry them in Sweden and at Edsbacka Krog. 'We do it like this in Sweden,' I can still hear myself uttering those words."

Was it after a workday at Edsbacka that they first started talking about starting their own restaurant together?

"No, we were first convinced that we wanted to start something of our own when we were living in England. In Sweden, we mostly talked about what we'd learned at work. The year at Edsbacka was amazing, but when we left for England, it felt as if we wouldn't be able to progress past the level the restaurant had already achieved. That was when we decided to go to England—it was a joint decision."

The stagnation at Edsbacka was not a downward spiral, but it was more of a resting period after the incredible success of being chosen as Sweden's best restaurant in the magazine

Gourmets 199 Bord (tables) and on the way to earning two Michelin stars. The natural course for Björn and Daniel was to try to work at a three-star restaurant—but that didn't work out. They applied to work at Raymond Blanc's Le Manoir aux Quat'Saisons in Great Milton in Oxfordshire near Oxford, as well as a few other restaurants including Michel Bras in Laguiole and Pierre Gagnaire in Paris.

LE MANOIR AUX QUAT'SAISONS

This was a two-star restaurant out in the middle of nowhere, and for Raymond Blanc, food was an art form where the four elements—water, air, earth, and fire—transformed into a palette of textures and flavors. "In the moment this art is short-lived, but in the memory it is endless," he stated.

It might sound pretentious, and is actually somewhat of a given today, but back then in 1999 it was an exciting philosophy.

"Björn had already been in England once before, but I hadn't. I had always been my own 'teacher' by flipping through books and trying to mimic and develop. The reason I wanted to go to England was to find someone I could learn more from, to bring new knowledge back home, and I wanted the head chef to be very knowledgeable and the restaurant to be great and have at least two stars."

When Manoir received their application, they immediately jumped on the two young chefs from a starred restaurant in Sweden.

Manoir turned out to be a great kitchen machine, and working there was completely different from working at Edsbacka Krog. Björn worked at the fish stove with four other chefs. Daniel made afternoon tea, creams, and petits fours. At that station, which was farthest inside the cold kitchen, there was one baker and three chefs—one who made all the ice creams and sorbets and two who arranged the desserts on plates. All in all, thirty-six chefs worked in the kitchen at Manoir.

"Most of the greats had worked there, and Manoir was a school for aspiring star chefs, but there was no joy in the work. There was a lot of yelling and screaming in the kitchen. Maybe necessary, but what do I know. We had one hundred guests every single service. On weekends alone, we had five hundred guests. It was incredibly labor-intensive."

The problem was that there was not much else to do besides work. Manoir is located far out in the countryside, the town is not especially inspiring, and the living conditions were not the best, at least not for Björn, who lived with a woman who owned poodles.

"We started in the kitchen at seven o'clock every morning, except the days the shellfish were delivered from Scotland; on those days we began at five o'clock in the morning. When we went home at night, it was so dark that we were forced to use flashlights to see the road. I had to tiptoe inside so that the dogs didn't start barking, and that was not particularly popular."

Daniel had somewhat better accommodations in a commune inside an old dilapidated house. He had his own room and a TV, which Björn didn't have at his place.

"I don't know if my accommodation was particularly good. It could almost be classified as

My name is Björn Frantzén. I am at the beginning of my journey as a cook. My ambitions are high and I am willing to put in much effort and time to reach my goals.

After 3 years of Restaurant School, I was lucky to get not just one job, but two. Firstly at Restaurant Edsbaka, which has earned one star in the Michelin Guide. I work there during the dinner service and at weekends. The second establishment is the Restaurant Circus in Stockholm, where I work at lunch-time. This restaurant often serves more that 1000 guests a day.

With these two jobs I have had a wonderful opportunity to study and work with many variations in cooking, which has suited me very well. It also has given me good experience as well as development.

Now, I wish to work at a restaurant where I am able to continue my development and be amongst the best chefs, in the hope that I myself will one day also become one of the best.

Björn Frantzén

Björn's first cover letter, 1996

a complete madhouse. It was shabby and had no hot water, and I lived with French chefs who smoked weed. However, both my accommodation and work were comfortable compared to Björn's situation. I was only in the kitchen twelve hours every day, and I would just stand there and prepare the mise en place. Björn, on the other hand, was working right in the middle of service, and I was never close to that."

"First the chef threw the plate with what was left at us at the fish stove, then he grabbed me and took the piece of shell and squeezed it into my palm so hard that blood spurted."

When Björn thinks back, many years later, he realizes that he was actually very worried about their health during their time at Manoir. "If it hadn't been for Daniel tossing me a Snickers bar now and then, I don't know how it would have ended. It was a useful experience, we learned a lot, and we don't regret a minute of it, but being in the middle of it was not fun. Everything was made fresh for every service, which meant that all the leftovers from lunch were thrown out. Not a single ingredient prepared for lunch would be used for dinner. That was wise, and today this is obvious to many. Between six and seven in the evening, they would serve food for the employees. That was exactly when I started preparing everything again. My responsibility was to make a new *beurre blanc*. All of the other chefs at the fish station were able to take a break to eat, but I was left with my sauce. Daniel saw how it was and brought me Snickers."

Björn and Daniel learned a lot at Manoir. Unbelievable things happened, things that become etched in your memory—things you never forget.

"I still have a scar on my hand. There had been a faulty order of a crab dish. It was sent back to the kitchen, and the French sommelier started eating the dish. Halfway through, he ran over to the kitchen manager and yelled that he had found a piece of crab shell in the food. The chef threw the plate with the remaining food at us by the fish stove, and then he grabbed me and took the piece of shell and squeezed it into my palm so hard that blood spurted. That night 'Limpan' was lying at home in his madhouse watching *Seinfeld* on TV."

"I often watched *Seinfeld* because there was nothing more inspiring to do. You've heard chefs described as horrific devils in the kitchen, yelling and screaming. And sure, we met a few of those in England. When something went wrong, as things sometimes do go wrong in restaurants no matter how well you prepare, all hell would break loose. I remember once when the pastry guy, a Frenchman, was making lemon cakes for afternoon tea. The recipe was for nine lemon cakes, but he could only find seven molds. I suggested that we calculate the recipe

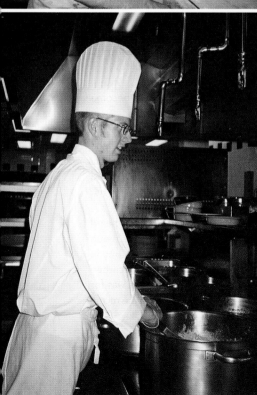

down to seven cakes instead. The Frenchman looked at me stubbornly and wouldn't budge because the recipe was for nine cakes. He ran off to find the molds. Finally, he found them in the fridge after a Norwegian had just used them for duck liver terrine. While the terrines were freshly made and still lukewarm, the pastry guy emptied them out before they set, took the molds, and left. You would think that the French pastry guy would be scolded for ruining the duck liver terrines, but he wasn't. Instead, the Norwegian was accused of sabotage."

"We never saw a hint of team building or team spirit. Everyone worked selfishly without thinking about the fact that they worked in the kitchen for the guests out in the dining hall."

The problem, Daniel and Björn soon realized, was that the restaurant was too large, and so they would never gain the experience of cooking on the star level that they were looking for. Instead, they got practice and experience in delivering hellish volumes of food.

"I was looking for a mentor, but I didn't find one, and it was so boring to live out in the middle of nowhere. Not to mention that the job paid next to nothing. On the other hand, there was nothing to spend money on. I hung out at the local pub now and then, but never Björn. He just worked."

The time had come for the first "walkout" of their careers, which means that you simply don't show up for service the next day.

"We don't claim that Manoir was bad, but it didn't represent the culinary turning point we were seeking; it simply wasn't the right place for us."

One morning, when they should have been at Manoir, they jumped on a train to York where they stayed with a friend and tried to figure out where to go next. They wanted to work with Tom Aikens at Pied à Terre. He was the youngest chef ever to receive two Michelin stars, which was impressive, and it was rumored that he was now even more invested in his work because he wanted to get three stars before Gordon Ramsay. Tom Aikens had twelve chefs in his kitchen for thirty-six seats in the restaurant.

"We wanted to go to Charlotte Street, but the question was only how to get through the door to Tom Aikens's kitchen."

PIED À TERRE AND TOM AIKENS

There was a link between Björn, Daniel, and Tom Aikens. The connection was a man who had a wider and larger network than any other in the restaurant world. Moreover, he was a close friend: Robert Benfield-White. He simply called Tom Aikens and told him about Björn and Daniel. And that was enough. Aikens always wanted to have a surplus of talented chefs so that he was never understaffed.

Tom Aikens had just returned to Pied à Terre after being in France where he had worked for Joël Robuchon in Paris and Gérard Boyer at Les Crayères in Reims. He went there to obtain even greater star experience in order to accept the challenge from Gordon Ramsay about the third star.

"At the pastry station, we were four chefs in total: me, two Swedes, and an Indian who never wanted to fry apples. When I asked him why, he told me that Tom Aikens had, unprovoked, repeatedly heated a frying spatula and had burned him on the arm."

Still, Daniel thought, because it was a decent pastry department, he would shadow some of the more experienced chefs in the place. Unfortunately, he was mostly left tempering chocolate because he was the only one who knew how.

Björn worked with the sous-chef Shane Osborn. In service, Björn did the plating (arranging the food) with Tom and Shane.

"Shane was nice in the beginning, but later he lost it, if you ask me. And Tom Aikens was really fanatical, a machine at doing good stuff. The only problem was that he wanted to do everything himself, even though we were twelve chefs in the kitchen."

"Tom Aikens was equipped with a crazy mood. Burning his subordinates in the kitchen was commonplace."

"Tom Aikens was equipped with a crazy mood. Burning his subordinates in the kitchen was commonplace. When he was pissed off at some chef, like the Indian who was going to fry apples, he went over to the gas stove with a spatula and heated it well before he set it against the underarm of the one whom he wanted to teach a lesson."

"That practice would eventually bite him in the ass."

Tom Aikens had hired a young chef whom he burned badly on the arm one day during one of his anger outbursts. What he didn't know was that the chef shared a room with another young chef who worked with Gordon Ramsay. Obviously, Gordon Ramsay heard about this and called the press. It turned into a big media debacle. This was how Ramsay got rid of his worst competition. When it all went down, Tom Aikens was fired from Pied à Terre.

"All in all, there was a lot of violence in the kitchen at Pied à Terre. Tom even hit a waiter once. When that happened, the owner and restaurant manager David Moore came down looking for the waiter and found him knocked out on the basement floor. Tom Aikens was furious and shouted at the restaurant owner: 'Get the fuck out of my kitchen.'"

"We started at seven o'clock in the morning, both Björn and I, and we were not done until midnight. Between lunch and dinner, we had a forty-five minute break, and all of the chefs met at the Oxford Circus McDonald's to eat. At Pied à Terre, there was hardly ever enough food for employees. And when there was enough, it was mediocre, to put it mildly: overcooked rice with bell pepper skin, for example. They also wouldn't let us use plates, so we had to find a pot or pan to hold the food and then eat with our hands."

"At McDonald's, we would eat and then lie down on the benches to sleep for a while. Tom Aikens thought resting was overrated, so he stayed back in the kitchen and did his thing."

"This went on six days a week. Sometimes Daniel and I would take the bus home around 2 AM just to set our alarms to 5:40 AM and do it all over again."

PETITS FOURS:
STORSLAGNA SMÅSAKER

Små söta avslutningar på måltiden har funnits i över tusen år.
Petits fours kallas de – "små ugnar". Innerestaurangernas bakelsebonsaier
har ett släktskap till Afrikas morer, romarnas överdådiga kalas
och Alhambras bagare i Grenada.
– Ett litet underverk av betydelse, tycker Daniel Lindeberg,
konditor på Edsbacka krog som här delat med sig av sina recept.

Daniel Lindeberg, 20 år, är till vardags konditor på Edsbacka krog utanför Stockholm. Där skapar han små söta konstverk som lustfylld avslutning på måltiden.

● ● ● Var kommer de ifrån? Vem kom på att middagen ska avslutas med det där lilla perfekta? Efter den söta desserten, osten, glassen eller kakan. Det är då, till kaffet, som de ska bäras in till bordet.

Små bakelser som ska se ut som sina släktingar på kondiset, fast mindre, lättare, intensivare i smak och fruktighet, balanserade mellan det söta och det syrliga. Små bakelser som understryker att middagen är en fest, att ätandet är en konst och att gourmanden i oss gärna tänjer gränserna för hur mycket vi egentligen tål. Redan mätta låter vi oss väl smaka.

– Regel nummer ett för en petit four är att den ska kunna smakas i en enda tugga, säger Jan Hedh, landets främste sockerbagare, som minns sitt 60-tal då dessa små bakverk serverades till kaffet vackert glänsande i korgar av dragen karamell.

Ett femtiotalsnamn på dessa små godsaker är friandiser, ett begrepp som åter framkallats av konditorerna på de fina krogarna. Som landets främsta "sockerbagare" eller "pâtissier" har Jan Hedh noterat dessa bakverks trendkänslighet.

Under trettio år har de gått från att vara tyskinspirerat ettersöta till fruktigt franska, från komplicerade till enkla med bara två hallon, ett litet flarn och vaniljkräm.

– Det är det senaste på petits fours-tallriken. Mycket hel frukt sammanfogat med en kräm eller en fruktpuré

och lite florsocker över. Bakade petits fours finns naturligtvis fortfarande, det är ju efter bakningen som bakelserna fått namn: "liten ugn", säger Daniel Lindeberg, på Edsbacka krog.

– Det finns fler recept på petits fours än det finns kockar i världen, säger han. Varje kock ska ha sitt eget personliga anslag. De små bakverken är konditorns lilla "tumavtryck", signum.

DAMMSUGARE PÅ STJÄRNKROG
Under en lång rad av år har svenskarnas favoritkaffekaka varit Delicatos "dammsugare". Den finns i varje kakautomat, på alla fik och alla vägkrogar och förmodligen på de allra flesta lunchrestauranger. En välkänd profil bland svenska kaffetilltugg alltså. På Edsbacka Krogs petits fours-fat dukas den lilla dammsugaren elegant upp tillsammans med åtta, tio andra munsbitar till varje gäst.

Dammsugare på en stjärnkrog, uppkäftigt, roligt och väldigt elegant. Den är bara som en pytteliten tugga, en centimeter i omkrets och bara två och en halv centimeter *forts på sid 28*

AV GÖRAN LAGER, RECEPT: DANIEL LINDEBERG, FOTO: ULF SVENSSON

26

From *Allt om Mat* (All about food), 1999

"One may ask why anyone would subject his or herself to something like this because it sounds completely bizarre, but Tom Aikens was insanely talented and incorruptible when it came to quality. He was manic in the kitchen, and he made very good food."

"One morning when we were on our way to work, we jumped on the train going the wrong way by mistake, and we didn't notice until two stations had passed. There we were, on a packed train car, headed in the wrong direction, exhausted, and we both thought at the same time: 'Tonight, we're leaving.'"

"In England it was, as we mentioned, tradition to just leave once you've had enough. Everyone in the business did it. If you decided to resign in the proper Swedish way, you would only be convinced to stay. And staying was the last thing you would want to do. Instead, the night you decide you've had enough, you stay late, gather up all your personal stuff, knives, and clothes, and then you leave and never come back."

DANIEL AT THE NK BAKERY AND BJÖRN AT RESTAURANT LETTONIE—A SMALL HOTEL IN BATH

When Daniel was working at Edsbacka Krog, he received an offer for employment from NK Bageriet, the respected patisserie in NK, a department store in Stockholm. Anyone with regular ambitions would have jumped at this opportunity right away, but not Daniel, who had already decided to get international experience. Now he felt it was time to call Stefan Johnson-Petersén.

"I flew back home and left Björn behind in England."

"When Daniel called NK and arranged a job, I decided to stay. I didn't feel ready to return home. I hadn't found that special something I couldn't find working back home in Sweden. Daniel and I had started talking about opening a restaurant together; the conversation began in London when we were living like rats and working like dogs. It might have been a survival strategy. We talked an unseemly amount about food, arrangements, porcelain, spaces, services, kitchens, tools, everything. It was like an explosion of ideas when we finally decided. I can't say exactly when we nodded at each other and said that we would open something together. We sort of glided into it all and ultimately it became a given. We would try to open a restaurant with the goal of making it into a starred restaurant. This much was clear."

The small place in Bath where Björn worked was a hotel restaurant called Restaurant Lettonie. Björn was at the stove and worked with vegetables. He worked long hours, but it was okay because he had Sundays and Mondays off.

"The owner, Martin Blunos, and his wife lived upstairs above the kitchen with their two children and a dog. Compared to London, this was peace and quiet."

At this time, most restaurants in Sweden worked with butter-based sauces and purées of various kinds. Martin Blunos had the direct opposite philosophy; he thought it was an embarrassing way of trying to conceal taste. The deep flavors should come from the ingredients and garnishes instead, with only the exception of light sauces.

"It was a pleasant job, and I had a nice time. The conviviality is what I remember most from there. Considering everything we had experienced in London before, Bath was paradise. What I learned from Martin Blunos was that it is actually possible to have a small kitchen and still make two-star food."

After this, Björn felt that he was done with England and wanted to move on to France. Together with a French sommelier from Bath, he put together a résumé in French and sent it out to restaurants where he wanted to work.

"I received a surprising number of answers. One was from L'Arpège. They wanted me to come over on a Monday to try out, which I did. Immediately afterwards, I received an offer to start, and then I traveled back to Bath to talk to Martin Blunos. We stood in the kitchen the next morning, and I told him about the offer from L'Arpège. He understood that the offer was attractive and that I simply couldn't say no.

"A little later, he came in with an English National Football Team jersey with the name 'Björn' printed on the back. He had so much heart that he knew I had the number five on my back when I played soccer for AIK, a Swedish football club. He also gave me a spatula that he had gift wrapped. At some point, there had been a quarrel about spatulas in the kitchen, and I had shouted irritably in English that I 'had definitely had four with me, and they had both been stolen.' He had that engraved as a proverb on the spatula he gave me: 'I had four and they both got nicked.' Then he wished me good luck. Talk about a good manager; he was the best I've ever seen in England. Now I was off to the dream restaurant L'Arpège and Alain Passard."

Back home in Sweden, Daniel began working at the NK bakery with Stefan Johnson-Petersén. Daniel was looking for a mentor and found one in Stefan. But the bakery was so much more than that. You could say that "everyone was there": Martin Isaksson, who later opened Chokladfabriken; Ted Johansson at Dessert & Choklad; Per Olsson, who now owns Pock Choklad and Konditori; and Mattias Wallmark at Söderbergs Bakery.

"Everyone who worked at the NK bakery was very driven, despite the fact that the work was not that well paid. There was so much knowledge to be gained that I would have worked for free if necessary. In the evenings, people stayed back to practice making sugar and chocolate sculptures—Stefan was, and still is, the best in the country at this. We were given a lot of room to be creative, great space. Stefan gave us the freedom, and the freedom made us work like crazy."

When Daniel first started his first week at his new job, he had only a vague premonition of the hierarchy that existed—despite the freedom. Certain stations and departments were considered finer than others, and Daniel was placed in the French patisserie to bake mousse cakes.

"I had no idea that this job had the highest status in the entire bakery. Now, looking back, I can remember how people would glare at me just because of that, but I had no idea back then. I was so focused on gaining knowledge that I didn't even look at other people, much less evaluate our relationships."

If it had been a regular recruiting, Daniel would have started at one of the classic stations and baked cakes, cookies, mazarin (almond tarts), and various kinds of chocolate.

"Martin Isaksson was responsible for my station. When he quit, the responsibility was given to me. After only a few months at NK, I was suddenly a supervisor, but now in retrospect I can say that I was far from ready to lead the station. There were girls who would literally cry because I was too hard on them. I had yet to realize that people are different, that they work in different ways, and that you have to learn to accommodate their individual skills and knowledge. Another thing I didn't really understand was that not everyone cared as much about the same things I was passionate about. In terms of knowledge, I was there, I dealt with my job in a professional manner, and I had the will to work. But I wanted to move on. I wasn't there to lead others; I wanted insight and knowledge, and I longed to bake bread."

This is how Daniel works. There he was, at the finest station at the NK bakery, doing what others dream of doing—and he went to Stefan Johnson-Petersén and asked to be transferred to the bakery instead.

"I went from 'flash-flash' to baking dough and buns, and I still think that I made the right decision. I stayed at the bakery for a long time, and I take that as a sign that I had much to learn. That was important, so much more important than making some sort of career at the NK bakery—that's not why I moved back home from England. Eventually I set my sights on the chocolate room. If I had been a novice, I would have had to get in line to be moved, but by that time I had been at NK long enough to be able to choose where I wanted to work. You could say that the line ended there in the chocolate room. I had spent two years at NK, and now I was dipping and making fork marks all day long. I recognized the situation from Le Manoir aux Quat'Saisons and Edsbacka Krog. I was finished at NK, and I needed to move on."

This is where the story could have ended. Björn was at L'Arpège on Rue de Varenne, and Daniel was making fork patterns on pralines in Stockholm—it all felt very far from a joint restaurant.

L'ARPÈGE

Björn called Daniel from "his" new kitchen every day. They didn't want to let go of their common ideas just because they were developing separately. Funnily, Björn was placed as chef de patisserie with Alain Passard despite the fact that he didn't know a word of French. It was mostly just because that was the only free spot in the restaurant.

The patisserie was located in the basement, and Björn was placed in charge of breads and pastry dough. To put it mildly, he was curious to see how it would end.

"Björn called me at NK to ask me how to get a chocolate pastry dough to rise like a regular pastry dough."

"Alain Passard suddenly wanted to make a pastry with chocolate. His regular pastry dough was amazing and was the base of one of his best desserts. When you add cocoa to a pastry dough, however, it makes it much heavier and you don't achieve the same height. And there I was, with a bunch of coworkers who refused to talk to me in any language other than French, attempting the impossible task of making cocoa-based pastry dough."

The start at L'Arpège could, in other words, have been better. The language barrier worsened because many French people refuse to speak anything but French to English people as part of a historically anchored tradition, and everyone thought Björn was English because he came to France directly from Restaurant Lettonie in Bath.

"'You have to show them who's in charge,' the kitchen manager said to me on the second or third day, and I thought, 'How the hell am I supposed to do that when I can't speak a word of French?'"

When Björn's French coworkers eventually found out he was Swedish and not English, they realized they could practice their English without having to be embarrassed, and it became possible for him to complete, lead, and delegate tasks.

"I had daily meetings with Alain Passard, a hero in the eyes of many, including mine, but I still say that I think he has some crazy ideas, now and then. One day, for instance, he was convinced that the vegetable suppliers had lied about the weight and measurements of their produce and had charged too much. As a result, every morning when the vegetables arrived, we had to receive them and note the exact price per kilogram compared to what they delivered. It took about half an hour of valuable preparation time for all of the chefs. All in all it was a trivial matter, but it still says a lot."

Björn had applied to work with Alain Passard because he liked his philosophy regarding the quality of raw ingredients. Passard had drilled his kitchen into a certain perfection based around "ingredient thinking."

"That, combined with the incredibly simple preparation. Despite the amount of butter used, the expression was still 'light,' with no heavy sauces, and we barely made any stock. We rarely used the kitchen oven, which can seem odd today. Alain Passard felt that the oven would dry out the ingredients; the sauté would constantly be warming on the stove for various fowl. There was an outstanding simplicity to the cooking. And the quality of the ingredients was striking. The duck liver was so fresh that it was still lukewarm when it arrived at the restaurant. The scallops were alive, the crayfish were energetic and jumped, and the blue lobster from Brittany was fantastic. I was taken aback by white peach and coriander, simple things that turn out amazing just because. This is when it becomes interesting: simple spices, a simple flavor that's added to a raw material. The combinations were dazzling—tomato and mustard, whole root vegetables baked in a large pot with seaweed. There were no special techniques other than making the food on the stove and preparing the ingredients whole. The atmosphere was country-like, almost sloppily arranged, as if in your grandmother's kitchen. It was food prepared with great care, tenderness, and foresight."

At L'Arpège, Björn built a personal friendship with head chef Günther, something that had been unimaginable in England.

"And I was involved in selecting the very best ingredients and learned to be careful with heat to avoid damaging them. When the food was plated, the portions were not large, and what was served was carefully chosen. There were almost never more than three pure flavors in one serving. When I was there, I didn't really consider this to be special, but in hindsight I realize Alain Passard's genius. I still have a menu from that time, and there's nothing bad on it. First and foremost, the food was very good in that we were never afraid of salt, and in the kitchen there was complete control in every station. I understood early on that as long as I kept my eyes open, I would learn a lot. And I did."

INTERLUDE

You could call it an interlude: Björn and Daniel back home in Sweden for a moment and the thoughts and conversations about a restaurant of their own continuing. They both had a clear idea of the direction they wanted their food to take, and they had written long descriptions, with drawings, photographs, and notes for various test preparations, arrangements, and tastings.

By now they had been talking about this for so many years that everyone around them was tired of hearing it—it never amounted to anything. Caught up in their enthusiasm and ideas, they seemed a bit confused. Dreamers.

"Johan Sörberg would become the sole individual who has meant the most to Daniel Lindeberg."

Every time they talked to people about the future restaurant, they would always say, "but don't tell anyone." Oh well, that didn't stop people from talking, and that was both good and bad. It was mostly bad in the short run, but good in the long run because the early buzz about what would "maybe" happen developed hype when it finally did.

Daniel was convinced he had achieved what he wanted to achieve at NK, and Björn was home from L'Arpège, mostly because he wanted to work on their plans to make something of their own. It had become somewhat of an obsession to plan and to look for financers and suitable locations for the restaurant. They were in constant contact with realtors who specialized in restaurants and had a seemingly never-ending hunt for ventilation experts who could give prices for renovating properties that existed or building those that didn't. It was a whirlwind of prices, loan negotiations, and bank contacts.

Daniel wanted to know more about bread and he knew that in Stockholm Johan Sörberg at Riddarbageriet was the greatest when it came to bread. So, Daniel called Johan and asked if he could come in for a trial. And Johan gave him a job.

Johan Sörberg would become the sole individual who has meant the most to Daniel Lindeberg.

"He is incredibly passionate, he is passionate about flavor, and he uses the absolute best ingredients. He was also first to look for the right biodynamic and organic flour and used chestnut honey in the bread dough because it made it better, despite the fact that it was expensive. He is completely uncompromising. It was just as easy for him to talk about things that went wrong as it was to talk about the things that went right. I inherited my uncompromising attitude from him."

After six months, Daniel was the manager of Riddarbageriet, and Johan Sörberg opened Rival.

The direction of what was produced at Riddarbageriet was very much in line with what Daniel valued. He despises sugar coating and chocolate spirals, and at Riddarbageriet they emphasized taking elements away rather than adding decorations.

There was also a freedom there for which Daniel had longed. The customers would never get used to expecting a set selection; rather, they were encouraged to try new bread varieties baked with various kinds of flour.

"We all trusted each other, every single person in the bakery knew what he or she was doing, and everyone was daring. Take, for instance, the idea of adding cloudberry flour to the bread as a flavoring. Cloudberries, leftover from the preparation of cloudberry wine, were dried and ground to an aromatic meal to create a totally new flavor."

For Daniel, this was the most instructive period. This was the first time he was able to really develop and bake sourdough.

"It is the thirst for knowledge that always drives me, and it was this thirst that drove me to Riddarbageriet. As a pastry chef and baker, you have many areas to specialize in. It takes time."

Björn wanted to find work as a chef while they searched to find the right venue for their own future business. Through the Swedish employment office, he was offered a job as the head chef at a failing restaurant called South of Siberia in Vasastan. It was a place to try out new ideas and new menus.

Björn spent six months working to get the restaurant back on its feet. To test his team spirit, Daniel would work in his spare time as an "extra" when needed.

South of Siberia became a platform where Björn and Daniel could test logistics in a minimalistic kitchen and try menus they had worked on for years. It was an opportunity to see if they were ready to do everything on their own and if they could awaken Sweden's stomachs.

They succeeded at everything except the last part. Food critics, writers, and journalists stayed away despite the fact that South of Siberia had now become a prestigious restaurant.

"I made a veal sweetbread with licorice that would come with us to F/L much later."

One can wonder why South of Siberia did not become the great success that Björn, Daniel, and the owner had hoped for. Maybe it was because Björn and Daniel were not allowed to fully launch their concept. There were other people who set requirements and got involved in the details. Later on, because of their experience at South of Siberia, they allowed no one else to be included in the creative process.

One guest raised his eyebrows more than the others, and that was Peter Bennysson, the manager at Tornvillan. He plainly "headhunted" Björn and Daniel for his restaurant.

Stockhuset owned Tornvillan along with Fabrikörsvillan and Restaurant J, all situated in Nacka Strand, a town near Stockholm. Björn and Daniel soon discovered that there was no real structure of ownership within the company, and many suspected that the restaurants would soon be sold. Peter Bennysson was, however, an ambitious restaurateur who was convinced that Tornvillan could get a Michelin star with the right staff in the kitchen. To achieve excellence in his staff, he hired his brother Robert Andersson, who was a restaurant manager and sommelier at Mathias Dahlgren's Bon Lloc at the time.

And so Björn and Daniel came to a set table, with the only drawback being the management structure, and soon Nobis (who owns Operakällaren among other things) bought the restaurants. Shortly before the restaurants were sold, Björn and Daniel got together with Robert Andersson and Peter Bennysson and arranged for established newspapers to write about them in order to get people coming through the doors.

Tornvillan was also a conference center. At the time, the conference guests received unexpectedly terrific food, and the evening dinner was served à la carte. After the restaurant was sold, the new owner decided the à la carte business was not appropriate for Tornvillan. Nobis already owned one Michelin-starred restaurant at that time, Operäkallaren, and that was where they wanted to invest their money and efforts.

Peter Bennysson, who had spent so much energy turning Tornvillan around, fell apart completely when he was told the news, and he quit the same day. Björn and Daniel finished their contracts.

You could say that the debacle with Tornvillan very much contributed to the intensification of Björn and Daniel's hunt for a space for a restaurant of their own.

> *"All of the landlords we talked with thought it sounded fun to have a restaurant, just not in their building."*

PRELUDE

During their time in England, there was one place Björn and Daniel sought when they wanted to be alone with their thoughts and plans for a restaurant in Stockholm. It was a small hotel in Tunbridge Wells, sixty miles south of London. It had been a place "to hide" when the crazy London kitchen was at its worst. This is where the plans for Frantzén/Lindeberg started taking real shape. This is where the term "casual elegance" was coined—the term that would be on every "content declaration" when the restaurant opened.

"We compiled a very thought-out program for how we would manage to create our own restaurant. It was a complete business plan that included an extensive financial analysis in an Excel spreadsheet of about thirty-five pages: the craziest thesis. Everything was very detailed and based on three different scenarios with various guests and conditions. This was the beginning of a completely insane time that accelerated as Tornvillan turned out to be nothing but a stopover."

The pipedream was to find a spot where there had not been any kind of restaurant before. Preferably, it would be a place with elevators from the street level that would open straight into the restaurant. The bar was set very high when they contacted a plethora of realtors.

"All of the landlords we talked with thought it sounded fun to have a restaurant, just not in their building."

There were alternatives, and there were most certainly spaces that could be rebuilt and used for Frantzén/Lindeberg, but it always came down to cost. One in a thousand wanted to rent to a restaurant, but they would absolutely not cover the costs of ventilation and grease traps.

"Every time we found a space that we thought would fit, we ended up in a state of euphoria, just complete happiness, and we were always convinced that 'this was the one.' It was very hard, especially because we did not have a financer. And so it became sort of like a catch-22. We had the space, but the landlord wanted to see how we would finance it, and we could not get a financer before we could present a space. Sometimes it would take months before we received an answer, and when the answer finally came it was usually negative. We kept at this for a long time."

"We weren't known within the Swedish culinary world. People didn't get it, we had good résumés, but no big names, so it would take a true food expert to understand the level we were representing. Our menus were innovative, but in hindsight we realize that maybe we should have presented ourselves with 'trout and spinach,' which might have gone better. It might have been easier to get a space that way."

It seemed to be completely impossible. Because of a lack of money and their very high demands for how a restaurant space should look, many good offers slipped through their hands.

"Saltmätargatan offered an elevator from the street level directly into the restaurant. Kungsholmen was a space with glass ceilings. Norrlandsgatan had a long glass hallway with a gigantic bright window and a square dining hall. Rörstrandsgatan had outside seating on the terrace. Blasieholmen—but there the contract said that we needed to serve lunch, and we weren't interested in that."

"There was never a question of giving up, but today we do understand how difficult it is to start a business without money. Naive? No, we don't think so because there was no road to take other than the one we chose."

Neither Björn nor Daniel comes from a wealthy family. Not even close. Working at Swedish or Scandinavian starred restaurants might have helped them get financers because they would have been more easily recognized.

However, they wouldn't have been as talented at cooking.

"Sure, we can acknowledge certain mistakes in our demands for the space. We got stuck on the idea that we needed a gigantic space with a lounge for our guests both before and after dinner. This was a flawed thought from the beginning."

In the beginning, the hunt for financers was very amateurish, with emails and letters to people who had both money and a claimed interested in food.

"We also went through all of our friends to see if they knew anyone with money. Then, we ran to different banks and actually obtained a bank contact: Swedbank at Norra Bantorget. Now, we could look for financers and inform them that the project was partly financed based on a promise from the bank. We imagined that it would be easier this way. On the other hand, we had been a bit sneaky at the bank because we told them that we had some financing for an eventual project. All's fair in love and war."

"After the conversation with the bank, we quickly realized that we would be forced to abandon the idea of a large space and of unfurnished spaces where there had never been restoration. Instead, we started looking at finished restaurants for sale. Mistral had been for sale for a while by then, it had even been posted on Blocket—the Swedish online marketplace. Talk about good guys."

21 LILLA NYGATAN

Mistral was a tiny space—about one thousand square feet—in an old dairy shop in Old Town in Stockholm. It had already peaked and won in every category, including a Michelin star.

"How could we develop the restaurant without destroying the place? We looked abroad and remembered how Alain Passard had taken over from his head chef and previous owner, and how Gordon Ramsay had taken over his restaurant on Royal Hospital Road after Pierre Koffman."

"Anders Malm at Realmäklarna is one of the few people who are really serious in the restaurant real estate business. We had many conversations with him, and he believed we could develop Mistral further. He said they only opened three days a week, and that they had another room where their employees ate. We decided to go to Old Town to look at the place, especially because the price was decent."

"We don't really know what happened that first day at Mistral. Everything moved very quickly. After so many years and so many spaces, so many delusions and failed deals, it suddenly looked like we were on our way to our own restaurant."

At Mistral, Fredrik Andersson, who moved out to Sockenvägen in Enskede, is an emotional guy for whom Björn and Daniel have a great deal of respect. He appreciated Björn's experiences with Alain Passard at L'Arpège, and despite the fact that a Japanese restaurateur had actually bid more than they did on the space, Andersson gave the restaurant to Björn and Daniel.

"Fredrik Andersson wanted to sell it to us so that we would continue to keep the flag flying. He didn't want to ruin the pride of the place, and that says a lot about him."

Obviously, this was a great opportunity, despite the fact that the multiple years they'd spent planning around a large space now went down the drain. Financially as well, the scenarios they had tested were no longer applicable; they were based on a much higher daily income than what was possible in the small space.

"We were forced to think again and to test things Mistral had not tried. We started working on the menu right away, and we decided on two: one with ten dishes and one with twenty. This meant that we had to change our long-planned food concepts. Because nothing would turn out the way we had planned, there was nothing wrong with introducing some humor and unexpected antics. We immediately got into the molecular trend with inspiration from elBulli and The Fat Duck with fire, air, smoke, and textures. It was the space and the ambition that became the basis of this work."

Those things were thought out quickly. Björn and Daniel had already informed Fredrik Andersson that they wanted to do business and that they "just needed a little confirmation from the bank that the finances were okay." This was a truth with some embellishment. There was only a small promise from the bank based on the condition that they had a larger financer to cover the majority of the capital needed.

"We called our friend Robert Benfield-White again and told him that we needed 500,000 kroner [about $90,000]. Strangely enough, at that very moment, he was sitting with his financer and bookkeeper, who in turn had contact with a client who had money to spare and who accepted the offer to be financer of Frantzén/Lindeberg, the first years."

"While we were dealing with the bank, our financer, and Fredrik Andersson at Mistral, we were standing with plane tickets to London, where we were going to prepare a fortieth birthday dinner. We felt the time-crunch from all ends."

Everything at Mistral was included in the purchase except Fredrik Andersson's handmade plates, which he took with him. The renovation was moderate. They moved the window niches 40 cm (16 in) out so that they could fit more tables and increase the seating capacity. Tiling and painting were, of course, also part of this remodeling.

"In what used to be the employee dining hall in the Mistral era, we built a wine cellar and a private room with a small office behind, where there was also room for refrigerators and the coffee machine. Frantzén/Lindeberg is 'compact restoration' where every inch is used to its full potential."

At the end of September 2007, Björn Frantzén and Daniel Lindeberg signed the contract to take over Mistral's space at the end of 2008.

"We had three months."

THE TEST KITCHEN AND THE BLOG
Then a strange thing happened—after a long planning period, they were left with one question: "What now?"

Despite the fact that everything to do with the new restaurant was already in writing, the planning didn't fit. They hadn't done any math for a small restaurant like Mistral at 21 Lilla Nygatan.

Their old friend Robert Benfield-White came to the rescue once again. He knew exactly what Björn and Daniel needed—a test kitchen.

"There was an apartment that was more or less just a kitchen. It was on Klara Östra Kyrkogata, and it had just been furnished by the television show *Roomservice* on Kanal 5. The kitchen would be our home base until we opened in February."

"It was an amazing kitchen, and we were there every day. It became our sanctuary. We needed that to be able to really talk things through. There were plenty of things we had never really done before and didn't know how to do."

At the first moment and as a first task in the new kitchen, they decided to start a blog to describe the work they were doing. A blog would serve as a cliffhanger by exposing the work behind the scenes, about the thought process, and the experiments in the kitchen.

It may have seemed unnecessary, but it turned out to be a very good decision. The blog became one of the most visited within Swedish gastronomy. It was mostly updated daily, all the while advertising that it would describe the journey from the starting point to a starred restaurant. The first blog post came on October 15, 2007:

"We will have twenty-two seats in the dining hall, and we will turn the 'current' bar into a seating area for ten people. We will serve two menus: one with ten dishes and one with twenty dishes. We will offer various drink packages with the meal. We will make European food with warm flavors from the Nordic countries. Slow cooking mixed with modern techniques and advanced humor. Our motto is casual elegance, and we want to create a casual environment in the dining room where our guests can really be themselves."

The blog was characterized by uncompromising optimism and an abundance of ideas that most certainly provoked many of the conservatives in the food world. Especially when they wrote about their new ideas: "Some special tools need to be bought in the United States or Spain, including a smoke machine where we can add flavor to the smoke."

"That warrants a comment because when we wrote about this new way of making food, the almost chemically based way of cooking, people assumed that we would only concentrate on the molecular kitchen, and that could not be further from the truth."

"Our cooking felt like something that had never been tried before. People who read about our efforts in our blog naturally reflected and immediately assumed that we were working with molecular food. It was the most influential readers who spread this rumor on their own blogs with the result that when we opened we had a misinformed hype as a molecular kitchen."

From the first moment, the blogging was about strengthening the brand Frantzén/Lindeberg—previously unknown in the cooking world. And so the hype and strong reactions were a good thing.

"It was fun to write, and it was an ego boost to see so many followed our blog and kept up to date with what we were writing."

The blog is left as a relic, abandoned, and has not been updated since the opening of the restaurant and since their website took over their Internet presence. The site has a whole different language and a completely different kind of communication with the readers.

"The blog was updated two, three times a day, and we received many comments. Many people were so provoked that they felt compelled to be rude."

Every comment, negative or positive, was still great PR for Björn Frantzén and Daniel Lindeberg.

"I would say that we did everything right. It was a smart move to present and strengthen our brand and also to create expectations."

This excessive marketing resulted in a fully booked restaurant for weeks, long before it was even open. This way they were guaranteed a packed restaurant from the first moment and until the media coverage came out.

"The test kitchen was, however, different, mainly because of the way we portrayed it on our blog. In the kitchen, we tested cooking methods, techniques, instruments, machines,

porcelain, practices, flavors, and dining utensils. The kitchen was a base where we could stay on course until the opening. Every idea would be tested there, the failed experiments would be left there, and the successes would be brought to the restaurant."

"I am not sure we understood that people thought we were only good bloggers and good braggers of what would happen in a few months' time."

"We posted a total of 151 posts on our blog from October 15 to February 4, and we had over 25,000 readers and several thousand hits daily."

In the comments section of their blog, some people wrote that it was careless and cocky to blog this openly. They said it would be a real wake-up call when their restaurant opened because there were many people who wanted to come after them.

The blog had created a fuss that nearly stabbed them in the back. But at the same time, this was precisely what made the blog interesting and the most important PR element for the restaurant. The posts and comments on the blog were later referred to by newspapers and other specialized media.

THE FIRST TRIAL DINNER, PRESS CONFERENCE, AND FIRST SERVICE
Not a single stranger was let into the test kitchen; the only preview was supposed to be the blog. This piqued the interest of journalists; many requests were denied, but they did make some exceptions.

"We chose to selectively invite media people, one at a time, without mentioning who else was invited. It was all to maintain the sense of exclusivity. Obviously, one could question if it was ethically correct, but the ends justified the means. Everybody wrote and everybody

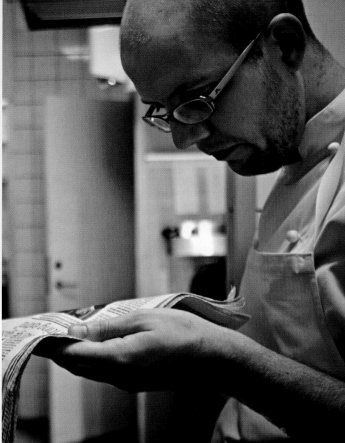

Björn and Daniel during the first services on March 3, 2008

published, despite the anger and jealousy from certain journalists when they realized that they hadn't received exclusive rights to the story. This jealousy was good for us when we were marketing the restaurant. At the same time, we did see the danger of making enemies: such people could be dangerous for us because we stand or fall on one good or bad review."

The journalist visits to the test kitchen were characterized by secrecy, whispers about methods, showings of strange, expensive, and imported specialty machines that could make both ice and heat, smoke, and various gases—it's clear that this contributed to the belief that the country's first real molecular restaurant would be opening in Mistral's old space.

What the journalists later wrote about and published in the newspapers really added to everybody's expectations.

"We simply gave the people what they wanted, but we never lied and we never promised exclusivity."

A short while before the opening day, they had two trial dinners, which meant a full restaurant with test customers and a real-life situation.

"We didn't invite any journalists to this. It was the great dress rehearsal."

"We can't remember anything. We didn't even realize that dinner service had lasted for seven hours until we had time to look at our watches during late service. There had been long breaks between each service."

"To be honest, we were so busy that we lost track of the whole picture, we just delivered. But I think it went okay."

Only Björn and Daniel were allowed in the kitchen, nobody else, and Jon Lacotte and Jonathan Hiljanen were out in the dining hall. Because they had set up the schedule with a deliberate fifteen minutes between each seating, this was also a test in managing to plate desserts and main courses at the same time.

"The only thing we remember is chaos. The trial dinner is basically just a big blur."

Not until after the trial dinner did Björn and Daniel realize that they had received positive feedback, and that what they had created during these two evenings was a rarely seen art of cooking. And so their confidence was back on top before the press dinner, which became a lunch with journalists where no individual was a shoo-in. It was their strategy to invite journalists who would really write about them in their paper, and not those who were just after a good meal, staying for a second, and then "gossiping" about it in some small blog. Björn and Daniel wanted the greatest possible payoff.

Some of the journalists invited certainly raised their eyebrows at their invitation. Others went green with envy when they realized that they weren't going to get an invitation. This is a way to definitely form friendships, but also to make enemies. The tactic did succeed and the result was that Frantzén/Lindeberg was mentioned on the radio, in trade magazines, and, among other things, in a well-read column in one of the largest evening newspapers.

The press was served what would become signature dishes for the restaurant for multiple years: the fired scallop, the French toast, followed by veal sweetbreads with onion and raw licorice. For dessert they served "tomato water" and small macaron cheeseburgers.

It was February 1, 2008; the restaurant was fully booked for an entire month.

FINALLY, SERVICE AND CRITIQUE

It seems there is something built into chefs: an inner drive that cannot be stopped. They can be friendly and sociable privately—outside the kitchen, outside of working hours—but as soon as it's time for service, they gain a completely different focus. Björn and Daniel suffer from this beneficial syndrome. They can long for service, long for a packed restaurant full of expectant guests, long for the sight of all the employees starting their workday. To start the large operation that begins in a second, no downtime, no wait once the time has come. You may wonder what the appeal is, what it is about the kitchen that changes personalities.

"That day was very special, the first day on the job, and a very real situation. A representative from *White Guide* attended the press dinner. There was space reserved in the *White Guide* for us, and the presses had been put on hold, waiting for his review. He didn't even have time to finish his meal, so it was a matter of minutes before the review would run."

"That may not be an answer to the question of what drives us, but it is what it's all about, the critique, both from critics who write in newspapers and from our guests. You focus on doing your absolute best. That's the main motivation, that's our satisfaction. In actuality, there is an uncomfortable tension every night, year-round, again and again; nobody can let food leave the kitchen unless it measures up. That's the challenge. In the end you can't work without that excitement and concentration every night, and so it becomes a longing: finally, service!"

Many of the blog's followers from the months before the restaurant opened booked a table for the first week after opening. Björn and Daniel felt as if they could feel their presence in the kitchen. They had come to the restaurant not only to enjoy, but also to "check us for our cockiness and, for that matter, for our absolute transparency." What the restaurant stood for and what they had advertised was something so new and modern that some didn't recognize it. And how do people who aren't familiar with something act? They lose it; they become scared, vengeful, not at all nice. There were those who laughed and mocked "all arts" at Frantzén/Lindeberg, "the smoke and chemistry." But the icing on the cake was that even these guests discovered that the food served was good.

"In all honesty, we had a kind of panic attack as we waited to read the first reviews. We had built up enormous expectations. It had taken years of planning since we first met that day at Edsbacka Krog. A review was supposed to show that we had 'made it'—the wait was crippling, it was a horrific feeling. When you've worked so hard and for so long on the development of an idea, it feels like nobody else gets it. You read a lot of reviews and think that what they write is not sufficient, that they don't understand, don't get the taste and, moreover, the technique and the mania that lies behind it all."

"We were prepared for the critics to write any number of crazy things."

The uncertainty was also emphasized by the knowledge that many editors send out the less talented journalists to write reviews.

The first review was posted online at half past one in the morning. The newspaper rated the food, service, and atmosphere with a numeric score. Only the scores were posted online, and the entire review was printed in the paper edition.

"We went to the distributors of the morning newspapers to find the paper and waited until the morning drivers started working. The score given was eight out of ten, which was disappointing, but in retrospect, we accept it."

"You can always connect the rate of table booking with the latest review, which is why it is so important, and it was incredibly important to us in the beginning. Yes, we received great reviews from many newspapers, but it still didn't feel as if we were being taken seriously until we were voted Best Food in the 2009 *White Guide* and when, after holding on to this hope for a year, we received our first Michelin star in March 2009. At the same time, we received the Stockholm Award in the young adult monthly magazine *Nöjesguiden* and were named 'Årets Guldkrog' ('gold restaurant') in *Vägarnas Bästa*, the annual guide to Swedish gastronomy. The success was fantastic, to put it mildly."

AWARDS

....

"We don't cook for a book or guides or reviews. We make the things we believe taste good and that we believe in. We make food for our guests, and if they don't like it, the restaurant will be empty."

Ever since F/L's inception, the awards have kept coming, including the two Michelin stars, the placement in the top fifty list of the world's best restaurants, and *White Guide*'s awards over several years, among them Restaurant of the Year in 2010 and 2012.

Awards are just as important as positive criticism from a single food blogger or an article in an important international food publication.

"You can't get away from the fact that awards and mentions are important for the restaurant because they allow guests to find us, but it is also important for our staff and in the hunt for competent coworkers and suppliers. The positive attention motivates our pricing and the guests' experience during their visits. The awards go hand in hand with success."

"We've been lucky enough to have never received a bad review."

Many view it as taboo to talk about success through the measure of what other people write or express about a business. Still, it is a fact that a restaurant needs awards to get visibility.

"It is no secret that our goal has been to work towards first two and then three Michelin stars. We've had this goal since we opened the restaurant. The star status can also be used internally to inspire the staff to hold a certain standard. This can apply to everything, from how the fridges look to how to treat a guest."

No other business in the world is put under the same pressure as a restaurant on the Michelin level, where they are scored every year depending on how that particular year has gone.

"A small restaurant like ours stands and falls on the grade given to us by others. And therefore everyone involved has a large responsibility to deliver. Not a single plate can enter the dining room unless it is up to par. There are easier ways to do business, to put it mildly. On the other hand, there is probably no other business that adds such an extra spice of life."

"To receive two stars in the esteemed food bible after two years is most likely one of the greatest things one can experience, next to the birth of a child."

OUR SPOONS ARE HYGIENIC INSTRUMENTS

The worst enemy of the kitchen is uncontrolled bacteria, the kind that causes food poisoning.

"From the very beginning, we've used disposable tasting spoons wrapped in plastic. Using disposable plastic spoons instead of tasting spoons that are inadequately cleansed in lukewarm water between uses is a simple solution to a problem that can have insurmountable consequences."

It is a cheap investment. During a day they go through more than one hundred tasting spoons at a cost of a few kroner.

IT'S NOT THE FOOD THAT CAUSES POISONI

THE
AT
OOD
NG

PHILOSOPHY

There is no dress code at Frantzén/Lindeberg. Guests should be able to visit the restaurant with no strings attached. It is the guests' night; the restaurant exists for their sake. In the dining room, there should be a welcoming and warm atmosphere. People who come here should experience that they not only buy food but also take part in a show that gives a whole experience.

"We think our generation is against stiffness and restriction. Whispering, gestures, and bows in the fine salon are things of the past. It just doesn't feel modern. A guest should never have to be anxious to visit us."

DETAILS

The whole depends on the details. The food and atmosphere correlate with the details in a direct and intimate relationship.

"To enhance the unique details, we have a network of artists, designers, and craftsmen with whom we work."

DRINKS

In the "homeland" of wine, France, the wine list at restaurants will often be less of a result of the philosophy of the restaurant and more a result of the geographical location and tradition. If the restaurant is located in the Rhône Valley, the list will be filled with Rhône wines. If it is in Champagne, it will be filled with champagne. In addition, the list will include—at least at ambitious restaurants—the obligatory wines from Bordeaux and Burgundy.

"If we worked the same way here in Sweden, our list would consist of beer . . ."

"If we worked the same way here in Sweden, our list would consist of beer, mead, and possibly some wine—most likely made of fruit, but in certain brave exceptions from actual grapes. In other words, we can't have the same approach to making a wine list that they have in wine-producing countries."

Swedes may be some of the world's most wine-loving people. They are trend-sensitive and somewhat nervous with money to spend on more than the necessities of life. That Sweden doesn't have a history of producing wine is not inhibiting; rather, it's the opposite. Ask a Frenchman from Avignon about wines from places in France other than southern Rhône, and you will most likely get a blank stare as a response. Ask about wines that are not from France, or even Europe, and he or she might not even know what you're talking about.

In wine-producing countries, you rarely meet people who haven't grown up close to a vineyard. In Sweden, you can find wines from all over the world in any little hole-in-the-wall that sells liquor. As a first choice, all Swedes drank rioja; then South African wines and later Amarone. Australian sémillon goes well with fish, American zinfandel with steak, and northern Italian rosé for . . . well, for anything actually. As a restaurateur, how do you create a wine list in a country like this?

"One option is to offer a little bit of everything. To let the wine list be a UN General Assembly where the whole world is represented. That was how we started."

But a list that belongs to everyone doesn't belong to anyone. It lacks direction. It lacks personality and character. Frantzén/Lindeberg does not want to be a restaurant that lacks personality and character. Just like cooking in a large kitchen shows a desire to express a specific vision, a good wine list is an expression of will and personality. This means that you

Gaston lit a candle.
In the kitchen, he saw the bottles
glimmer from the shelves, beautiful,
old, dusty, untouched, row upon row.

"Alain, Victor, Justin, come.
Here is all we've longed for."

Together they took a beautiful
bottle and poured.
The enjoyment was complete.

"To a new place in a new time
in another room."

Unknown, France, 1892

have to opt out of certain items to make room for others. A sommelier chooses drinks as a chef chooses ingredients.

"This way the wine list was transformed from a wine list to our wine list. It is a reflection of our food, of our thoughts, a reflection of what our gardens produce, and a reflection of our personal taste. Simply put, we serve wines that we would drink. Right now, the list is centered on a few wine districts: Burgundy, Rhône, and Champagne in France; Rheingau and Mosel in Germany; Jerez in Spain; and Piemonte in Italy."

That was the idea, but then suddenly another question came up: Why do we have a wine list?

"The work of developing the wine list had been continuous since we opened the restaurant. Much work, meetings, and money had been dedicated to finding just those producers, places, and vintages we wanted. The wine list had grown from a few measly pages to a hefty stack of tightly written papers rewarded by two prestigious glasses in the American wine magazine *Wine Spectator*. At the same time, a certain sense of frustration had crept upon those of us who had lovingly created and nurtured this list. Almost none of our guests do more than quickly flip through it before they choose one of our drink packages. The wine treasures in our basements have been left almost untouched, and the list has slowly changed from a living entity to a museum where the guests look, but don't touch."

This is not unique to Frantzén/Lindeberg. The wine world is changing more and more into an investment market. Bottles change owners and are shipped around the world without any of these owners ever intending to uncork a bottle. High scores in publications and from reviewers mean money rather than flavorful experiences and memories.

"We are not interested in being a part of this. We don't want our wines to be letters and numbers on paper. Therefore, we will now forego most of our wine list. Instead of sitting around and waiting for someone to choose from our bottles, we have decided to try as much as possible to make them part of our wine packages."

Remaining will be a short list of the best of the best. The time of the large wine list is past.

A very tiny part of the daily job of the sommelier is to choose between the wines of the world. More importantly, his job is to develop the drink package: the opportunity for the guests to try various wines that suit the menu.

"A combination of food and drink is just as personal as the drink in itself. You have to make a choice. Do you want to present proven safe choices, or do you want to challenge taste buds and convention? We've done both. We've served oolong tea, coffee from Panama, beer, and white, red, and rosé wine from all over the world. We've fought hard to make the guests appreciate what we appreciate, to see the world the way we see it. Sometimes we've succeeded and sometimes we've failed. Going against convention can easily turn the relationship between the guest and the waiter into a fight, or make it like a classroom where we are the teachers and the guests the students. We don't do that anymore. We want our guests to enjoy the hours they spend with us, not to make them feel conquered or leave with a vague sense of discontentment. We are no longer that interested in performing our most advanced somersaults. Instead, we want to provide our guests with the opportunity to drink some of the world's best wines."

THE SPACE AND CONTINUITY

Mistakes happen and always should, but as long as they stay in the kitchen, there is no harm done.

At 21 Lilla Nygatan, there are no marble floors, mirrored walls, crystal chandeliers, or golden faucets. The decor is simple, comfortable, color-conscious, and can sometimes be perceived as minimalist. All of the focus is on the food, the drink, and the service.

"Sometimes we talk about a larger space, but we wonder how that would look. We are convinced that the food and the flavor would be different in a different space. There is a mirroring between the kitchen and the dining room, between the craft and the spirit in the dishes and the guests at the table. Sure, we can sometimes think that the old dairy shop is less than practical, but it is also a space you remember. The impression of the dining room and kitchen is important; it is a framework for the flavors and provides a picture of the visit. We view our space as very much alive. What we have worked for is personality and intimacy."

The advantage of the small dining room is that it is easy to get an overall grasp; it is almost always fully booked, and it has a manageable logistic, which is one of the prerequisites of the white menu that depends on serving directly from the stove to the table. Everything is cooked in front of the guest.

Nobody can ever build safeguards against mistakes, human factors, and technical flaws.

"We are under the firm belief that it is not about who makes a mistake, but how we react when it happens. The minimal kitchen sets extreme demands on those who work there, and we value our coworkers' loyalty, humility, and responsiveness immensely."

There are many advantages to a limited number of guests for each service.

"We have a maximum of 120 guests a week and the same high-quality staff five days a week. This not only creates safety and prevents all kinds of stress in the kitchen and dining room, but it also helps maintain the same high continuity."

FOOD

At Frantzén/Lindeberg there is no menu in the traditional sense.

"What we create and serve is presented as a series of surprises at your table. It is important to us to allow the availability of ingredients to determine and direct what we will serve that evening. The ingredients we ultimately get for our kitchen are a result of intensive daily discussion with breeders, farmers, cultivators, fishermen, and winemakers with the intent of making sure that they deliver the materials of the very best quality to us.

"Everything in our kitchen is based on immediate cooking and direct serving. To us, this is a given. . . ."

"The space, our restaurant, is our stage and it's not irrelevant to the experience. It's here that the dairyman Alf Forsberg ran his dairy shop. It was over 120 years ago, but it still affects us today, like everything else that has happened before us—what we choose to call experience.

"In our world, and out of respect for the guest, we strive for perfection.

"At the cost of traditional menus, we get the opportunity to use the ingredients that have the absolute best quality. Welcome. Share in our world tonight."

All guests receive this letter when they arrive at F/L—a manifesto, words on concentration.

"Everything in our kitchen is based on immediate cooking and direct serving. To us, this is a given, a natural and necessary priority."

In the immediate and uncompromising kitchen, it is the potential of the ingredients and the flavor that rule, in combination with cooking temperatures, ending temperature, and season.

DINING ROOM AND WORK

They quickly dropped the idea of the old-fashioned maître d' who watches over the guests, pulling out chairs, and showing them to the bathroom five times during one night.

"This is a kind of service that seems obsolete. There is no need to reduce the employees to mere plate carriers. Instead, they should be a part of the whole philosophy, the focus, time, and energy of the dining room; helping with the clearing at the end of service and sometimes preparing food at the table, among other things."

MENUS

"We created our own freedom with the 'white menus,' which means that there is nothing in print on the website or in the restaurant saying what we will serve on that particular night. This fact creates expectations in a different and new way."

The head cultivator in Malmköping

The reason for this longing for freedom is the continuous hunt for the best ingredients. In an uncompromising kitchen, the best ingredient of the day cannot wait until tomorrow.

White menus set high demands for creativity; the work in the kitchen becomes a never-ending movement. It creates great possibility for spontaneity, which is very satisfying, but it also makes it so that the kitchen can never stagnate. It demands a high level of presence both craft-wise and idea-wise. Before each service, there is an outline for the evening. Some people call such an outline dramaturgy.

"It comes down to this—we trust our own instinct and talent, the confidence we have as creators. A keyword for this security is restraint."

BUILDING THE MENU

"We usually say that it is not the chefs who decide what will be served in the restaurant in the evening; it is nature, the farmers, and the cultivators. Obviously, this is very true, but we are the ones who choose the best level of ripeness, of flavor concentration, of fat content, and of texture among what is presented to us. It is the uncompromising kitchen that acts; certain in-season ingredients have a maturing limit of just a couple of days. It is, therefore, useless to set up menus that last for many months."

A meal should always be experienced as escalating. From the first dishes offering small variations of lean, concentrated raw flavors, for example, via a richer truffle sauce in the scallop, to the later desserts with sweetness, salt, and tartness.

The cooking methods are always decided based on what that day has to offer. This creates a large variation in preparation methods between raw, poached, fried, fired, and oven-baked. During the evening, there is no room for repetition, not even between hot, cold, temperate, crispy, soft, and silky.

The bread service has been the source of much love and questioning. A bread should, if it is part of a menu, be freshly baked in the restaurant. But bread has a heaviness in its flavor and a filling quality that should not really fit into a tasting menu. Nevertheless, bread is still served at F/L. This is because there is something innately human about eating bread with a meal; something about gathering around bread to talk and share. Home-churned butter is served with the bread. The butter is escalated as well by serving a browned butter, for instance, perhaps followed by butter with roasted bone marrow.

"At our restaurant, the bread is solitary, situated in the middle of the menu, or rather, at the very second it is ready and out of the oven, it goes straight to the table. We don't want the end of the menu to be a grand finale, but rather a continuation of satisfaction and careful escalation. That is what we always strive for."

This restaurant will, therefore, never end with a large chocolate and sugar bombardment, even though the expertise and resources to do so are there. "The desserts here should never feel like you've moved from Frantzén/Lindeberg to another restaurant for your dessert. The finish should be in harmony with the rest of the menu, like a detail."

PRESENTATION

"Together with Swedish designers, we have developed the exact plates and porcelain that we feel add to the presentation of the food; that serve as a kind of scenography. Our handmade porcelain is like our food—a craft—and it helps highlight the things that may not always be as predictable. In this way, we do care about form. But the content is always first and foremost about flavor. Our philosophy about an uncompromising kitchen where everything is prepared in front of the guest in the moment does not leave room for anything else."

What you experience at F/L can only be experienced there: atmosphere, porcelain, textile, and food.

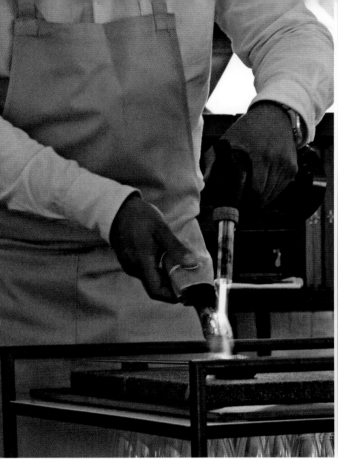

"When it comes to the food, we try to create unique dishes. Every chef longs to create something unique. For example—bread is not unique, scallops are not unique, butter is not unique, cauliflower is not unique, but seared scallops with burnt bread pudding, flavored with tobacco honey, served with browned butter, hay ashes, and caramelized cauliflower should be a candidate for something unique—a classic in our restaurant, by the way."

THE RAW MATERIALS

"An excellent herring is preferable to a less than perfect lobster."

The ingredient philosophy is comparable to soccer: Let's say that there is an unlimited amount of money, and Björn Frantzén and Daniel Lindeberg are the coaches for a Stockholm team with the goal of winning the Champions League. They would naturally start by trying to find the best players as the "raw material" of the team. In order to do this, they would probably be forced to look outside the Stockholm area. The best right-back for their team might live in Brazil or Argentina, and even though he wasn't from Stockholm, it would be a given to try to hire him to play for their team. This is exactly the philosophy applied to the ingredients they use in their restaurant. If you are going to serve carrot, then you want the absolutely best carrot, no matter where it is grown or what its nationality or origins may be. The ingredients are the star players of the restaurant.

"This means a continuous search to find the best raw ingredients. Unfortunately, a raw ingredient has never knocked on our door asking to be served, and so we spend half of our working hours looking for suppliers to work with. We never forego our principle that quality and taste are more important than local and organic. Luckily, the best produce is often organic or biodynamic and usually local. The reason we think this is positive is because the quality of many products deteriorates during a period of long transportation."

Glass artist, Ebba von Wachenfeldt

Pottery maker, Ulrika Brüderle

COOKING TEMPERATURES AND TECHNIQUES

The uncompromising principle when preparing food is that everything should be based on temperature. Cooking temperature combines with room temperature when serving. Every ingredient, whether vegetables, fish, shellfish, fowl, or meat, will reach an optimal point of taste and texture at a certain temperature. This is the moment when it should be served.

Generally, and as a clear example, you can purely scientifically say that fish is cooked when its temperature is 100.4°F (38°C), but there are exceptions in the search for perfect taste and texture. Monkfish is best at 104°F (40°C) and turbot at 108°F (42°C). The pike-perch needs an internal temperature of 113°F (45°C) to be good. The prerequisite is that the fresh fish has been treated correctly, cleansed by the Japanese *ike jime* method and allowed to come out of rigor mortis while maturing on a bed of ice, which can take up to twenty days for turbot, for instance.

"Fish is almost impossible to control when you cook it in a frying pan because it cooks so quickly. Therefore, with certain exceptions, we avoid serving fried or grilled fish. Preparing fish slowly allows us to maintain complete temperature control and also to ensure the fish is evenly cooked."

"Few industries have as many myths about what is right and wrong as this one. Generations of chefs have followed these myths in the belief that they are cooking the best way possible (cooking times are one of the myths). We believe temperature is the only element that is pivotal in cooking because it is based both in science and experience. In our world, where we strive for uniformity in our products, we take great pains in finding these exact temperatures depending on the ingredient and the season."

They aim to cook the ingredients gently, if at all. Some of the raw ingredients have such intrinsic texture and taste that cooking is unnecessary.

In the kitchen, the various appliances support the philosophy of the sensitive preparation of food. Ovens from the brand Delta, for instance, allow slow and gradual rising heat. A Roner creates the perfect temperature of water baths, and a Gastrovac cooks the ingredients using atmospheric pressure.

"To obtain a caramelized surface, a so-called maillard effect, we also sometimes use gas burners, coal ovens, and frying pans, but it is still equally important that the temperature decides when the ingredient is ready."

COOKI
TECHN

MANY CHEFS ARE SETTING UP LABORATORIES to research the food they serve. But this is a development that has already passed. Ingredient and cooking research has become incredibly specialized and requires expensive tools and a new kind of competence among the people who lead the research.

"We were almost a 'research center' of our own when we had been running our test kitchen before we opened the restaurant. It was basic research where we simply tested boundaries and wanted to see what was possible. The rapid development and thirst for knowledge that have characterized us ever since guided us into collaborations with some of Scandinavia's most distinguished professors and scientists. We view the scientific level today as so high, and the results of the research so dependent on qualifications, that our own role in this is mostly to embrace the knowledge and evaluate it based on flavors, textures, scents, and aromas. The competence we have on our side makes it possible for us to act as inspiration and as a sounding board for qualified researchers."

During the past year, not least thanks to the production of this book, they have helped to "force" a basic investigation of every assumption that has lived as a truth in the kitchen, assumptions that might be based on inspiration as much as experience. This is a kind of self-criticism where everything that's been said about cooking—technique, ingredients, everything

that's made, and everything that's claimed—should be proven, preferably through science.

"It's not instinctive to use science to refute taste, aroma, scent, and texture. There is no way to objectively measure things that are based on heritage, experience, and orientation. On the other hand, we can measure the basic ingredients, both chemically and physically. We can scientifically and biochemically prove when the sweetness in a fish is at its most concentrated, or when a piece of meat is at its peak of maturity. It is in the meeting between the most trusted scientific results and our own taste buds that the research becomes valuable to us."

One example of how research and flavor work together is when scientists recommended simmering kombu—Japanese seaweed that has been cultivated for its flavor since the sixth century—for an hour at the exact temperature of 149°F (65°C) when making dashi bouillon, in order to extract as much glutamate (umami) as possible.

"We did as the researchers and many Japanese recipes recommended, but we felt that the result was surprisingly weak."

"The umami concentration was maxed out, but we understood that there were other elements of the raw ingredients that affected the flavor as well. That is exactly where our own work began, and we tested multiple methods before we found the one that gave the most flavor on every level."

1 ¾ oz (50 g) of kombu kelp is stirred in with 4 ¼ cups (1 liter) of water and placed in the refrigerator for sixteen hours. The water should be kept at a constant temperature of 41°F (5°C). Lift the kombu from the water and set it aside.

Carefully warm the water to 175°F (80°C) and add 1 ½ oz (40 g) of bonito. Remove from the heat, wait for fifteen seconds, and then strain the mixture without pressing it. Save the bonito that's left in the sieve. Cool the liquid.

Add the saved kombu and 0.9 oz (25 g) of fresh kombu, and heat carefully. When the mixture comes to a boil, lift all of the kombu and add the saved bonito and an additional 0.7 oz (20 g) fresh bonito to the water. Simmer on gentle heat for twenty minutes and strain the mixture.

"Scientific research gives us a priceless tool in the hunt for uncompromising flavors in raw ingredients. Our dashi preparation is just one example; we took it further and focused on the mechanisms that make the combination of kombu and bonito in a dashi bouillon so satisfying. The foundational work done by the scientists explained the physics and chemistry behind our discovery. The umami in the kombu and the inosine in the bonito are elements known to accelerate the brain's outgoing neurochemicals, such as beta-endorphins, by almost seven times the normal activity. This makes our experience of umami so much stronger. The scientific interpretation in this instance also explains why we appreciate Japanese cooking. Despite the fact that they never use animal fat or dairy products, a kaiseki meal is just as filling as a gourmet meal served at a starred restaurant in Europe."

Another example of how science has influenced the way these chefs work with raw ingredients in the kitchen is regarding aroma and texture; it is obvious that these two factors directly influence how food is received. Food with identical flavor but with a different smell and texture can taste completely different.

"You may ask what we can learn from this undisputed fact, and how we can use this to change our way of working with the raw ingredients to achieve the flavor we want to achieve. By using structure, among other things. One way of maintaining a consistent quality, with the importance of texture in mind, is to work with the very best knives, ones you can sharpen to perfection. Slicing the finest fish with a bad knife will change the whole texture of the fish and the flavor will be overpowered by the texture instead of the other way around. In this way, we have analyzed more or less every ingredient we work with and make sure that everyone in the kitchen has the best understanding, consciousness, knowledge, quality, and interest in every aspect of preparing food in our restaurant. We know that nothing can be left to chance—even if chance is very often what will carry a kitchen's innovation forward."

SHELLFISH

Inhabitants of the Nordic countries are spoiled by exceptionally good shellfish, for which they can thank the cold waters. Crayfish, lobster, and scallops are all world-class. The oysters from the western coasts have a very different sweetness from the ones from the banks farther south, and the crayfish have an astonishingly good meat structure. The shellfish delivered to the restaurant are live, a necessity to achieve a high-class gastronomic result. But, being situated on the east coast and in Old Town has not exactly made attaining live shellfish easy. Logistics has been a major problem.

THE SCALLOPS ARE HAND-PICKED IN HITRA, which is south of Trondheim in Norway. From there, they are usually flown to Oslo right away and then transported to Gothenburg where they are repacked and flown to Stockholm. The long journey is destructive for the scallops because they have time to enter into a kind of dormancy during which they lose much of their sweetness, and the decomposing process has already begun. This was a problem because scallops have been on the menu right from the beginning at F/L.

The goal was to get the scallops to the restaurant within twenty-four hours after they were caught. "We managed, after much negotiation, to get some live crayfish and some very fresh live scallops to Old Town. For a Stockholm restaurant, this is not easy. Not for any restaurant, for that matter."

To fly scallops separately is an expensive affair, as anyone who has tried will know, but by using direct transportation in unbroken cold containers, the scallops are now delivered directly from Trondheim to the restaurant.

The crayfish are from Fjällbacka, Sweden, where immediately after being caught, they are packed individually into tubes that imitate the natural tube-like environment of the crayfish on the bottom of the sea. Prior to this, they were delivered packed together on ice. Many died during transportation, and it was not uncommon for the crayfish to start eating one another. In addition because they are nocturnal creatures, crayfish are quickly completely blinded by light, and are most likely in a lot of pain when treated in this way.

THE SWEETNESS OF SHELLFISH

"We believe that ethical treatment is important not only for our conscience, but first and foremost for the taste. Stress causes chemical reactions, even with shellfish (see the chapter on fish, page 109) and makes the ingredient unusable in our kitchen. The shellfish have a special sweetness in the meat for two to three hours after being killed, which is especially important if they are being served raw. We are dedicated to the preservation of this sweetness, and that is why it was so important to us to get living shellfish delivered to our kitchen. It would have been idiotic to place so much emphasis on obtaining perfect raw ingredients only to prepare them in a general way by putting them in hot water or in a pan for a number of minutes."

Because the shellfish are delivered alive to the kitchen, they are often served completely raw, first and foremost to surprise guests with the unique and easily lost sweet flavor that a

freshly killed shellfish offers.

"When we prepare shellfish, the focus is on less rather than more."

"It is often jokingly said that there are as many ways to cook lobster as there are fishermen from Gothenburg. Everyone has their own method with three minutes this way and six minutes that way. But we forget to ask the important questions: Where do I want to go with this? How do I want it to taste? How do I want the texture to turn out? These are the important factors, and so you can wonder what it is that controls all of this. As we have previously stated, we never cook based on time, but rather on the inner temperature. And that goes for vegetables, meat, fowl, game, fish, and shellfish. Because everything is important: Which liquid do I use for poaching? Is the shellfish tied up or not? What is the pH value of the water, and how is that affected by what we are cooking? What is the temperature of the liquid? Certain liquids can't exceed 113°F (45°C). For us, working without compromise means that temperature is the only measure of preparation quality. The inner temperature of a cooked crayfish should be exactly 109.4°F (43°C) when it is placed in front of the guest."

NET-CAUGHT LOBSTER WITH SOFT SHELLS

"For larger services of lobster, for instance, we understand that we need to do a careful double-cooking to save time. Instead of being boiled, the lobster is warmed in a water bath that maintains the temperature at exactly 100.4°F (38°C). When the lobster meat reaches 100.4°F (38°C), it is placed at room temperature to cool for fifteen minutes. Then, it is placed in an ice bath for fifteen minutes. Right before serving, the lobster meat is quickly fried. This preparation allows the meat to maintain its texture when the frying rises the inner temperature to 109°F (43°C)." It is obvious to only use lobster of the very best quality. Sub-par lobster is the planet's most expensive and toughest seafood, no matter if it's Swedish, blue from Brittany, American, or Irish.

*"Sub-par lobster is the planet's
most expensive and toughest . . ."*

"We bought the guaranteed best lobsters of the best brand, and still they sometimes had an off-taste, something lightly muddy, and we couldn't figure out why. Today we know better."

After multiple years of testing, they have found that net-caught lobsters are much better than lobsters that are caught in creels because the latter will most likely absorb some of the flavor from the creels. Such "cage-caught" lobsters have to get rid of the off-taste of what they last ate. They are left in water tanks for over a week, which is bad for the quality as the meat goes through a texture change that makes it watery when cooked, and then it dries. A period of starvation in the water tank is also stressful for the lobster, which is even more damaging to the quality; the meat will become hard and woody.

"Before, we sometimes received lobsters that were about to molt their shells. These tasted like nothing. A lobster that is about to molt absorbs water in order to 'knock' the old shell. In contrast, a lobster that has a recently grown new soft shell will often have the very best quality, if it is net-caught. This kind of lobster will also have eaten a lot of minerals to make the shell harden."

"Generally, we say that lobster should have a shiny beautiful shell that is preferably somewhat softer, and it should have both antennae intact. Clearly, it is out of the question to buy cooked or dead lobster. The best lobsters come from nutrient-rich and clean cold waters. We mostly take females to our kitchen for the sake of the roe."

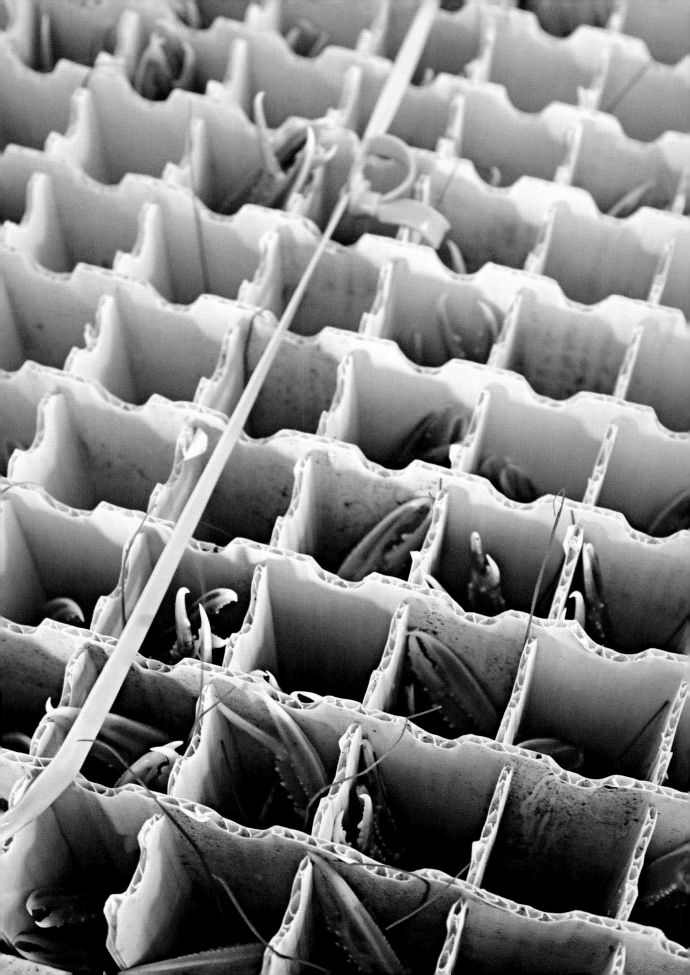

RAW SMÖGEN SHRIMP MARINATED IN PINE NEEDLES AND PINE OIL

Confit, scorched pieces of turnip. Grated Brazil nut and ground elder with small leaves of sorrel, oil of crushed coriander seeds and chlorophyll.

The original taste of shrimp with all the sweetness and taste of the sea can only be detected in the right condition. There are many shrimp varieties, everything from the Swedish seaweed shrimp to the larger tiger prawns. Boiled with salt, they all taste pretty much the same, but when served raw, they represent an entire palette of tastes and flavors.

"We count the Smögen shrimp as the best, and we combine them with the flavors of the forest, pickled pine needles, and a perfuming of pine oil. With this, we serve the curse of the garden, ground elder, which has a hint of lemongrass. We choose the turnip because it goes so well with Asian flavors. Confit pine oil brought forth both the harshness and the sweetness. For the same reason, we use Brazil nuts with their clear coconut flavor. The acidity we get from sorrel."

IN FURTHER DETAIL

PINE OIL

Rinse freshly harvested pine needles and cover with rapeseed oil. Pour into a can with a tight lid and leave it in a cool place for three to four weeks, then sift.

DIVER-PICKED SCALLOP
FROM HITRA IN TWO SERVINGS

First fired in its shell with a cream made of duck eggs,
grated truffle, browned butter, and a salt made with dried
chanterelles and roe. Then, raw-marinated and combined
into the confit roe and served with bouillon of dried
scallop, sea algae, and chanterelles.

Naturally, you should preserve as much of the scallop as possible. When the kitchen was equipped with a coal oven, it became possible to develop the shell-prepared scallop.

"At the exact moment when the guest finishes the first dish, the second is served, during which our Swedish version of dashi bouillon is drunk straight from the shell with the raw marinated scallops, which are placed on a small stone on the board. This is the surprise element of the serving, when the guests don't know that the scallop will be served in a warm and a cold form. The second serving happens unannounced."

IN FURTHER DETAIL

BOUILLON OF DRIED SCALLOP, SEA ALGAE, AND CHANTERELLES

Slice the scallops thinly. Dry in a drying cabinet or in an oven until they are paper-dry and completely brown. Rinse the chanterelles and clean them quickly in 4 ¼ cups (1 liter) of water blended with two tablespoons of wheat flour. The mushrooms will then be completely clean of any sand or other dirt. Dry the chanterelles in a warm cabinet until they are completely dry.

Cut the algae (kombu) into smaller pieces and place it in a saucepan. Pour water on top and carefully heat to 194°F (90°C). Remove the algae and add the dried mushrooms and scallops in the stock. Wait until you see the first boiling bubble, shut the heat off, and let it sit and stew until the bouillon is cold. Sift through a fine sieve with a sifting cloth and store in an airtight container in the fridge.

ROUGHLY CHOPPED CRAYFISH UNDER A MELTING LAYER OF PIG FAT

Served with vanilla-perfumed applesauce, roasted almonds, fresh lavender, and rosemary. Emulsion on last year's pressed apple core oil from Blaxsta, almond oil, apple cider vinegar, and lavender honey.

The condition is completely fresh and alive crayfish. The Swedish crayfish are simply the best in the world and especially those delivered to the restaurant from Ingemar Johansson at SD 137 Myra, who fishes outside of Fjällbacka. They are unique because they are packed individually in small individual boxes that imitate the crayfish's natural environment. "The crayfish we serve have not gone through stressing ice beds where they have either committed suicide or been eaten by another crayfish."

In actuality, these are classic flavors with shellfish: apple, vanilla, rosemary, almond, and lavender. You can vary this dish infinitely.

"What I love about this dish is the creamy emulsion, and a vinaigrette with an internal match of the sweet and tart. It creates a massive aroma. The apple cores are reminiscent of almond paste in their flavor. To the natural sweetness of the crayfish, we've added the pig fat that is carefully melted over the crayfish with a burner. Pork and shellfish are a perfect combination.

IN FURTHER DETAIL

EMULSION ON APPLE CORE OIL FROM BLAXSTA, ALMOND OIL, APPLE CIDER VINEGAR, AND LAVENDER HONEY

Seventeen tons of apples will give about 154 pounds of apple core, and when they are pressed while frozen, it is possible to extract about 13 cups of apple core oil.

1 oz (35 g)
2 oz (70 g) lavender honey
1 ½ oz (50 g) almond oil
3 oz (100 g) apple core oil

Blend vinegar and honey, and slowly whisk in the oil (as with mayonnaise) to a creamy consistency.

"The dishes were fun, but utterly mediocre in flavor . . ."

RAW COCKLES MARINATED IN SAFFRON

Slow-cooked rabbit leg stewed with tart cream made with Alströmer's Leksands Vit potatoes spiced with Ceylon cinnamon. Served with cold mussel juice and carefully perfumed with allspice.

"Alain Passard got me a table at elBulli in 2001. This was during my time at L'Arpège. The dishes were fun, but utterly mediocre in flavor. On the other hand, they served a dessert that made us obsessed with the combination of saffron and cinnamon. During our opening in February 2008, we served rabbit and crayfish in a clarified onion bouillon. The dish was served in a cellophane bag that was cut with scissors, and with the help of ice, ground cinnamon, and boiling water, we created a cinnamon mist to go with it."

Here the flavor combination is further developed with rabbit,* and complemented with raw cockles instead of crayfish and a mussel juice instead of onion bouillon.

"We try to keep to simple flavor combinations in one serving, like here with three different flavors: allspice, saffron, and cinnamon. They marry each other while they still complement the individual raw materials respectively: cockles, rabbit, and potatoes.

IN FURTHER DETAIL

ALSTRÖMER'S LEKSANDS VIT

One of Sweden's oldest potato varieties brought to Sweden from England by Jonas Alströmer, who is referred to as the father of the Swedish potato. Leksands Vit is a mealy variety with a high starch content, which makes it perfect for binding different kinds of liquids, flavors, and fat. It has an enormous cell structure, which feels nice against your palate. The flavor is very rustic.

At F/L, they love rabbit because the light meat is not overpowering in flavor. If you can't get rabbit, you can use chicken thighs. Chicken is also a classic in combination with lobster or crayfish, and so the road to cockles was not long.

BOILED SWEDISH NOBLE CRAYFISH WITH LATE FALL FLOWERS

Raw vegetables and oil of roasted crayfish head.

In fall, when the Swedish noble crayfish are in season, it can be hard to find a place for them on the menu.

"In order for crayfish to belong with the other dishes and 'fit' on the menu, our idea was to create something 'decadently surreal.'" In August, the gardens are filled with the edible flowers of fall. There are, however, still leftovers of certain summer vegetables. "It would be thoughtless *not* to create this dish." The crayfish taste is elevated by the classic shellfish oil made from roasted crayfish heads. Also on the plate are sprouts, beans, carrot, radish, black radish, and cauliflower, with beer-boiled Swedish crayfish.

IN FURTHER DETAIL

OIL OF ROASTED CRAYFISH HEADS

Save the heads when you peel the crayfish and roast them in the oven at 530°F (275°C) with a little tomato paste until they darken. Take them out and let them dry until completely crisp. Finely crush them and place them in a saucepan with a thick bottom and pour natural olive oil* on top. Carefully heat and let it slowly simmer for two to three hours. Stir occasionally so that the crayfish bits don't stick to the saucepan. Sift through a fine sieve and cloth, let it cool, and then bottle.

*In all cases of boiling bouillon and gravy, it is better to remove than to add—the idea is to preserve the flavors and not to compromise the quality of the ingredients. The shellfish oil is the exception that proves the rule through the addition of a pinch of saffron for color and some lovage to enhance the flavors.

PAN-FRIED CRAYFISH
WITH BOILED PIG TAIL

Smothered in homemade sour cream, flavored with saffron and sandalwood. Roe from Kalix, grated carrot flavored with meadowsweet and violet.

"The combination of pork and shellfish is a favorite with us. The pig tail has a rich flavor and the classic stringiness of rillettes."

The more delicate crayfish turns the flavor upside down with sandalwood and meadowsweet. The Kalix roe enhances the ocean flavor of the dish with its saltiness. Saffron, carrot, and violet enhance the flavor combination. Sandalwood (with inspiration from Holland) is a classic spice in almost every kind of preserve.*

IN FURTHER DETAIL

HOMEMADE SOUR CREAM
WITH SAFFRON AND SANDALWOOD

8 cups cream
3 tablespoons sour milk
Saffron
Sandalwood

Blend sour milk with cream and leave it to stand in a dark place at room temperature for two days. Add saffron and sandalwood, let it sit to mature, and then whisk before serving.

Saffron, sandalwood, and violet are classic ingredients in finer perfumes.

JAPAN OFFER A PRON

THIS PROMISE IS FULFILLED by the unprecedented quality of the ingredients used and the appreciation shown for them. Passionate individuals create and prepare these ingredients and make them complex based on seasons, with respect and great trust for the individual history.

In these Japanese kitchens, great cultural connections and the best of culinary traditions are bound with innovation and curiosity.

No matter the direction of the kitchen, there is a great respect for both the raw ingredients and the preparation, tools, and machines used.

This is combined with a technical skill and large humility before the task.

The Japanese chef often takes personal responsibility for the restaurant by giving it its name and opening the kitchen to the guests. This invites an intimate and personal experience with an almost unreal welcoming spirit and direct open cooking in front of the guests.

The Japanese tradition says that raw ingredients can never be manipulated because the origin of the ingredient disappears and the greatness of it will be

S
MISE

ruined. "Japan has, in other words, had a great influence on our way of thinking in the sense that we are willing to apply these lessons. The Japanese restaurant culture is important because it clearly identifies the fundamental purpose of every ingredient and its preparation and presentation. And it does so in a world where the boundaries are fading."

"We are classically trained, and so we approach dishes from a classical basis and add unexpected elements to make it feel unique and not boring."

At F/L, everything is prepared in front of the guest in an open kitchen.

This food philosophy is built on time. Everything is cooked simplistically right before serving.

"We cut the chives right before serving instead of chopping them three hours before service. All ingredients should be treated this way."

CREAMY GOAT MILK PUDDING AND BOILED CRAB FROM BOHUSLÄN WITH LIVER

Flaked macadamia nuts, wild black pepper,* and steeped onion, with roses and cold-pressed rapeseed oil from Julita.

A visit to Shanghai motivated an inspirational trip to Tokyo. "At a three-star restaurant, they served a combination of goat milk bavarois with macadamia nuts and salt—it was good."

"Often, what you taste is considered and developed further. This dish is from the Japanese three-star restaurant developed and complemented with the best crab you can find."

Boiled and gutted, the meat is extracted. The liver is mixed and combined with the meat shreds. Instead of making bavarois, you bake a small pudding with fat and lukewarm goat milk, which has a texture reminiscent of kalvdans, a Scandinavian dessert.

The pudding is then mixed to a lean cream. For the blossom, you add roses; for nuttiness, you complement the dish with the cold-pressed rapeseed oil from Julita, which has an extremely pretty color and a good nutty flavor.

IN FURTHER DETAIL

WILD PEPPER

In many kitchens and recipes, food is automatically spiced with black or white pepper, which is often of mediocre quality. Why should you always add pepper over everything you make when there is really no reason? Pepper tastes like pepper and does not elevate the flavor of the ingredients the same way as salt, for instance, does.

"We have to make it clear that not everything will taste better because pepper is added. When we use pepper, it is motivated by flavor, just like any other spice or flavor enhancer we use. In other words, there should be an idea behind the use of pepper; that we want the dish to taste of a certain kind of pepper."

In this dish, wild black pepper from Madagascar was chosen. The flavor has a hint of citrus and is flowery and fresh, not especially sharp, but intense and lingering. Exactly the flavor sought in the crab.

PAN-FRIED, DIVER-PICKED SCALLOP FROM HITRA IN NORWAY

Served with purée of burnt bread pudding perfumed with tobacco honey, caramelized cauliflower, old bread, and the ashes from burnt hay, and browned butter.

The scallops that are hand-picked by divers received a lot of attention when they were served to the first guests for the first time on the first day of opening. This is another dish that's been on the menu for a long time, created in the test-kitchen in the weeks before opening.

"I saw a recipe for a bread pudding somewhere. When we made it, we left it in the oven for too long and it got burnt pretty bad. Still, when I tasted it, there was potential. It didn't taste burnt, just bitter. I mixed the pudding, and to break the burnt and bitter, I made a tobacco honey; I've always wanted to use something off the tobacco plant, mostly because it is exciting and interesting. What happened was that it tasted and smelled like toasted bread, and I love that smell and flavor."

The question was, what could be served with the "toasted bread"?

"First, we tried veal sweetbreads, but it didn't have the sweetness we needed. And so, the scallop was perfect."

"It isn't about hiding the bitterness with honey, but rather to lightly perfume it. The bitterness should not be completely neutralized; it should just be balanced, to create a break. To increase the sweetness even more and to help the scallop, we chose caramelized cauliflower cream. Another kind of bitterness comes through the ashes from the burnt hay and is complemented by the nuttiness of the browned butter. We added the dry bread and small raw cauliflower bouquets for texture. It is important to add good texture with the smooth scallops.

IN FURTHER DETAIL

CARAMELIZED CAULIFLOWER PURÉE

Make a purée with lightly boiled cauliflower. Melt sugar in a pot with a thick bottom. Quickly stir in the cream. Watch out for hot splashes! Let the caramel melt into the purée. It is ready when it has blended completely and has a light brown color. Flavor with salt and freshly squeezed lemon.

BURNT BREAD PUDDING

Place slices of French bread in a bowl and cover with whipped eggs. Let it stew for an hour, turning the bread slices every so often. Transfer it into an oven-proof pan and heat it to 437°F (225°C). Remove from the oven, and let it cool until lukewarm. Place in a mixer and add some water, salt, lemon, and honey—mix until smooth.

HAY ASHES

Buy a small bag of sterile hay from an animal store. Place in a deep heat-resistant pan and go outside. Light the hay and make sure that it burns down to ashes. Sift through a sieve.

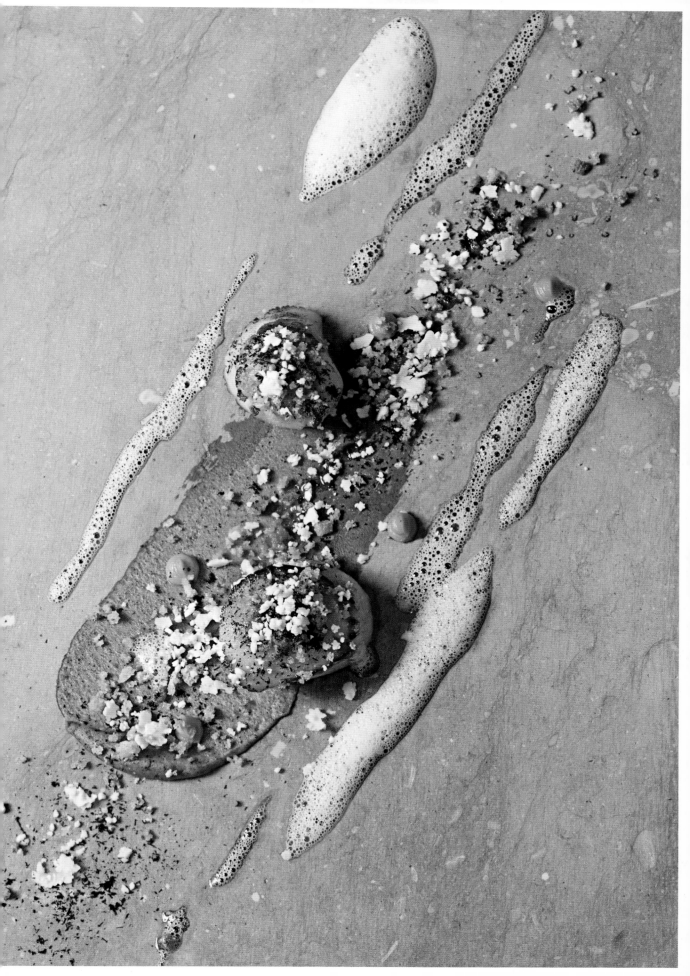

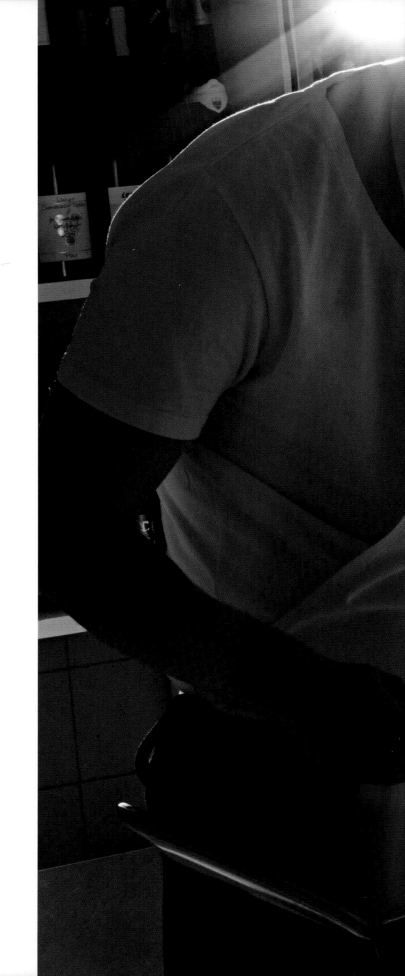

Lightly Pan-Fried Crayfish with Boiled Pig Tail

MANY ROOT VEGETABLES LOOK GOOD with some of the green parts left on, but around the stem fastening you can often find dirt and soil that should be peeled or scraped away with a small knife. The work takes time, and the result is often sad.

"We solved this by using an electric toothbrush that quickly, carefully, and effectively rinses away the dirt under cold running water. It is part of our daily work to find ways to simplify practical tasks to create more time for creative work."

UNEXP
SOLUT

ECTED

ONS

FISH

A fish should never be stressed when it is caught. Research done on fish caught with a fishing pole shows that generally they enter rigor mortis almost right away at the pier. A fish that's been caught in a trawl and then thrown on top of a ton of other fish on the boat will end up in the same immediate death cramp, with the meat filled with waste products that are not pumped out of the body. Line-caught fish is an alternative if the fish is picked up right away and not left on the line for multiple days, causing it to become very stressed.

THIS WAS A COMPLETELY NEW TASK FOR US, but it was information we expected to find. We had witnessed the great variation in fish quality at the various restaurants at which we worked. We had a feeling that stress-inducing ways of catching fish were relevant and wondered if fish, despite the fact that their muscular structure is so different from mammals, needed the same caring consideration as our beef, fowl, and game."

"Among our detailed descriptions of why and how we make food, what we do and what we don't, it is clear that we are uncompromising with our fish, as with anything else. We are located in the Old City in Stockholm, far from the fishing ports on the North Sea. It has been difficult to make this an advantage. For a long time, we felt that the fish we used were out of our control. We thought it was too hard to obtain newly caught and fresh fish—today we know better."

It is not without reason that Frantzén/Lindeberg can look enviously to Japan and the total care the Japanese show fish, partly in the actual catching and partly when it comes to slaughter and freshness. It becomes very clear why the Japanese restaurant has chosen to bring the fish into the kitchen while it is still alive, to kill it ethically, and to serve it immediately and raw.

In order to maintain the fresh taste, there are a few important elements to note about the muscular structure of fish. These elements are the same for all biological creatures and are easily disrupted through careless handling. The most sensitive of these elements is called ATP—adenosine triphosphate—and is a requirement for the quick movements of fish. It allows it to run away quickly, or hunt fast, or get away from danger in the blink of an eye. This element is vital, but it can disappear quickly. ATP, scientists say, has a special sweet taste, and it is that little extra element that makes the fish especially flavorful. But, the taste disappears only a few hours after slaughter. To catch this flavor, you have to kill the fish or shellfish in the restaurant kitchen and serve it right away.

"To catch this flavor you have to kill the fish or shellfish in the restaurant kitchen and serve it right away."

The scientists that Frantzén/Lindeberg worked with to try to understand how various elements influence the maturity and flavor of fish and shellfish found that other elements, for instance glycogen (bodily glucose) and IMP (made from ATP=>ADP=>AMP=>IMP) enhances the sweet flavor in newly slaughtered fish and shellfish.

Professors Bo-Sören Wiklund and Anders Kiessling at SLU, Swedish University of Agricultural Sciences, say:

"We think that if we research this more, we'll find that glycogen and IMP influence the taste, but in another time span and with other flavors such as the ones we've talked about. These flavors are the ones we perceive as 'superfresh' and that you only find right after slaughter, and that you first and foremost find in seafood. It is also interesting that shellfish have a higher content of these elements than fish. Furthermore, shellfish contain other flavor-enhancing elements, like betaine, in addition to more living amino acids."

"Our work with Wiklund/Kiessling at SLU was first started to try to figure out what was really fresh fish and shellfish."

After just a few minutes to a couple of hours, the flavor enhancers are broken down to diphosphates and monophosphates, and it is then completely unnecessary, not to say a pure waste, to use the fish.

"Others are welcome to use it, but not us; at that point the fish and shellfish no longer have the freshness we demand for serving raw. The enhancement of flavor from the adenosine triphosphate is the only reason it may work."

RIGOR MORTIS

In the real meaning of the word, fish and shellfish are only fresh for a couple of hours after slaughter, and only if they've been treated sensitively and have not been stressed. Frantzén/

"The fish we serve is always tenderized after rigor mortis in order to bring forth all of the best flavors of the meat."

Lindeberg often receive fish at the restaurant kitchen that are completely stiff as if the fish were cramped up. And this results in fish that is absolutely impossible to work with, despite the fact that the commercial fishing world we live in will call it "fresh."

"In our world, not even cod caught that morning is fresh, even if it is better than cod that's been transported for days, been placed on ice, and exposed to uneven temperatures, and may have even been damaged when slaughtered, so that bacteria-rich and protective mucus has entered the fish and has begun breaking down the meat."

The alternative to stiff fish with a gummy-like texture is to see fish meat the same way as we view pork meat—it is about maturity and tenderness.

The stale, cramped fish that's delivered under the guise of "fresh fish" have entered rigor mortis. Every caught fish enters this stage sooner or later. A stressed fish (like one that has been rod-caught) will enter rigor mortis almost immediately, whereas a carefully and ethically caught fish will take a little longer before entering rigor mortis.

When the fish is still alive, calcium is released into the muscle when it receives the signal that it should move; you can say that calcium is a "green light" for the muscle to contract. When the fish is resting, the calcium will be pumped out of the muscle, which is now relaxing. We can use ourselves as an example. The calcium exchange in our body is the same as our entire weight during twenty-four hours, and it can be satisfying to know that when we sleep the excess calcium is drained from our muscles, and this expends much energy. In other words, we lose weight the easiest when we sleep.

Sometimes this whole system falls apart and we get an excess of calcium in our muscles that makes them cramp up. When you're alive, the mistake can be repaired and the cramping

will stop, but when you are dead, the cramp will be permanent and is then called rigor mortis. It is the same with fish.

When a fish is caught, large amounts of calcium are released into the muscle for it to move. In order to get enough energy for this, it transforms its API and monophosphates. The energy is released when the phosphate breaks loose. When it is brought on shore and dies, it is very stressed and has depleted its ATP. When the fish dies, the muscle becomes very confused. It is just "annoyed" that there's no acid that propels it into metabolism, when the only way of creating energy, or ATP, is to transform sugar to lactic acid. This moves very slowly compared to when the fish is alive and receives acid. Therefore, a dead fish that's been killed under stress will never obtain high levels of ATP. This, again, means that the muscle is empty from ATP and full of di- and monophosphates, calcium, and acidic substances. Then, little by little, all of the energy disappears from the fish muscle, which can no longer pump calcium. The fish will first cramp up and then enter rigor mortis.

The course described here is very simplified so that it is understandable, because there are obviously many other chemical processes that take place during the death of a fish and the subsequent rigor mortis. But the processes that are interesting and important for a restaurant are the ones that remove flavor and the ones that enhance flavor.

IKE JIME
There are alternative ways of handling fish. The ethical catching without stressing the fish is important. The actual killing is also an important process for the fish.

"We follow ike jime. This is a more than three hundred-year-old method of killing fish, and in our restaurant, this means sedating the fish with a strong thud against the head and then

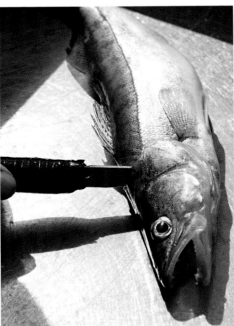

The fisherman Per Vidlund performs "ike jime"

sticking a thread into the spine to drain the blood. One of the advantages of this method is that there is no discoloration of the fish meat, but more importantly, that it decreases the risk that the iron and acid in the blood will react with the fat of the meat. In addition, leftover blood can become 'food' for bacteria that enters the fish during rinsing. Following the ike jime method means that, when the thread is inserted into the spine, the nerves responsible for the release of calcium are stimulated, so that the muscles along the body will contract and push out as much blood as possible. Because the fish is drained of blood in an effective matter, early staleness or growth of bacteria will be halted, resulting in cleaner and better-tasting fish meat. This rapid killing process also prevents the muscle from accumulating lactic acid, which is found in great quantities in industrially fished fish."

After ike jime, the fish is placed on ice to give it an inner temperature of 32°F (0°C). An ike jime-slaughtered fish will go into rigor mortis like any biological organism, though without blood and with as much as possible left of the various phosphates and glycogen from its energy storage. If the fish were to be prepared right away, it would go into rigor mortis as soon as it was exposed to heat, with the result that it would harden and lose flavor. The rigor mortis is controlled by proteins, but when the muscle cells have "understood" that it is dead, other proteins will starts loosening the retraction and the rigor mortis will stop. We can compare this to pork meat that hangs on bones, in the beginning hard and chubby, but after a week almost falling off the bone.

  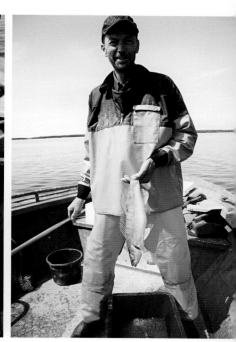

The fish should never be prepared until rigor mortis has disappeared. With certain kinds of fish, this process only takes a couple of days, but may take longer for others. The length of rigor mortis depends on how the fish was caught, killed, and stored. For turbot and halibut, for instance, the quality after rigor mortis can last for a maximum of twenty days, which underlines the importance of draining the blood and killing the fish with clean and sterile tools to avoid bacterial growth.

In time, a careful breaking down of the fats in the fish will happen parallel with a dissolution of proteins that are transformed into free amino acids, which are very flavor enhancing. At F/L, they simply get a controlled and positive tenderizer that will slowly move into another process as the bacteria grow in the meat.

"The fish we serve is always tenderized after rigor mortis in order to bring forth all of the best flavors of the meat."

CONFIT CHIN OF COD

Morels, roasted turkey bouillon, bread toasted in thyme butter, unfiltered olive oil, as well as reduced cream flavored with juniper-smoked bacon. Finish off with a generous amount of really old vinegar.

In the Basque country of Spain, they prepare fish chins called "kokotxas." Usually, the dish is prepared with garlic sauce and parsley. At F/L, the cod is prepared *sous-vide*. They first remove the skin and then place the cod with unfiltered olive oil in vacuum bags in a water bath that maintains 100.4°F (38°C).

The chins are not the main attraction of this dish. You could say that it is like a hotchpotch where all of the details create the flavorful whole. The Basque preparation is where country-style and robust cooking blend, which has inspired powerful flavors with the smokiness of bacon, a roasted rich taste from bouillon, and thyme bread, which also adds character to the texture.

GRILLED MONKFISH BAKED ON BONES

Sot-l'y-laisse from a forest hen, yellow chanterelles, cream on oven-baked artichokes, enriched with the bone marrow from the monkfish and served with a buttered chicken bouillon flavored with fermented beans and yellow wine.

There is most likely no other fish that is this appreciated in the kitchen. "The monkfish is the best of all food fish," they say, knowing that the preparation is a real challenge. The meat of the monkfish has a very different structure from other fish, reminiscent of light veal meat.

"Our monkfish is caught in the cold and clean waters outside of the Norwegian coastline by Møre og Romsdal and outside of Sogn og Fjordane, where the fishing quotas make it legal to extract a specific number of monkfish each year. This is where it is the absolute best."

The meat and flavor of the monkfish is autumn-like, which may be because of all the notes of minerals naturally contained in the fish (which can also be verified through chemical analysis).

In order to enhance the sense of autumn, the fish is served with newly picked yellow chanterelles, fermented beans, and freshly cut artichokes.

"Most people buy monkfish to grill. We've brought this tradition into our autumn arrangement, but it is completely impossible to control the temperature of a fish on the grill. The heat of a grill is so high that the inner temperature of the fish gets carried away. If it is even a little bit overcooked, the monkfish turns into rubber—in other words, inedible. Therefore, we only give the fish a quick turn on the grill before we cover it with lardo di colonnata, and then later carefully and slowly bake it in an oven that holds steady at 140°F (60°C) until it is ready. The monkfish is perfect at an inner temperature of 100.4°F (38°C). We've found that this is when the fish gains the best texture and releases all of its flavor."

IN FURTHER DETAIL

BUTTERED CHICKEN BOUILLON

The sauce, which is a buttered chicken bouillon, is built on the fact that the butter emulsifies with the yellow wine. *Vin jaune* is from Jura in eastern France and is made using only Savagnin grapes. The wine is stored in oak barrels and is left completely undisturbed for six years. During this time, it develops a layer of yeast fungi that covers the surface and prevents the wine from oxidation. That is why the finished wine is yellow.

If you can't get ahold of vin jaune from France, you can replace it with sherry, which is somewhat similar in flavor. The difference, however, is that sherry contains added alcohol, often in the form of brandy, whereas vin jaune is a naturally strong wine.

Vin jaune is boiled down to half in a saucepan and lightly whisked with a little ginger powder. In a separate saucepan, a blonde chicken bouillon has been boiling down. The wine and the bouillon are mixed together with unsalted butter and spiced with a white miso paste made with fermented beans, which provide the right saltiness.

GRILLED FISH

Turn the fish in 40-percent cream before you place it on the grill. This way, the fish will obtain a grilled surface more quickly, and the fat in the cream will prevent the meat from sticking to the grill. A quick grilled surface adds flavor before the fish is removed from the heat and baked slowly on a low temperature in the oven, which allows even cooking of the entire fish.

SLOWLY BAKED WILD-CAUGHT WHOLE FLOUNDER WITH FRIED AND CRISPY YELLOW ONION

Roe from Mälaren, white wine sauce flavored with anchovy brine and chive butter, served with dill.

This is Sweden: dill, roe, anchovies, and chives. It is the flavors of the Swedish casserole Jansson's Temptation that inspired the anchovy stock, onion, and cream; ingredients that have specific and Swedish personalities.

The flounder is a tough fish in flavor and willingly absorbs other flavors and helps develop them. It is best after slow maturation in an ice bed, that is to say it has an enhanced flavor and better texture. Freshly caught flounder is not as flavorful as it is after maturing.

"Flounder is a large fish, so we don't have room in our kitchen to prepare it whole on the bones, which is otherwise a rule in our kitchen. But with the flounder, such a demand would be unreasonable. We therefore fillet the fish, save the skin on the upper side, and cover the cut surface with either thin lard or stored pig fat, lardo di colonnata, to protect the fish and cover the 'sore.'"

The slowly baked flounder has been very much appreciated by the restaurant's international guests, who have also raised their eyebrows in surprise. They have obviously had flounder before, but never with such a pure flavor. There is no better fish than the wild-caught flounder fished in the cold northern seas. The cold water gives the flavor character.

The flounder should be baked slowly, and there is a slightly moving story behind this:

"When we bought the restaurant, we took over a lot of equipment from the previous owner. Our own money was not enough for a new oven, and the one we took over had many years on its back and was difficult to use because it could not hold an exact temperature during longer baking. It made it impossible to bake fish slowly because the temperature would vary. We soon found an alternative: our plate-oven. It is built to warm plates, so that the food will maintain its warmth from the serving hatch to the table and the guest. The plate-oven kept a steady and perfect temperature of 150°F (65°C), and from that day on, it became our fish oven. People who've been served flounder in our restaurant can be certain that it has been prepared in the plate-oven because, even today, that oven is best for cooking fish. After a while we had enough money to buy one of the most modern restaurant ovens available, but even though it keeps an even heat, it is still too humid for the fish to turn out well."

"It is said that at Frantzén/Lindeberg we never boil sauce. That can't be more wrong. The difference is that we never make reduced stock because we can't understand covering the natural flavor of an ingredient with its boiled, spiced liquid. Instead, we use gravy. A blonde bouillon or white wine sauce, and on the latter we might as well bestow the title 'most magnificent sauce,' which is why we add it to our serving of flounder."

IN FURTHER DETAIL

FRIED ONION

Thinly slice yellow onion and place in a bowl. Add butter at room temperature and carefully massage into the onion. The liquid of the onion will emulsify with the butter and bind the flavors together. Place in a nonstick pan and fry on medium heat until it starts caramelizing. Finish it off with a little good-quality sea salt. Shape into a quenelle with two spoons and top with a little finely chopped fried onion.

MÄLAREN WALLEYE BAKED IN THE EMBERS WITH STRAW, JUNIPER, AND HERBS

Raw chopped Swedish lobster, roots from the garden boiled in whey, served with homemade sour cream flavored with roe and chives.

"Before the walleye is prepared, we show it whole to the guest in an open foil package on a bed of straw, herbs, and juniper. We want to recreate the feeling of sitting by the fireplace after a fishing trip, having gathered juniper and wild herbs to place in a package with straw and wet newspaper, and then later cooking the fish in the glow of the dying embers."

"We wanted to get ahold of the flavors, the feeling, and the scents. We first tried with wet newspapers and made a fish package that we placed in our Josper oven.* This didn't work, or rather, it worked, but the entire restaurant was filled with smoke. We had to take a shortcut, just for once, and bake the fish in foil. We do this right after we've showed the fish to the guest." The package is placed in the glow bed at the bottom of the Josper oven, where the fish is baked until it has an inner temperature of 110°F (43°C).

"We've always been careful about cooking fish too rapidly just because it is difficult to keep track of the inner temperature. This is the exception that proves the rule. The cooking demands constant watching and constant turning and moving the package many times in order to control the temperature. The fact that the fish is covered with straw helps because when the straw carbonizes, it steals heat energy from the fish and gives it a pleasant and mild smoky flavor. We take the fish package out right before the walleye has reached 110°F (43°C). Because it has been cooked in such a hot oven, the afterwarmth continues to bake the fish once it has been removed from the oven."

Walleye is one of Sweden's most flavorful fish (it tastes a lot like fish, so to speak), and therefore it can also survive the rough cooking.

There is something very Swedish about this way of cooking and the idea behind it, and so the "Swedishness" of the dish is further enhanced by the garnish—black salsify, salsify, and burdock. "Cultural roots" they could be called because they have traditionally been farmed in Sweden for hundreds of years. "They grow in our gardens in Malmköping and Askersund. These are sensitive roots, which oxidize easily when you peel them. The only chance of maintaining their blonde freshness is to add acid. Because we make cheese, we have a lot of whey that we can boil the walleye in. This also provides a tart flavor."

"You ask why we choose Mälaren roe instead of Kalix roe, and it's an easy question to answer—it has nothing to do with quality because they are both just as good—but the walleye is from Mälaren outside of Enköping, and the same fisherman also catches the bleak roe."

*Spanish oven that allows coal grilling inside.

BUTTER-FRIED SOLE SPICED WITH GREEN TEA AND FENNEL POLLEN

Pickled cucumber and the first green zucchini of the season, with apple mint and zucchini flowers.

Exactly when the gardens start delivering the pre-summer's first zucchini or green squash, or courgette, as they say in Sweden, the sole is at its fattest and best.

The sole is, like all F/L's delivered fish, slaughtered by the ike jime method and matured until all "waste products" in the muscles of the fish have been transported away. This process takes from a couple of days to multiple weeks depending on the kind of fish. During the tenderizing and maturing time, the fish is packed in ice (see more in the introduction of fish, page 114).

The sole has a sweeter taste and has to be balanced with salt, but first and foremost, acid. The cucumber turns into a very nice complement for the fish. The fruitiness of flavor, the freshness, comes from the green zucchini with apple mint.

The whole dish contains light, but not fleeting, flavors where the Japanese green tea, through its own rich ocean taste, binds the sweetness in the fish, the acid from the cucumber, and the anise from the fennel pollen.

SATIO TEMPESTAS

Satisfaction based on season and time of year.

Why give this dish that's always on the menu a Latin name? It is not to be pretentious, but rather because the Latin *Satio Tempestas* perfectly describes a dish that varies from day to day depending on what is at its best in the two gardens.

The base is some sort of fish; which fish is used also depends on what has reached the best maturity and texture that day.

"In a 'Satio' we also gather many flavor components from the forest depending on the season. We are very meticulous about only using ingredients that follow the course of the year. A Satio Tempesta in wintertime is very different from the one you will get in spring or fall."

The background to the F/L's Satio Tempestas is the great production of vegetables in the two gardens. "They delivered more than we used. Instead of notoriously throwing away some of the best produce in this country, we needed to find a way to use everything we produced."

In spring, 2009, the base of the Satio Tempesta was composed; a basic dish that could be varied infinitely.

It will almost always be shaped around the tenderized and mature fish delivered by the fisherman in Gothenburg and Ängsö.

"What we receive from the gardens and the forest is served raw, boiled, dried, creamy, and fried. The fish is prepared in the same way as the other fish—whole and protected with a thick layer of lard—slowly in a warming cabinet until the inner temperature is between 100.4°F (38°C) and 113°F (45°C) depending on the kind of fish used.

FOURTEEN-DAYS' MATURED TURBOT POACHED IN SHEEP MILK FROM BREDSJÖ

Flavored with fresh bay leaves, served with its own skin and the milk from the preparation. Burnt béchamel sauce, fried oyster mushrooms, yellow onion, and onion flowers in browning butter.

The skin of the fish contains many amino acids that are flavorful. You could say that the fat reserve of the turbot is placed there, and the fat is a flavor carrier, even with fish.

"A couple of years ago, we began to poach fish in milk. The whiteness was maintained and we use sheep milk because it holds a natural sweetness that complements a mild and fine fish like turbot. It is also fattier and protects the fish during cooking. The bay leaves are added as a perfume. To make it clear, we serve the fish with the poaching milk that has absorbed the fish flavor and the slight harshness of the bay leaves.

The fish is poached to an inner temperature of 100.4°F (38°C)."

The oyster mushrooms are delivered from the Frantzén/Lindeberg garden in Askersund.

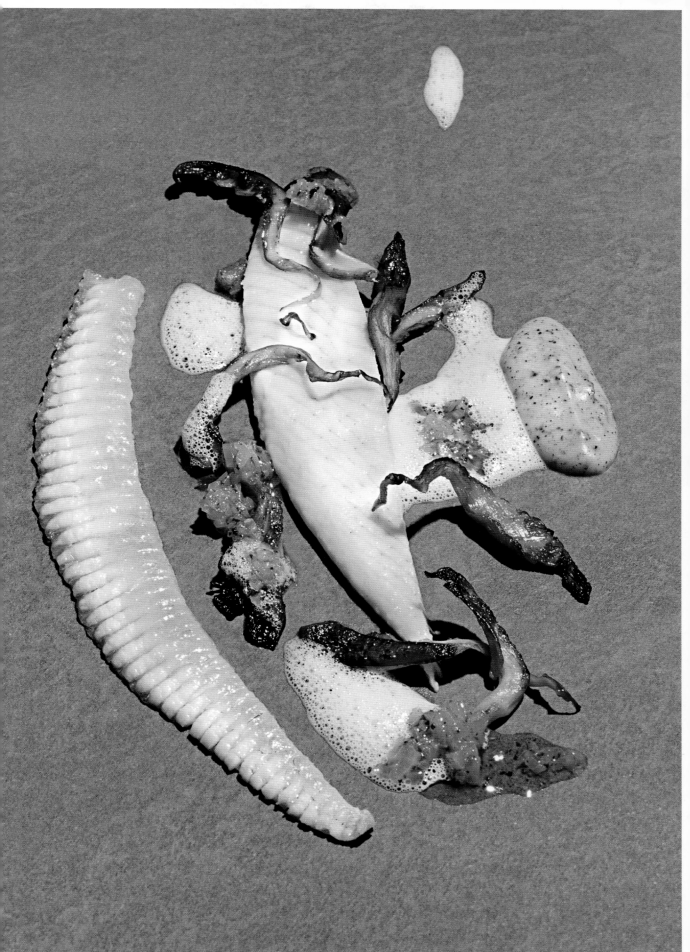

IN FURTHER DETAIL

BURNT BÉCHAMEL

This should not be considered a sauce in the proper sense but rather a cream in which the taste of the roasted flour still remains.

"Often, when we serve burnt flavors, we've discovered them by mistake. In this burnt béchamel there was never a mistake, rather it was a conscious burning of butter, milk, and flour with the purpose of making garnish for the turbot. The flavor is reminiscent of hazelnuts and mushroom."

Roast regular wheat flour in an oven without a fan at 355°F (180°C) until it is nut brown, stirring every now and then. Cover the bottom of a 12-inch (30 cm) thick bottom pot with old-fashioned milk or farm milk.

Set on high heat, boil, and burn so that it sticks to the saucepan. Scrape it out with a spatula and place it in a bowl. Repeat this up to ten times for quantity. Blend the burnt milk with about 2 ½ cups of farm milk and mix with a handheld mixer to a light chocolate color. Add four tablespoons of unsalted butter, and brown harshly while stirring. Finish by adding the roasted flour. Whisk the flour to a smooth béchamel. Flavor with a little salt and some lemon. If you prefer, you can also add a little finely crumbled dried Karl Johan mushroom.

Butter-Fried Sole Spiced with Green Tea and Fennel Pollen

EVERY EVENING, THE SCENARIO is that the guests place a linen napkin on their laps, use it to wipe their mouths, and sometimes for other things.

The guests leave the napkin when they step away from the table for some reason.

"We ask ourselves if it should be part of our service to run back and forth and re-fold the napkin because it looks pretty and is part of the care, but is this acceptable hygiene?"

Many guests view the napkin as part of their own private sphere. Is it then right that the waiter touches it and folds it, or should it be exchanged for a new one?

"No one in our service has the time to clean his or her hands before and after touching every napkin during one evening. To exchange the napkin every time the guest leaves the table (which can be six or seven times) is not ideal from an environmental point of view with washing, starching, ironing, and transport. And so we have a problem to solve."

"We have tried to fold the napkin with pliers so that we don't touch the linen. However, the napkins are so stiff that it is impossible to fold them nicely and they looked worse after the plier-fold than before." The guest could also perceive it as a sign that the server did not want to touch the napkin.

"Another solution was to use a cotton glove that is used only for this purpose. This solution was not successful either because we had to use many cotton gloves. It also became difficult to keep track of which glove should be used for what."

"The best solution from an environmental and bacterial point of view was a disposable napkin that you could lift with pliers and exchange, but this solution didn't really feel like us at all."

"We have yet to find the ultimate solution, but we are working on it. Today we are taking a kind of middle road; we exchange napkins that have been on the floor or have become very dirty during dinner. The rest of the napkins are simply folded and placed back on the chair."

BREAD/DAIRY

The first thing you encounter at Frantzén/Linde-berg is the bread. As soon as the guest is seated, a small teak box with a glass lid is presented. In the box, there is a baguette-shaped dough. It now only needs to finish rising before it is baked in the coal oven.

"I think it shows how much weight we place on bread and dairy products. When the bread later returns baked, it is in the company of home-churned butter. In the beginning, we had a whole array of different kinds of bread, rolls, rye, and crisp bread. Slowly, we concluded that it is the light bread, the baguette, which is the optimal to serve in a tasting menu. If you even serve bread, that is."

"You can never say exactly when the bread is taken out to the guest . . . "

A BAGUETTE IS A LIGHT BREAD with a deep flavor. It fits with meals when it is first presented and is later served as a kind of a middle-snack before finally becoming a part of the peripheral.

You can never say exactly when the bread is taken out to the guest; it simply depends on when it is ready. Some days it can take longer, other days it is quicker, depending on the humidity and temperature. Bread is living. You can't set the clock according to bread, and this is true about the rising box on the table.

The bread's journey to the table starts as a poolish, a pre-dough, a day before it is served. It is made out of water, flour, and some yeast that ferments in order to develop the wheat flavor. The flour is stone-ground with the wheat ash content maintained, which makes the natural wheat flavor deeper and more flavorful. You can call a poolish for "direct sourdough" with the long fermenting time in mind.

At three o'clock in the afternoon the same day as the guests arrive, the dough is blended and is allowed to rise for two hours before it is weighed, rolled out, and wrapped in French linen cloth couche and placed in the refrigerator. At the same moment as the guest arrives, the dough is taken out of the refrigerator and placed in the teak box, which is then presented at the table.

The dough shows the importance of dramaturgy by the table. That is one of the reasons the bread is served to the guests immediately after it is out of the oven.

"We always serve it with a salt butter because we are convinced that butter should be salty. We usually stay at a salt-content between 2.1 and 2.3 percent fleur de sel."

"To get the exact butter we want, we churn it in the restaurant."

"In the beginning, we bought good butter from various suppliers, even from France, but in time we've developed a taste for our own butter because we had the opportunity to learn from

Patrik Johansson at Vallmobacken's Dairy in Alingsås. He has great knowledge about how to sour the cream before churning. The acid and salt is the secret behind our good butter. Today, we churn the butter at the table in about two minutes."

   Unlike any other nationality, the Swedes like butter with a high-acid content, and this was established as early as the old mountain communities. The cream was extracted and placed in large dishes. When they had enough cream to churn butter, it would often be naturally acidified. Since then, they've been very much in love with butter with a high acidic content; this is even true for the home-churned butter at Lilla Nygatan 21. A fun fact is that there used to be a dairy shop at this exact address, and the Old City's best cheese and butter shops used to be located right across from the small restaurant.

Do you know why the
bread is so filling?
Because it is baked with
love.
Bread is love.

It is a luxurious enjoyment
to have real bread and
then add premium butter.

Notes of Astrid Lindgren

LUKEWARM HOME-CURDLED CHEESE IN ITS OWN WHEY

Cold-pressed unfiltered rapeseed oil from Julita, sea salt, and grated macadamia nut.

"We've had difficulty finding a place for cheese in our tasting menu. A cheese plate can be terrific with a three-course meal. In that case, the kind of cheese served needs the space and time to enjoy—ideally, cheeses with flavor and a lot of character. In Sweden, there is no set culture of eating cheese after the main course and before dessert. Still, with our great interest in dairy, we wanted to find a cheese that could be created daily in our kitchen. We ended up with a soft cheese that is now part of our menu."

IN FURTHER DETAIL

CURDLED CHEESE

Eight cups (2 liters) of sour milk is heated to 100.4°F (38°C). Hang a sifting cloth over the stove so that the cheese stays lukewarm. Save the whey and pour it over the cheese dish as a sauce.

HOME-CHURNED BUTTER
BROWNED BUTTER
BUTTER WITH ROASTED BONE MARROW FAT

At the opening in 2008, it was impossible to get ahold of butter that lived up to their high demands for quality. Therefore, they started to experiment with their own.

"First, we whipped pure cream until it separated into butter and butter milk. The butter was churned with two-percent salt and served with the bread in portion pieces as butter cubes."

In a happy meeting with a dedicated dairy specialist, Patrik Johansson at Vallmobacken in Alingsås, it was revealed that butter is so much more than whipped cream. Still, the home-whipped butter had a much richer flavor than the butter you could get from the industry, with an added butter aroma and a quick preparation in a butter churn.

The secret is a combination of acid and salt where the acidification happens naturally with the help of lactic bacteria.

"Before every service, we home-churn the exact amount of butter we need for the evening, and based on experience, we know that it is at its best in both texture and flavor right after churning. This means that there is a constant acidic culture that needs to be encouraged."

"The consequence of doing this was that we could not offer seconds of our home-churned butter. Instead, we serve a browned butter as a second serving and a butter made with roasted bone marrow fat as a third serving with the bread."

IN FURTHER DETAIL

BROWNED BUTTER

Brown a part butter to *beurre noisette*. Empty into a bowl and cool to about 104°F (40°C). Whisk in one part butter at room temperature. Flavor with salt.

BUTTER WITH ROASTED BONE MARROW FAT

Roast rinsed and well-cleaned bone marrow in an oven at 355°F (180°C) until the fat separates from the marrow. Sift and let cool to 104°F (40°C). Weigh the fat, and blend with butter with ten parts butter to seven parts bone marrow. Flavor with sea salt, and refrigerate. Whisk before placing on plates and serving.

BAGUETTE

The kitchen is equipped with a coal stone oven. This allows the oven to keep a natural humidity and extreme heat.

"Generally, you say that you should never open the oven door while you are baking bread. We don't care about that."

"In the same oven, we also make the scallops, which are ready in minutes. This basically means that there is a continual opening and closing of the oven door, even when the bread is baking in there."

A coal or wood oven is very organic. You can't set the temperature as you would do in your regular oven at home. Sometimes the coal oven will reach about 750°F (400°C). The only way to bake bread without burning it is by constant surveillance and continuous turning.

"We break all the traditional rules and restrictions to bake the bread we like best: a baguette with a clear wheat flavor and a chewy and powerful crust. It creates an inside with random air pockets, which shows a sensitive touch of hand."

IN FURTHER DETAIL

BAGUETTE
Day 1, Poolish
> 1.3 lb (625 g) water
> 15 oz (430 g) stonemeal wheat flour
> A small pinch of yeast (the size of half a sugar cube)

Place all the ingredients in a bowl and blend with a whisk. Cover with plastic, and let it sit at room temperature for four hours. Place in the refrigerator.

Day 2, Baking
> 6 cups (1.4 L) water
> 2 lb (1 kg) stone-ground wheat flour
> 3 lb (1.375 g) Manitoba meal
> 0.8 oz (25 g) chestnut honey
> 0.7 oz (20 g) compressed yeast
> 2.2 oz (65 g) fine salt

Place everything, except the salt, in a dough blender. Blend for four minutes on the lowest speed. Then, increase the speed and blend for another four minutes. Add the salt and blend for another four minutes at the same speed. Let it rise for two hours.

Divide the dough into 1-oz (130-g) pieces and shape into oblong baguettes of about 10 inches (25 cm) length. Let it rise for one and a half to two hours.

Bake at 480°F (250°C) for about seven minutes.

JUST
SEA SA

DIFFERENT KINDS OF SALT create different sensations in your mouth and work in different ways in different kinds of cooking. "At Frantzén/Lindeberg, we use our own salt."

Regular salt grains—table salt—have a less dramatic salt flavor that may fit well when you need to salt water for boiling an ingredient that demands salt water. Not potatoes, however, but other ingredients such as leaf vegetables.

"Then we have the many flaked salts that we believe gained popularity through a well-known TV show, but were created as early as the Viking days when the Vikings learned the method for creating salt in order to preserve meat and fish. They created flaked salt next to fishing stations they had along the Bay of Biscay. The salt was used to preserve the fish that was brought onboard for further travel. Some of these travelers went to Normandy, and it is assumed that they would have shared their knowledge of salt with the French there. Tell this to any Frenchman, however, and he or she will revoke your friendship. That the Vikings could make butter as well, knowledge they also brought to the French, makes the ignominy complete. But these facts about butter and salt are warranted and completely true."

Patrik Johansson and Zandra Bring at Vallmobacken's Dairy in Alingsås are friends and mentors of Frantzén/Lindeberg, both when it comes to the making of butter and as producers of the restaurant's salt, a traditionally made flake salt. A salt made without cheating. Patrik Johansson shares his story of how he came up with the idea:

"We were living at Styrsö in Gothenburg's southern archipelago. We built a houseboat that later sank, but before that Zandra and I puffed around a lot in it, and one day we ended up in a heavy storm. When we survived the storm, we kissed each other, and I realized that Zandra's lips were salty. This became the beginning of a research project that began with finding out how salt was produced in southern Sweden in earlier times.

"Swedes have produced salt by simmering and reducing salt water for a very long time. The goal has always been to extract flakes of salt because they work better with fish and meat. A granular salt doesn't enter the meat in the same way because it takes so long to melt that it sucks out the meat juices instead of salting the meat.

"The Vikings had a fishing station by the beach below the mountain at Île de Ré, where they made Bayonne ham, which is viewed by many as the best dried ham. One can easily conclude that it was the Vikings' salt production that made it possible to dry large hams there. In Île de Ré, the salt was created through reducing ocean water by allowing the sun to do its work in large pools. But they also reduced ocean water in large iron pots.

"Anyone can extract salt from ocean water. It becomes granulated if you simmer the water down, but making larger crystals such as flakes is a lot harder. The crystals appear at the water surface when the salt content is 25.8 percent, but in order to get the crystals/flakes larger you have to make them float on the surface. It took two months of experimenting every day and night before we found how to do it, with the help of a journey to Stockholm and studying old documents at the National Heritage Board, as well as a journey to London in order to study old documents

there. Two expensive 5-gallon (20 L) pots cracked during testing, but then one night the crystals appeared as they should.

"You can cheat and add butter or animal glue to the water, for instance, and in that case the crystals will become larger. But, the only thing we add is seaweed because the salt then becomes mineral-rich and the flakes become larger. We tried adding butter, but quickly stopped. It was during my experimenting with salt that I had to make my own butter exactly how my grandmother once taught me.

"Today, we get the water to our salt production from outside of Gothenburg's archipelago. Then, it is transported in a tank-car that holds 2,600 gallons (10,000 L), from which we extract between 330 and 550 pounds (150-250 kg) of flaked salt. In other words, our production is very limited.

"In the whole world, it is only we and the salt producers at Laso in Denmark who produce salt in this old-fashioned and complicated way."

"We have chosen this Swedish-made salt because it is honest, clean, and because it tastes good with its mineral undertones. It is sad that the kind of salts we used previously were a result of cheating with animal glue and other elements in the production. Now we have a salt that takes no shortcuts and hates cheating! Another interesting anecdote, although not completely historically proven, is that during the 200s, Lombards emigrated from the south of Sweden and settled down in Lombardy. There, they taught the people to salt hams and make cheese. What today is known as prosciutto and Parmesan!"

MEAT

The standards Swedish slaughterhouses have for grading meat are based on European general regulations. The highest score is granted for the most economical meat with the least fat and the greatest amount of meat development in the shortest amount of time. This kind of meat is tasteless, and this development of the meat business is unfavorable for the flavor and the quality.

For a long time, Frantzén and Lindeberg couldn't find any Swedish supplier that met their expectations of quality in flavor, so they imported their meat to provide the quality their guests expected.

"**THE PRINCIPLE OF FOLLOWING** the season means serving many different kinds of meat throughout the year: deer in hunting season, the first suckling lambs in early spring, veal in early summer, goat when it has matured a bit in summer, and pig whenever one likes.

"When we prepare meat dishes, we try to use all of the parts of the animal, and as much as possible, we try to mimic the old Swedish farms and use everything, even the blood. I often find it more amusing to show my expertise as a cook by using unusual and inferior butchering parts and putting them together with finer ingredients. For instance, beef brisket with goose liver, pig blood and Kalix roe, and pig tail and crayfish."

Finding good pig meat has been very difficult. It is easy to find a lean industrial pig that has been slaughtered at about 110 lbs (50 kg), but hard to find a real farm pig that has been slaughtered at closer to 220 lbs (100 kg). But Frantzén and Lindeberg suddenly got in contact with the responsible breeder of Linderöd pork—the original Swedish pig.

"That contact introduced us to a lot of other suppliers of a pork meat that meets our demands for flavor and maturity. Since then, we have found a number of suppliers of pig parts from purebred Linderöd pig. Pigs that are allowed to walk outside in large areas and live naturally before slaughter. This creates a good fat content and a maturity of flavor. These Linderöd pigs immediately became the trademark of Frantzén/Lindeberg."

Are Frantzén and Lindeberg conservative?

"Yes, you could actually say that, we believe that an animal tastes significantly better if it is allowed to mature, grow older in the best circumstances of life, eating the best food, and when it is slaughtered without stress. We know how good the meat you can buy from Japan or France, for instance, can be, and we know that it should be possible to get the same quality meat here at home. The Linderöd pork is a good example of how one single breeder has taken responsibility. The journey to the experience with us begins with him."

Linderöd pigs from Askersund

The pigs are bred, among others, at Gustaf Söderfeldt's farm, the same farmer who raises F/L's chosen chickens. This means having almost daily contact with the breeder and making many visits to the farm. Söderfeldt boils 220 lbs (100 kg) of potatoes daily for his pigs, potatoes that are partly grown at the farm, partly in the local area. The pigs also eat other root vegetables from the vegetable garden. The cultivator Lars Feddeck keeps his horses in the same area.

"We had no idea that it would be in Åmmeberg in Askersund that we would find our pork, but the one who seeks shall find, and it took many years of seeking before we found the right place."

The younger meat—young goat, suckling lamb, and veal—is delivered from breeders in Sweden and France.

"It would be great if we could use Swedish lamb as well, but we have yet to find a lamb meat that has the quality the French can deliver. Unfortunately, we have realized how people try to rationalize within the sheep industry and allow the sheep to go indoors on straw beds in the belief that it will be possible to get quality meat this way. It is pure idiocy because they need to walk outside with lots of pasture in order to obtain flavor-carrying fat from herb-holding grass. Our suckling lambs have been allowed to walk naturally under the sky."

After a little more than three years, we were able to form bonds between the restaurant and some Swedish beef suppliers as well. One of them is Odd Norman, from Gotland, who owns Ejmund's farm.

"One may wonder why we would choose such a large farm in Gotland to find the meat that suits us, but the reason is simple: Here they breed animals that are treated right, that get the right kind of food, and that are slaughtered ethically. In short, Ejmund's farm can deliver the meat we want. It is always flavor and texture that decide."

"We were surprised by both the texture and the flavor . . ."

At Ejmund's farm in Gotland, in actuality a genuine Gotland farm and today a large grain farm of 450-acre self-owned fields and a 740-acre lease that's been passed down through four generations, Maude and Odd Norman have started producing a "royal meat." Many years back, crossbreeding was begun at Stenhammar's estate outside of Flen. Stenhammar was leasing from King Carl XVI Gustaf since 1965, and the crossbreeding began and was supervised by the Agricultural University in Uppsala. The goal has been to find a breed that's reminiscent of the Japanese kobe, and to make sure that the animals are treated similarly, with, among other things, massages and draff (a product from beer brewers) in the food that otherwise consists of silage and pasture. As heifers, they arrive in Gotland and stay there for three years before they are sent to slaughter. In other words, enough time for the meat to mature so that the fat has entered and mottled the muscles.

"We were surprised by both the texture and the flavor when we visited Gotland and Ejmund's, and we were happy to see how well these animals were treated during breeding with good flavor-enhancing food."

Odd Norman says that the Swedish kobe meat is a cross between Simmental and Angus, which in common conversation is called Simgus. Whether or not the massage does anything for the quality might be debatable, but the animals like it, and so the massage can be placed under "workplace satisfaction and quality of life," which naturally can't be wrong. The massage is done with large rotating brushes, reminiscent of the ones you find at a carwash, hanging here and there. The animals voluntarily walk under the brushes and agree to the massage, which is performed in the same way on Japanese kobe meat animals.

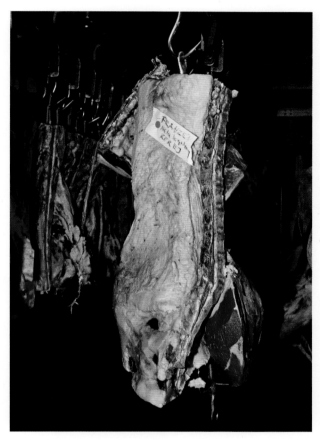

A forty-month-old beef carcass from a Simgus heifer from Ejmund's farm

BUTTER-FRIED PANCAKES OF ALMOND POTATOES AND PIG BLOOD

Roe from Kalix, small leaves of sorrel, fried duck heart, veal bacon, and dried browned butter, served with home-made applesauce and freshly cut chives.

In 1999 Georges Blanc from Vonnas made a guest appearance at Edsbacka Restaurant. As one of his guest appearance dishes, he made his famous and classic potato pancake based on his grandmother's recipe.

"We were working at Edsbacka then and were in the kitchen during the guest appearance. The memory of the potato pancake stuck, and now we've brought it further, added pig blood, and made it our own."

The advantage of this pancake is that it is airy and light because it is based on egg white and therefore lightly soufflés when fried in butter.

"To obtain a real saltiness in the dish, we added the roe. George Blanc placed the pancake on salmon. Under our blood circle, there is some veal bacon for a slight smoky flavor."

The tradition at the gold restaurant is usually Russian caviar and blini with sour cream.

"I want to associate this with other blood pudding or other blood dishes that are served with apple and bacon—the fruitiness is a must against the somewhat harsh iron flavor of the blood. Because there is also need of a little acid, the Lingonberry could be compared with the blood pudding if you wish; we use small leaves of sorrel."

IN FURTHER DETAIL

RECIPE FOR THE BLOOD PANCAKES

16 oz boiled sifted almond potatoes
9 oz pig blood
1 tablespoon potato flour
1 egg
4 egg whites
1 tablespoon dark syrup
3 tablespoons dark beer of a Bavarian variety
Veal bacon

Cut the veal bacon brunoise (very tiny cubes) and fry. Blend all of the ingredients except the egg whites. Later, fold in the unwhisked egg whites carefully so that they keep their structure.

Fry in a generous amount of butter in a griddle. Sprinkle some veal bacon on top of the raw surface before you turn the pancake over. Fry the sides quickly so that the pancake is still creamy on the inside.

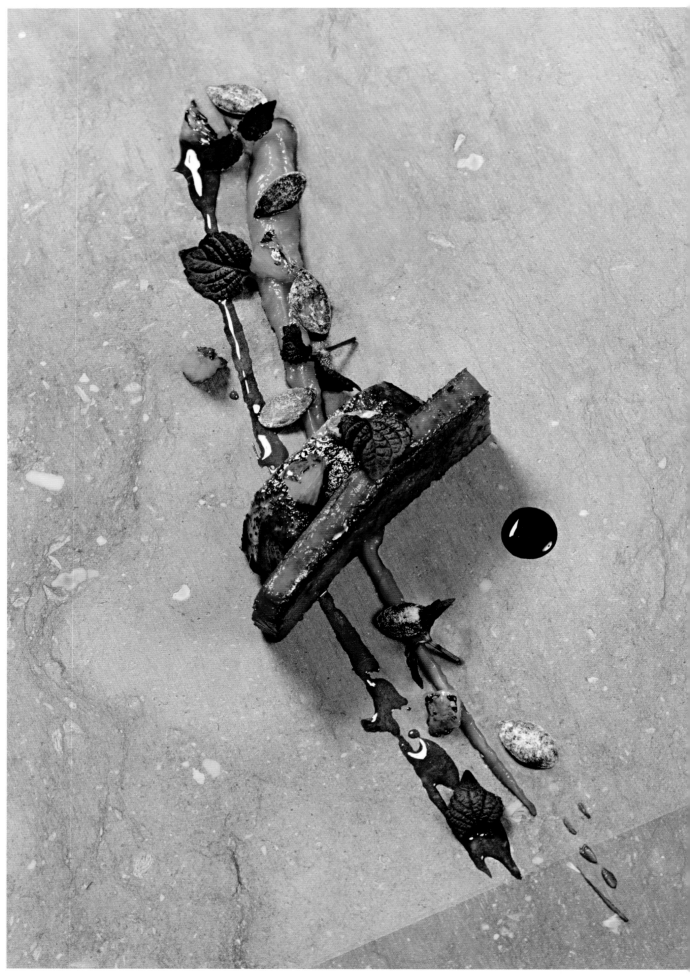

FRIED SALTED BEEF BRISKET WITH SEARED FOIE GRAS

Caramelized orange with seeds, oil, cream, and juice from hokkaido pumpkin served with reduced wine.

"I am in love with this combination, and I remember that I created it as early as in 1998 back at Edsbacka Restaurant at Christer Lingstrom's. The salty, dense, and somewhat dry meat of the fried beef brisket blends well with the buttery texture of the foie gras."

In season, the hokkaido pumpkin is delivered from the restaurant's own vegetable garden in Malmköping.

"When you cultivate your own fruits and vegetables, it makes you want to use them with extreme care. Therefore, we bake the pumpkin meat in the oven, press, and stir it into cream. We juice the other parts of the pumpkin in a juicer (see p. 248), mix it with raw sugar, and boil it down into sweet and sour syrup."

The orange is filleted and sprinkled with sugar and caramelized using a gas burner. The sweet and sour of the orange breaks the fat in the foie gras and also the sweetness of the hokkaido pumpkin.

VEAL LIVER MARINATED IN ALMOND MILK

Fried with suet in a frying pan, sprouted almonds, preserved yellow chanterelles, and dried apricot are served with carrot porridge, bitter cocoa, and freshly grated truffle.

Something about dried apricots and chanterelles makes them similar in taste, but they have different textures and a different level of sweetness. Chanterelles have a spicy and interesting aroma reminiscent of apricots. Just as interesting is offal when combined with surprising ingredients. In France, for instance, they fry kidneys on skewers over an open fire. The kidney is never fully removed from its tallow membrane, which is instead allowed to slowly melt over the kidney as a kind of self-basting roast.

Cookbooks still say that you should marinate liver in milk to "draw out the liver flavor." In reality, this method helps to enhance flavor and remove the elements that destroy the flavor: blood, proteins, egg white substances. The taste is then pure liver.

"We have used almond milk to marinate our veal liver. If it is allowed to marinate, it absorbs part of the almond flavor, but it also becomes lean, de-blooded, and stronger. The flavor of the liver grows through the almond."

"We almost never use slow-cooked stocks or sauces. Instead, we use quickly made juices from the frying of the ingredients. The broth from the liver is too rich to waste and is enhanced by the melted suet that is scooped over the liver continuously while frying in the pan. Liver should be fried very quickly and should have a somewhat moist core to allow the flavors to release. That way, the almond milk also works as a perfume for the liver's otherwise somewhat harsh flavor."

IN FURTHER DETAIL

CARROT PORRIDGE

Peel carrots and juice them in a juicer, save the juice, and, most importantly, save the dehydrated carrot leftovers. Dry the dehydrated carrots in an oven or a dry oven until completely dry. Mix into a fine powder. When serving, mix a little of the carrot juice with the powder, add a pat of butter with lemon, and salt. Warm the blend in a saucepan. The carrot powder will expand and form a liquid porridge. This is a technique you can use for many vegetables. For instance, celeriac porridge flavored with truffle and nutmeg, red beet porridge with walnuts and goat cheese, or parsnip with apple and vanilla.

RACK OF LAMB MARINATED
IN WHEY FOR FORTY-EIGHT HOURS

Then slowly cooked in a frying pan. Baked and compacted garden tomatoes, unfiltered olive oil, and sheep milk. Crispy olives, dried tomato skins, as well as a small salad with lilac and green basil.

"It is summer, and if you have a head cultivator like Jan Andersson in Malmköping who adores tomatoes, then it is also tomato time. In our garden, we grow over one hundred varieties of tomatoes, and we use some of them for the lamb. For variety and to take care of all the different flavors of the tomatoes, we have, among other things, saved the skins from large, red, ripe tomatoes and then dried them to a crisp. The smaller tomatoes are vacuum-packed as tightly as possible with tomato water. The vacuum packs are placed in water baths and carefully simmered. The most beautiful tomatoes are oven-baked at extremely low temperatures with apple cider vinegar, sea salt, and a touch of sugar. They are baked for a long time until most of the water has evaporated and the tomato flavor is concentrated."

Frantzén/Lindeberg's lambs have walked freely through fields. They have received the advantage of both Swedish meat processing and the open countryside. Lamb that has never been outside and has never tasted herbs in the grass provides uninteresting meat.

"After such a reasoning, it might be perceived as amusing, if not controversial, when we speak for the highly debated thrombin."

IN FURTHER DETAIL

TOMATO WATER

Mix ripe tomatoes into soup. Pour into a fine sieve with a filter cloth and let it drain and cool overnight. The transparent liquid is a tomato water that may be used for both warm and cold dishes, even desserts. In our lamb dish, we use tomato water to further enhance the flavors of the tomatoes, almost infusing them with tomato flavor while in the vacuum.

LAMB

Debone the rack of lamb and cut away the fat layer. Brush both the upper- and underside to remove any tendons. Coat the meat with thrombin and replace the fat layer. Press it down so that it sticks. Bind the roast together with thread leaving ½ inch (1 cm) between each row so that the lamb will become a hard, tube-like, and compact roll.

Cover the lamb completely in whey, and let it marinate in a cold place for two days.

Sauté the fat in a dry pan until it is crispy. Towards the end, add a piece of butter so that you can baste the roast. Remove the thread and bake in the oven at low heat until it reaches an inner temperature of 133°F (56°C).

THROMBIN

This is commonly called meat glue, but is referred to as thrombin by professional chefs. It is an enzyme that forms cross-links between muscle fibers.

It can also be used to glue pieces of meat to larger entities. For example, the meat industry wants to use thrombin to glue bad parts of pork together in order to make it look like ham. You can even use it to glue the rind back in place.

Thrombin was first used in kitchens that were fascinated by molecular cooking, mostly to test the boundaries. For instance, gluing chicken skin onto shellfish or bacon onto beef fillets.

To receive the best of both worlds—the crispy sweetened lamb fat and the tender meat of the rack—all the tendons need to be removed. The only way of doing this is to lift the fat layer, remove the large tendon, and place the fat back. The use of thrombin does not mean that F/L supports the use of meat glue in the meat industry. It is rather proof that how a substance is used is more important than the substance itself.

WHEY

The enzymes in whey cleave the meat and make it more tender. At F/L, they use it to tenderize lamb, veal, and chicken. There is also a natural acid in whey that makes it excellent for poaching shellfish.

"We like the traditional English home cooking . . ."

FRIED SHANK FROM GOAT WITH PRESERVED PEAS AND OYSTER LEAF

Served with goat milk, mint juice, pea shoots, and broth.

The road to Frantzén/Lindeberg passed through England, and obviously this was influential. England is "the world of minted lamb and peas."

"We like the traditional English home cooking where lamb is served with mint and peas. The fried goat is our own version of this English classic."

Goat is reminiscent of young lamb, but it is even milder in flavor. Careful use of garnish is advised.

"Light flavors of peas and mint go together well and are ripe and at their best in the garden at about the same time as goat is at its best. In France, we learned to use oyster sauce with lamb. We have found an oyster herb that grows along the stony beaches of Bohuslän, but that we now also grow in our own garden. The oyster leaf has a mild flavor of sea, and it breaks the flavor of the goat nicely."

The goats served at Frantzén/Lindeberg are from Skåne and are of "Northerns Skåne Lantra" or commonly known as "Göinge goats." After all, it was in Göinge where this old forest goat was first discovered and saved not that long ago. It is still viewed as an endangered species today, which does not mean that you compromise the species by using it in your kitchen, but rather the other way around.

"This unique mild goat meat with spice flavors from forest grazing is unmatched as far as we've experienced, and our own breeder in Klippan is determined that the best way to preserve the breed and the genuinely good flavor it offers is to create a market for these goats to encourage more responsible breeders to breed them. 'Göinge goats' have always roamed freely in the forests in southern Sweden, helping to keep the woodlands open and clean. These goats are an important part of Sweden."

AIR-DRIED BOSTON BUTT WITH SIGNE BEANS

Cream on oven-roasted, garden-grown red bell pepper, and oil from chorizo, served with dried olives and fried stored pig fat.

This dish was first made in 2007 when it was broadcast on the radio as part of the food program Menyon Swedish Radio's P1.

"During the long radio program, we cooked over twenty different kinds of beans that were grown by the 'Program for Cultivated Diversity' seed project where people were asked to send in their Swedish historical beans. Through testing and tasting during the radio program, we fell in love with the signe bean, which we found to be beautiful, mild, and tasty with a fine balance of salt and tart. We decided there and then to create a dish around this bean."

Signe Andersson in Aby first grew the bean, and later his daughter Johanna inherited it from him. Today, the grandchild Ake Karlsson is keeping the bean alive.

"Our Swedish Linderöd pigs contain the exact fat content that's needed for good flavor after drying. They are fully comparable with their black-cloven cousins in Spain known as Pata Negra. Drying pork is a long process. At our meat supplier, the meat is first placed in a blend of salt and juniper. This way, our meat decreases in size and weight and is then hung in well-ventilated rooms where the cut surfaces are covered by corn dough to avoid bacteria spreading in the meat. The method is ancient and well tested. Slowly, umami develops in the pieces, and the flavor is concentrated as the liquid dries, or rather is ventilated away. This is our pork from Linderöd pork, dried for long over a year. The dish is composed after a Mediterranean image we have, naturally on our own Swedish pork meat. A contrast is formed in the combination of dried aromatic and mild pork and the more fiery chorizo oil that holds the spiciness."

IN FURTHER DETAIL

FRIED STORED PIG FAT

Use well-stored pig fat like lardo di colonnata. Cut in cubes of about ½ inch (1 ½ cm). Fry in a hot pan until they have shrunk to half their size. Empty in a sieve. Save the fat for frying. Keep the cubes on paper at room temperature. For flavoring, you can spice the meat with thyme, marjoram, rosemary, or another herb; the pig fat easily absorbs all kinds of flavor.

CHORIZO OIL

Allow pieces of chorizo to slowly stew on the stove until they release oil. Then pass through a filter cloth and pour into a bottle. The oil can be used for added flavor in a variety of things: mayonnaise, pasta, and butter. If you like the chorizo flavor, the oil is very practical.

PORK SHANK FROM A ONE-YEAR-OLD LINDERÖD PORK

Stewed in its own fat for three days and later grilled over an open fire. Razor clam, spiced with homemade mild curry, seeds and oil from sesame, small caramelized onion boiled in apple juice.

The shank is lowered into a hot bath of lard, really in the same way you would confit duck. The shank is cooked slowly and, therefore, loses a minimal amount of weight as all the flavors and tenderness is encapsulated by the warm, covering fat. To enhance the flavor and make the surface crispy, the shank is then baked over an open fire.

"With this kind of preparation that takes three days, the apples of fall and the classic curry go together perfectly. The razor clam is a friendly acquaintance that enriches the pork with umami the same way it has been done with shellfish, fish, and pork for thousands of years."*

IN FURTHER DETAIL

LINDERÖD PIGS

"A pure Linderöd is a rare pig. Our breeders are dedicated to their pigs and their piglets, which are allowed to walk around for at least one year before butchering. It is not before then, with a weight of almost 220 lbs (100 kg), that the Linderöd pig is fully mature. The meat is then dark red, with a yellow fat layer. The pigs we use are protected through the Association of Landtsvinet (native pigs)."

In total there are now about 104 boars and 274 sows used for breeding. No semen collection center is involved with this pig, as it is not yet profitable enough. It grows slowly and demands care and attention. It likes the outdoors best and lives with its family until butchering and until the sow births new piglets, just like the wild pork in nature.

"To obtain the absolutely best meat, we have focused on the best care and feeding. In each detail we want absolute control for the best result. We feel that if we can be part of promoting the excellence of these pigs we can secure the future breeding and survival of the race—we find this important, not the least for flavor's sake."

HOMEMADE CURRY

4 teaspoons coriander seeds
2 teaspoons turmeric
1 teaspoon cumin
1 teaspoon black pepper (Tellicherry)
1 teaspoon rose pepper
½ teaspoon green cardamom
¾ inch (2 cm) cinnamon stick
½ teaspoon grated ginger
2 spice carnations
2 teaspoons yellow mustard seeds

Roast all of the spices whole in a dry frying pan. Crush in a mortar and mix into powder.

In his famous cookbook De re coquinaria, the Roman writer Marcus Gavius Apicius recommends to always use a spice with garum, a yeast fish and shellfish blend, for meat.

SLOWLY COOKED CRISPY PORK CHEEK SERVED UNDER MELTING PIG FAT

Lemon-infused red endive, pork broth, and dill, served with salt herring, potato aioli, as well as a marmalade made with white Belgian endive.

Pork cheek is a tough detail piece that demands a lot of attention during preparation. All of the work, however, is rewarded in flavor.

"I almost have to laugh when I look at this dish.* It is so genuinely Swedish with herring, pork, potato, and dill, yet still it is not. It is a complex dish and one of the most appreciated at our restaurant. It has returned in many different shapes: for a while as a canapé served on a spoon where the pork meat was covered in potato aioli, with a small anchovy for added flavor."

IN FURTHER DETAIL

PREPARING PORK CHEEK

Brush the pork cheeks clean from tendons and membranes. Place the cheeks with white wine, bay leaves, black pepper, a few thin strips of fresh ginger, and crushed stalks of dill in a vacuum bag and close with maximum vacuum. Marinate in the refrigerator for seven days.

Open the bag and rinse the cheeks in cold water. Move into a new vacuum bag, and cover it with melted lard. Poach the pork cheeks for two days at 158°F (70°C).** Cool at room temperature for 15 minutes, then 15 minutes in the fridge, and lastly ice bathe.

SERVING PORK CHEEK

Remove the cheeks and place them on a cloth. Let the fat run off at room temperature, dry carefully. Fry them over medium heat in a dry frying pan. Be careful about frying the entire cheeks so that the whole surface is crispy—let it use the time it needs, usually 30 to 40 minutes. Finish the last 10 minutes of the frying by adding a large spoonful of good country butter. Increase the heat a tad until the butter starts browning. Complete the frying by repeatedly scooping the browning butter over the pork.

Season generously with sea salt. Place the cheeks directly onto a warm plate and cover with a thin layer of stored pig fat (lardo di colonnata or similar).

*"The year was 2000, and I was in southern France. Don't ask me what the restaurant was called, it had no great advantages except for one: it served a combination of salty fish and pork meat as part of a buffet. The stringy meat was lying in melting spiced fat on a raw endive leaf—I was completely obsessed with the flavor, and I must have helped myself to at least ten portions."

**"We often work with slow cooking the same way we describe here with the pork cheeks; it is actually suitable for many different kinds of meat. Only spicing, marinating, and poaching are varied to fit, depending on what we would like to achieve."

BUTTER-FRIED LICORICE-SPICED VEAL BRAIN BREADED IN HAZELNUT FLOUR

Confit root from fern, raw cooked root of Spanish chervil. Served with an emulsion of caramel, buckthorn, and hazelnut oil.

"It was 1996, I can't remember where, but they had taken a veal sweetbread and stuck it through a licorice root before finally frying it on the root. It had a mild licorice flavor, and it was very good. I wanted a more distinct flavor and decided to use raw licorice instead. This was one of the first dishes I ever created myself, and it was even part of our opening menu at Frantzén/Lindeberg, but then served with artichoke, almond, and lime—different ingredients but the same function: nuttiness, acid, and root. I have made a very Swedish version that, in season, lies somewhere between cherry and lilac, as the Spanish chervil and the fern is warm and aromatic. The fern has a short licorice flavor, bordering on both sweet and bitter. Spanish chervil has a milder, almost perfuming flavor of licorice and anise.

IN FURTHER DETAIL

SPANISH CHERVIL

In addition to the distinct taste of licorice and anise, it has another important and practical use, namely making sour flavors milder. When we work with rhubarb and gooseberries, for instance, we may add a leaf of Spanish chervil, which allows us to use less sugar.

EMULSION

Make a blonde caramel in a thick-bottomed pot using 2 ½ oz (75 g) cane sugar, add 1 cup (2 dL) buckthorn juice, boil together, and reduce to medium heat. Sift into a tight container, and let it cool at room temperature. Add five tablespoons of hazelnut oil in a fine ray during mixing. When the sauce emulsifies, it will thicken to a cream. Flavor with some salt.

HAZELNUT FLOUR

In this dish, we breaded the brain with hazelnut flour to enhance the nuttiness. If, for some reason, you do not wish to use hazelnut flour, you can oven-roast regular wheat flour to a golden color. This way, you obtain nuttiness in the flour without adding nuts.

"The naturally soured kimchi is closest to our hearts . . ."

THYME-FRIED LIGHTLY SMOKED COW HEART

Sour cabbage, unripe juniper, and softly dried and butter-fried apple lightly perfumed with jasmine.

"Elements from Asian cooking interest us, and mostly when the flavors can be presented through Swedish ingredients. For instance, giving green junipers a careful scent and taste of lemon and lemongrass, but still with the aromatic gin flavor intact."

In Sweden and the rest of the world, we have made sour cabbage for ages. In France, sour cabbage is served as choucroute, in Korea as kimchi—they are basically the same, but vary in flavor based on the kind of cabbage and the technique or souring.

"The naturally soured kimchi is closest to our hearts with its ability to make the cabbage blossom with freshness and earthiness. The sour cabbage helps the smokiness of the heart. I think it is important not to limit myself, but rather to find combinations of different flavors in one and the same material. Sometimes after it has been changed through souring, boiling, storing, or drying."

"To us, it is a rustic while at the same time elegant dish, with the heart at the center and the jasmine-boiled, dried, and butter-fried apples at the side. The whole thing may appear simple, but it is the result of many preparation processes."

IN FURTHER DETAIL

SOUR CABBAGE FRANTZÉN/LINDEBERG

Use 2 cups (5 dL) of fine jasmine rice. Save the first rinsing water and sift it into a clean glass container. Clean the cabbage and cut it into wedges. Place in the rinse water. Let it sit at room temperature for three to five days. Already in the first twenty-four hours, you may experience a mild fresh scent from the cabbage. Before serving, remove the cabbage and let it dry on a kitchen towel. Melt a good salted butter in a saucepan. Pour over the cabbage and let it sweat in the butter, but not brown. Pour apple cider of good quality on top with a few splashes of thyme oil. Braise until the cabbage is soft, but still has some of its crispiness left.

JASMINE-INFUSED, SOFT DRIED, AND BUTTER-FRIED APPLES

Remove the core of the apples and cut in four pieces. Boil water and make a good jasmine tea. Cook the apples in a Gastrovac.* Dry. Just before serving, fry them a little in apple seed oil and salty butter.

*A Gastrovac is a vacuum machine in which the ingredients are prepared by atmospheric pressure.

TARTARE OF SWEDISH HORSE

Tied in melting tallow flavored with black pepper. Home-acidified cream with cold smoked cultivated eel from Landskrona, served with raw grated frozen duck liver, dried onion, and caviar.

Horse is too rarely served and not appreciated enough as an ingredient.* The meat is tender and tasty, and therefore, perfectly suited for tartare. "To carry the lean meat, we melt a fat layer from steak and add it to the tartare."

"Cultivated eel has a naturally high fat content. It is carefully smoked and creates a contrast to the horse-meat. Duck liver makes the dish luxurious and adds richness."

"We have long discussed if we should use eel at all because it is blacklisted as wild caught. However, we did find a company in Skane, Scandinavian Silver Eel, that catches glass eels from Île de Ré in France. The glass eels weigh only 0.01 oz (0.29 g). In nature, 90 percent of all glass eels are wasted because of environmental waste and as food for other fish and birds. They are brought to Landskrona where they are quarantined for ten weeks to make sure they are healthy. During this time, they fatten up and weigh about 0.03 oz (1 g). Most glass eels, three million out of about four million, are set out in Swedish oceans and lakes to strengthen and develop the Swedish eel life. The rest are saved and allowed to grow before they are carefully smoked. The restaurant name for the glass eel is 'Silver Eel.'"

The eels that are let out into the wild later have a survival rate of 15 percent. After fifteen to twenty years the eel will have fed enough that it has the strength to swim to the Sargasso Sea. It makes the journey of 9,950 miles (1,600 mil) without eating, and over there, it disappears after mating. We really don't know where the eels go. What is left is fertilized roe stuck to the seaweed in the ocean, which is brought back to the European coasts by the current. The journey takes years.

"The story of how the eel ends up on our table is both unbelievable and beautiful. These cultivated glass eels are purely an advantage for the Swedish wild eel, which is why we allow ourselves to serve this with a good conscience."

Something that makes the life cycle of the eel even more mysterious and mythical is that it decides its gender on its own, depending on the circumstances. It is said that opportunity to give birth is one factor and living space is another. In captivity in Landskrona, for instance, over 80 percent of the eels that are saved for smoking become male. This is because the living space is so small. Still, it takes great foresight because eels don't mate before they have reached twenty years and conditions may very well change during this time. An eel that is let out in Swedish waters will not decide on its gender before it weighs about 2 oz (60 g). The glass eels that return from the Sargasso Sea return to the female waters in Sweden.

IN FURTHER DETAIL

HORSE MEAT
The kind of horse meat we use in our tartare varies. It all depends on what is best on that day, and for this we keep constant contact with our suppliers.

BLACK PEPPER
We have chosen Tellicherry, which is grown in Kerala in India. It is aromatic and fruity with a powerful warmth and heat. The pepper fruits are left on the branches for a long time so that they have time to develop a deeper and richer flavor. When the pepper is harvested, an elimination process removes anything but the best pepper (only 10 percent) which can bear the name Tellicherry. We view Tellicherry as one of the best peppers in the world.

*At Frantzén/Lindeberg, they only use meat from Swedish butchered horses.

BONED SADDLE OF VENISON CONFIT IN COCOA BUTTER, LATER PAN-FRIED

Raw marinated root vegetables, butter-braised cabbage, thyme-fried yellow chanterelles, and a lukewarm vinaigrette of venison broth, homemade blueberry vinegar, and bitter chocolate oil.

It is fall. The combination of venison and chocolate has become a classic tradition over the last fifteen years. Everything else on the plate is seasonal, the best from the garden and forest.

The root vegetables are marinated for at least twenty-four hours in their respective raw-pressed juices for enhanced crispiness and intensified flavor. A fruity sweetness comes through with the preserved blueberries and homemade blueberry vinegar.

"We know that the deer season starts with the hunt in August, but it is not until after the rut that the meat is free of all the hormone and urine substances and becomes flavorful. Therefore, we never serve venison until October. By then, it is also cold enough that the deer keep fresh during the transportation from the forest. We want the meat to be matured, so we do not take the youngest animals where the flavor is underdeveloped nor the oldest animals, for they have too much bitterness in the meat. Simply put, we could say that we choose a middle way, the classic 'Svensson way.' With all the garnishes, this venison dish is excellent as a tartare, that is to say with scraped saddle."

IN FURTHER DETAIL

CHOCOLATE FOR OUR VENISON

Preparing venison is a controlled adventure of its own. To enhance the slight bitterness that you find in all game, and so to underline the flavor, we add chocolate. This way, the harshness and wild flavor of the venison is increased. You could say that chocolate has the same flavor-enhancing function as a strongly reduced bouillon.

Veal Liver Marinated in Almond Milk

A SWED PORK

FOR SOME TIME NOW at F/L, they have used a Swedish-produced breed of pig for their pork. It comes from multiple smaller farmers who keep pigs just like the olden days, as household pigs. This means that the Linderöd pigs are outside year-round and have a small sty to hide in when they need protection from weather and wind.

An uncompromising demand for flavor and quality is always the deciding factor, and it has made the Linderöd pork the obvious choice for the restaurant. But there is also another important reason, and that is to support the preservation of Swedish country swine. Over the years, pigs have been bred into industry pigs, whose meat is ugly, tasteless, stale, and impossible to cook with.

The Linderöd pig is the small remnant left of the Swedish household pig, and it was found by stocktaking at the beginning of the twentieth century. There were only eight pigs back then that turned out to be from variegated land-race pigs. The remaining pigs were delivered from Liderodsasen to Skane's animal park at the beginning of the eighties. Wild pigs have broken into the pigpen multiple times and mated with the sows there. But those offspring were removed

right away. These first, or rather last, "Linderöd pork" became the base in a gene bank. Ronny Olsson in Klippan is one of the most knowledgeable people in the Association of Landtsvinet (native pigs), and he has played a big role in "saving the race."

"Through him, we get to take part in the behind-the-scenes of pig breeding, which is important as our ambition is to gain control over the entire chain that leads to the delivery of the ingredient to our restaurant."

Another supplier is Patrik Johansson in Alingsås. He is a dairy farmer who also breeds Linderöd pork. To the feed—a blend of rough grits (a mixture of crushed grain and water), root vegetables, and apples—he also adds milk from butter manufacturing. You can taste a tartness in the flavor of the fat in these pigs, which distinguishes them from the other pigs we get partly from Ronny Olsson in Klippan in Skane and partly from Gustaf Söderfeldt in Åmmeberg in Askersund.

"We demand that our pigs should be of 100 percent genetic lineage. This means that they should be the offspring of the 104 purebred boars and 274 purebred sows that are registered breeding animals. Another uncompromising demand is that the butchering happens ethically. To us, this means that the pigs are brought to slaughter one at a time and that the slaughterhouse only ever receives the pig for slaughter. We do not want our pigs to wait in line in a slaughtering chutes and 'wait their turn.' We know that stress hormones in pigs taste awful no matter how you prepare the meat."

The Linderöd pigs have an appealing muscular structure, just like the old Swedish domestic pigs used to have. This means that they are round and slightly plump with big fat layers that are built during winter with pure lard.

"We know that our breeders care for their pigs and feed them the exact amount they need to be comfortable, and that they are able to move around enough in order to produce excellent meat."

The Linderöd pig is always a result of a physical meeting between boar and gilt or sow. In the Linderöd world, no boar is placed on stations where its only task is to produce sperm as often as possible to later be used to inseminate gilts or sows. No such station is interested in breeding Linderöd pigs because the Association of Landtsvinet protects them, so that they cannot be mated with anything but a purebred sow.

Linderöd pigs are viewed as worthless in the commercial world because they do not grow fast enough and demand much care. These are pigs that need to be scratched behind their ears now and then. The existing boars are transported around to the purebred sows in order to both secure the purebred and the good meat.

"The pigs, for instance ours that walk around on that large field in Askersund's Åmmerberg, receive many apples and potatoes in their food, which also affects both the meat, fat, and blubber."

Today, there is a fear for everything animalistic and white, in other words fat. This after decades of indoctrination that fat is fatal.

However, the fat is the carrier of flavors. It also absorbs most of the flavor from what the pig eats.

"The fat is great to melt and use in the cooking process of shanks and shoulders of pig, for instance. The pig boils in its own fat (confit). It is easy to forget that all of the flavors are stored in the fat, and because we are looking for flavor, it seems natural to choose parts of the pig where the flavor is most concentrated. Feel free to call it flavor sense because that is what it is."

They say that the quality of the Linderöd pig varies, but the Linderöd pig in itself doesn't really vary that much in quality. Rather, less meticulous breeders are tempted to try to improve an already good product by adding more of wild swine or industry pigs to the Linderöd pork with the result that the breeding work is compromised and the taste varies.

"We would never buy pigs from anyone outside of the Association of Landtsvinet. Our Linderöd pigs are slaughtered at their very best, which means that they have reached their top weight of 220 lbs (100 kg) with the head and skin left on. At this time, the pig is twelve or thirteen months old. After this, the growth, when it comes to meat and fat, plateaus. In extreme cases, we have bought Linderöd pigs well over 440 lbs (200 kg) to get as much fat as possible."

An extra twist that should be mentioned is that this Swedish swine, which most likely have genetic lineage from the migration period, now face the fact that they will be used as a brand within Carlo Petrini's slow food movement.

"That's how we like it."

FOWL

The hunt for a somewhat larger chicken that had matured in age and gained a real fat layer under the breast skin by walking freely in the woods went on for a long time.

These birds exist in France.

One of the restaurant's two gardens is in Askersund. Close by, in Åmmerberg, lives a young man who is one of many farmers breeding the pure Linderöd pigs, which sometimes end up in Lilla Nygatan 21.

"Because we were so happy with the pigs he delivers, we began a conversation about getting chickens that are flavored by Swedish forests and fields, chickens that have been allowed to walk outside, and that have been partly eating what is grown at the farm/garden, and partly eating what they find on their own."

"And so why not serve the one thing Sweden is undeniably the best at . . ."

SINCE THAT DISCUSSION, Gustaf Söderfeldt, the "Åmmerberg Farmer," acquired the original Plymouth Rock chickens, an American land breed with a heritage dating back to the 1800s. Gustaf Söderfeldt says that he feels like he is in the American South with all these chickens flying around:

"They need to walk in the forest for the best flavor. After all, much of what we appreciate the most when it comes to flavor comes from the forest. The forest is a mature ecosystem that, among other things, offers the minerals and enzymes that makes flavor possible. But it is also about time—the time the forest takes to put all of the complex substances together and the time it takes for a chicken to mature. A Plymouth Rock weighs over 6 lbs (3 kg) when it is slaughtered. That is a real chicken with a huge layer of fat under the skin at the breast, beneficial bird fat and flavor."

It is a privilege to become self-sufficient with poultry.

The slaughter of the poultry is important; it is crucial that it happens ethically. Birds should not be scalded in hot water right after death or before plucking, which is usually routine at fowl slaughterhouses. The skin turns flabby, and the fat underneath decreases. Another routine is to flush the fowl in cold water after plucking to cool the bodies. The water makes the bird lose a lot of flavor.

"We have found a small country slaughterhouse that lives up to our demands, where the fowl are close to dry-plucked and later sprayed with cold air for cooling."

And so why not serve the one thing Sweden is undeniably the best at: wild birds like black grouse, grouse, quail, woodcock, and wild duck.

"Obviously, the forest fowl brings the forest with them to the table, but in our kitchen it is also about diversity. We wanted our own chickens where the lowest quality was equal to the best French quality, and we got it."

Everything on the bird is appreciated, from the chubby breast to crispy fried skin as spice, piece details like sot-l'y-laisse, the small muscle in the indent of the back, the wings, confit-boiled thighs, fried hearts, and fowl liver, which is often transformed to a cream.

The lighter birds are excellent to combine with fish or shellfish—for instance, fried wing with turbot, and chicken breasts with crayfish. The hull gives flavorful but light broths. The chicken fat that melts out of the chicken when cooking is used as added flavor for potato purée, for example.

All birds are best prepared on the hull. Therefore, whole doves and chickens get a quick fried surface in the pan before they are placed in the Delta oven with increasing heat for an exact inner temperature.

Gustaf Söderfeldt

BLOOD DOVE FROM LOIRE FLAVORED WITH PISTACHIO AND GREEN PEPPER

Raw roasted king crab, purée of salt-baked carrots saturated in crab broth and tonka bean. Served with fermented garlic, raw liver cream, and a vinaigrette with dove broth, pistachio oil, and blood orange vinegar.

The blood dove has a mild gamy character in color, flavor, and texture. Swedish forest dove tastes too much like game. Therefore, the French dove from Loire is better.

The blood dove is served with roasted king crab, which has a powerful flavor but a soft texture.

The dish demands some perfumed, etherial flavors such as pistachio, which adds nuttiness and freshness; green pepper, which provides mild heat; and the tonka bean with its mild vanilla tones.

Instead of making a powerful dove broth, at F/L they boil a broth based on the hull to lukewarm vinaigrette with blood orange vinegar and pistachio.

During the preparation, the dove is basted with hard reduced blood orange and green pepper broth strengthened by a blonde caramel. The idea brings to mind the sweet and sour heat found in the Chinese kitchen. Since the dove is basted, it maintains its own juiciness during cooking up into an inner temperature of 127°F (53°C).

IN FURTHER DETAIL

TONKA BEANS

Scents with hints of freshly mown green hay and vanilla, and picked from a tree that can be over a thousand years old. In previous days, perfumers would extract an isolated substance, "coumarin," and use it in perfumes. Coumarin forms in the tonka bean first when it has fallen off the tree and started to yeast.

In Latin, the tonka bean is called *Dipteryx odorata*, referring to the scent of the beans.

"We are in love with the mild scents and flavors, which we recognize and which are so well blended in the tonka bean: vanilla without being vanilla and freshly mowed green hay without being green hay."

FERMENTED GARLIC

Fermented garlic comes from Korea, like so many other fermented and acidified dishes. It is fermented naturally and is later transformed from being hot-tempered and stubborn in taste to giving mild licorice tones and a somewhat sugary deep molasses.

The process in itself fills the garlic with umami tones from broken-down proteins. This is just one example of how nature can change an ingredient on its own, so that it can be used in new contexts and help complement other flavors.

GREEN PEPPER

The green pepper is almost vanquished from finer cooking and referred to in the context of road tavern, which often serve it in sauces with overcooked meat. Unfortunately.

At Frantzén/Lindeberg, they use it with lobster, duck, and blood dove. All of these main ingredients are tough enough to stand up against strong, tough flavors, which are even enhanced by mild heat from the green pepper.

RAW CREAM MADE WITH LIVER

Liver in general challenges many guests, especially when it is almost raw.

The dove liver is quickly broiled in a hot pan. After a rapid cooling, it is mixed with nitrite salt and cream before serving.

LUKEWARM BLOOD CREAM WITH BAKED AND PRESSED GOOSE LIVER

Swedish sea salt from Patrik Johansson and white peach infused with its own juice and almond oil.

In order to follow old Swedish traditions with classic blood foods, and from fowl blood especially, a goose farmer has taken on the task of delivering pure goose-blood that is used in a blood cream at F/L.

"We are traditional when it comes to goose liver terrine. The livers are picked free from membranes and tendons, salted with nitrite salt, and placed in a terrine pan lined with foil. Before we place the terrine in the water bath in the oven, we make sure that there is space between the baking sheet and the pan, so that the cooking will be as even as possible. For the same reason, we use a 'careful oven,' by which we mean 185°F (85°C). The terrine is baked to an inner temperature of about 98°F (38°C). It is then cooled down under pressure and later left in the refrigerator for three to four days, so that the flavors mature."

IN FURTHER DETAIL

LUKEWARM BLOOD CREAM

1 cup goose blood
0.7 oz (20 g) butter
1 pinch of nitrite salt*
3 tablespoons dark beer
2 teaspoons dark syrup

Blend all of the ingredients and warm them in a simmering water bath while whisking until it turns creamy.

INFUSED PEACH

White peach is juiced in a juicer. The juice is blended with almond oil and placed with whole peaches in the Gastro-vac without heat until they are completely infused.

*Nitrite salt is most often used for color. Blood dishes and some meats have a tendency to turn gray before serving, and with the help of a little bit of nitrite salt, the color of what is served is enhanced. Nitrite salt also has an antibacterial function, and among other things, it prevents the growth of the dangerous botulinum bacteria.

POACHED AND GRILLED GUINEA FOWL WITH FRIED RHUBARB AND SAGE

Small turnips with light leaves and flowers of dandelions, as well as a tart rhubarb sugar.

Bitter flavors in combination with acidity and sweetness. A dish for early spring, exactly around the time the first dandelions grow. Turnips, which also grow early, have a tendency to be peppery, which helps the sweeter guinea fowl.

The meat structure with a wilder bird such as the guinea fowl has the ability to manage its own fat under the skin and baste itself during roasting. It feels like it can take "a turn on the grill" without a risk of losing flavor or texture.

The guinea fowl is lightly poached in hen bouillon boiled on the hull. The grilling is rapid and light; the main goal is just to scorch the skin and enhance flavors.

IN FURTHER DETAIL

TART RHUBARB SUGAR
Slice rhubarb thinly and dry in an oven. Mix into a fine powder. Blend with granulated sugar.

GROUSE BAKED IN HAY

Lucky clover, dried cranberries, browning butter, dried onion, and purée made with baked fall apples.

It is fall; it is hunting season. Grouse, capercaillie, and hazel grouse are legal to hunt starting on August 25. A few weeks after this, the grouse becomes the carrier of the flavors of the forest to the F/L table.

The dark meat of the grouse, the tender resistance, needs the browning butter to enhance the nuttiness, and the concentrated dried onion rounds off the wild flavors. The fall apple and lucky clover add acidity and fruitiness and balances the forest sweetness of the grouse. The cranberries add a little balancing bitterness.

IN FURTHER DETAIL

LUCKY CLOVER

Many are content with common or wood sorrel. The small Mexican clover that grows in the garden in Malmköping does not have such a distinct acidity and is therefore perfect for finer cooking, where it usually presents as a small flavor surprise. The lucky clover's root fruit is also well worth saving. In texture, it is reminiscent of the tender water chestnuts. Lucky clover is this plant's popular name, and it is sold as a red blossoming pot plant in the flower shop.

COUNTRY CHICKEN ROASTED IN NETTLE BUTTER

Homemade yogurt flavored with roasted fresh garlic, small artichokes poached in melted animal fat, served with garlic mustard and ground elder.

The spring chicken breathes hope and is served with the very first flavors of the garden, the things that have a fresh peppery flavor, such as the freshly harvested pre-summer garlic that is small and tender, the ground elder with its distinct cabbage flavor, and the garlic mustard that has a green onion flavor full of chlorophyll. The artichokes have just grown out of their rosette.

IN FURTHER DETAIL

HOMEMADE YOGURT

4 cups (1 L) whole milk
4 tablespoons plain yogurt

Bring the milk to a boil and let it cool to 98°F (37°C). Pour into a thermos and add the yogurt in scoops, which will now function as a culture. Close the thermos and let it sit for fifteen hours.

THE GARLIC

Peel and divide the wedges lengthwise. Remove the small green sprouts. Slice the wedges thinly and soak them in milk for twenty-four hours, replacing the milk now and then about eight times. Sift the milk off. Dry the garlic on paper, and dry-roast in the oven until golden brown. Later, press the roasted garlic slices and blend with the yogurt. Flavor with a little salt.

"Alain Passard added sesame oil and lime, but we've removed these ingredients."

ROASTED WILD DUCK GLAZED WITH WHITE MISO

Served with coffee-scented and lightly whisked country cream, yarrow, butter-fried yellow chanterelles, and sour and dried red cabbage.

"At L'Arpège, we did a glaze with coffee and miso. The flavor was fantastic, and we have carried this with us for many years. I thought that this flavor was important to remember and use at a suitable time. One fall, I received newly caught duck, and it is a special feeling to take care of hunting game; it feels so natural, and it smells of oceans and forest. Suddenly the memory of the good coffee glaze popped into my head, and now was the time to use it. I thought that this good flavor from L'Arpège I had gotten to know ten years before was just what the ducks needed. I brushed them during baking, so that the glaze 'boiled in' them and left flavor. When I tried, after making it right out of flavor memory, I concluded that it tasted just as good as it had at L'Arpège and would be great for the wild duck. The only difference is that Alain Passard added sesame oil and lime, but we've removed these ingredients."

The glaze is easy and a tiny bit genius. Boil a strong wild duck bouillon on the hull. When the bouillon has obtained flavor, it is concentrated in a serious reduction. At the same time, you add miso and coffee.

The dish is served without sauce except a lightly whipped cream flavored with coffee. The duck and coffee make a great combination, which is repeated in the glaze.

The sour cabbage is acidified with apple, the salt comes from the white miso, and the chanterelles add a nuttiness and fruitiness.

The yarrow is somewhat bitter in taste and gives a pleasant texture to the wild duck.

TARTARE OF DUCK'S BLOOD STIRRED IN TART RASPBERRY AND BLACK CURRANT VINAIGRETTE

The first red beets from the garden marinated in their own juice and bitter cocoa, the dried liver from the duck, as well as roses and coffee.

There is no use rushing beets to grow. If they are sown too early, they start flowering because it is too cold. It is best to sow them as close to summer as possible, and the best beets are ready for harvest at the same time as the raspberries.

"The most difficult task for me as a chef—and I am talking on a personal level—is to create cold meat dishes that are not duck liver. It mirrors the small kitchen at Lilla Nygatan well because we rarely have cold dishes on our menu. This is partly because of my lack of creativity, and partly because we have space issues, and cold dishes take up space. I don't want our kitchen to be a plating kitchen; it is just too uncompromising for that. Still, there have been some cold dishes over the years, and the tartare of dove's blood is one of my favorites. It maintains a naturally high acidity combined with earthiness from the beets and surprising tones of roses, coffee, and cocoa.* Furthermore, it is a fun dish because you can play with the choice of drink. The right choice will highlight the flavors even more."

*This dish has even been served as a dessert with the exact same ingredients except the duck, and then with a certain heightened sweetness.

Grouse Baked in Hay
Page 209

SOMEON
MOVE FO
FOR ALL (
BECOME

IT IS CLEAR THAT THE NEW KITCHEN represented a temptation for most cooks who wanted to try a new way of thinking or a new adventure. During the years Frantzén/Lindeberg was starting out, molecular cooking reached its highest peak.

"I think it would have been a mistake to not be a part of it. The molecular kitchen offered a new kind of knowledge about cooking that no one had ever reflected over before. I am convinced that both Daniel and I became better cooks after familiarizing ourselves with this kind of kitchen that builds on deep-seated knowledge about chemistry and physics with a whole new range of tools in the kitchen."

The problem was that the new molecular kitchen

offered resistance as well. The techniques and understanding can't be conquered just by buying certain Texturas products.*

"Our approach, when we were standing in our test kitchen that we created before the opening of Frantzén/Lindeberg, was molecular, just like the world would perceive us, and that is not something we can hide. When we opened, we worked with all senses: smell, flavor, sight, and on a molecular and slightly brutal way. Here were fragrant smoke and air, caviar pearls of clams, and warm and cold jellies of pumpkin and peaches. It was supposed to pop in your mouth, smell, and be a sensation in each bite."

E HAS TO RWARD OF US TO BETTER

"Both Björn and I thought that this was very exciting. We didn't find any faults with it. Frantzén/Lindeberg became a success, and the way we worked with ingredients gave us knowledge that helped us form a new raw ingredient philosophy."

"If you look through a magnifying glass at something beautiful, it stays beautiful. But if you look at something ugly, it becomes even uglier."

"What we are saying is that there is no chemistry or preparation method in this world that can hide a bad ingredient or change it to something better than what it is."

"If we had been more clear with ourselves and filtered the influx of new ideas, you could say had we been more mature in our approach, then the molecular kitchen would have become really good. Instead, we chose to take the best out of that era and use the knowledge to become wiser."

"Our molecular kitchen, we conclude, was a historical necessity to move on and to see the forest despite all the trees."

*Texturas Products is a line of tools created by elBulli.

VEGETARIAN

Flavor is the decisive factor. From the first baby vegetables to the fully matured ones at harvest in the fall, it's never showmanship—just pure nature. During winter, the root vegetables are placed in the press and refined through flavor concentration.

A long time ago, at the time when the deepest seriousness started to color Frantzén and Lindeberg's discussions of opening their own restaurant, there were plans for a garden of their own. Maybe at first these were romantic ideas about how they could walk out and choose what was ready for harvest, to be standing there with the shovel themselves.

Angela broke into the
pea garden, was showered by the
raindrops that had been resting
on the leaves, and shoved a handful of
peas in her mouth.

They were sweet and cold and crunched
delightfully when she chewed them.

The air was so fresh on these mornings.
A tangy scent of dew-covered
flowers and soil filled it.

Text by Agnes von Krusenstjerna.
"The chorus rows describe the exact feeling and intimacy of having
your own garden: beautiful, sensitive, flavorful, and elegant."

". . . with a rich umami that you can feel far into your mouth."

OFTEN IT IS THE PURELY AESTHETIC values that become the decisive factor when one chooses a vegetable. There are large businesses that have created this system, very well aware that this is how it works. They buy from farmers who grow rationally, often with guarantees that only natural fertilizers are used, but completely without thought for the genetic conditions of what kind of seeds they use. The main issue, it seems, is that the sprouts grow and are protected against insect attacks and pesticides. Later the vegetables are cleansed, rinsed, and packed up for a restaurant customer. They are clean, and they look pretty. This is the way most restaurants get ahold of all their greens.

"We wanted something different. We wanted the feeling of water drops that shower you when you pick tender peas, and we wanted to maintain the sense of the sour flower scent and the warm humid soil."

"To achieve this, there was only one road we could choose: we needed to find a farmer with good fields, who was just as uncompromising in attitude as Frantzén/Lindeberg."

It needed to be a farmer dedicated to the task, uncompromising when it came to fertilization and weed prevention.

"One of them contacted us on his own: Jan Andersson, with a garden outside of Malm-köping. He saw himself as a unique cultivator of oyster leaf, and called us because he wanted us to buy from him." Right away, he was asked about all things green, edible flowers, unique mints, licorice root, tomatoes, and lucky clover, as well as all kinds of peas and beans."

This was not about prices or making a profit.

"Björn and Daniel wanted exclusive rights in Stockholm on everything I grow, and they got them," Jan Andersson says.

His garden is on fields that he leases and is situated on a slope so cleverly that the growth always "turns its head" towards the sun. In rapidly built greenhouses, he grows over one hundred

Malmköping

different kinds of tomatoes, in real soil without the fertilizers in which industrially created tomatoes grow. Jan Andersson's tomatoes taste, as commonly expressed, of the warmth of the sun and with a rich umami that you can feel far into your mouth. The skins are extremely thin because they are older varieties that have not been created to travel far or be treated roughly through rinsing, washing, and packaging.

"We have kept an eye on the treatment of animals for a long time in this country, but we have not reflected on how the vegetables taste and why," he says.

THE HUNT FOR FLAVOR
Swedes have understood some things over the years, and they have learned to choose organic, KRAV (a Swedish organization and product label for organic and sustainable agriculture), or biodynamic. They obviously see that these vegetables are a little bit more expensive, but because of the faith that they will get better taste and that they are more honest with nature, many still make this choice.

Unfortunately, even most of the organically grown industrial sprouts have been cultivated to be resistant to various attacks, can handle pesticides, and have hard skins so that they can survive the packaging and the long transport from where they are grown to the stores. All of this endurance is obtained through crossing and sometimes through genetic modifications.

"I don't know how they think, but flavor is never mentioned. Therefore, most of my time is spent looking for the old varieties that are not modified through crossbreeding, but that are naturally rich in flavor as a vegetable should be," Jan Andersson explains.

Part of the art is also that different kinds of soils create different kinds of flavor. The diversity about thirty years back was huge compared to now. To go back to von Krusenstjerna's verses, we only have two kinds of peas to choose from today: green or yellow.

Jan Andersson—Malmköping

"The weeds help attract bees, butterflies, and bumblebees, and that's good for the growth."

During Krusenstjerna's time, there was a whole ocean of pea varieties, all with different names and flavors.

"The flavor depends on the soil as well, depending on where you grow the pea. Therefore, I look for an old kind of pea that has the rich taste and fits my clay soil on the slope in Malmköping."

Jan Andersson was born and raised on a farm in southern Rada in Värmland. After working as a preschool teacher, he wanted a garden, just the kind of uncompromising garden he owns today.

"I took a class at Capellagården at Öland, where they teach what I am inclined towards: nontoxic cultivating without anything other than pure manure and compost as soil enhancers and for added nutrients."

Milk thistle and other weeds stand proudly and are part of the vegetable garden. In times of pesticides, we are not used to seeing such vegetable gardens, but rather black soil between the rows. Jan Andersson cleans his growth beds up until midsummer. After that, the vegetables have claimed their space, and because weeds are no longer competitors, he lets them stay.

"I sometimes remove the worst of them—guess it is a question of aesthetics as well—but otherwise, the weeds help attract bees, butterflies, and bumblebees, and that is good for the growth. Furthermore, it is an advantage because the weeds help keep the soil moist."

"It is the unspoiled flavor we are looking for and that we have found in a garden in Malmköping. A garden that delivers most of what we need when it comes to vegetables that grow above ground. We have reasoned the same way when it comes to root vegetables. We went on a journey to London the same week that we opened the restaurant; we went with Lars

Askersund

Feddeck, who at the time had a cultivation field in Katrineholm. Since then, he has been our second cultivator."

MINERALS IN ÅMMEBERG

Lars Feddeck was born and bred in Germany, where he received his degree as a farmer through apprenticeships at farms. He is a traveling man who likes to stay where it suits him; a horseman with, for the time being, three Ardennes horses and a foal.

Before he moved to Sweden, he lived with the Amish in Canada for a while. It was his interest in horses that had taken him there, and since then, he has also worked with the construction of cultivation tools to be pulled by horses. The horses play a very important role in the root vegetables he delivers. Everything is maintained with horses in his fields: fertilizing, plowing, planting, seeding, and weeding. It seems that Lars Feddeck's horses know that they shouldn't trample on white beets, red beets, circle beets, yellow beets, greater burdock, salsify, and carrots in many different colors and shapes, no matter how small the plants are.

"When we first came in contact with Lars Feddeck, he was growing on leased fields in Katrineholm." Soon he found a better place for his germinates, in Åmmeberg in Askersund, next door to another friend of Frantzén and Lindeberg, Gustaf Söderfeldt, who delivers pigs, ducks, and chickens.

"We have understood that Lars Feddeck is a mover. He lived in Norway for a while with his own farm, but decided to move to Sweden. We don't know what controls him, but he can deliver the most fantastic root vegetables, and that is all that matters to us. We have an idea that the quality is connected to the lifestyle of the supplier—simply an uncompromising attitude—and we are prepared to follow him no matter where his crops go. It is that good!"

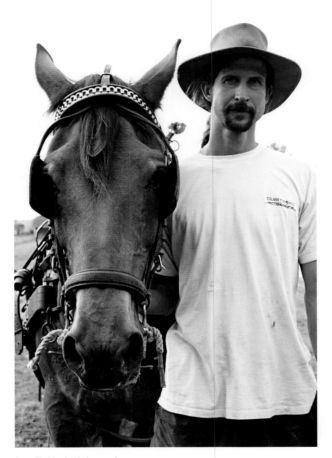

Lars Feddeck—Askersund

"Another sign of an uncompromising lifestyle is that he packs up his vegetables once a week and travels with them to us. That is impressive and large."

He has yet to decide if the soil is good enough in Askersund, or if he can achieve even better flavors somewhere else. Right now, Småland and Kalmar seem tempting, where there is also an opening to become a more permanent farmer on self-owned land. It may very well be that the root vegetables will be grown there in a short time.

In Askersund, the farmland lies in a valley among fields that used to be the bottom of the sea. It may be, therefore, that the root vegetables seem high in minerals and full of flavor. Cobalt has always been present in the surface of the ground, and the fields in the area are so full of zinc that it is still mined in the neighboring area of Åmmeberg, Zinkgruvan. Zinc is the one substance the body has the most trouble surviving without, but for Frantzén/Lindeberg, the flavor is most important, and nobody knows for sure if it is the zinc, cobalt, or other minerals in Åmmeberg that make the vegetables taste so good. Maybe it's simply the craftsmanship of Lars Feddeck that makes the difference.

"Like Jan Andersson, a huge part of my time as a cultivator is dedicated to finding older,

sustainable, and flavorful varieties: seeds that have the tradition and flavor built-in," Lars Fed-deck says.

"Once, in May, I ran out of my own potatoes that I keep in my basement, and I was forced to buy potatoes from the store—it had nothing close to the same good flavor. It was then that I truly understood that the biodynamic cultivation I perform does not only value and protect the earth, but it also adds flavor."

"Both of our vegetable gardens are not only incredibly beautiful; they are run by people who are completely uncompromising and have realized that there are no shortcuts to quality and good flavor."

MILLE-FEUILLE OF CELERIAC

Chestnuts and truffle. Served with grated nutmeg, argan oil, chestnut honey, and bee pollen.

Jokingly, you could say that this dish is built on height. A mille-feuille is supposed to be constructed so that it is built on "one thousand floors." One over the other like a cake in multiple layers.

The flavors have changed again and again throughout Frantzén/Lindeberg's existence, and the combination has been on the menu since the first winter at Lilla Nygatan 21. The dish is served as a fine tartlet with ox marrow, as a soup, and as a consommé.

"Celeriac and truffle are two corms that work well together. We take advantage of this through layering celery chips with shaved truffle, layered with a cream made with baked celeriac, shaved chestnuts, and bee pollen, carefully spiced with grated nutmeg and with chestnut honey and argan oil. The process is repeated until we have the height we want on the plate."

IN FURTHER DETAIL

ARGAN OIL

Argan oil comes from the argan tree in Morocco, which is only grown in the southwest part of the country and in a special area, but in great numbers (about twenty-one million trees). The fruit contains a stone-hard nut with up to three almond-shaped seeds. These are cold-pressed to produce argan oil, a nut oil with the strongest flavor.

"The idea was to serve a frozen and later fired bread briquette."

FRENCH TOAST WITH STEWED SILVER ONION

Cream of Vacche Rosse, hundred-year-old vinegar, and truffle. Served with white soy and truffle infusion.

On the day prior to the press lunch before F/L's opening, they test-made all the dishes one last time. The idea was to serve a frozen and later fired bread briquette. A piece of brioche would be rolled with squid ink so that it turned completely black. It then would be rapidly frozen in liquid nitrogen. The idea was to make it look like a piece of grill coal.

"We were convinced about the elegance of the dish. The frozen, coal-black piece of bread would be carried out to the guest on a plate with flammable liquor. At the table, the bread would then thaw over the burning liquor while the guest was busy eating other dishes."

"We had tested the procedure multiple times in the test kitchen, and it had worked perfectly. At midnight before the press lunch, at the last test cooking, we suddenly could not get the liquor to light up."

"It simply didn't work, and we tried with all different kinds of liquor, everything from pear cognac to rum. We were left with a soaked, soggy, liquor-saturated black piece of bread that tasted awful."

"Late that night, we were able to get hold of strong smuggled liquor through a friend's Finnish mother to save the show. There was general panic with only twelve hours left before the lunch, the menu had been mailed out to all the journalists, and the dish was not even close to working. Getting ahold of the illegal liquor failed, thank God, and we were forced to rethink everything."

"We made a silver onion casserole with lemon and Parmesan instead."

"With the casserole, we served a cube of bread rolled in egg flavored with truffle juice, truffle oil, and balsamic vinegar. The bread was fried in butter and served with grated Parmesan and grated truffle."

And so, a classic was born at Frantzén/Lindeberg: French toast.

Over the years the dish has been refined to become what it is today.

IN FURTHER DETAIL

FRENCH TOAST

Slice silver onion and boil with a little cream. Grate Parmesan on top and squeeze a little lemon, flavor with salt, and cool. It is important that the blend is not too loose.

Cut the edges of brioche or form bread and slice into about ½-inch (1 ½-cm) thick slices. Scoop the silver onion blend on top of half the slices and glue together.

Make a loose egg blend out of cream in the ratio of one and a half eggs to ½ cup (1 ½ dL) of liquid. Flavor with truffle juice, truffle oil, and balsamic vinegar. Dip the bread in the egg blend and fry on both sides in a generous amount of butter over medium heat until golden brown. Let them cool and cut into even cubes or elongated pieces. Top off with sea salt and a little truffle oil (it is important to use black truffle oil because the white truffle oil is for perfuming).

PARMESAN CREAM

14 oz (400 g) grated Parmesan
7 oz (200 g) butter at room temperature
1 egg

Here we mix everything in a thermo mixer and keep it going on medium speed at 140°F (60°C). Alternatively, whisk in a water bath to a smooth cream.

WHITE SOY AND TRUFFLE INFUSION

2 ½ lb (1,140 g) water
3 ½ oz (106 g) white soy
0.2 oz (7 g) vermouth
0.1 oz (3 g) Madeira truffle oil

Blend all the ingredients, warm, and then whisk in a few drops of truffle oil right before serving.

VACCHE ROSSE

"We wanted the best Parmesan cheese and found it in the middle of the Italian Parmegiano district. Made out of milk from the antique race Antica Razza Reggiana, commonly called "Vacche Rosse,"* a type that's been on the brink of extinction but has been saved thanks to the rediscovery of the milk's advantages for creating Parmesan. The milk contains a strong casein, which is the protein that contributes to the curdling of the cheese as well as the quality."

The cheese is stored for 28 to 30 months before it is delivered.

Before serving, the bread is carefully heated in a 355°F (180°C) oven. Finish off with spritzing the Parmesan cream over the French toast and topping it off with shaved truffle.

Serve with four to five drops of hundred-year-old balsamic vinegar and white soy and a truffle infusion as tea.

*The variant is the same as Swedish "Rödkulla."

POTATO PURÉE MADE WITH STEAMED ALSTRÖMER'S LEKSANDS VIT

Served with lightly boiled and butter-fried biennial potatoes, the dregs from spring rape, black pepper, sorrel, dill, and roe from Kalix.

"We have to make sure we always question our actions. Like this thing where we always set an equal sign between potato purée and pots."

In this pronounced potato dish, which is classically combined with roe from Kalix, the potatoes are steamed to enhance the grassy and summery flavor. The potato is one of the oldest varieties of Sweden, Leksands Vit, which the "father of the Swedish potato" industry Jonas Alström of Alingsås brought back from England during the early 1700s. Leksands Vit is good, rich in starch, and mealy. The starch in the chosen potato allows it to bind a lot more butter than, for instance, the almond or the French ratte potato (a potato that was created and developed in cooperation with Joël Robuchon, who wanted a potato that could bind its own weight in butter). The old Swedish Leksands Vit has proved to be even better at binding butter, thanks to the natural high concentration of starch.

"After oven-baking our Leksands Vit and adding enough butter that the mash cracks, in order words, when the butter separates from the potato, we sift it. Then we fold in whole milk that makes the potato and butter emulsify and become a solid smooth purée, which is flavored with salt and lemon. We make this purée for every service."

The biennial potato refers to those that have been left in the soil after the harvest of the previous year. These potatoes often show up in free land at the farmer Lars Feddeck's fields in Åmmerberg outside of Askersund.

"That potato will often give smaller tubers, and these are the ones we use for this dish. We carefully boil them, then cool them down, and smoke them in our smoke machine. Right before serving, we warm the potatoes in a pan with browning butter."

IN FURTHER DETAIL

DREGS FROM COLD-PRESSED SPRING RAPE

Spring rape is the rape that is sown early in spring and turns the fields a light shade of yellow after midsummer, the ones that smell of wonderful butter, honey, and nuts, of which they have an abundance of in Sweden.

"At the Tibasthouse at the Nordic Museum's Julita Farm, beautifully situated by Lake Öljaren, we have found Julita Raps and Erica Larsson. From them, we have been able to get just what we are looking for from the rape's nuttiness and oily, fresh character. To get as much intensity as possible, we asked to get the dregs from the pressing early on. It is cloudy and so nobody else wants it, but we find it optimal for pulling out nutty flavors without using nuts. The oil also holds a richness that is rare in oils. We choose the dregs from the spring rape because it offers a nutty flavor, which in the fall rape is replaced by a rather stubborn grassiness. If you look carefully at the color, you can see that the oil from the fall rape is a lot greener than the oil from the spring rape."

ROOTS FROM THE GARDEN BOILED IN SHEEP MILK

Then slowly fried in a pan with good butter. Served with toasted wheat bread, lightly whipped cream flavored with smoked lard, cold-pressed rapeseed oil, dried sea urchin, and small leaves of sorrel.

In an old book from 1660 by Schering Rosenhane, there are recommendations as to what should be cultivated in a real vegetable garden. "There we got the early history of roots and understood the Swedishness in the salsify, which is at the top of the cultivation list, followed by Ranunculaceae root, and skirret."

The salsify does not look like much to the surrounding world. You could almost describe it as ugly, filled with side roots and completely wooly on the surface. The flavor, on the other hand, is mildly spicy with a nod towards carrot, greater burdock, and scorzonera. It has fluffiness and crispiness that doesn't seem to be compromised through cooking.

"We've used salsify this time, but when we serve this dish, we use the roots that are available that day."

Salsify oxidizes the moment it is peeled, just like every other similar root. Therefore, it needs to be placed in liquid right away in order to prevent oxidation. At F/L, they usually use lemon water or water with vinegar.

"We place the salsify in sheep milk, which will later be used to boil it in. The sheep milk* enhances the whiteness of the root and helps lift the sweetness."

The following frying gives a somewhat crispy surface on the otherwise meltingly tender root.

*If you can't get ahold of sheep milk, you can use goat milk or whey instead.

SOUP OF SMOKED CAULIFLOWER

With lightly whipped country cream perfumed with chamomile. Dried lavender and nettle oil.

....

Cauliflower is one of the vegetables that can be varied infinitely. It welcomes truffle, browned butter, bacon, toasted bread, curry, and dill. It helps lift other flavors, especially lighter ones.

In the garden of Jan Andersson in Malmköping, most of the flowers have already blossomed when the cauliflower is at its best. The solution is the flavor-concentrated dried flowers that are delivered from there around this time.

"The cauliflower is lightly smoked and transformed into a soup in our thermo mixer together with cauliflower juice, butter, salt, and lemon."

Before the soup is served, it is flavored with a little oil from the nettle of the spring and with dried lavender. At the table, they add a lightly whipped cream flavored with chamomile.

THE MO
IMPOR
TOOL

"**WE HAVE ALWAYS DREAMED** of finding a way to not have to boil all the flavors out of the vegetables, which is what happens if you prepare them in water. One alternative has been the microwave, but in that kind of cooking you lose control over the inner temperature, and when the inner temperature is too high, it destroys many of the flavors a root vegetable offers."

The juicer has, therefore, become one of the most important tools in the Frantzén/Lindeberg kitchen.

"Looking back, we don't understand how a vegetable that has been so carefully picked when it comes to care and soil could ever be placed in water where all the flavors go and are later drained off. Firstly, when a juicer is allowed to juice a vegetable, you appreciate the richness of flavor a single root vegetable contains. The juice is a magical elixir and I don't mean solely juicing for drinking, but also the pulp you are left with after the vegetable is pressed. It would never occur to us to stew vegetables in anything but their own juice, or we would use the juice to infuse the vegetable in a Gastrovac (where the raw material is cooked by atmospheric pressure)."

The vegetable fibers that are left over are excellent to use later to create different kinds of textures, from dried and powdered to refined as "porridge."

"The pulp has a texture that is very different from anything else, and that is especially true when you juice carrot, parsnip, red beetroot, and other root vegetables."

There are three different kinds of juicers on the market. The most common that you can find in any appliance store is a rapidly rotating disc that tears whatever you need to juice apart and then sifts the juice through a fine net into a container. The disadvantage with these is that the high speed has a tendency to warm the juice, which can disturb the flavor. Furthermore, it is not very effective for leaf vegetables, berries, or herbs.

Another juicer crushes what you would like to juice and presses that crush against a fine net. The advantage of this is that it moves slowly, which prevents heat that can affect the juice. You can recognize this by the fact that no foam appears at all in this juice, which is common in the grating juicer.

The third juicer is also grinding, but instead of a twister that crushes the fibers, it has two rust-free screws that face each other. This juicer is the most effective and also the most expensive.

Because it is the slowest juicer, it protects the juice from oxidization and protects living enzymes, flavor substances, and nutrients.

SINGED LAMELLAE OF POTATO ONION FROM LINNE'S RASHULT

Roasted almonds, melting marrow, and aged vinegar, with creamed almond milk and raw licorice.

Rashult is located in Småland, and it is the place where Carl von Linne was born. It has been proven that the potato onion was grown there back then.

The potato onion is reminiscent of the potato in how it grows. You sow an onion, and you get so much back—like potatoes. That is why they are called potato onions. They grow like large wedges from the bud, and the flavor is mild and sweet. This sweetness is naturally enhanced when cooked.

"Onion with licorice has been a classic with us from the beginning. Licorice removes the sharpness of the onion. Almond and licorice are also great together, which the pastry world has proved multiple times. For the sake of acidity, we have added fifty-year-old balsamic vinegar. If the vinegar is stored for longer than that, it tends to be too sweet, and we already have sweetness in this dish from the licorice."

The potato onion is both durable and resistant, and it is one of the vegetarian favorites. You can store it for over two years.

"We are definitely happy that we have been able to take part in the exclusive cultivation from Lena and Michael Michaelsson at Rahult in Småland, but we still wonder why there is no greater production. The first answer we receive when we ask is that the onion wedges are too 'tedious' to peel, and modern people don't have the time. The other answer is that nobody really knows why this historical and delicious onion is not grown commercially."

The small-scale production may still be the best because a loving and protected crop tends to give the best results. Lena Michaelsson describes the flavor of the onion as mild, soft, and a little spicy. She also says that the advantage of the onion, just like garlic, is that it can be planted in fall and harvested in spring. This way, you can get two crops per year, which says a lot about the unexpected abilities of this onion.

MOUSE MELON WITH COUNTRY CREAM

Black currants, Sarawak pepper, broad beans, yellow and green squash, as well as fresh herbs and unfiltered olive oil from Ivar Günther.

....

"You slowly fall in love with these small melon-like cucumbers. The first time they came from the garden, we were initially struck by their appearance—they look like mini melons—and then later by the flavor: a striking green cucumber flavor that can be caused by the thick skins where the flavor seems to concentrate, but also with a distinct salt and acid flavor, almost like a pickled cucumber. It is our ambition to enhance the green flavor of the mouse melon by using currants and squash blossoms."

Natural cream is poured over the plate so that the vegetables can develop their flavor through the fat.

"Except for drying the flowers and the lightly soaked broad beans, everything else is raw and untouched straight from the garden."

Because all the flavors appear subtle, F/L serves a pepper with an equally subtle aroma: the Sarawak pepper, a black variety from Borneo. It has fine tones of lime and flowers and a good balance between heat and tartness.

IN FURTHER DETAIL

"We found Ivar Günther's olive grove through a family member who married into the farm Le Mas d'Eole, which has 120 olive trees in Bargemon, outside of Nice."

Many of the olive trees are close to two hundred years old, the farm having been established in 1817. The oil that is produced for Frantzén/Lindeberg is unfiltered and mild and has been pressed in the town's old olive press from the early 1700s. There is no use of pesticides or artificial fertilizers at the farm. Possible infestations are fought biologically, and the olive grove is fertilized with goat manure.

WHITE AND GREEN ASPARAGUS WITH CILANTRO, LIME, AND LEMONGRASS

Prepared for three hours in the oven. Served with saffron and curry cream, the buttery juice from the cooking as well as pistachio nuts and oil.

To instruct "three hours in the oven" is obviously impossible. It depends on the thickness of the asparagus. There should be a little chewing resistance in the asparagus, and the oven should never exceed 212°F (100°C). Large asparagus can take four hours or more.

"We tie up the asparagus, both the green and the white, with lime, cilantro, and lemongrass. It is important that the stalks of asparagus are somewhat similar in size."

"The asparagus is placed upright in a tin, and white wine is poured on top. When the asparagus is

left standing, the heat comes from underneath and moves through the thick bottom first and later upwards through the herb bouquet, so that the asparagus is evenly cooked. The leftover juice is mixed with butter."

The worst thing you can do with asparagus is to boil it on the stove. All you need to do is taste the water after boiling, which becomes a rich asparagus bouillon while the asparagus itself has lost much of its flavor.

The alternative is baking in an oven or frying in a pan. The white asparagus needs to be peeled, whereas the green only needs to be cut at the bottom and rinsed at the end (where dirt can get stuck).

Asparagus has a slight bitterness, but also sweetness. The bitterness is released in the wine and becomes part of the buttery sauce. In this way, the bitterness "is returned" to the asparagus to make the flavor complete.

"Pistachio and asparagus are a good combination. I can't explain why, but it tastes great."

IN FURTHER DETAIL

SAFFRON AND CURRY CREAM

Slice four large silver onions thinly. Slice the middle part of a lemongrass stalk as thinly as possible. Grate ginger the size of a thumb and add saffron and the homemade curry (alternatively Madras curry). Place everything in a frying pan with high edges and let it sweat in butter until soft and transparent. Mix until smooth and pass through a sieve, flavor with sea salt and a little lime juice.

DELICATE LEEK SIMMERED IN WHEY

Sour cream with caviar, smoked yellow bell pepper from Malmköping, oyster leaf, dill juice, and borage flowers.

. . . .

A clear example of how thoughts and inspiration can work when composing a dish:

"When we were at the garden in Malmköping, we saw the finest yellow Swedish-grown bell peppers we had ever seen. They were almost ripe. Yellow bell pepper is a difficult ingredient; it does not belong in our list of ingredients. We traveled back to the restaurant convinced that we would only use the bell pepper in the food we serve to our staff."

"At the same time, I had moved and had found some old notes from our time at Raymond Blanc at Le Manoir aux Quat'Saisons. I'd written something about a soup made with yellow bell peppers and smoked haddock, and I thought: 'Why not smoke the bell pepper and combine it with the acid in the whey-boiled leek?' And that is what we did. The following week, we went to our garden and harvested our yellow bell peppers."

VARIATION OF CABBAGE WITH WINTER TRUFFLE

"We've carried the simple but also deep flavor of a browned cabbage consommé with us since we worked at Edsbacka Restaurant in 1998. We think it is the flavor we remember the best from that whole time."

At Edsbacka Restaurant, they made it as a consommé meant for ravioli stuffed with truffle and duck liver.

"Our variation of cabbage with winter truffle is an homage to Christer Lingström shared among him and his two head chefs at the time, Håkan Thor and Fredrik Pettersson."

To bring the flavor into the twenty-first century, the dish is now developed from Edsbacka's consommé on browned white cabbage.

"Here we choose to serve the consommé lightly solidified with cabbages of various kinds and textures."

THIS IS PLATED:
A browned Savoy cabbage purée
Butter-sautéed green cabbage
Steamed leaves of brussels sprouts
Raw white cabbage
Truffled cauliflower velouté
Dried heart leaves of chinese cabbage
Gelé of white cabbage consommé
Shaved winter truffle sprinkled over the cabbage

IN FURTHER DETAIL

BROWNED WHITE CABBAGE CONSOMMÉ
Frantzén and Lindeberg make the consommé in a slightly different way from the way it was done at Edsbacka Restaurant in 1998. Firstly, they make the bouillon their own way with ice filtration.

Cut white cabbage in rough pieces, except the stem. Brown in oil until the cabbage has a significant color, but is not burned. Move into a deep saucepan and cover with water—twice as much water as cabbage. Simmer slowly for twenty-four hours, remove the dregs that float to the surface, and replace the water that evaporates. The bouillon should have a nutty brownish color. Sift through a sieve with a double layer of filter cloth. Bring to a boil and reduce to half.* Ice-filtrate and warm. Flavor with salt and lemon. Melt two gelatin leaves per 4 cups (1 L) of water into the pot, and let it stiffen into a smooth gelé in a cold place.

ICE FILTRATING
Traditionally you whisk egg whites in the bouillon to make it clear. The problem is that it loses a lot of taste and volume.

You obtain the same clear result with ice-filtrating, which is basically adding one gelatin sheet per 4 cups (1 L) of bouillon and placing the pot in the freezer. The gelatin will bind all of the dregs in the bouillon, which is later allowed to slowly thaw in the refrigerator over a sieve with a filter cloth. The gelatin will form a net, or a "membrane," that will let liquid through but prevent dregs and leftovers from the boiling pass into the bouillon. The clean flavors are not affected at all by this filtrating. The result is an almost crystal clear bouillon.

*Reducing before ice-filtrating is only recommended for vegetable bouillons that lack gelatin as a binding substance. For animal bouillon, Frantzén and Lindeberg recommend reducing after ice filtration.

Potato Purée Made with Steamed Alströmer's Leksands Vit
Page 243

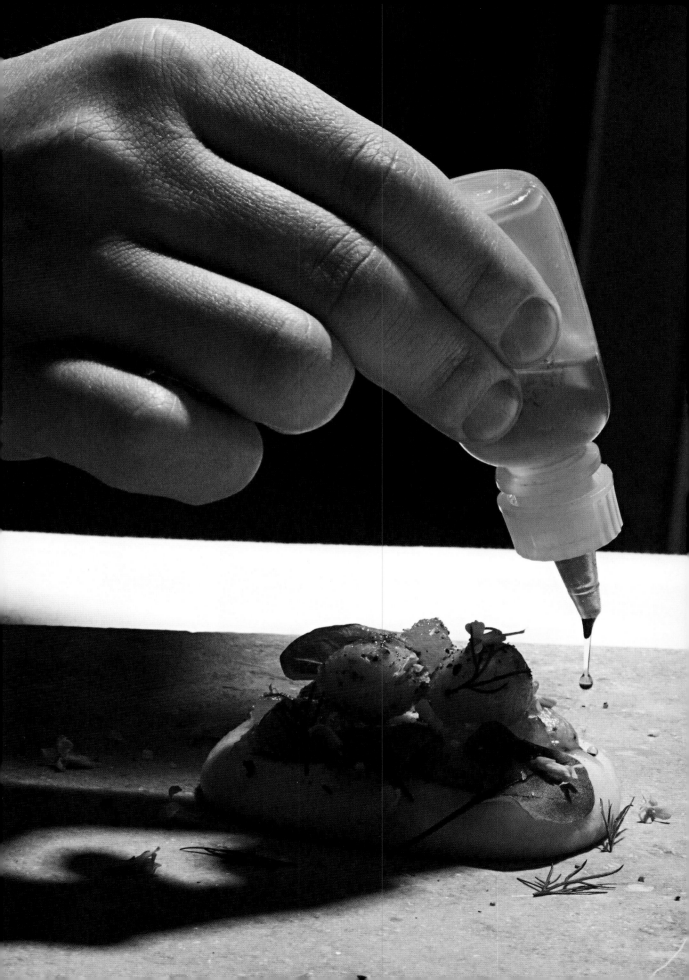

"**THERE ARE INSTANCES** when we wish to enhance the green in dishes, but not to do it with the green ingredients we use because the flavor will be too evident."

The solution is to add chlorophyll, the substance that makes all plants green and plays a huge part in photosynthesis—the plants' ability to transform, among other things, carbon dioxide into oxygen.

"Chlorophyll is without flavor and does not influence the dish in any away except the color."

At Frantzén/Lindeberg, they extract their own chlorophyll by making juice out of spinach leaves in a juicer. The juice is slowly heated up until the point where it stratifies. The chlorophyll is released from the liquid and is sifted finely with a filter cloth. The liquid is allowed to drain overnight. Whatever is left in the cloth is pure chlorophyll.

GREEN
GREEN

DESSERT

Desserts are traditionally the great finale of dinner. It is, therefore, easy to believe that you have to use the entire battery to make the guest as happy as possible, with fat, sweet, and chocolate galore. But, Frantzén/Lindeberg chose another direction.

It is a myth that meals have to be finished with a bombardment of sugar and chocolate. Most likely, this is from an old German tradition, seeing that Sweden was inhibited by German cooks and bakers at the beginning of the last century. By dessert, the guest is already so full of impressions that something very different is needed in order to create new energy and curiosity. The desserts cannot, and should not, become a separate department.

"**I HAVE TO BE THE PASTRY CHEF** and the one who designs the desserts, but I can never be blind to what the guests are served before it is time for dessert. This means that I can never work with banana, pineapple, and mango, which are such good materials to make desserts with, because they would never go with the big picture, and the sense of wholeness is what we uncompromisingly work towards."

And so many would now conclude that in reality, it is Björn Frantzén who decides what should be placed on the dessert plates because he is the one who decides what is served first on the testing menu, and that Daniel Lindeberg as pastry chef is some sort of second rank.

"No, I am not a cowed pastry chef; to the contrary, I see it as a challenge and a given that I should bridge the menu to the dessert service and make the meals become one, uninterrupted, whole."

It has taken a long time to find the "country style" in desserts. The simple way out would be to do tricks on the plate and make sugar sculptures or chocolate spirals.

"But I don't think it tastes good, I have never liked those things, and I will never work with that kind of dessert art."

A chocolate bomb is completely uninteresting, but when Frantzén/Lindeberg's three finishing dessert plates arrive at the table at the same time, something very unexpected and interesting happens.

"I realized early on that there is no logical explanation for the excess of dessert. A good pastry work is all about holding back, to make choices and embrace carefulness, something that is part of the whole philosophy of the restaurant."

Daniel Lindeberg started using salt in desserts very early on. Salt enhances the cocoa flavor in chocolate, lifts flavors of caramel and nuts, and balances out acid.

"When the seasons and the ingredients permit, it does happen that I compose the three desserts after the base flavors of sweet, salty, and sour. But the concept never controls the flavor."

Every self-respecting restaurant serves large cake plates on multiple levels with "coffee sweets." When Frantzén/Lindeberg was completely new, it didn't deviate from this rule—quite the opposite. It offered an abundance of coffee sweets: sour rims hanging from specially designed teak and plexiglass stands, racks for homemade lollipops, traditional candy, and huge amounts of petits fours, chocolate truffles, marshmallows, raspberry jellies, marmalades, French nougat, and Punsch rolls (cylindrical Swedish pastries of crushed cookies and punsch liqueur, covered in marzipan with the ends dipped in chocolate).

"I think that we, in some kind of eagerness and innocence, wanted to recreate the French starred restaurants, where they come rolling in with the abundant dessert trolleys to show the magnificent skill of the pastry chefs. I don't necessarily think that what we did was so bad. It was good and much of it was innovative, but today it feels somewhat immature."

For a period of time, all of the coffee sweets were replaced with classic jellyrolls with buttercream. With it we served various complements: blackberry, raspberry, blueberry jam, buckthorn jam—all the berries the garden could offer.

"Jellycake and Swedishness in all its glory, but at the end it felt like we just wanted to go back and make simple macarons. It is the world's best pastry and can be varied infinitely."

The first thing that is placed in front of guests when they arrive at the restaurant is a wooden box with rising bread dough. The last thing that is placed on the table is a small teak box, now with three macarons that capture the flavors from the gardens depending on the season.

TOASTED HAY AND PINE NEEDLE ICE CREAM

Soft dried apples, praline on salt-roasted sunflower seeds, walnut meringue, apple purée, pickled spruce shoots, and hay ashes.

"We want to make malt-tasting ice cream. A rounder, milder, and less smoky malt flavor than the one from the malted rye we got through toasting the hay."

The whole dessert is based on a forest theme. The garden in Malmköping is situated in a billowing forest and meadow. From the nearby forest, the young pine needles are delivered depending on the season with a mild flavor of resin and turpentine. The soft dried apple with its sweet tartness helps to bind together the "malt flavor" from the toasted hay and the forest flavor of the pine needles.

IN FURTHER DETAIL

ICE CREAM

Roast a fistful of clean hay in a pan in the oven; add sweetened milk, cream, and a few fresh pine needles. Let it simmer in the oven for forty-five minutes in 355°F (180°C). Sift through a chinoise and later bring to a boil in a saucepan on the stove, add yolk, and simmer to 180°F (82°C). Let it mature in the fridge for at least twenty-four hours. Freeze to ice cream and make scoops, and then freeze on a sheet. Roll the scoops in lightly whipped cream and later in crushed walnut meringue. Freeze until serving.

PRALINE

9 oz (250 g) sugar
⅓ cup (70 mL) water
Seeds from one vanilla pod
9 oz (250 g) sunflower seeds
A pinch of fleur de sel

Boil water, sugar, and vanilla to 242°F (117°C). Add sunflower seeds and caramelize. Empty onto parchment paper and let it cool. Mix in a mixer, and flavor with fleur de sel.

SOFT DRIED APPLES

Peel, core, and wedge the tart apples. Simmer gently in water. Rinse under cold water and place on a rack. Dry at 120°F (50°C) in the oven.

BROWNED BUTTER ICE CREAM WITH BUCKTHORN CURD

Manjari chocolate cream, dried milk chocolate mousse, crispy honey, and dried browned butter.

Browned butter is a treasured product with Frantzén/Lindeberg, and it is used in both cold and warm cooking. One reason for using browned butter is that it gives a nutty flavor without having to use nuts.

"Butter is often used in ice cream in Belgium and France, but rarely here. It gives the ice cream a different character: a softer, leaner taste. Because butter contains about 80 percent fat and about 40 percent cream, I use milk from Järna Mejeri to balance the fat content—in other words, my ice cream is not more fattening even though I use butter—rather it's the opposite if you compare it with the classic Swedish restaurant ice cream. Nevertheless, it is more flavorful because the butter enhances the flavors."

If you have ever tasted buckthorn, you know that it has a tart flavor. The butter makes the tartness milder and gives the buckthorn a more balanced flavor. You might say that the butter helps draw out the fruitiness of the berry. Buckthorn is also the closest you come to a tropical dessert at Frantzén/Lindeberg; it has a slight tutti-frutti taste.

"When I tasted the browned butter in the ice cream, buckthorn, and chocolate, I added a 'farmer's cake' to soak up the ice cream and cream. I made a mayonnaise with browned butter and added meringue and flour before baking. It ended up as an airy cake with a taste of browned butter."

Crispy honey may puzzle some. In English-speaking countries, we'd call it honeycomb. Honey and sugar are caramelized and then bicarbonate is added. Bicarbonate makes the caramel expand to five times its volume. If you later cut the caramel, the sides will have a structure that looks like the interior of a beehive.

IN FURTHER DETAIL

BROWNED BUTTER ICE CREAM

5 ½ cups (1 kg) butter
8 ½ cups (2 L) milk, fat content about 4 percent
1 ⅕ cup (300 g) sugar
Zest from one lemon
1 lb (600 g) yolk
1 pinch (5 g) Swedish sea salt

Brown the butter and add cold milk. When the butter has turned a nutty color, whisk. Add the sugar and lemon. Bring to a boil and add the yolks, whisk quickly, and then heat to 180°F (82°C) while stirring. Cool down and let it "mature" overnight.

HONEYCOMB

1 tablespoon (40 g) honey
2 oz (65 g) glucose
⅘ cup (200 g) sugar
2 ⅓ tablespoon (35 g) water
2 teaspoons (10 g) bicarbonate

Boil everything except the bicarbonate to a light caramel in a large saucepan. Remove from the stove and stir in the bicarbonate. Be ready for the reaction—it will expand significantly. Pour onto oiled parchment paper and let it cool. Break into smaller pieces.

CHOCOLATE CONSOMMÉ WITH SALT-BAKED PARSNIPS AND THYME ICE CREAM

Served with sliced fresh almonds and roasted cocoa beans.

In the gardens, there is an abundance that needs to be taken advantage of: Swedish root vegetables gain a natural sweetness through the constant flooding light and the somewhat cool climate during the short summer. This is a sweetness that goes well with chocolate. During fall and winter, we store the root vegetables in a basement buried in sand. There they mature, that is to say they age into an even more concentrated sweetness. This is when they are best for the dessert kitchen, unless you wish to use the softness of the flavor and the crispy structure that is most evident in season."

Salt-baking a root vegetable is a gentle method for the root vegetable to become a unified boiled buttery purée filled with concentrated flavor.

"I see it this way: There is a common denominator for parsnip and chocolate, and that is earthiness. Thyme is from the wild landscape and is a common flavor accent for both the chocolate and the parsnip."

IN FURTHER DETAIL

CHOCOLATE CONSOMMÉ

Chocolate consommé should have a pure chocolate flavor that is light and fruity. Simmer roasted cocoa beans, bitter chocolate, and water for one to two hours. The texture should be like bouillon. Instead of using the classic clarifying substance, whisked egg whites, clarify with ice filtration. Sift away the cocoa beans and add 1 percent gelatin. Freeze the consommé and later thaw it slowly in the refrigerator through a filter cloth.

SORBET OF FRESH-PRESSED GRANNY SMITH APPLES
Flavored with lemon verbena and chamomile.

Intermezzo is Italian and means "between" or "in the middle": something that happens in between two other elements. In the world of music, it can be the name of a part of a symphony. In the world of opera, it is used to create a segue between two scenes.

"In our world, we use it as a break after serving something with powerful flavors that has a tendency to linger in your mouth. Without a break like this, the next dish would have difficulty displaying its flavor registry. Still, it did take two years before we began serving intermezzos, what they in the Tore Wretman kitchen often called granité or flavor cleanser. Early on, we asked ourselves the question of why one serves a flavor cleanser between fish and warm meat dishes. If it was so important to cleanse the flavors between fish and meat, then shouldn't it be served between every dish, before the fish dish, and even before dessert?"

It was really the classic at Frantzén/Lindeberg, the French toast, that pushed the decision and almost forced an intermezzo. The French toast is full of umami from the soy and the Parmesan, not to mention a lot of shaved truffle and hundred-year-old balsamic vinegar—in other words a lot of flavor. This made it a hard act for the next dish to follow.

The most important thing to keep in mind when you make a granité or sorbet that is going to be served as intermezzo is to lower the sugar content.

The worst thing possible is a sweet sorbet that grows in the mouth instead of cleansing.

"We agreed that all the flavors of the French toast needed to be broken before the next serving. We made our own slightly surprising sorbet with Granny Smith apples and lemon verbena, which had a very nice balance of tart and sweet. It was sufficiently breaking against our classic French toast."

IN FURTHER DETAIL

SORBET

2 cups (500 g) Granny Smith juice
2 tablespoons (35 g) lemon juice
3 ½ oz (100 g) glucose
3 ½ oz (100 g) dry glucose
⅓ teaspoon (1.5 g) chamomile rum
2 pots lemon verbena/Pacojet beaker

Add the lemon juice to the Granny Smith juice so that it doesn't oxidize. Take one third of the apple juice, glucose, and dry glucose, and warm carefully on the stove until it has all dissolved. Blend in the remaining apple juice. Pick two pots of lemon verbena and place in a beaker, add a sorbet layer to the line, and freeze. Mix the sorbet once and let it freeze again before you mix it once more. The sorbet will then end up completely smooth.

INFUSED, DEEP-FRIED MUSCAT PUMPKIN

Homemade licorice on black olives, caramelized almonds, and toasted bread. Served with salt-roasted pumpkin seeds, milk ice cream, pumpkin seed oil, and pumpkin cream flavored with Carlshamn's Flaggpunsch liquer.

The garden in Malmköping produces a large number of muscat pumpkins every fall. This is a pumpkin with a distinct natural sweetness and fruitiness. If you roast the pumpkin, the sweetness will be even more evident. To meet the sweetness, at F/L they use the buttermilk that is left over from their own butter production and transform it into tart ice cream.

"Obviously, I've been inspired by the American pumpkin pie in combination with their buttermilk."

On the plate, you can also find Atsina cress and fennel dill, which, with the homemade licorice help enhance the natural sweetness of the pumpkin.

CLOUDBERRY FLOUR PANCAKES WITH SWEDISH MAPLE SYRUP ICE CREAM

Served with stirred cloudberry from Jämtland, vanilla crème, and jelly, with Swedish maple syrup.

Pancakes at Frantzén/Lindeberg don't seem quite right, but they do it anyway. Like in this case with pancakes that are baked with cloudberry flour developed with Grythyttan wine, from a leftover product from the development of their cloudberry dessert wine. The sifted cloudberries are dried and ground to an aromatic flour, which can complement the wheat flour in the pancakes.

"I have never liked the thin Swedish pancakes, but the American pancakes on the other hand are a little thicker, creamier, and richer. And when we wanted a warm dessert, the choice fell on the combination of pancakes and maple syrup.

"The idea was still to work with Swedish expressions and Swedish raw materials. We didn't think Swedish maple syrup existed because sugar maples in Sweden are very rare. The production of maple syrup is also virtually nonexistent."

The producer of the restaurant's apple seed oil, Göran Amnegård in Blaxsta, could, however, deliver a Swedish hard-tapped maple syrup, which is, actually, better than the Canadian because it has a more balanced, round, and mild sweetness. The ice cream for the warm pancakes is flavored with the syrup, and they serve a maple syrup jelly as a soft complement to the whole cloudberries.

IN FURTHER DETAIL

HARD-TAPPED MAPLE SYRUP

Göran Amnegård writes about the chemistry of Blaxsta hard-tapped syrup:

"Our maple syrup contains exactly 68.4 percent sugar. It is an absolutely pure cellulose sugar. The remaining 31.6 percent is mostly water, but also various carbon-hydrogen compounds, minerals, and proteins. The latter makes up about 6 to 8 percent and works in the finished maple syrup as a binding element, which means that it can be whipped like whipping cream and transformed into maple butter."

PANCAKES

1 ½ cup (400 g) milk
⅘ cup (200 g) wheat flour
½ cup (165 g) cloudberry flour
1 teaspoon baking powder
½ teaspoon (2.5 g) bicarbonate
1 pinch Swedish sea salt
½ cup (150 g) egg
2 ½ tablespoons (40 g) honey
2 ½ tablespoons (45 g) melted butter

Blend all of the dry ingredients. Then blend the milk, egg, and honey in a separate bowl. Add the dry ingredients while whisking. Finish off with the melted butter. Let it sit for at least fifteen minutes. Fry in clarified butter.

SWEET MACARON

Chocolate macaron with white chocolate truffle flavored with dried parsnip and vanilla. Boiled apple.

SALT MACARON

Macaron with salt caramel cream flavored with roasted rapeseed oil.

TART MACARON

Violet macaron with homemade rhubarb jam.

Macarons are the ultimate pastry because they can be varied infinitely. People often have the mistaken idea that they are supposed to be crisp and immediately disappear as a kind of dust, like a crispy meringue. That is not true. A macaron should never be served fresh; it has to have time to mature and soften. Through storing for a couple of days, the macarons enhance their own flavor. The texture should be the same throughout the macaron, including the filling. A macaron should have a brief chewiness and take time to eat.

People often talk of the perfect macaron, and as always when it comes to pastry, it begins with a batter. That is where the secret of the macaron lies.

It demands a touch and experience to blend a macaron batter, where the basis is Italian meringue with egg white and warm syrup. When the almond meal is added with powdered sugar, it is important to press the air out of the meringue batter. You can see how the meringue falls together under real turns of the whisk. When the batter flows slowly, or rather, rolls off a rubber spatula, it is time to pipe it out on parchment paper.

"It is important that freshly baked macarons are cooled on a cold baking surface to stop the baking and not left on the warm baking sheet or they will be over-baked. A macaron can, and actually likes, to be frozen."

IN FURTHER DETAIL

SWEET MACARON

Pour warm cream over broken white chocolate, stir into ganache. Leave it to cool.

Press a peeled and cleaned parsnip through a juicer. Save the parsnip meat and dry it on a baking sheet in the oven at 122°F (50°C) until dry. Blend the dry parsnip with the ganache, and round out with some of the juice.

For the boiled apple, boil equal parts white wine, water, and sugar with a vanilla pod. Add the entire peeled Åkerö apples. Slowly simmer so that the apples do not turn into mush. Move into a glass container and keep with the poaching blend in the refrigerator.

Construct the macaron through spritzing a little ganache, place dice of apple on top, and cover with more ganache. Close the macaron.

CHERRY MARBLED
ALMOND MILK ICE CREAM
Served with cherry mousse, cherry meringue,
preserved sour cherries, and Swedish morello cherries.

"We have found our own morello tree. It is surely eighty years old, tall, and mighty. During the blossoming, the air is filled with pollinating bees and bumblebees. This provides sweet, dark, summer breeze-filled morellos to our cherry dessert. What I work for is a visually beautiful expression, with a sauce of sour cherries, a marbled almond milk ice cream that is spread out on the plate, and our own, pitted morello cherries. Everything should be in contrast with the molded cherry mousse that's placed diagonally on the plate."

"I admit that I love sour cherries preserved in sugar and alcohol, which are then allowed to mature for months. We use sour cherries, and there we also present a contrast against the sweet morello cherries. Almonds and cherries are of the same spirit. The almond milk ice cream pulls out the fruitiness and makes the two different cherry flavors complete."

IN FURTHER DETAIL

MARBLING
The almond ice cream is marbled with a syrup that is developed through reducing Kriek (Belgian cherry beer) with fresh cherries and sugar.

CHERRY MERINGUE
3 ½ oz (100 g) cherry purée
½ cup (100 g) water
0.7 oz (20 g) egg white powder
1 oz (30 g) granulated sugar

Blend water, cherry purée, and egg white powder with a hand mixer. Whisk with the sugar into meringue. Spread out thinly on parchment paper, dry in an oven at 195°F (90°C) for about three hours. Turn the oven off, open the door, and let it sit overnight.

MILLE-FEUILLE WITH RHUBARB MOUSSE

Tender rhubarb poached in pomegranate apple juice.
Violet crème, dried, and crystallized violets.

Mille-feuille is actually a puff pastry, and the intent is to create "a thousand leaves." Here we use phyllo dough to obtain a lighter and crispier feel.

"The violet flavor is a strong memory of mine from the violet candies of my childhood. In other words, I use violets in desserts with great enthusiasm. The violet flowers are crystalized with sugar and egg whites, and the flavor is a ready aroma from Catalonia."

Rhubarb, with its persistence in tannin and texture, is helped along by the round, mild, and violet common to Swedish childhood sweets. Violet flowers do the same for rhubarb as strawberries: they tone it down and soften, even out the acidity, and balance the roughness. Rhubarb and violets make a different and very tasty dessert with flavors of candy history.

"The rhubarb comes up at the same time as the scent violets in spring. This is the timely spring dessert, a nod to the coming summer."

IN FURTHER DETAIL

PHYLLO DOUGH

The phyllo sheets are brushed with hot butter, a little powdered sugar, and powder from crystalized violets and then layered in three layers. The sheets are baked in the oven under pressure at 340°F (170°C).

RHUBARB POACHED
IN POMEGRANATE APPLE JUICE

Scrape the core, meat, and juice. Pass through a juicer. Boil the juice with sugar, and let it cool. Cut tender rhubarb into 3-inch (8-cm) long stalks, and vacuum-pack with the pomegranate apple juice. Marinate overnight and later poach in the vacuum bag at 140°F (60°C) until they are completely soft, but still have texture.

SALTED CARAMEL ICE CREAM WITH CHOCOLATE AND ROASTED RAPESEED OIL

Served with chocolate cream made with chocolate from Ecuador, chocolate crumble, milk chocolate powder, mud cake, and chocolate oil.

Mixing nuts, chocolate, and caramel is usually a given, but on a tasting menu, there is no way to make moderations if you are serving a guest with nut allergies, for instance. This dessert is nutty, but does not contain nuts.

The roasted rapeseed oil is brought back from France, where it has been produced since 1878 under the brand Nouvelle huile de colza grillé à l'ancienne, an oil that the Swedish rapeseed oil producers are trying to copy. A roasted rapeseed oil has an aged, rich flavor with tones of both the blossoming rapeseed meadow and lots of roasted peanuts.

The salt in the dessert is distinct, as intended. What makes the ice cream is caramelized cane sugar—this way you get a sharper and rawer character of the caramel, which is completed when fleur de sel is added.

The reason why they use chocolate from Ecuador is that it is fruity despite its cocoa content of 72 percent. Other chocolate varieties have a short and bitter flavor at this height of concentration.

"It is no secret that I am personally very in love with Gold Nougat, Snickers, and Daim. When I was a child, we would make Daim out of the *Cookbook for Children* with my grandmother. That was when the lust for flavor was first awakened. I was about twenty years old at her funeral, and to keep the heavy sorrow at bay, I thought of her mud cake and cardamom balls all the way through the funeral service—it helped.

"In this dessert, there are small pieces of my grandmother's mud cake, full of chocolate from Ecuador.

"It is sort of an homage to her, I would say."

IN FURTHER DETAIL

CHOCOLATE CRUMBLE

Blend butter, sugar, cocoa, and wheat flour to a crumble dough. Bake on a baking sheet at 330°F (165°C) until the crumbs are dry. Allow to cool. Mix rapidly in a mixer—the crumbs will then get a texture that is reminiscent of soil.

CARAMEL ICE CREAM

Melt sugar, and let it darken a little bit. Pour lightly whipped cream on top. The air in the cream is "sucked up" into the hot caramel that will then not get lumpy and stiffen. Add milk, Swedish sea salt, and an egg yolk.

CHOCOLATE OIL

Warm rapeseed oil with dark chocolate and cocoa powder. Let the chocolate melt slowly in the oil.

SALT
Oxidized pear sorbet with hazelnut
emulsion flavored with fleur
de sel and burnt mead.

SWEET

Buttermilk ice cream flavored with vanilla and rose water.
Served with homemade raspberry jam, confit cocktail
tomato, compressed garden tomatoes, and tomato seeds stewed
in rose water and vanilla as well as fresh rose leaves.

TART

Variation of lemon and buttermilk.
Lemon cream and buttermilk shake
flavored with lemon and
vanilla, lemon meringue, preserved
lemon peels, and tart caramel.
Topped off with whipped buttermilk.

When guests are finished eating the white menu and have also enjoyed the drink package, this means there is a dulling of attention and taste buds. In that case, it seems inhumane to force people to take in even more information. The three desserts that are placed in front of the guest are a surprise and a new beginning. They are colored by the dessert chef's play with the guest's thoughts, ideas, and taste.

SALT DESSERT

"Mead sounds like an exciting ingredient. Traditionally, mead is an alcohol containing honey wine with a furiously long tradition in history. In Northern Europe, a rye malt base was often used because honey was very expensive. Rye, on the other hand, was cheap. We have found desserts that are based on wheat beer and pears. The fat in the hazelnuts goes well with the freshness and deep flavor of the oxidized pears. A hazelnut emulsion also brings a soft saltiness."

The oxidized pears were discovered by accident.

"Oxidization happened for the first time when we forgot the pear juice in the juicer. It was placed directly in the refrigerator, and after a few hours, it was completely brown. Obviously, we should have added lemon juice to prevent the color change and oxidation. Yet, when we tasted it, we were very surprised: the oxidation had lured a deep and intensive pear taste to the surface, a fruitiness you never experience when you prevent oxidation with lemon."

SWEET DESSERT

"Tomatoes have a natural sweetness, and we use all kinds of varieties. In our garden in Malmköping, Jan Andersson grows over one hundred different kinds of tomatoes. Because these tomatoes grow in good soil and come from seeds that have never been adjusted to industrial cultivation, we can use the entire tomato for the dessert. We dry the thin skin, we stew the seeds with rose water and vanilla, the fruit meat is compressed with tomato water in a vacuum machine for the most flavor, and all the smaller tomatoes are confit in olive oil with sugar and salt."

We also receive many roses from Jan Andersson.

"They have a very perfuming flavor and go great with vanilla. We make an ice cream with buttermilk, vanilla, and rose water. Roses with raspberries are a classic flavor combination, and here the acid from the raspberries is connected with the little acid in the sweet tomatoes. The raspberries make a sweeter jam."

TART DESSERT

"A dessert that, besides from being tart, builds on many different textures. The lemon cream is baked in the oven, boiled on the stove, or simmered in a water bath to give it an off-flavor and slow it down. Baked in the oven at 195°F (90°C) allows the freshly pressed lemon juice to be savored. Before the lemon cream is placed in the oven, we break pieces of buttermilk cake (sponge cake in buttermilk) on top. We want a rich feel where the cake soaks up flavors from the cream. The inspiration is the English bread and butter pudding."

"Buttermilk has a friendly acid, but because it doesn't really contain fat, it can't be whipped. We therefore add a flavorless stabilizer from 'Sosa' that is otherwise used in siphons to make foam. 'Pro espuma.'"

CAKE* FOR ANYONE WHO HAS SOMETHING TO CELEBRATE

White chocolate mousse flavored with vanilla, pistachio brûlée, orange flower water, and soft jelly made with wild strawberries, Arctic strawberries, strawberries, and raspberries, flavored with St. Germain.

Many guests come to Frantzén/Lindeberg to celebrate something, often a holiday. Swedes traditionally serve cake when they celebrate. It is a kind of a Swedish seal, proof that it is a holiday or party.

There are guests who say they will be coming to celebrate something when they book, and sometimes the waiters pick up on it. For some time now, they've always prepared a cake serving.

"It is a way to show that we care, often to the guests' surprise and joy. This belongs under our general motto: 'relaxed elegance.' Besides, it is completely unexpected to be served cake in a restaurant like ours."

*The cake varies depending on access to the ingredients and on the season.

OVEN-BAKED RASPBERRY ICE CREAM WITH LICORICE MOUSSE

Boiled in root from Spanish chervil, compressed apricot, fresh wild raspberries, dried apricots poached with muscovado sugar, licorice caramel, and freeze-dried raspberries.

It is always exciting to see transformations in both flavors and texture. This is based on the old classic glace au four where a meringue cloaked warm sugar cake has a filling of ice cold vanilla ice cream.

A glace au four à la the twenty-first century became something completely different, and the idea that it has been in an oven for an entire hour at 390°F (200°C) is staggering. The truth is that it is only the ingredients for the ice cream that are baked: cream, milk, sugar, and raspberries. Then the eggs are whipped and the ice cream is frozen. The transformation is there. The ice cream tastes like baked, cold, and tender raspberry pie.

Desserts at Frantzén/Lindeberg often contain an ingredient that feels like texture: something crispy to accompany the smooth. Except for the crispy and aromatic freeze-dried raspberries, the oven-baked ice cream is soft and smooth all the way through.

Licorice and raspberries, anise and apricot are old classic flavor combinations; the acidity in raspberries goes very well with licorice flavors. You can say that the concentration is based on three different flavors besides the fruit: muscovado sugar, licorice, and the root from the chervil, all with an anise aroma as a common denominator.

IN FURTHER DETAIL

ROOT OF SPANISH CHERVIL

Harvest the smallest roots but ones that are still about ⅓ inch (2 cm) or more. Clean in lukewarm water and later peel with a sharp knife as if you were peeling rhubarb. Preserve the roots by lowering them into a saucepan with equal parts water, sugar, and white wine brought to a boil and cooled.

Vacuum-pack the roots with the syrup and poach in a water bath that holds 150°F (65°C) for two hours. Store cold in the syrup.

COMPRESSED WATERMELON AND SORBET OF XINTAI CUCUMBER

Salad with grapefruit, red currants, Arctic strawberries, melissa, sorrel, and dried wild strawberries.

This is a simple and "straightforward" dessert, a small fruit salad inspired by summer, with very high fruit freshness without dairy products.

Cucumber sorbet sounds very much like a "middle dish" or a "palate cleanser," but the cucumber's fruitiness and clear flavor can be used in desserts and as sorbet, somewhat sweetened, but with care not to destroy the bitterness. The sorbet is great against the garden berries.

"One of the goals for our own gardens has been an uncompromising focus on season. Daily contact with the cultivators makes such a focus almost automatic."

Arctic strawberries, red currants, and wild strawberries ripen at the same time. The melissa and sorrel grow, more or less, throughout the whole cultivation season. The watermelon is from somewhere else; it is Swedish-grown and has a high sweetness and juiciness enhanced though compression. The sour that is needed against the sweet berries comes from the bittersweet and tart grapefruit.

IN FURTHER DETAIL

XINTAI CUCUMBER

Xintai is a kind of cucumber that is grown in northern Korea. It is fresh and has a minimal bitterness of flavor. It has even been grown in Sweden with success, and in later years, in the F/L gardens.

XINTAI CUCUMBER SORBET

2 lb (900 g) Xintai cucumber
6 ½ tablespoons lime juice
½ lb (260 g) sugar
3 ½ oz (100 g) pro sorbet from Sosa

Mix cucumber with lime and sugar to a smooth purée. Add pro sorbet, which has the ability to stabilize the sorbet and remove the freezing cold, somewhat splintered crystal feel you usually experience when you eat sorbet. Use an ice cream maker to give it an ice cream texture.

COMPRESSED WATERMELON

A simple and interesting way to change the structure of berries or fruit is to vacuum-pack them. When the air is sucked out of the fruit, in this case the watermelon, it lets go of all the juice, and the meat goes gray. When the vacuum lets go, all of the juice is sucked back into the fruit. The advantage is that the melon gets the same texture and quality throughout the entire fruit, and the color and juiciness is heavily enhanced.

Cherry Marbled Almond Milk Ice Cream

THE FULL SCANDIN ICE CREA

THE LOVE SCANDINAVIANS have for fatty ice cream seems to be deeply culturally rooted.

"We Scandinavians generally, and the Swedes especially, have since the beginning of time been fostered with fatter dairy products than other people. It seems that we love fat as a flavor carrier, fat cream in ice cream that takes hold of the flavors and makes them last for a long time, in contrast to, for instance, a lean Italian ice cream in which the flavors explode in your mouth and then disappear just as quickly."

You don't have to travel very far south before you find leaner ice cream varieties. These are also praised, like the Italian ice cream: so fruity, direct, and fresh.

"You could maybe seek an explanation in the climate. The Italian ice cream is fresh and works as a thirst quencher, or at least you can eat it to cool down immediately. A more creamy and fatter ice cream is not experienced as equally cold or fresh in flavor. This reasoning may seem logical. I have experimented with ice cream at the restaurant, and I have tried different kinds of ice creams on the personnel after closing. They all chose the fat ice cream over the leaner and more fruity, which they called 'watery.'"

The base of F/L's ice cream is the simplest imaginable:

The ice cream consists of 2 cups milk (500 g) and the same amount of cream, mixed with ½ lb sugar (200 g) and the same amount of yolk. It is not unique to Frantzén/Lindeberg, but it is a traditional ice cream, significantly richer than the southern European ice cream, in which the relationship is 4 cups (1 L) milk to ¾ to 1 cup (2-3 dL) cream. "Based on the way we express our philosophy in other aspects, it would be natural for us to serve the continental ice cream, but it wasn't. The tradition and the cultural heritage seemed to play a large role and influenced our choice. Furthermore, I personally like the fatty ice cream better."

In the restaurant kitchen, there is no ice cream maker. Instead, the ice cream is prepared in a mixer, a Pacojet. The frozen ice cream mass is chopped to pieces in the mixer and come out as a smooth and lightly worked ice cream with a texture more like soft ice.

"Through decreasing the influx of air in the machine, I can fool the Pacojet into making an ice cream that is reminiscent of that made in an ice cream maker."

Sometimes you want to use some of the elements from, for instance, Italian ice cream, which has a different flavor intensity. To manage to make such an ice cream, yet keep the experience of the fat structure.

"Because we produce our own butter at the restaurant, we are left with large amounts of buttermilk. Buttermilk contains only 1 percent fat and has a light tart flavor. Buttermilk is also rich in phospholipids that have an emulsifying effect and can replace the cream in the ice cream despite the low fat content. We blend 3 cups (7 dL) buttermilk with 1 ⅓ cups (3 dL) cream, and the buttermilk has become one of the most important ingredients for making a leaner ice cream that still has a sense of the fat."

THANK YOU

BJÖRN
My girlfriend Sara Sandberg for all the support and for bothering with it all. Thank you Stella and Leiah for existing, you give me so much energy and joy despite early mornings . . .

DANIEL
My girlfriend Kristina Linder and our children Cornelia, Hugo, and Esther for being there, for putting up with it, and for all your love!

TOGETHER
Göran "Tabberaset" Lager for all the text and knowledge. Without you, it would have never been a book. What unparalleled strength you've shown during the work with this book! Not many people would have managed this while also going through the things you have gone through.

Photographer Fredrik Skogkvist for your uncompromising attitude to this book, the only thing you've cared about is that the pictures and the book turn out exactly the way we want it. Respect.

Art Director Stefan van der Kwast Gissberg for your enormous work and your ability to visualize our food and our ideas in the graphic world, and not least your great patience with us and our ideas.

And, of course, everyone who works at Frantzén/Lindeberg. Especially our kitchen manager Jim Löfdahl, who has had to pull a lot of weight during the work with this book.

Norstedts for the opportunity to make a book about our greatest passion—food. And Johanna Kullman who has really made sure that all of our ideas and whims have been made possible . . .

And Jon Lacotte—for everything!

RECIPE INDEX

INGREDIENT INDEX

METRIC AND IMPERIAL CONVERSIONS

(These conversions are rounded for convenience)

Ingredient	Cups/Tablespoons/ Teaspoons	Ounces	Grams/Milliliters
Butter	1 cup=16 tablespoons= 2 sticks	8 ounces	230 grams
Cream cheese	1 tablespoon	0.5 ounce	14.5 grams
Cheese, shredded	1 cup	4 ounces	110 grams
Cornstarch	1 tablespoon	0.3 ounce	8 grams
Flour, all-purpose	1 cup/1 tablespoon	4.5 ounces/0.3 ounce	125 grams/8 grams
Flour, whole wheat	1 cup	4 ounces	120 grams
Fruit, dried	1 cup	4 ounces	120 grams
Fruits or vegetables, chopped	1 cup	5 to 7 ounces	145 to 200 grams
Fruits or vegetables, puréed	1 cup	8.5 ounces	245 grams
Honey, maple syrup, or corn syrup	1 tablespoon	.75 ounce	20 grams
Liquids: cream, milk, water, or juice	1 cup	8 fluid ounces	240 ml
Oats	1 cup	5.5 ounces	150 grams
Salt	1 teaspoon	0.2 ounce	6 grams
Spices: cinnamon, cloves, ginger, or nutmeg (ground)	1 teaspoon	0.2 ounce	5 ml
Sugar, brown, firmly packed	1 cup	7 ounces	200 grams
Sugar, white	1 cup/1 tablespoon	7 ounces/0.5 ounce	200 grams/12.5 grams
Vanilla extract	1 teaspoon	0.2 ounce	4 grams

OVEN TEMPERATURES

Fahrenheit	Celcius	Gas Mark
225°	110°	¼
250°	120°	½
275°	140°	1
300°	150°	2
325°	160°	3
350°	180°	4
375°	190°	5
400°	200°	6
425°	220°	7
450°	230°	8